Psychoanalysis and Black Novels

Psychoanalysis and Black Novels

Desire and the Protocols of Race

CLAUDIA TATE

New York   Oxford
Oxford University Press
1998

Oxford University Press

Oxford   New York
Athens   Auckland   Bangkok   Bogota   Bombay   Buenos Aires
Calcutta   Cape Town   Dar es Salaam   Delhi   Florence   Hong Kong
Istanbul   Karachi   Kuala Lumpur   Madras   Madrid   Melbourne
Mexico City   Nairobi   Paris   Singapore   Taipei   Tokyo   Toronto   Warsaw

and associated companies in
Berlin   Ibadan

Copyright © 1998 by Claudia Tate

Published by Oxford University Press, Inc.
198 Madison Avenue, New York, New York 10016

Oxford is a registered trademark of Oxford University Press

Library of Congress Cataloging-in-Publication Data
Tate, Claudia.
Psychoanalysis and black novels : Desire and the protocols of race
/ by Claudia Tate.
   p.   cm.—(Race and American culture)
Includes bibliographical references and index.
ISBN 0-19-509682-7; ISBN 0-19-509683-5 (pbk.)
1. American fiction—Afro-American authors—History and criticism.
2. Psychological fiction, American—History and criticism.
3. Psychoanalysis and literature—United States.   4. Afro-Americans
in literature.   5. Desire in literature.   6. Race in literature.
I. Title.   II. Series.
PS374.N4TT36   1998
813.009'896073—dc21   97-8423

Page v constitutes an extension of the copyright page.

9 8 7 6 5 4 3 2 1

Printed in the United States of America
on acid-free paper

For Ma and Daddy

Acknowledgments

Many people helped me to address questions about enigmatic textual representations that eventually evolved into this book. Marshall Alcorn spent hours instructing me on how to use the language of psychoanalysis. He also read each chapter several times, checking my use of psychoanalytic theory and the cohesion of my arguments. Ann Kelly read and reread every draft. She challenged me to make my argument accessible to scholars who were neither African Americanists nor psychoanalytic critics. Mark Bracher also read several chapters and challenged me to organize my arguments in such a way as to make my use of psychoanalysis as cultural criticism more forceful.

I thank Fred Bowman and the staff of the Library of Congress for facilitating my work on W. E. B. Du Bois. I thank Ellen Wright and Patricia Willis, the curator of the Beinecke Library of Yale University, for permission to reproduce unpublished materials from Richard Wright's private papers contained in his archive at Beinecke Library at Yale University. I thank David Graham Du Bois and Linda Seidman, the special collection librarian, for permission to reprint unpublished material from the W. E. B. Du Bois Library, University of Massachusetts at Amherst. I also thank Janet Sims-Woods and the staff of the Moorland-Spingarn Research Center at Howard University for their congenial assistance, so varied as to make its articulation here impossible. I thank Esme Bhan, formerly of the Moorland-Spingarn Research Center, and the staffs of the Beinecke Library, the Gelman Library at George Washington University, and the Washington Area Consortium Libraries for assisting me in locating books and private papers.

I thank the members of "First Draft"—Vicki Arana, Eve Hawthorne, Jennifer

Jordan, Ann Kelly, and Alinda Summers—for not tiring of my requests that they read yet another draft of the chapters for this book. I thank Carla Peterson for allowing me temporarily to draft her into "First Draft." I thank the members of "Jeffrey's House Party"—Jeffrey Stewart, Marilyn Mobley, Francille Wilson, Gilbert Morris, and Saundra Nettles—for helping me to write the introduction. I thank David Levering Lewis for generously answering my questions about Du Bois. Other colleagues—Arnold Rampersad, Jean Wyatt, Nellie McKay, Bill Andrews, Hazel Carby, Gayle Wald, Wahneema Lubiano, and Priscilla Ramsey—critiqued chapters at various stages and offered me their encouragement and suggestions. Several people whom I met on the Internet also read chapters and offered me their valuable critiques: Sander Gilman, Virginia Blum, Lynne Layton, and Kalpana Seshadri-Crooks.

I thank Judith Plotz and Chris Sten, the recent and current chairs of the English Department, and Lee Salamon (the former dean of Columbian College and Graduate School) of George Washington University for their support. I am grateful for the financial support of the George Washington University Facilitating Fund and the Office of Research at George Washington University, both administered by Don Lehman. I thank George Washington University for sabbatical leave and the American Council of Learned Societies for a postdoctoral fellowship that afforded me the time to work through the most difficult stages of this project.

I thank my students at George Washington, who allowed me to test my various theories on them and who offered their questions, resistance, and commentary. I thank the students, faculty, and guests who attended my lectures at Emory, Johns Hopkins, Princeton, Temple, and Rutgers Universities, the University of Virginia, and the University of Tennessee at Knoxville. The audiences at these lectures challenged aspects of my arguments at key moments in the evolution of this project.

I thank Susan Chang, the senior literary editor of Oxford University Press, and her assistant, Rahul Metha, for helping me to bring this project to closure. I thank Liz Maguire, formerly of Oxford University Press; series editors Arnold Rampersad and Shelley Fisher Fishkin; and an anonymous reader for recognizing a book in the premature manuscript I sent to them after the completion of my sabbatical. Again, I thank Arnold Rampersad for reading the penultimate draft of the manuscript and challenging me to clarify my argument about the relationship of canonical and anomalous works. I also thank psychoanalysts Joseph Smith and E. Victor Wolfenstein for their attentive readings of the manuscript.

My sons, Jay Lindsey and Read Hubbard, helped me to complete this project by keeping me sane, in good humor, and in touch with the demands of the "real" world. I thank my grandmother, Mozella Austin, who still remembers that I loved books as a child, and my brother, Dr. Harold, for simply expecting me to finish a project once I started. My deepest appreciation is for my parents, Harold and Mary Tate, who are my empathic mirrors.

All of these people and probably others whose names I've inadvertently omitted helped me to produce this book. Their questions, skepticism, resistance, and encouragement greatly enhanced the final product. Its limitations are mine.

Princeton, New Jersey   C. T.
July 1997

Contents

Abbreviations

The following abbreviations are used throughout the text.

BB   *Black Boy*, Richard Wright. 1945. Reprint. New York: Harper Perennial, 1993.

"BC"   "Black Confessions," Richard Wright. Unpublished manuscript. Wright Archive, James Weldon Johnson Collection, Beinecke Library, Yale University (Wright Papers, box 9, folders 202–8).

DP   *Dark Princess, A Romance*, William E. B. Du Bois. 1928. Reprint. Jackson: University Press of Mississippi, 1995.

DT   *Dust Tracks on a Road*, Zora Neale Hurston. 1942. Reprint. New York: Harper Perennial, 1991.

M   *Megda*, Emma Dunham Kelley. 1891. Reprint. New York: Oxford University Press, 1988.

NS   *Native Son*, Richard Wright. New York: Harper & Row, 1940.

P   *Passing*, in *Quicksand and Passing*, Nella Larsen. 1928 and 1929. Reprinted in 1 vol. Edited by Deborah E. McDowell. New Brunswick, N.J.: Rutgers University Press, 1986.

Q   *Quicksand*, in *Quicksand and Passing*, Nella Larsen. 1928 and 1929. Reprinted in 1 vol. Edited by Deborah E. McDowell. New Brunswick, N.J.: Rutgers University Press, 1986.

S   *Seraph on the Suwanee*, Zora Neale Hurston. 1948. Reprint. New York: Harper Perennial, 1991.

SH   *Savage Holiday,* Richard Wright. 1954. Reprint. Jackson: University Press of Mississippi, 1994.

TE   *Their Eyes Were Watching God,* Zora Neale Hurston.1937. Reprint. New York: Harper Perennial, 1990.

UTC   *Uncle Tom's Children,* Richard Wright. 1938. Reprint. New York: New American Library, 1963.

Psychoanalysis and Black Novels

The subject of the dream is the dreamer.

—Toni Morrison, *Playing in the Dark* (1992)

The essence of the word is its ambivalence.

—Ralph Ellison, "Twentieth-Century Fiction and
the Black Mask of Humanity" (1953)

Introduction

Black Textuality and Psychoanalytic Literary Criticism

Perhaps the ideal approach to the work of literature would be one allowing for insight into the deepest psychological motives of the writer at the same time that it examined all external sociological factors operating within a given milieu. For while objectively a social reality, the work of art is, in its genesis, a projection of a deeply personal process, and any approach that ignores the personal at the expense of the social is necessarily incomplete.

> —Ralph Ellison, "Twentieth-Century Fiction and the
> Black Mask of Humanity" (1953)

What happens to the writerly imagination of a black author who is at some level *always* conscious of representing one's own race to, or in spite of, a race of readers that understands itself to be "universal" or race free? In other words, how is "literary whiteness" and "literary blackness" made, and what is the consequence of that construction?

> —Toni Morrison, *Playing in the Dark* (1992)

Protocols of Black Textuality

What constitutes a black literary text in the United States? Must it be written by, about, and/or for African Americans?[1] The conventional answer to this question is that a black text is one written by an African American. However, the racial protocol among African Americans has also demanded that a black text explicitly represent their lived experiences with racial oppression. Given the origins of the African American novel in the slave narrative, such a viewpoint is understandable, for the very purpose of the slave narrative was to justify the abolition of slavery by characterizing the humanity of the slave and the inhumanity of the peculiar institution.

African American literature and literary criticism have continued to respond to Western concepts of race. So much so, in fact, that we readers and scholars—black and nonblack—generally expect literary works and critical studies by African Americans to contest racist perspectives and the resulting oppression. Conse-

3

quently, we require these texts and especially those of canonical status to foreground the injustice of black protagonists' persistent and contested encounters with the material and psychological effects of a racially exploitative distribution of social goods, services, and power. We might call this the manifest text of black literary discourse. For African American cultural history has consistently venerated those works that explicitly portray such contestation as "the black experience," even though black writers have frequently debated what constitutes this experience, its depiction, and its analysis.[2]

Before the 1980s, when protest-oriented directives dominated the African American critical viewpoint, a literary work of even renowned black authorship risked intraracial censure if it failed to manifest the sociological factors of an oppressive "black experience." At that time scholars and readers all seemed tacitly to agree that such works, which focus on the inner worlds of black characters without making that world entirely dependent on the material and psychological consequences of a racist society, were not black enough, and they cast them aside.

Richard Wright's *Outsider* (1953) confronted such marginalization.[3] Because Wright did not confine his conception of freedom in the novel to the typical depiction of black social protest, the novel puzzled its reviewers. They had no ready strategy for constructing the novel's meaning. Wright's "Blueprint for Negro Writing," published almost two decades earlier, in 1937, gave them little preparation for sympathizing with *The Outsider*'s refusal to center around the familiar racial paradigm of social oppression and resulting protest. Indeed, the essay directed them to consider black individuals as reflections "of the history of their race as they in one life time had lived it themselves throughout all the long centuries" (qtd. in A. Mitchell, *Within the Circle*, 105). Rather than performing the predictable role of the racial victim, though, the protagonist of *The Outsider* escapes a conflict with his wife and mistress by exploiting the consequences of a subway accident. This experience makes him realize that he can also manipulate others' perceptions of racial difference in order to establish sites of free agency for himself. He goes so far as to create a new identity and a new life for himself. In doing so he demonstrates that his personality transcends the conventional understanding of a racially performative self.[4] Consequently, his behavior complicates the novel's political argument in ways Wright's reviewers have failed to appreciate because the novel depletes blackness of the usual expressions of racial grievances.

Instead of addressing the significance of the marginality of race on the actions of this protagonist, the reviewers—white and black alike—frequently made trite observations and justified them with allegations about the novel's aesthetic flaws and its violations of conventional wisdom. For example, when Granville Hicks of the *New York Times Book Review* explains that the protagonist of *The Outsider* is not so much a Negro as what Wright describes as a "psychological man" (qtd. in Reilly, *Richard Wright*, 201), the not-so-subtle assumption that these are contradictory identities dictates his analysis. For Hicks, a Negro protagonist is categorically defined by the demands of racial politics. Rather than asking what desires drive this character, Hicks obliges him to fit into an inappropriate critical template of racial needs and political demands only to complain about the failure of the work to depict universal concerns.[5]

Black reviewers were not much better at imagining the subjectivity of Wright's protagonist. Writing in the *Saturday Review,* Arna Bontemps, for instance, claims that *The Outsider* is a product of Wright's "roll in the hay with the existentialism of Sartre" (qtd. in Reilly, *Richard Wright,* 208). Rather than probing what the novel suggests about human subjectivity and existential freedom, Bontemps dismisses the opportunity by trivializing his own perception. Bontemps's remark was meant to consolidate the cultural identity of black literature by invalidating discussions of Wright's depiction of *both* a freedom that exceeds the typical experiences of a homogeneous black folk and an intellectual inquiry that challenges the representational proficiency of social realism.

While I extend my analysis of *The Outsider* in Chapter 3, I refer to it here to illustrate the failure of a very provocative novel by a canonical black author to fascinate its first audience—black and white. Detecting why this was the case, I argue, will be instructive for understanding the tension between the discourses of personal desire and political demand in black texts that cohere around what might respectively be called their latent and manifest narratives. Through my investigation I hope to demonstrate how the racial protocol for African American canon formation has marginalized desire as a critical category of black textuality by demanding manifest stories about racial politics. Moreover, I contend that we can illuminate the manifest racial meanings of the prominent texts by canonical black writers by probing the latent content in their corresponding noncanonical works.

Because I refer to psychoanalysis to advance my investigation of desire in black textuality, some will no doubt claim I'm having my "roll in the hay" with Freud and company. Such a charge would, first, insinuate the misgivings that many African Americans have about the relevance of psychoanalysis to black liberation, thus the general absence of psychoanalytic models in black intellectual discourse.[6] Second, the claim would thwart the possibility that psychoanalysis has anything significant to say about a black writer's work as constituting a meaningful projection of personal and social longings—acknowledged and unacknowledged. As I argue throughout this study, psychoanalysis can tell us much about the complicated social workings of race in the United States and the representations of these workings in the literature of African Americans.

That the protagonist of *The Outsider* experiences life as a Negro is a social consequence of his identity in the novel. But such experiences seem infinitely variable rather than reducible to any racial formula. The meaning of the protagonist's experiences are not simply the unmediated effects of the racist reality in which he lives. Rather, such meaning evolves from the *conjunction* of that reality and the protagonist's (as well as Wright's) personality. In addition, this protagonist's desire is never reducible to racial politics. His desire includes and exceeds racial liberation. Instead of regarding *The Outsider* as irrelevant to racial politics because of these circumstances, we might investigate what it can tell us about the relationship between personal desire and the social conventions—protocols—of race.

Certainly, race matters. It matters precisely because in the United States "race remains a salient source of the fantasies and allegiances that shape our ways of reading" all types of social experiences (Abel, "Black Writing," 497). These racial fantasies and allegiances have historically conditioned all social exchanges, and they continue to do so. Indeed, the racial conventions of the United States seem to have sentenced black subjects to protest forever the very deficiencies that white subjects presumably do not possess. Racism allows white subjects generally to assume that they have "fully developed, complex, multi-layered personalit[ies]" (Prager, "Self Reflection[s]," 357).[7] By contrast, racism condemns black subjects to a Manichean conflict between their public performance of an essentialized, homogenous blackness, which is largely a by-product of white "ideological formations" of racial difference (Althusser, "Freud," 219), on the one hand, and a private performance of individual personality, on the other.

While dominant racial ideologies attempt to reify the "categorical, essentialist, representational languages depicting black life and experience" as deficient, what we identify as *blackness* is "continually being reconstituted as African Americans inhabit widely differentiated social spaces" (Anderson, *Beyond Ontological Blackness*, 11). One prominent cultural theorist refers to the term "postmodern blackness" to designate the complicated ways in which other positions—those of gender, class, sexuality, region, nationality, and so on—also determine the performance of African American identities (hooks, *Yearnings*, 23–31). What this means is that different occasions and social contexts allow individuals to activate and to be perceived by one or more of the various constituents of their identities. For example, a black resident of the United States can activate self-identity as "basically African American at one time, American at another time, could activate class identity at one time, a gender identity at another time, a professional identity, and so on" (Goldberg, "Conversation," 182),[8] while another person may simultaneously perceive similar or different constituents of that first person's identity.

Western conventions additionally regulate the social authority of males and females—white and nonwhite—by placing them in a hierarchical arrangement so familiar that I need not describe it here. In short, white patriarchal power determines how we—blacks and nonblacks, women and men—are to *mis*-recognize ourselves. Yet other personal factors, like those mentioned earlier, intervene and often interrupt the effects of dominant discourses on us all. Because social power is unstable, we are not powerless in this exchange. Whether we realize it or not, we all mediate in different ways the hegemonic effects of white male power with whatever authority we personally claim.

In *Playing in the Dark,* Toni Morrison explores such subjective mediations in

African American literary history. Indeed, these novels could be called anomalies, primarily because they resist, to varying degrees, the race and gender paradigms that we rather spontaneously impose on black textuality. Yet, as I will argue, Du Bois's *Dark Princess*, Wright's *Savage Holiday*, and Hurston's *Seraph on the Suwanee* respectively present a set of rhetorical features for expressing enigmatic emotional meaning that not only conditions that work but also characterizes the more prominent novels of each respective author. *Quicksand* also contains such meaning, although it is usually effaced in readings that center race, gender, and class. The category of canonical cannot be associated with either Kelley or *Medga*. Kelley presents, as I will explain, a different critical problem—the complexity of literary recovery that involves the interplay of cultural codes no longer current.

By contrast, Du Bois, Wright, and Hurston are indisputably canonical authors. For this reason, I position their respective marginal novels—*Dark Princess, Savage Holiday,* and *Seraph on the Suwanee*—against their widely read works. This strategy allows me to provide intertextual readings of the more prominent and marginal works so as to reveal the consistent representation of the emotional conflict that forms the narrative core of each writer's works. For example, by referring to Wright again, I demonstrate that *Savage Holiday* is an exaggerated representation of the theme of maternal (or female) betrayal that regulates the unfolding narratives of Wright's more celebrated *Native Son* (1940) and *Black Boy* (1945). Hence, by using *Savage Holiday* as a fictive lens for reading the rest of Wright's fictional corpus, I argue that the anomalous work not only inscribes but exaggerates a primary narrative, an "urtext," that is repeated but masked in the canonical texts. While the primary narrative dominates the anomalous text and becomes its manifest story, this primary discourse is repressed in the corresponding canonical ones. Like the latent content of a dream, though, the anomalous work of a prominent writer can illuminate the rhetorical logic and deep emotional meaning of that writer's more successful works.

Because the five novels at the center of this study stage meaning that is more concerned with personal longings than public conflict, the meaning is not readily accessible to our social paradigms of race and gender. For example, the central characters of *Medga* appear white, and the novel effaces the interracial hostility of the 1890s that caused historian Rayford W. Logan to call this period "the Dark Ages of recent American history" (*Betrayal*, 9). Similarly presenting its protagonists as white, indeed poor white "Crackers," *Seraph on the Suwanee* seems drastically to depart from the rich vein of black culture that had characterized all of Hurston's other works. Even though *Dark Princess* acknowledges racism and subscribes to racial propaganda as the sanctioned discourse of black novels, this work also undermines its polemical effectiveness with an extravagant display of a personal erotic fantasy. Traditional scholars like Alain Locke and Arthur Davis have regarded the blatant intrusion of private desire into a work of social commentary so problematic that they probably would have relegated *Dark Princess* to the women's section of the black literary canon had the novel not been written by Du Bois. So they did the next best thing: they generally ignored it. Such a response is clearly sexist; it adheres to patriarchal conventions that delegate the realm of the emotional to females and that of the political to males.

Quicksand encountered a slightly different fate. Until the women's movement, this and other novels by black women were marginalized, probably because they did not present "the black experience" from what traditional African American literary scholarship has assumed to be the representative position of a working-class black man. Because *Quicksand* relies on the inner-world perspective of a middle-class black woman, it eludes the material paradigms that focus on the effects of economic deprivation and political exploitation. Yet when this novel was reprinted in 1971, black scholars fashioned it as a racial protest story, and shortly thereafter feminists refashioned it as a story protesting sexist victimization as well. But its black female protagonist is not simply an innocent victim of racial oppression and sexual repression. Rather, she is also an aggressive and defensive seductress, implicated in her own tragic fate. In order to make the novel fit the racial and/or sexual paradigms, their respective proponents discarded these troublesome aspects of the protagonist's personality.

Finally, the critical response to *Savage Holiday* has been extremely negative. Wright's U.S. critics categorically dismissed the novel as an embarrassment to him—so much so, in fact, that this novel is frequently omitted from discussions of his works. This response is undoubtedly the result of Wright's abandoning the familiar racial protest plot, for in *Savage Holiday* he dramatizes another plot about a latent heterosexual conflict, played out in an insular white social setting and saturated in Freudian allusions.

The general marginality of these five novels is probably the effect of a distinct characteristic that all novels share but that these accentuate. They inscribe complex discourses that reveal what scholars of African American literature have heretofore largely neglected or intentionally suppressed: the residual surplus meaning of unconscious desire.[9] Such desire manifests itself in what I call implicit (or unconscious) discourses or narrative fragments of a text. They form an enigmatic presence that produces textual meaning, which in turn complicates the explicit social message of the text.

The five novels accentuate personal and unsocialized desire that, while commonplace, is seldom acknowledged because it engenders in us what I suspect to be vague feelings of emotional discomfort—anxiety, shame, and/or guilt. For this reason we have often justified our reluctance to recognizing the unsocialized desire inscribed in these and similar texts by referring to their curious relationships to racial politics and therefore their erratic attention to the materialist or sociological analyses that constitute the familiar racial paradigm. Because these novels are external to the sanctioned social discourses of traditional black literature, they express what can be said to be the *repressed* of that tradition. These suppressed novels express psychological forces of subjectivity—which are potential social forces as well—that are not readily visible in the typical racial story.

Given the ubiquity of the effects of racial politics in the United States, "the writerly imagination of a black author is at some level," as Toni Morrison contends, "*always* conscious of representing one's own race" (*Playing*, xii; original emphasis). This condition marks the text, even in those instances in which the text is not otherwise racially designated. Furthermore, such works inscribe a process by which the respective author negotiates explicit, public, racial identifications—or what I am calling *the protocols of race*—with the implicit, private psychological effects of narrative subjectivity. Thus, the black text mediates two broad categories of experience: one is historically racialized and regulated by African American cultural performance; the other is the individual and subjective experience of personal desire signified in language. Together, these two types of experience constitute textual desire, which is different from, though contiguous with, authorial desire, as I will further explain.

By desire, I do not simply mean sexual longings but all kinds of wanting, wishing, yearning, longing, and striving—conscious and particularly unconscious. Whether in the text or the world, we seldom recognize the surplus of desire associated with black subjectivity because, like Wright's *Outsider*, expressions that transgress the social and political have been silenced by the master discourses of race. If we persist in reductively defining black subjectivity as political agency, we will continue to overlook the force of desire in black texts as well as in the lives of African Americans.

While desire is constitutive of a loss, desire also generates by-products even as it makes that deficiency conspicuous. For desire is not only "a pure absence striving for an impossible completion, fated evermore to play out or repeat its primal or founding loss," but "a pure positivity, a production" as well (Grosz, *Space*, 179). Hence, desire is itself "the force of positive production, the action that creates things, makes alliances, and forges interactions" (Grosz, *Space*, 179). Desire "experiments; it makes: it is fundamentally aleatory, inventive" (Grosz, *Space*, 180).

Wright's *Outsider*, for example, dramatizes desire as the protagonist's daring production of his experimental life. However, traditional African American criticism has been much more invested in defining desire as—indeed, confining desire to—the consolidated aspiration for black civil rights than appreciating desire as the performance of existential freedom. Desire as political prerogative was probably efficacious when the color line regulated all aspects of black life because the objective was clear. Still, the color line has produced curious distortions in what the black and white literary establishments have recognized as *black* works. Both establishments have confirmed the existence of that "line." Both have referred to race in determining intelligibility for these works. But race has had different meanings for each establishment. For white reviewers, *The Outsider*'s claim to universality and blackness were mutually contradictory. By contrast, *The Outsider* was not quite black enough for African American reviewers because it did not focus on a politicized racial loss. Thus, reductive definitions of race have hindered the performances of both establishments.

It is common knowledge that during the post-Reconstruction era (1876–1915) extreme forms of racial prejudice, discrimination, and segregation undermined the material needs, nullified the political demands, and frustrated the personal ambitions of all African Americans. The legacy of such practices remains with us today. During the New Negro Renaissance of the 1920s and 1930s, the ambitions of black artists were further regulated by a system of white patronage that imposed its prescriptions on their creativity. By the 1940s, social protest became the endorsed topic of African American literature no doubt due to the rise of such protest in the society at large. Thus, in each epoch historical exigency was a key factor in constituting protocols of racial identity and subsequent codes of black artistic expression. These codes sanctioned certain topics—principally stories of frustrated aspirations arising from racial oppression—and suppressed others. These exigencies demarcate the conditions of "black modernity" and make the term "black modernism" an appropriate label for the African American literary works canonized during these periods because in responding to racist conventions, the endorsed social discourses in these works assume the authority of black master narratives.

But now that the law of the land forbids racist covenants, the gap between law and practice has not so much eliminated the color line and its covenants as complicated them both. Although it has mutated, white patriarchal privilege still functions. Its regulatory power resides in presumptions of a color-blind, gender-neutral society, while narratives of social equality exist largely as rhetoric. The slippage among identity, law, lived experiences, and unstated supposition has complicated color-line issues with postmodern multiplicity. At different times, black master narratives seem both irrelevant and necessary to safeguard the civil agency of African Americans. This paradoxical racial situation has further confounded our understanding of what constitutes a black novel, indeed black subjectivity in general.

If a black modernist canon defines a black novel as one that centers a racialist agenda, then what are the critical imperatives of a black postmodern canon? Does it simply reject race as a primary focus? Or does it place historical racial proscriptions in a broad context among other social issues and personal concerns? Would desire be a category of investigation in postmodern black criticism? Would this approach produce information about black textuality not accessible to a modernist inquiry?

One way to address these questions is to examine novels written by African Americans that do not fit the typical racial paradigm because they did not conform to modern conceptions of black identity. Rather than subordinating their expressions of private longing to racial politics, the novels mentioned earlier exaggerate the distinction between the prevalent discourses of racial protest and the resonant expressions of personal emotional meaning—in short, between race and desire—by accentuating the latter. Because these works do not conform to the protest agenda of black modernism, they are repressed in the traditional black canon. Yet these works make visible the ways in which we readers have circumscribed black subjectivity and black textuality by a reductive understanding of racial difference that has in turn made concepts of race and desire seem incompatible.

I hope to illustrate the fallacy of such thinking by drawing on Freudian and post-Freudian theories about the roles of the conscious and the unconscious in the creative process.[10] I hypothesize that in each of these five novels, indeed in all novels, there are unconscious discourses or implicit narrative fragments that fulfill latent wishes, much like dreams. These discourses accompany the novels' social meanings. Although contiguous with the writer's intentional social story, the unconscious discourses are generally ex-centric to that story, and they cohere much like the background details in a work of visual art. But in these five novels the unconscious discourses are so pervasive that they refuse to remain subordinated to the intentional story. Their repressed and unspoken desire forms the surplus meaning that unsettles the sanctioned social plot. As I shall demonstrate, the tension between the intentional social story and the unconscious discursive fragments makes the novels appear both reactionary and revolutionary because the unconscious discourses in each work partly support and ultimately abandon the public argument in exchange for a solitary and forbidden fantasy that we readers seldom want to share.

Despite the rich payload of personal meaning that black anomalous novels offer, analyzing them is a frustrating task. They inscribe more content about the emotional significance of various experiences—the enigmatic surplus meaning—than traditional African American literary criticism typically addresses. Because psychoanalytic criticism evolves from a set of theoretical propositions that has been the most concerned with examining the manifestations of such surpluses in language, it can, I believe, help me illuminate the workings of desire in these novels.

Since my primary audience is composed of those interested in African American literature, I am not interested in consolidating or privileging the theoretical demands of individual schools of psychoanalysis. Rather, I will construct my critical model by referring to basic Freudian, object-relations, and Lacanian theories about the development of the personality[11] as well as to black literary and cultural criticism. I connect these psychoanalytic schools in my critical model because object-relations theory supplements Freudian theory by addressing regressive (or aspects of infantile) subjectivity and because Lacanian theory further develops Freudian tenets by elaborating on both the expression of unconscious desire in language and the subversive effect of desire on the subject. While other schools of psychoanalysis (like American ego psychology and the psychology of the self) offer additonal ways of constructing textual meaning,[12] I selected Freudian, Lacanian, and object-relations theories for my critical paradigm because they facilitate my analysis of unconscious textual desire in the novels as unacknowledged fantasies of lost and recovered plenitude.

Although I explain the principal tenets of these three schools in each chapter, here I simply mention the central hypotheses from which my model evolves. It (1) draws on a contemporary psychoanalytic premise (which I elaborate by referring to the work of Peter Brooks) that regards the structure of a novel as somewhat analogous to that of the psyche. My model (2) distinguishes a novel's conscious and preconscious discourses from its unconscious ones, which are cryptically inscribed in the novel's rhetorical expressions and plotting structure. Finally, my model (3) analyses the novel's representation of attachment, loss, and fantasized plenitude by referring to object-relations and Freudian tenets about the pre-oedipal and oedipal stages of subjective development. While I realize that combining different schools of psychoanalysis may seem problematic, especially to some cultural and literary theorists, my point is to show how psychoanalysis can illuminate aspects of desire not otherwise examined in these texts rather than to illustrate the virtue of a particular school. Theorists tend to be purists, whereas clinicians often refer to different psychoanalytic schools, depending on the stage of subjective development, psychological structure, or psychopathology under examination.[13]

I take a moment here to explain what I mean by *conscious, preconscious, and unconscious discourses. Conscious discourses* form the explicit social content disclosed in the plot, characterization, and dialogue (though these elements also harbor the unconscious). Conscious discourses typically inform thematic readings that are grounded in social realism. In order to produce a coherent social meaning, the racial paradigm usually either disregards the disruptive content arising from implicit or unconscious discourses in black novels or attributes such content to aesthetic defects. By *preconscious discourses* I mean the stylistic features (like figurative language) that contain implicit meaning that is accessible to conscious understanding. By *unconscious discourses,* I mean those longings that are inscribed in the novel's most deeply encoded rhetorical elements. Like the cryptic images of dreams, the unconscious of a text must be deciphered within the dynamics of its representational design.

My intention, then, is to tap the critical potential of psychoanalysis to demonstrate how a black text negotiates the tension between the public, collective protocols of race and private, individual desire, thereby forming an enigmatic surplus—what I will call a "textual enigma." As we all see, the enigma is a puzzling rhetorical performance that generates meaning in the novel that is external to its racial/social argument. For this reason, the enigmatic surplus disrupts the novel's conscious plot about racial/social protest or affirmation. We have typically disregarded these enigmas or designated them as aesthetic shortcomings, but the enigmas are not so much flaws as characteristics of textuality. In successful works, the enigma is carefully concealed so that its inscription of the writer's desire does not interfere with the reader's pleasure. Rather than marginalize works that do not safeguard reader's racial expectations, I want to concentrate on works that fail to do so in order to analyze aspects of black textuality that exceed traditional literary demands or what I am calling "modernist" conventions of blackness.

My critical ambitions are summarized in the title—*Psychoanalysis and Black Novels: Desire and the Protocols of Race.* I include "and" on both sides of the colon, first, to maintain rather than resolve the tension between the psychoanalytic venture of detecting a black writer's "personal psychological uniqueness" (Chodorow, "Gender," 521) and the canonical imperatives of modern black literature and, second, to emphasize the transgressive force of desire in language that complicates a unified racial perspective in African American cultural discourses. My intertextual model will demonstrate that black texts are composed not only of candidly stated social meaning but of implicit surplus content as well. Textual meaning, then, is a construction of both kinds of content.

In each chapter I refer to a central Lacanian axiom about language that proposes an interconnection between the novel and the psyche. This supposition proposes, according to Peter Brooks, that "the structure of literature *is* in some sense the structure of mind—not a specific mind, but what the translators of the *Standard Edition* call 'the mental apparatus,' which is more accurately the dynamic organization of the psyche, a process of structuration" ("Idea," 24–25). The convergence of the structure of the text and the psyche facilitates an analysis of the text by using the topographical model Freud identifies for the psyche constitutive of the conscious, the unconscious, and the preconscious. According to this model, desire and prohibition are the basic animating forces in the psyche and in the text. As a consequence, textual meaning is dependent on the mediation of a text's explicit, conscious discourses and its implicit, unconscious ones. The latter are in turn dependent on a compromise formation to express a prohibited wish. Because the unconscious wish is forbidden, its expression is veiled and evolves as the "psychic investments of rhetoric" in a text (Brooks, "Idea," 44). The unconscious desire of a text is so subtle that rather than "speak" itself, it is "performed" as "dramas of desire played out in tropes" (Brooks, "Idea," 44). By contrast, conscious textual desire is explicit. A text literally "speaks" such desire as specific personal, social, material, and political longings.

Since Lacanian theory designates subjectivity as structured in and by language, it is especially pertinent to literary criticism. Lacanian theory identifies the text itself, specifically its stylistic devices and rhetorical structure, as the appropriate object(s) of the psychoanalytic critical enterprise. In this context the subjectivity of a text is constitutive of the attributes of language in that text. By contrast, practitioners of Freudian and object-relations psychoanalytic literary criticism have often identified the object of critical investigation to be the author (see, for example, Marie Bonaparte's classic Freudian reading of Poe in *Life and Works of Edgar*

Allan Poe), the character (see, for example, Norman Holland's Freudian analysis of Hamlet in *The Shakespearean Imagination* or the object-relations readings of characters in Lynne Layton and Barbara Schapiro's *Narcissism and the Text*), or the thematic situation, like literary depictions of the pre-oedipal dyad of mother and child (as in Marianne Hirsh's *The Mother/Daughter Plot*). According to the Lacanian formulations of psychoanalytic literary criticism, these are the misrecognized objects of investigation. Characters are signifiers of meaning, thus meaningful symptoms, and not real subjects.

What I hope to accomplish in the following chapters is to demonstrate the analytical possibilities of psychoanalysis for articulating complicated conflicts of narrative desire in African American literary texts. My readings of *Megda, Dark Princess, Savage Holiday, Quicksand,* and *Seraph on the Suwanee,* in conjunction with those of corresponding canonical works, suggest ways in which psychoanalytic theory can inform African American literary scholarship by revealing how the material and cultural paradigms of race and gender that typically frame this scholarship do not entirely address the complex textuality of this literature. While such paradigms can effectively describe the external conditions that produce personal experience, they cannot explain how individuals internalize or represent those conditions so as to construct personal meaning. It is precisely this process of internalization—the dialectical engagement of the material and the psychical—that I am attempting to analyze in black textuality.

While examining narratives of desire in these novels is my objective, I am not attempting to psychoanalyze the writer, though my strategy clearly incites such speculation. Rather, I want to investigate some of the resonant inscriptions of desire in these novels that reflect how their respective authors uniquely combined emotional and cognitive meaning in the production of the works. My investigation will, I hope, illustrate how black texts construct textual meaning out of specific material and cultural circumstances as well as personal authorial longings—conscious and unconscious. Textual meaning and textual desire are more complicated than and therefore different from authorial meaning and desire because the former mediates conscious *and* unconscious yearnings, aspirations, longings insinuated in the language of the text. By contrast, authorial meaning and desire are generally constitutive of the author's conscious intentions about expressing social themes and personal passions.

My use of psychoanalysis in the context of the five novels at the center of this study is intended as a method of examining issues we have routinely dismissed because they seemed to be transparent conveyors of information or were, by contrast, so troublesome in their opacity that we disregarded them. Thus, my inquiry produces a "way of interpreting" by asking questions that consider but do not privilege racial meaning. What I seek is a methodology for reading black textuality rather than advancing a "specific product or interpretation" (Skura, *Literary Use,* 3).

Race and Psychoanalysis

When I mentioned to one prominent scholar of African American literature that I was working on a book project that combined black textuality and psychoanalysis, the response was, "Why do you want to do that?" This reply seemed to be a castigation of my inquiry. Didn't I know that psychoanalysis is inappropriate and perhaps even detrimental to black agency? I realize that psychoanalysis offers no clear and immediate path to greater freedom and justice of the sort that at least at one time appeared to be offered by demonstrations, sit-ins, and legal battles. By no means am I suggesting that these strategies do not work. Rather, I want to turn to literary culture to ask, how do we read black texts that engage competing, even contradictory needs, demands, and desire? My investigation suggests that while traditional activist responses may offer relief from racial oppression, racist attitudes produce unpredictable, irrational, and complicated effects. Psychoanalysis, I believe, can help us to not only analyze black textuality but also effectively explain important aspects of the deep psychological foundations of the destructive attitudes and behaviors of racism.

But while psychoanalytic theory can help us analyze the social pathology of racism, its practice has carried a lot of irritating baggage that has made it virtually an anathema in the black intellectual community. Rather than simply denounce psychoanalysis or regard it as a metadiscourse, I try to understand its own compensatory defenses by questioning the cultural effects of its Jewish origins in anti-Semitic Austria at the turn of the twentieth century. Such origins have produced a psychoanalytic practice that silences its own ideological history by presuming the culturally neutral family as its object of investigation. This displacement is important because it designates the family as primarily responsible for the tragic fates of real individuals who, for example, are like Bigger Thomas of Richard Wright's *Native Son* (1940) or Pecola Breedlove of Toni Morrison's *Bluest Eye* (1970).

By isolating the family from society—specifically its economic, political, and technological factors that condition the family—psychoanalytic practice has avoided examining the relationship of social oppression to family dysfunction and the blighted inner worlds of individuals.[14] Instead of regarding individuals and their stories as products of a dialectic of material circumstances *and* their internalization of them, psychoanalysis, as it generally operates, centers the individual's primary nurturing environment, not the external circumstances that precondition that environment. As a result, psychoanalytic practice relegates the bleak material circumstances of real lives to the background and blames the dysfunction on personal or familial deficiency. No wonder scholars of African American literature and culture shun this model and instead endorse materialist analyses of black novels, for mainstream psychoanalysis effaces racism and recasts its effects as a personality disorder caused by familial rather than social pathology. Hence, there is hardly a leap between shifting the blame from the social trauma of chronic racism to pathologizing the black family, as the infamous *Moynihan Report* does.

Similar pathologizing was largely the fate of the white women's encounter with Freudian psychology until white feminists took on the project of rewriting Freudian discourse to expose its hidden ideological suppositions about gender. A similar venture on the part of scholars of African American culture can also expose the racialist ideology in psychoanalysis posing as objective findings. In fact, such a venture will reveal that many discourses of scientific "fact," in general, are neither absolute nor truisms but belief structures that reproduce the status quo of white master and black slave as well as male plenitude and female deficiency.

Feminist and gender studies have persistently and effectively undermined the reign of biological determinism in the construction of the Freudian gendered subject. By contrast, though, black critical theory has seldom engaged psychoanalysis,[15] despite the theorists' various undertakings in other areas of structuralism and poststructuralism. With the recent intersection of postcolonial studies and psychoanalysis, though, particularly the revisionist studies of the works of Frantz Fanon, race has reappeared with a vengeance in discussions of psychoanalysis, much like the return of the repressed.[16]

A racially contextualized model of psychoanalysis, I argue, can help us analyze black textuality by identifying the discourses of desire generating the text. Such a model, I suggest, can advance our understandings of racialized behavior in other social settings as well. By referring to psychoanalysis, I am not suggesting that black texts err when contextualizing their narratives with the material circumstances of racial oppression. But I am asking black literary criticism to consider the roles of the narrator and protagonist in constructing various racial dilemmas and also suggesting that we probe such conflicts within and beyond their attribution to race.

I pursue such meaning in this study by considering a black text as a partly self-conscious fantasy. This conceptual framework facilitates our speculating about the author's inscription of pleasure as well as pain in the text. While we cannot gain direct access to the inner world of authors, we can detect and analyze the traces of emotional meaning left behind in print. Ascertaining how this process works in black textuality can, I believe, provide a model for understanding how individuals transform the material circumstances of cultural experience into personal emotional and cognitive meaning.

Given the persistence of racial oppression and the demand for black literature to identify and militate against it, the impulse to make the representation of such oppression the primary critical criterion for a black text is understandable. Under these circumstances, black literature evolves so as to prove that racism exists in the real world and is not a figment of the black imagination. As a result, the modern black text functions like a racially sensitive psychotherapist. To borrow the words of one, such works teach black readers to recognize "the parameters of the negative, racist and patriarchal boundaries which traditionally define [black people]" and to dare "to step outside of them" so as "to understand their own individuality, worth and ability [and] to utilize inner strengths in the service of growing and coping" (Greene, "Black Feminist Psychotherapy," 34, and "Considerations," 389). While this type of instruction teaches black readers to project the neurosis and psychosis of racism outside of themselves, unremitting racial trauma demands an unending supply of stories about the black victims of white racism in order to teach new generations of black people how to recognize both gross and subtle racist assault as well as to foster understanding among new generations of whites. For as we might expect, black and white people have very different perspectives about "how prevalent or threatening racism may be" (Greene, "Considerations," 390). Yet racism is only one type of assault, and it too is complicated by—and hence either mitigated or exacerbated by—other forces of subjectivity.

By repeatedly inscribing the negative effects of racism on black characters, the modernist black text perpetuates fantasies of white power and black victimization that take on lives independent of the material circumstances of real black and white experiences. Consequently, we come to understand social privilege and disadvantage according to racial prescriptions. Other factors are silenced. While things "white" signify entitlement, liberty, and power, things "black" signify penalty, lack, and defect. Such racialized allotments of good and bad are omnipresent. According to another psychotherapist, blackness becomes for many "a focal point for projections of all that we find most unacceptable," while we unconsciously equate whites and whiteness with "safety, goodness and abundance" (Holmes, "Race," 1).

What I want to do in this study is to recover from psychoanalysis what is useful for the work it can do to distinguish the workings of desire in black texts that are not direct expressions of racial alienation and to show how desire and race become mutually overdetermined in textual expressions. My objective, then, is not simply to use psychoanalysis to read the five novels; I also want to suggest that the novels can demonstrate how psychoanalysis has repressed race under the mask of gender in the family domain. While I frequently refer to this latter concern throughout this study, I give it the most attention in Chapter 4, on Larsen's *Quicksand*.

By making race and gender a part of the psychoanalytic literary project, I hope to encourage others to formulate new questions about the dialectical relationship between representations of desire and race in black texts, indeed in all kinds of social situations. Such questions will offer us opportunities, to borrow the words of Ralph Ellison, to probe "into the deepest psychological motives of the writer," while also examining the "external sociological factors operating within a given milieu" ("Twentieth-Century," 136n; see the first epigraph). Such an exploration will suggest factors that not only clarify the creative impulses of writers but also condition the behavior of human subjects.

In an attempt to read the five novels at the center of my study as the products of their authors' interior and external world experiences, each chapter of this study presents a critical model that questions by contextualizing the presumption of the social neutrality of psychoanalysis with the material effects of a historicized black culture. Because these novels reflect the power dynamics of the period of their production, they inscribe complex psychological strategies for adapting to the disturbing effects of social oppression, and they reveal surplus content, as mentioned earlier. Because a black critical perspective has been sensitive only to the effects of racial oppression, the surplus content has generally remained blurred or buried. For this reason, like the five novels, I de-center racial oppression in order to locate this other content. My method does not mean that race is unimportant but simply that it is not the only site of conflict. Race is one important element of an individual's social character and personality. But there are others that are not so easily discerned.

In the chapter on Emma Kelley's *Megda* (1891), I explain why the feminist paradigm of gender inequity (associated with contemporary readings of Louisa May Alcott's *Little Women*) and the racial paradigm of social oppression (associated with Frances Harper's *Iola Leroy*) are inadequate for reading a work that evolves from a perplexing tangle of social positions—a historically black, woman-centered, evangelical cultural context that silences the discourses of race. I use psychoanalytic theory in the context of cultural studies to address the weaknesses of both paradigms. In addition, I explain how this novel constructs an imaginary plenitude by using facsimiles of pre-oedipal and oedipal discourses to construct and resolve its narrative conflicts. I refer to these two psychoanalytic discourses because textual conflicts and their resolutions have a striking correspondence to the oedipal and pre-oedipal stages of subjective development.

Chapter 2, on William E. B. Du Bois's second novel, *Dark Princess* (1928), also combines cultural criticism and Freudian/Lacanian psychoanalytic theories to call attention to this novel's implicit but nevertheless comprehensive plot about the lost mother that forms the novel's enigma. This plot energizes the novel's eroticism and propagandistic mission. Desire and propaganda not only organize *Dark Princess;* they also form persistent themes in Du Bois's other writings, especially, I will explain, in his "Criteria of Negro Art" in *The Crisis* and his *Quest of the Silver Fleece*. The overdetermined relationship of desire and propaganda prompts me to ask under what conditions a personal fantasy can sustain a successful work of propaganda and indeed inspire the social activism that characterized Du Bois's life and works.

In Chapter 3, on Richard Wright's *Savage Holiday*, I refer to object-relations theory to uncover a basic plot line of maternal betrayal and character splitting that appears throughout Wright's works, particularly *Black Boy* and *Native Son*. But in these more celebrated works this plot and this character technique are masked under the compulsive plots of interracial violence. I argue that *Savage Holiday* gratifies the unspeakable desire of matricide that Wright's other major works conceal. Disclosing the centrality of the matricidal desire in Wright's fictions also helps me to clarify his narrative logic, which repeatedly produces rapid and often confusing transitions between heterosexual tension and racial hostility.

Chapter 4 examines the relationship between desire and death in Nella Larsen's *Quicksand*. Here I reread the protagonist's fate as not simply the demand of black bourgeois sexual repression but as the overdetermination of female fetishization, self-alienation, racism, and abandonment. Because *Quicksand*, like the other novels in this study, has been the object of traditional racialized and/or gendered readings that have routinely disregarded enigmatic content in the novel, it exemplifies the mediation of two often conflicting domains of meaning: the mimetic representation of social protest and the rhetorical performance of unconscious desire.

In Chapter 5, I argue that *Seraph on the Suwanee*, by Zora Neale Hurston, critiques the sadomasochistic tendencies of romantic love and the essentialized constructions of race by encoding these issues in a story about female self-discovery and romantic fulfillment. *Seraph* employs the mask of white privilege to depict these critiques and to explore stories of class and gender oppression that are denied to the black female protagonists Isis of *Jonah's Gourd Vine* and Janie of *Their Eyes Were Watching God*.

While it is my hope that these chapters provide provocative readings of the five novels and related canonical works, my engagement of psychoanalytic theory and African American literature is meant to demonstrate how black cultural studies and psychoanalytic criticism can help us to appreciate the covert and often latent content inscribed in writing (and other forms of expression) and thus to obtain a more thorough understanding the role of desire in the creation of meaning.

In the conclusion to this study I ask what we gain by articulating the subjective complexity of black textuality. To answer this question, I refer to Du Bois's often repeated visiting-card incident, which he claims teaches him the meaning of race, and to two photographs of him as a child. In studies of Du Bois, these three sites are presumed to be transparent conveyors of historical information. I endeavor to detect the heretofore overlooked expressions of surplus emotional meaning invested in these three representations by referring to the material and social history of Du Bois's early life, to the culture of photography, and to psychoanalytic visual theory about the gaze of desire.

The ultimate goal of my project concerns a question not about the text but about the world: can psychoanalysis help us increase our understanding of the oppressive emotional meanings associated with racial difference? Although I can offer no definitive answers, two points become clear: repeating the popular racial story calcifies our roles in the prescriptive racial plots; and referring to familiar psychoanalytic models does the same thing. Freudian and Lacanian theories are overinvested in their own historical anxieties. But object-relations theory offers a "transitional space" between past circumstances and future possibility—what psychoanalyst D. W. Winnicott calls a "play space" (*Playing*, 41). By establishing a dialectic between desire and the cultural/material effects of racial difference, *Psychoanalysis and Black Novels: Desire and the Protocols of Race* offers what I believe to be a compelling model for reading the complexity of black textuality. My model invites us to imagine a future for African American literary and cultural studies as well as a multicultural American society that doesn't compulsively repeat past regimes.

CHAPTER ONE

Fantasizing Plenitude

Re-Reading Desire in *Megda,*
by Emma Dunham Kelley

Now, I had no idea of writing a love-story when I began, nor have I any idea of making it into one now; I am giving the facts of the case, and no more. If I put more sentiment than wisdom in it, pardon me; it is the fault of the age we live in. Yet a little sentiment now and then, has never been known to hurt anybody; it is only when it is carried to extreme that it is objectionable, and then—it but verifies the old adage—"Extremes are dangerous."

—Emma Dunham Kelley, *Megda* (1891)

In the girl's oedipal fantasy, the mother is split into two figures: the pre-oedipal wonderful good mother and the oedipal evil stepmother. . . . The good mother, so the fantasy goes, would never have been jealous of her daughter or have prevented the prince (father) and the girl from living happily together. So for the oedipal girl, belief and trust in the goodness of the pre-oedipal mother, and deep loyalty to her, tend to reduce the guilt about what the girl wishes would happen to the (step)mother who stands in her way.

—Bruno Bettelheim, *The Uses of Enchantment* (1991)

In other societies, and in most subcultures of our own, women remain in adulthood involved with female relatives—their mothers, sisters, sisters-in-law (or even co-wives). These relationships are one way of resolving and recreating the mother-daughter bond and are an expression of women's general relational capacities and definition of self in relationship. A second way is by having a child, turning her marriage into a family, and recreating for herself the primary intense unit which a heterosexual relationship tends to recreate for men.

—Nancy Chodorow, *Feminism and Psychoanalytic Theory* (1989)

Recovery and Meaning in *Megda*

The recent reprint of Emma Dunham Kelley's *Megda*, originally published in 1891 by James T. Earle of Boston and reissued in 1988 in the *Schomburg Library of Nineteenth-Century Black Women Writers* by Oxford University Press, presents contemporary readers with a fundamental reading problem that arises from its presumably white social context. Conventional racial paradigms do not fit this novel. If there were only a few such novels of black authorship, which eschew our expectations for central, manifestly black characters, this problem would be inconsequential. However, the Schomburg series contains several additional "white" or "raceless" works: *Megda*'s sequel *Four Girls at Cottage City* (1898) and two of the extant novels of Amelia E. Johnson—*Clarence and Corinne; or, God's Way* (1890) and *The Hazeley Family* (1894).[1] At the turn of the twentieth century, well-known black writers also wrote "white" novels. These novels include, for example, Paul Laurence Dunbar's *The Uncalled* (1898), *The Love of Landry* (1900), and *The Fanatics* (1901); and William Stanley Braithwaite's *The Canadian* (1901). And at mid–twentieth century, Frank Yerby and Willard Motley exclusively wrote "white" novels, while Richard Wright, Zora Neale Hurston, William Gardner Smith, and Ann Petry occasionally did so. African American literary scholarship has typically dealt with such novels by relegating them to obscurity. However, our recent efforts to construct a more complete understanding of the literary culture of African Americans by recovering marginalized works demands that we ask new questions to determine what we mean when we say a work is "black."

I participate in this process by asking a series of questions: How are we to read these "white" novels of black authors? How do we fit such works into the corpus of a black writer's works, into African American literary tradition? What desires, pleasures, and defenses does such a narrative suggest? For even when *Megda* contextualizes its characters as white mulattos, the absence of explicit racial signifiers still makes the novel resistant to traditional racial paradigms. Because *Megda* seems more similar in plot, character, and theme to Louisa May Alcott's *Little Women* (1869), a popular girls' novel of white female development, than to the conventionally racialized and, therefore, routinely canonized *Iola Leroy, or the Shadows Uplifted* (1892), by Frances Watkins Harper (a work contemporaneous with *Megda*), the nonracialized feminist paradigm about gender inequity may seem more appropriate. Does this mean that we should read *Megda* as we read *Little Women*, since we cannot read *Megda* like *Iola Leroy*?[2] Or does *Megda*'s evangelical optimism, idealized domesticity, and reticent racial context also make this feminist model problematic? I argue here that the resistance of *Megda* and works like it to both the feminist and the racial paradigms means that we need other critical models. I offer one that centers desire as a significant topic for critical analysis.

While *Megda* looks like a story about white people, its cultural matrix is black. Yet it is precisely this hybridity that resists formulaic racial readings. Although *Megda* forsakes an unambiguous black milieu, it nevertheless conditions the novel's expression of evangelism and domesticity as enhancements of Meg's maturation rather than as occasions for her "regression . . . from leadership, self-reliance, and personal responsibility for her actions," as one prominent feminist reading of the novel suggests (Hite, Introduction, xxxiii). Granted, the meaning invested in the repression of blackness regulates *Megda*'s expressions of desire; still, though, we must also submit that the novel's refusal to gratify our contemporary racial expectation for explicitly identified black characters and the social-protest plot demands that we question conventional racial reading-models. By making racial difference unimportant, this novel already presumes as gratified the political objectives of racial equality depicted in traditional black works. Such a view makes a typical reading of racial oppression obsolete. Moreover, because the novel idealizes the domestic sphere, it also makes the typical feminist reading of gender inequity inappropriate. With these issues in mind, I restate the problem posed by the novel: How do we read the hybrid bodies of these characters? What is the relationship between their ostensible whiteness and their less visible cultural blackness?

From our vantage point, there seems to be little opposition between race and color but rather an intense competition between gender and contested patriarchal power. Despite all of our recent talk about the constructedness of race, whiteness is still presumed to be the standard signifier of social privilege insofar as the general population is concerned. I take a moment here to question the conflation of color and race because *Megda* offers us a striking illustration of its defamiliarization that necessitates my historicizing the construction of whiteness for one particular group of European immigrants to the United States who were commonly stereotyped in the same manner as blacks.

During the last half of the nineteenth century, Irish Americans labored to repress the midcentury appellation commonly associated with them—"Black Irish." While this label now designates Irish with black hair, in the nineteenth century, according to David Roediger, the term signified a partly black heritage resulting from large numbers of Irish "intermixing with shipwrecked slaves" (*Wages*, 4). The *Oxford English Dictionary* defines the "black Irish" as "Irish of Mediterranean appearance." Regardless of the source of the dark coloring, the term was also routinely associated with racial ridicule.

Megda's temporal and spacial locations present an intriguing possibility. Would *Megda*'s first readers have recognized its characters as racial hybrids? Zora Neale Hurston exploits the term "black Irish," suggesting that it was in social currency, by identifying the hero of *Seraph on the Suwanee* (1948) as "obviously Black Irish" (7). Regardless of whether this term designates mythic or factual hybridity, the black population during the late nineteenth century did observe how various white ethnic groups—the Irish, the Italians, and the Jews—renegotiated the racist stereotypes formerly applied to them into white privilege for ensuing generations.[3] Such instances of social mediation no doubt revealed to Kelley and her black contemporaries that racial privilege was not automatically associated with white skin color.

Kelley appropriates "the pleasures of whiteness" for *Megda* and her first audience by revealing the arbitrariness of racial categories (Roediger, *Wages*, 13). By repeatedly mentioning the characters' white skin, blue eyes, and even blond hair, she naturalizes their racial identities by making their textualized white bodies specular objects, realizing full well that a drop of black blood would make an apparently white person black. Kelley signifies that drop by having her narrator name the resort on Martha's Vineyard as Cottage City, a real African American resort at the time of the novel's production, now named Oak Bluffs. The naming of this actual place, in contrast to designating the story's setting as near the city of B——, suggests Kelley's intention to deconstruct conventional racial boundaries in order to form a site of pleasure for those readers who share this aspiration.

Yet *Megda* so repeatedly invokes white skin color as the signifier of beauty, goodness, piety, and affluence that it creates surplus meaning for whiteness. This process both promotes and interrogates the conflation of whiteness and virtue. In fact, the extreme whiteness and corresponding goodness of one character ironically identifies her as an antagonist. Her excessive virtue mobilizes the story by creating a series of internal conflicts, idealizations, and identifications for the heroine to resolve. Such a plotline suggests psychoanalysis as particularly germane not only for questioning the novel's accentuation of whiteness and its suppression of racial discourses but also for speculating about the pleasure such a narrative might hold for a black woman writer in the 1890s and her first audience as well.

In this chapter, I formulate a culturally informed psychoanalytic model for reading *Megda* that is also appropriate for other black novels. My model, to reiterate, emanates from a proposition of psychoanalytic literary criticism, advanced by Peter Brooks: that the rhetorical organization of a literary work is similar to that of the psyche ("Idea," 24–25). According to Brooks, "we sense that there ought to be, that there must be, some correspondence between literary and psychic process, that aesthetic structure and form, including literary tropes, must somehow coincide with the psychic structures and operations they both evoke and appeal to" ("Idea," 25). If this is so, then we could say that the discourses of a novel, which constitute its subjectivity, function somewhat like the conscious, preconscious, and unconscious domains of the psyche. In the case of *Megda,* the Freudian model seems particularly apropos because the novel inscribes the narratives of erotic love, conversion, and domesticity in the dynamics of desire that correspond to the Freudian family romance.

I want to emphasize here that textual subjectivity is different from textual meaning. Textual subjectivity, like its human counterpart, is structured by the mediation of desire and prohibition. However, textual subjectivity is dependent entirely on the language that constitutes the text. By contrast, textual meaning is an intersubjective product of the text and the reader. For African American literary works, textual meaning has routinely focused on the social demand for civil liberty. Thus, we have produced such meaning for these works by devising thematic narratives about social justice while discarding discourses about personal desire that seem irrelevant to this social mission.

Through my critical model I hope to articulate a more comprehensive narrative of *Megda*'s textual meaning by integrating discourses of political demand as well as surplus desire and by referring to all three realms of textual subjectivity—the conscious, preconscious, and unconscious. This model attempts to reveal the limitations of the materialist paradigms of race, gender, and class that concentrate on social discourses of material need and political objective by presenting a more profound, indeed a more penetrating understanding of *Megda* and black literary texts, in general, by reconciling a work's—here *Megda*'s—social demands, inscribed in conscious discourses, with its preconscious and unconscious discourses of desire.

By *conscious discourses,* I mean the explicit social content recorded, for example, in the plot, incidents, characterization, and dialogue (though these elements also harbor the unconscious). We typically refer to these discourses to formulate thematic readings. In explicitly black novels, the racial paradigm directs our construction of textual meaning by focusing our attention on a novel's direct social statements about race and class. (Gender paradigms proceed similarly.) However, such statements more directly concern the subject's material needs and social demands than what Jacques Lacan has identified as an insatiable, unconscious, and prohibited desire for pleasure. According to Lacan, such desire resides in language in signifying chains. It is this type of desire that forms the textual unconscious that I define later.[4] In order to produce a coherent social meaning, the racial paradigm usually either disregards the disruptive content arising from implicit or unconscious discourses in black novels or attributes such content to aesthetic defects. Such a model would regard *Megda* as a reactionary work because it eludes the racial paradigm altogether.

Megda's *conscious discourses* form a story of female development that includes narratives of ambition, conversion, courtship, and marriage. These plots incite, frustrate, sustain, and ultimately gratify the desire of the central character— Meg(da) Randal.[5] The conversion narrative transforms Meg's worldly ambition, pride, and willfulness into exemplary Christian attributes. The courtship and marriage plots idealize rather than problematize domesticity and feminine submission in order to make their achievement enhance and not curtail Meg's character. The plots of spiritual salvation, romantic love, and domestic fulfillment, I will explain, all draw on the respective oedipal and pre-oedipal scenarios of unrequited love and the plenitude of libidinal gratification. Because these plots engage the same developmental structures, *Megda*'s narratives of salvation, erotic pleasure, and refined housekeeping seem mutually generating and, thus, overdetermined. The overdetermined structure of these narratives indicates the text's conscious attempt to affirm its own social values and thereby deny deficiency. However, this overdetermination also signals the operation of unconscious textual desire in achieving satisfaction by means of displacements, which similarly comprise the novel's preconscious discourses.

By *preconscious discourses,* I mean stylistic features (like figurative language) that contain implicit meaning that is accessible to conscious understanding. *Megda*'s preconscious discourses, which I illustrate in detail in the next section of this chapter, form a complex libidinal semiotic of romantic settings, clothing, and sensory perceptions that also nurture Meg's development. I invoke Julia Kristeva's terminology of the semiotic because the pleasures associated with these sensations are accessible not to linguistic analysis but to prelinguistic models of blissful unification of mother and child, commonly identified as the pre-oedipal stage. Although the delight of these sensory discourses is not explicitly expressed, it has access to textual consciousness because its content is not censored. This libidinal semiotic bolsters Meg's self-esteem and preserves her desire during the novel's depiction of her unrequited love by anticipating her gratification in the overdetermined narratives of salvation, love, and domesticity.

In the third and fourth sections of this chapter, I examine the effect of the novel's vacillating pre-oedipal and oedipal plots so as to recover the novel's *unconscious discourses* of desire and gratification, which is to say, its implicit narrative fragments of desire and pleasure inscribed in the rhetorical organization and language of the text. According to Lacan, desire is determined by "the desire of the Other [the unconscious]." "Desire begins to take shape in the margin in which demand becomes separated from need," where there is no possibility of satisfaction ("Subversion," 311). Thus, discourses of unconscious desire are those that implicitly express a subject's unacknowledged longings. Language stages such desire in a signifying performance and its satisfaction by means of a masked fantasy in which enigmatic signifiers create a specter of surplus pleasure—what Lacan calls "the phantom of Omnipotence" or "JOUISSANCE" ("Subversion," 311). By means of signifiers language performs the plenitude once experienced but now inaccessible to consciousness.

Megda's discourses of unconscious desire are inscribed in the novel's most deeply symbolized discourses. Like the string of cryptic images in dreams, the textual unconscious must be deciphered within the dynamics of its representational design. But unlike the dream, the novel is self-conscious in its choice of closure. Because *Megda*'s last scene terminates all textual desire by gratifying it in language that both conceals and reveals the impression of plenitude, this is the site I will examine in an attempt to ascertain *Megda*'s unconscious desire.

The model that I am proposing, then, constructs textual meaning by combining its discourses of social demand and personal desire—conscious, preconscious, and unconscious. The unconscious discourses are the most difficult to determine because, like dreams, they are enigmatic. As I shall demonstrate in this chapter, Lacanian psychoanalysis allows me to ascertain the unconscious desire of this text by detecting discourses that repeat the psychosexual plots of pre-oedipal attachment and oedipal loss. Before I venture to explore the desire inscribed in *Megda*, I need to reconstruct the cultural expectations of its first readers and summarize its plot for those readers who are unfamiliar with the novel.

Megda's silencing of race makes it appear racially ambivalent to us. At the time of *Megda*'s publication, though, its first readers—black and white—would have identified it as "a race novel." For they would have understood "[r]ace literature," according to the 1895 lecture of black activist Victoria Earle Matthews, to be "all the writings emanating from a distinct class—not necessarily race matter; but a general collection of what has been written by the men and women of that Race" (3).[6] From the vantage point of the 1890s, the new century was to be a time of "prosperity and progress" for the virtuous regardless of race (Harper, *Iola Leroy*, 280). But unlike Kelley's contemporaries, we turn-of-the-twenty-first-century readers are ambivalent about and often very critical of novels without explicit racial designations because for us race has become a quintessential signifier. In its absence, we understand a novel to be set in a white social milieu because dominant U.S. convention associates racelessness with white identity and culture.[7] Consequently, *Megda*'s "whiteness" was sufficient to banish it from African American literary scholarship. However, when *Megda* was initially published, it was popular enough to warrant a second edition, one year after the first edition, also published by James T. Earle of Boston. I cannot determine the size of the print runs for the two editions, though I suspect that *Megda*'s readers were largely black women, like Kelley herself, in the Northeast, where literacy rates among African Americans were the highest.

From the vantage point of the 1890s, as I have argued elsewhere (*Domestic Allegories*, 97–112), *Megda*'s racelessness supports the viewpoint that the characters' social positions are more dependent on their morality, spiritual condition, intellect, decorum, and good taste than on the circumstances of their births. In fact, spiritual salvation not only sanctions but appears to engender their worldly rewards. Yet these revolutionary stories about social equality are hard to detect because we are not familiar with black novels that forfeit opportunities for candid racial protest and black activism, objectives that are emphasized in *Iola Leroy* as well as other contemporaneous works by black writers like Sutton Griggs and Charles Chesnutt. To us, *Megda*'s implicit endorsement of the unquestioned assimilationist values of whiteness as the sign of virtue—piety, purity, and classic beauty—make the novel endorse the status quo even while it blurs class and caste distinctions. Yet if we, like Ann duCille, read *Megda* as an "evangelical allegor[y]" (54) or historicize its gender discourse in the context of black post-Reconstruction expectations as I have done in *Domestic Allegories of Political Desire* (121–23), the novel appears less racially ambivalent. The same is true for the novel's stories of spiritual conversion and refined domesticity. Historicized, these stories mitigate the plot of female submission by becoming parts of the novel's liberational discourses about social equality, professional advancement, and female volition. Still, the novel's accentuation of whiteness cannot be entirely eliminated with contextualizing. What pleasure can there be in this "color-struck" text to explain its popularity in the 1890s among a black readership?

Variations of this question are fundamental to literary archeology and literary scholarship in general because it demands that we reexamine the critical process. The recovery of lost works makes us aware of how the politics of identity has controlled literary scholarship. Many works were lost because they were written by women with a different social agenda and/or because high culture celebrates only those so-called major writers whom modernist canonizers have endorsed. Some were lost because they aged poorly and their meaning became increasingly opaque with time. Others were lost because they failed to achieve the popularity of a writer's more famous works or to depict race, gender, class, sexuality, and so on in ways more contemporary audiences have endorsed. Twentieth-century African American literary scholarship has dealt with these problematic works by marginalizing them in favor of those with more traditional social agendas. As a result, novels of perplexing racial hybridity—like Kelley's *Megda,* Zora Neale Hurston's *Seraph on the Suwanee* (1948), and Richard Wright's *Savage Holiday* (1954)—or novels of complex sexuality—like William E. B. Du Bois's *Dark Princess* (1928) and Nella Larsen's *Quicksand* (1928)—rapidly went out of print. The scholarship further erased their historical presence by characterizing black writers and black literature in terms of only well-received works. The recovery of lost works demands that we ask new questions in the hope of making ever more incisive observations.

Megda is about the trials of friendship, salvation, love, and marriage among a circle of presumably white, middle-class girls at the threshold of womanhood. The center of this circle is Meg(da) Randal, who lives in modest comfort with her widowed mother, her brother Hal, and her sister Elsie. As in Alcott's *Little Women,* *Megda*'s "little women" form a "loving sisterhood" (*M* 248). The central cluster is composed of Meg, Ethel Lawton, Laurie Ray, and Dell Manton, while the outermost group includes Ruth Dean, May Bromley, Lulu Martin, Lill Norton, and Maude Leonard. Like Jo March, Meg Randal possesses an array of talents, if not clearly defined virtues; she is proud, ambitious, independent, and self-assured. She plays Lady Macbeth, indeed the very scene that Jo wants to perform in the March sisters' Christmas frolics.[8] By contrast, Ethel is "a perfect lady," "one of God's angels," whose "skin was as white as the driven snow" (*M* 135, 224). Laurie is "one of the sweetest, lovable kittens that every purred" (*M* 70). Dell is as plain-spoken and independent as Meg.

Through repetitive scenes, mirrored characters, and repeated events, *Megda* outlines their submission to divine will as Meg and her girlfriends become Christian wives. Because this plot also adheres to the conventions of nineteenth-century narratology,[9] Meg's development, like Jo's, is mapped on the landscape of sentimental domesticity, in which women are exalted as mothers or future mothers and the home is consecrated as their domain (Leach, *True Love,* 100–101). But unlike *Little Women,* *Megda* does not critique domesticity or its appropriation of the virtues of true womanhood. In *Megda* the domestic realm is idealized as a tastefully decorated and happy sanctuary for women as well as men. But unlike the patriarchal ideal, in which the wife is to be the angel in the house, to invoke the title of Coventry Patmore's 1854 poem, *Megda* sanctions the spirited woman of good character as the model wife.

While marriage ultimately circumscribes the lives of both Meg and Jo, their attitudes and the novels' demands on them are substantially different. At the end of the two-part sequel of *Little Women,* Jo renounces the integrity of her character by relinquishing her independence, ambition, and courage to fulfill the patriarchal expectations of her husband, Professor Bhaer. By contrast, after Meg's marriage, her husband loves rather than spurns "every little fault in her—the little flashes of temper, the spirit of pride that shows itself now and then, the natural willfulness of her disposition" (*M* 376). *Little Women* resigns itself to female subordination to patriarchal culture, whereas *Megda* celebrates female piety as an effective mediator of patriarchal proscription.

Meg has two human adversaries, rather than the cultural antagonist of patriarchal law that Jo encounters. The first is Meg's spiritual rival, Maude Leonard, who Meg maintains is a liar, a cheat, and a hypocrite. Although Maude repents and is baptized early in the story, she fails to live a Christian life of humility, faith, and love. Rather, she gratifies her vanity with arrogance and extravagant displays of herself. As the disingenuous Christian, Maude is both the obvious villain of the story and Meg's alter ego. Meg compares herself to Maude, despite her "lovable nature" and many talents (*M* 182), for "[p]ride was Meg's besetting sin; it often kept her from converting noble thoughts into noble actions." Unaware of the need for self-criticism, Meg finds herself growing more and more haughty.

Meg has a personal intercessor in the angelic Ethel, who will help Meg become an exemplary Christian. Meg idealizes Ethel and wants to identify with her. However, their relationship is much more ambivalent than that between Meg and Maude. The text constructs the triangular relationship among the three girls much like object-relations theory constructs the pre-oedipal stage. During this period, the daughter defends her attachment to the mother by splitting the mother into good and bad parts. Thus the daughter's devotion to the good mother is dependent on her repudiation of the bad mother. Meg repeats this familiar ploy by embracing Ethel and renouncing Maude, although Meg is more like Maude than she cares to acknowledge.

When Meg becomes infatuated with Reverend Arthur Stanley, whom she will marry, the relationship between Meg and Ethel becomes more ambivalent. It changes from the surrogate daughter's maternal identification and attachment to her estrangement from the mother figure as she heeds the demands of heterosexual love, much like the oedipal father's seduction of the daughter. Thus, with Arthur's growing importance to the story, the oedipal plot of triangular desire becomes dominant. Arthur supplants Maude, but the text does not entirely abandon the daughter's pre-oedipal desire for the figurative mother. Meg fulfills this desire by becoming like Ethel. The pre-oedipal plot of fusion with the mother is further enhanced by Arthur's role as a minister and intercessor for God, whose maternal attributes the text accentuates.

Ethel's first role has much in common with the mother during the pre-oedipal stage because Meg longs to be like the ideal Ethel. Meg loves and idealizes Ethel to the extent that she becomes the paragon of feminine beauty and virtue with whom Meg identifies. Early in the story Meg relates her adoration of this idol: "'I honor and respect Ethel Lawton above all my acquaintances. I am proud to think she has called me her friend'" (*M* 67). As an ideal model of feminine "sympathy and sacrifice," Ethel is, for Meg, both a mother surrogate and a Christian identificatory ideal.

After Meg's infatuation with Arthur, Ethel also becomes Meg's unacknowledged sexual rival in a plot of unrequited love. In this second plot, Ethel and Meg respectively play the mother and daughter in the female version of the classic oedipal triangle, in which the daughter represses her aggressive feelings toward the mother because she, rather than the daughter, is the object of the father's desire. Meg's idealization of Ethel intensifies her unacknowledged envy of and aggression toward Ethel. Meg "'wish[es] to be good, to be true, to be noble'" like Ethel (*M* 13). However, the process of idealization makes her suffer a "vague, undefinable feeling" that "will make itself known to her and fill her whole being so that she will know no peace and happiness until the longing is satisfied" (*M* 14). Meg's distress originates in her idealization of Ethel and Arthur's unrequited love. The text denies these effects, though, and misrecognizes them as Meg's spiritual longing. In so doing, the text replaces the unrequited love story between Meg and Arthur with the travail of Meg's idealization of Ethel and the demands of the conversion narrative. In resolving the unacknowledged rivalry between Meg and Ethel, as we shall see, the text capitalizes on its investments both in Meg's hidden hostility and in divine providence to eliminate Ethel from the text.

According to the dictates of the pre-oedipal and oedipal plots, respectively, the pressure from Meg's identification with Ethel and aggression toward her would respectively produce Meg's conscious desire to emulate Ethel and Meg's unconscious desire to replace her. The narrative plays out both desires, all the while preserving Meg's innocence by obscuring oedipal guilt with pre-oedipal loyalty, much like that of the enchanted girl in the Bettelheim epigraph who mitigates her guilt by splitting the mother into the good (pre-oedipalized) mother and the wicked (oedipalized) stepmother. *Megda's* intentional and therefore conscious narrative evolves into the conversion story in which Meg not only achieves spiritual salvation but also duplicates Ethel's piety, charity, and purity. Because plot causality indicates the force of unconscious textual desire, we can identify its effect in the elimination of Ethel from the romantic triangle.

While we tend to associate characters with representations of people, characters are actually internalized projections or the novel's imagos. Characters may appear mimetic, but they are "generated subjectively" according to the dynamics of the novel's subjectivity and not according to the demands of reality (Moore and Fine, *Psychoanalytic Terms,* 19). Characters, then, are signifiers of textual desire and not replicas of historical people. Meg in the signifying roles of the oedipal and pre-oedipal daughter allows the text to express and conceal the aggression and hostility that will erupt as the story moves to closure.

Other structural and rhetorical features of the novel—for example, repetition, exaggeration, ellipsis, suspension, anticipation, digression, irony, coincidence—also signify unconscious desire and its satisfaction in the expression of a hidden wish (Lacan, *Écrits,* 169; Brooks, *Reading,* 105). The expression of this wish creates textual pleasure and brings the story to its close. By referring to several of these rhetorical and structural elements in *Megda,* I hope to demonstrate that while the salvation story temporarily displaces the matrimonial plot, neither of these explicit and therefore conscious narratives expresses the dominant unconscious wish. For neither Meg's baptism nor her marriage to Arthur brings the novel to closure. The gratification of another unstated desire determines *Megda*'s conclusion. What is this desire? In an attempt to locate it, I return to incidents in *Megda* that are profusely symbolized, insinuating unconscious wishes.

Early in the story, long before Meg realizes her vague longing, she develops a crush on young Reverend Arthur Stanley as a consequence of an exhilarating chance encounter during a windstorm. The wind blows off his derby and makes Meg lose her balance. She accidentally falls to a sitting position and just happens to land on his hat. After Arthur helps Meg to stand up and recovers his crushed derby, he offers to escort her home. This important incident is full of sexual innuendo. In the novel's sartorial semiotic, their mutual exchange of the crushed hat for her neck ribbon as souvenirs are erotic signs that foreshadow the exchange of vows at their marriage. Moreover, by the late nineteenth century, stormy weather was a conventional signifier of rising sexual turbulence. This scene alerts us to the novel's practice of symbolizing desire by means of displacements, a practice that is accentuated in texts of black authorship undoubtedly because of white society's persistent allegation of black hypersexuality. By introducing the hero as a minister, this scene also prepares us for the replacement of the romantic plot with the conversion narrative.

Meg's infatuation with Arthur continues to build, even though her brother Hal tells her several weeks later on the way to church that "'Mr. Stanley is setting his cap for Ethel'" (*M* 109). Disregarding that remark, Meg daydreams in church about him. During his sermon, "[f]astidious Meg was thoroughly charmed, though she could not have told his text five minutes after she heard it, nor could she remember one particular thing that he said. He appealed only to her admiration; he demanded that and received it" (*M* 113). The text attempts to efface Meg's sexual attraction to Arthur with a sermon about the "infinite love" of "Our Heavenly Father" (*M* 113). This sermon is very important, as I will explain, because it provides the protocol for Meg's spiritual conversion and the text's romantic development. This incident also begins the process of transforming Meg's sexual rivalry into her spiritual need.

As the evidence builds that Arthur has indeed "set his cap for Ethel," Meg experiences acute distress (*M* 106). We remember that Arthur has already given his real derby to Meg, an act that makes us associate her feelings with sexual jealousy, even if the text insists that Meg is covetous of Ethel's attention rather than Arthur's. For example, "[w]hen Meg looked at Ethel . . . it seemed as if she were looking on one of God's angels" (*M* 224). Meg's admiration for Ethel silences her jealousy. In fact, the narrator insists that jealousy was unknown to Meg until the moment after Laurie reveals her intention to become a Christian and Ethel "took both her hands in hers, and kissed her" (*M* 196). Ethel's embrace of Laurie causes Meg to feel "a jealous pang shoot through her heart—the first she had ever known" (*M* 196). The text clearly wants to cast Meg's affliction as sibling rivalry instead of unrequited love before replacing it with spiritual longing. However, the text overstates its denial of Meg's jealousy of Ethel. As a result, this disclaimer is unconvincing, an issue to which I shall return. Insofar as Meg and the conscious narrative are concerned, though, the denial is successful. However, Meg's jealousy resides in the novel's unconscious. Even though she maintains her dignity, the text increasingly connects the "vague, undefinable feeling" associated with unacknowledged jealousy to her conscious wish for spiritual reverence (*M* 14). This powerful but indistinct feeling makes her conversion possible.

The text represents Meg's "strange, unaccountable feeling of dissatisfaction" as evidence of the yearning of her unrepentant soul rather than jealousy from unrequited love or guilt from repressed aggressive and hostile wishes (*M* 104). Hence, the following passage aligns Meg's latent romantic distress with conscious spiritual disquiet in a very poignant scene in which Arthur proposes to Ethel:

> "I love you, Ethel. Will you be my wife?" And Ethel answered simply and gravely, with the lovely wild-rose color dyeing her white cheek, "Yes, Arthur, for I love you with all my heart."
>
> . . . .
>
> "Oh, dear!" sighed Meg, at the dinner-table that day. "I feel so—so"—
>
> "I pity you, my dear," said Hal, gravely. "I know what it is to feel that way myself. A disagreeable feeling, isn't it?"
>
> Meg smiled, too *spiritless* to reply. (*M* 264–65, ellipsis in the original, my emphasis)

The ellipsis in this important scene links Arthur's proposal and Meg's strange malaise to an inadequacy of faith with the word "spiritless." This juxtaposition deliberately aligns spirituality and unrequited love; it also suggests that unrequited love prepares Meg for salvation, refines her character, and purifies her love for Arthur, thereby making her into a Christian wife at the end of the novel. In addition, this scene directs our attention to a series of amorous displacements among

Meg, Ethel, and Arthur in the plot of unrequited love as the effects of eroticism and spirituality become mutually signifying. Meg's "strange, unaccountable feeling of dissatisfaction" reveal both her spiritual and sexual longings (*M* 104). These displacements occur with increasing frequency as the narrative reaches its climax, much like the classic conversion narrative.[10] Kelley's first audience would have been very familiar with this narrative and also would have known how to read the dual plotlines of spirituality and eroticism.

The symmetry between Meg's desire and her subsequent unacknowledged jealousy of Ethel, on the one hand, and Meg's piety, on the other, anticipates another congruity between her spiritual conversion and erotic gratification. The text has repeatedly foreshadowed these events by having Meg stand in for Ethel. At the theatrical rehearsal and presentation early in the novel, for example, Meg's performance of Lady Macbeth displaces Ethel's Ophelia (*M* 41). When Meg is struck dumb in church school, "Ethel took her place" and greeted Arthur as their substitute teacher (*M* 133). While teaching at the institution that Meg and her girlfriends had attended, Meg routinely and self-consciously sits "in Ethel's chair" (*M* 315). Thus, the requirements of the conversion and romantic plots converge as Meg becomes Ethel's spiritual and erotic replacement. But Ethel's death signals the return of the love story, insinuated by the fateful meeting of Meg and Arthur on the night of the windstorm. The novel has suspended the love story in order to enhance its spiritual plot by preparing Meg to take Ethel's place as Arthur's wife. When Meg assumes this role, she knows she has not earned this role through her own abilities. Rather, Meg is consciously aware that God has prepared her for it with the "supreme educat[ion]" of spiritual love (Gay, *Bourgeois Experience,* 1:138).[11]

Megda, then, is both a conversion narrative in which spirituality has been eroticized and a love story in which passion has been spiritualized. The correspondence between piety and eros is no accident, for during the nineteenth century, evangelical novels like *Megda* "were to erotic faith what Bibles, churches, and chapels were to Christianity: the ways, means, and sites for the propagation of faith" (Polhemus, *Erotic Faith,* 4). By the end of the century, this equation favors eros, for Kelley cautions her audience to focus on the novel's wisdom rather than on the market demand for sentiment (see this chapter's first epigraph).

Undoubtedly, *Megda*'s erotic titillation contributed to the novel's popularity. *Megda* envelops the titillation within a moral allegory that sanctions Meg's desire, talent, and determination by making their gratification the signs of her virtue and the reward of a loving, magnanimous God. For the conversion narrative "gave women—both tellers and readers—a measure of free play, a vehicle for the expression of their feelings, and a testimony to their abilities" (Brereton, *From Sin,* 34). Divine power then supports Meg's claim of "spiritual individualism" that in turn supports "female self-determinism" (Brereton, *From Sin,* 31; Andrews, Introduction, 2). Even more important, though, divine power authorizes the novel's erotic desire by sanctioning and resolving the plot of unrequited love. Such an endorsement adheres to the tradition of evangelical domestic novels written by women of this era, a tradition that Kelley also invokes in *Four Girls at Cottage City* with reference to the then popular evangelical novel *Beyond the Gates* (1883) by Elizabeth Stuart Phelps.[12]

Thus *Megda*'s spiritual plot is not hostile to Meg's development because evangelism provides expression not only for the heroine's religious quest but for self-definition and sexual gratification as well. Unlike the ultimate demands of patriarchal law on *Little Women* that eclipses its maternal household and exacts Jo's obedient containment within an oppressive domesticity, *Megda*'s evangelical conversion story resists the patriarchal economy of girls' fiction and engenders a pervasive semiotic of gratified female desire. In addition, spiritual faith in *Megda* further conditions domesticity by transforming it into a holy agency with a woman at its center for redefining the individual and resocializing the community. Conversion then legitimizes Meg's desire and redefines domesticity as the site of her material, spiritual, and sexual pleasure and power.

These discourses of desire are a part of the novel's preconscious structure because they are accessible to Meg, the text, and the reader. The gratification invested in sartorial and residential elegance is also available to the novel's conscious and further supports the novel's economy of pleasure.[13] This somewhat oblique signifying pattern was especially appropriate for an African American reading community because it alludes to erotic desire while deflecting white society's allegations of excessive black sexuality.

Insofar as black post-Reconstruction subjects are concerned, possessing the accoutrements of taste signified social distinction, indeed social equality. While Meg may need lessons in piety to win the additional prize of ideal sexual pleasure, she is already an expert in all matters of taste. Indeed, *Megda* is replete in lessons about appropriate dress, polite speech, entertaining, and domestic elegance. In this way the novel revises the conventions of the traditional conversion narrative to make them compatible with emergent consumer capitalism. Whereas the pre-elect once were destined to go to heaven, in *Megda* they are destined to live graciously in commodious, earthly homes.

The conversion narrative, the discourses of good taste, and the presumption of a white social context are parts of the novel's conscious. They appeal especially to black readers and disrupt the standard scenario of black female submission in *Megda* by making Meg responsible for acting out her own convictions. As the subject and object of her salvation, religion offers Meg a position from which to reconcile desire—hers and the text's—within Christian paternalism. In addition, the plots of love, bourgeois consumption, civility, and family reformation in the context of presumed whiteness further enhance Meg's position as the novel's desiring subject by eliminating the material boundaries of her aspirations. More important, though, these conscious discourses distract us from recognizing the novel's restaging of social and spiritual aspirations as the family romance. For example, the conversion story, as we shall see, combines the desire of the oedipal and pre-oedipal plots by granting Meg a husband who is like the divine father who cares for his children like the omnipotent pre-oedipal mother. What distracts us from recognizing the plot of the family romance is the novel's display of a libidinal semiotic of romantic settings, clothing, and sensory perception.

Megda's Semiotic of Pleasure

In the episodes in which Meg suffers unrequited love, the imagery of sensory sensations becomes so profuse that it forms a semiotic of libidinal desire and pleasure like that associated with the infant during the pre-oedipal developmental stage.[14] This semiotic arises from textual representations of sensory delight that engage sight, touch, smell, sound, and taste. These experiences provide Meg with gratification and fill the lack caused by Arthur's unrequited love, hence Meg perceives other forms of satisfaction in lieu of his love. This semiotic sustains Meg's pleasure by diverting her attention from her own distress and enhances the reader's anticipation of the happy ending.

For example, not only do Meg's mother, sister, and brother as well as her friends idolize her, literally "hovering around the[ir] heroine . . . their pride and queen," "every face smiled a welcome on Meg" wherever she went (*M* 156–57, 110). Particularly important is Arthur's persistent display of pleasing reactions to Meg. Even though he expresses his preference for Ethel, the text repeatedly reveals that Meg is the most constant object of his gaze. For instance, in the chapter before he asks for Ethel's hand in marriage,

> [h]e sat beside Ethel, attentive to her slightest wish, but he also sat where he could watch Meg's fair, sparkling face, shining pure and white . . . with the soft, moonlike light upon it. She pleased him; she made him feel as if he would give the world, if he had it, if he could have just such a sweet, pure, loveable girl for his sister. He could have taken her to his heart, with all her faults, and cherished her as only a brother can cherish the sister he loves. (*M* 258)

The persistence of his focus on Meg reveals his attraction to her. The guise of brotherly affection does not conceal the true nature of his ardor from late-nineteenth-century readers or us, for "the ideal of falling in love with one's 'duplicate' image, rather than with a 'contrast,' was an increasingly familiar part of turn-of-the-twentieth-century romantic ideology" (Boone, *Tradition*, 11).

Megda explicitly instructs us in this expectation by investing Meg's brother with the seductive posture usually associated with the oedipal father and then displacing it onto Arthur. When she "accepts [her brother] Hal's invitation to a seat upon his knee," we are reminded of the storm scene in which Meg accidentally sits on Arthur's derby (*M* 27). Nineteenth-century sartorial symbolism understood the derby as a phallic signifier (Steele, *Fashion*, 224). Near the novel's close and after Arthur and Meg marry, the narrator feels compelled to "confess" that Meg can frequently be found "sitting upon his knee" (*M* 381). When Meg finally sits on Arthur's knee, the novel invites sexual titillation that readers in the 1890s and the 1990s cannot miss. But until the gratification of the titillation, the novel engages other sensual delights to comfort Meg. For example, confectionery treats habitually satiate her taste buds (*M* 241–43, 252, 258). "[D]elicious music" floats through open windows (*M* 259), and fragrant flowers surround her. Such sites of delight are accentuated in the novel's representation of clothing and settings.

We cannot escape noticing Kelley's preoccupation with describing the exquisite dresses of Meg and her friends, Ethel's unusual room, or the enchanting setting of Meg's baptism. However, Kelley's contemporaries probably experienced the eroticism arising from the discursive and semiotic displacements of Meg's desire more acutely and with less ambivalence than we do, for they were better conditioned to invest libidinal energy in nonsexual objects. No doubt they were also more adept than we are at obtaining pleasure from such objects because we have come to expect more direct and explicit graphic representations of sexual passion and pleasure. Such iconography, as David C. Miller explains, has been "subject to periodic change as the conceptual apparatus of seeing responds to cultural reconstruction" (*Dark Eden*, 152).[15] The semiotic of beautiful objects—pretty young women, exquisite clothing, lovely flowers, and delightful settings—presented throughout *Megda* were particularly resonant icons of Victorian eroticism on both sides of the Atlantic. Readers of that period were likely to have understood them as the powerful evidence of Meg's gratification. In addition, this lush iconography and the promise of salvation undermine any evidence of Meg's distress. Although she experiences libidinal depletion, this lack is initially filled with sartorial and sensual signifiers of gaze, taste, smell, touch, and hearing.

While there are numerous descriptions of the attire of Meg and her female friends, the fashion semiotic centers on Meg.[16] Her large and tasteful wardrobe is sartorial language for her captivating charm and bourgeois marriageability rather than evidence of her vanity. This sartorial code designated delicate fabrics as indicative of a lady's (presumed) delicacy (Lurie, *Language*, 187). Moreover, the light color of Meg's dresses as well as the elaborate ornamentation of artificial flowers represent her sexual purity and bourgeois social status. These elaborate dresses were signs of conspicuous consumption and conspicuous leisure (Lurie, *Language*, 116). In the context of post-Reconstruction black culture, as I have argued elsewhere (*Domestic Allegories*, 97–108), evidence of material wealth and leisure were proof of black people's acquisition of social parity with the white bourgeoisie.

Meg's attire also appeals to the senses, especially sight, making her presence into a pictorial representation to be interpreted. The colors and textures of the fabric please the eye, evoking tactile sensation, and the artificial flower-trimmings project and displace her sensual and sexual presence onto aesthetic objects. The reader sees Meg and approves of her appearance not only from a neutral external vantage point but also, and more important, from Arthur's perspective. By dressing up, Meg defines herself as both the subject of her own desire and the object of Arthur's. In the context of eroticized spirituality, Meg's good taste in sartorial elegance is an important signifier of her erotic desire which could not, at least for a respectable young woman, become either conscious or verbal.

Erotic signification in *Megda* is further amplified by Kelley's sensual rendering of nature and interior decor. Sexualizing nature was a very familiar practice by the nineteenth century. With the increased commodity consumption of the industrial age, interior space also became a repository for displaced eroticism. *Megda* depicts this practice in the episodes concerning Meg's baptism and her visit to Ethel's room. The first incident occurs on Easter Sunday. Meg selects this symbolic day for her baptism, and the text concurs by making that Sunday "one of the most beautiful days that ever dawned. The morning was perfect. . . . The place of the baptism was the most beautiful spot in that section of the country. The river lay between two groves" (*M* 321). The beauty of this fecund setting, complete with singing birds if not buzzing bees, underscores a similar solemnity found in Ethel's room, which we see through Meg's eyes. Like Ethel's skin, her room "was all white" (*M* 108, 217).

> From where Meg sat, she could look through into a large, airy, beautifully-furnished bed-chamber, also furnished and decorated in white. The pure whiteness was relieved in the boudoir by trailing vines of the delicate-green English ivy. . . . White marble busts of Shakespeare, Dickens, Hawthorne, and Irving glistened through the trailing ivy, from the various corners. (*M* 271–72)

While the idyllic riverscape incites the pleasure of spiritual rebirth, the interior of Ethel's room is a tranquil site of repose. The lush foliage and white marble furnishings of the cemetery-like room signals the displacement of libidinal energy from Ethel to Meg.

The text endows these settings with erotic meaning that nineteenth-century readers were particularly adept at discerning, for appreciating pictorial and verbal representations of landscapes was an important cultural activity for middle-class Victorians on both sides of the Atlantic. Also, from the middle of the nineteenth century, as David C. Miller explains, idyllic bodies of water were a safe and codified repository of "unchanneled libidinal energies" (*Dark Eden,* 34). According to him, the changing attitudes of Americans at this time "from moralistic preoccupations to a concern with psychic fulfillment and self-exploration was effected to a surprising extent by attention to landscapes that . . . had never before been awarded particular notice, much less positive value" (*Dark Eden,* 2). In addition, the nature poetry of William Wordsworth and his numerous U.S. imitators, including African Americans like Charlotte Forten Grimké (1837–1914) and Henrietta Cordelia Ray (1852?–1916), undoubtedly helped to transform the landscape image into a socially respectable and yet a "sentimental icon" of desire—but desire safely diffused and thus arrested (Miller, *Dark Eden*, 44). The poetic image masked the frightening aspects of nature with moral overtones that had been pervasive since the eighteenth century and reclaimed the picturesque tradition for oral and religious purposes, as pastoral landscape became an ideal symbol of the beauty that reflected God's nature (Miller, *Dark Eden*, 44, 135, 143). To ponder nature was to ponder the infinity, "unity, repose, symmetry, purity, and moderation" of natural beauty and to gain access to the sublime (Miller, *Dark Eden*, 143). Hence, the iconography of the sublime landscape became a most appropriate image for popular, nineteenth-century evangelical novels whose plots spiritualize the experience of erotic love by freezing it into visual imagery and by making the spiritual transformation of eroticism the supreme cultivator of the human character. The descriptions of the settings in *Megda*, then, are not simply neutral accounts for locating the novel's action; they are indirect erotic discourses. But there is still more pleasure that psychoanalytic criticism can mine from this novel.

Vacillating Plots of Desire

The vacillating pre-oedipal and oedipal plots,[17] respectively about Meg's desire to be like and to possess Ethel, on the one hand, and Meg's desire to assume Ethel's position with respect to Arthur, structure Meg's relationship with Ethel. The first plot conceals the hostility of the second by displacing Meg's jealousy of Ethel onto an idealized identification with her. Such recognition evolves implicitly as "a relationship of fatal rivalry" that culminates in the text's elimination of Ethel and the installation of Meg in her place (Silverman, *Threshold*, 42). The tension between these two plots prevents Meg's devastation from her initial unrequited love for Arthur, secures her confidence, and supports her denials of jealousy of Ethel.

While the vacillation between the two plots appears repeatedly until Ethel's death, for purposes of illustration I will focus on two conspicuous instances. The first occurs shortly before Ethel's wedding and desexualizes Meg's infatuation with Arthur by displaying her devotion to Ethel, whom Meg has all the while emphatically revered as her ideal woman. During this incident Meg prays that Ethel will survive to marry Arthur: "Meg went about her daily work with always this prayer in her heart and often on her lips: 'Dear Father, spare her; do not take her from us.' It seemed as if she had never loved Ethel half so well as she did now" (*M* 327). The pre-oedipal idealization of Ethel intensifies to keep Meg's oedipal jealousy repressed, while the text reports the circumstances leading to Ethel's death. As the following extracts indicate, the two scenes depicting her death are particularly erotically charged.

The first occurs on the evening before Ethel's death, as she presents herself to her bridegroom after the wedding rehearsal. The scene is cast from the perspective of Meg, who is Ethel's maid of honor.

> Ethel's dress was an ivory white silk. Her wreath was of orange blossoms, her bouquet of orange blossoms and white hyacinths. Her fair hair gleamed like gold underneath the misty bridal veil of costly lace; her blue eyes shone softly; her lips were like a scarlet line; a lovely pink color was in her cheeks. Mr. Stanley looked at her long and earnestly, and then, oblivious of Meg's presence, he took her in his arms, and held her close to him.
> "My wife," he whispered. (*M* 334)

This scene, replete with references to flowers, purity, luxurious commodities, and Arthur's passionate embrace, represents the couple's erotic fascination that anticipates sexual fulfillment. However, on the morning of the day of anticipated consummation, Ethel "was taken suddenly ill . . . with a hemorrhage" (*M* 335).

In this second scene,

> Ethel was lying on the bed, her face as white as the pillow on which it rested, her fair hair surrounding it like a golden cloud. . . . He [Arthur] bent over Ethel in speechless grief, and Meg slipped from her place beside the pillow and stole softly to the window. She would have left the room, but Ethel asked her not to.
>
> Meg never forgot that scene. It didn't seem as if Ethel were dying; she and Arthur talked together as if it were a parting for a few days or weeks at most. . . .
>
> "I am going, Arthur, but—it—won't—be—for—long; only—just a little—while—before. I will—wait for—you—and—watch for you. You—will—come—soon, Arthur?"
>
> "Yes, my darling; when I have finished the work He has set for me to do here." . . .
>
> Meg crept from the room, unable longer to bare [*sic*][18] the sight. Ethel did not see her go; she saw only the face bending over her, unutterable love and anguish in the dark-blue eyes. It was his turn to sooth her.
>
> "It is only for a little while, my darling—my wife."
>
> A look of ineffable joy passed over her face as he called her by that dear name. . . . Ethel was dying the death, as she had lived the life, of a Christian.
>
> "Only—a little—while—before," she whispered dreamily. "Then—no—more—parting,—Ar"—
>
> The word died on her lips. She turned her head slowly until her cheek rested against his; and thus, lying upon his breast, she fell asleep. (*M* 337–40)

The image of Ethel "lying upon [Arthur's] breast" is cast from Meg's perspective. She relates what the entire passage has intimated, that the deathbed scene is an erotic cultural fantasy, a displacement for a sexual embrace. The pervasive descriptions of Ethel's extreme whiteness throughout the novel preclude allusions to blood everywhere but in this erotically charged scene. Might the reference to hemorrhage also allude to the blood of the ruptured hymen and therefore strengthen the intimation of the sexual meaning for "dying," especially since the reference to "dying" precedes that to sleeping in the passage?[19] In order to preserve the subtlety of the erotic displacement of this scene and to foreshadow another involving Meg, the narrator brings the death scene to an abrupt ending by shifting our gaze from Ethel and Arthur to Meg, lying on her bed, not dying but, rather, crying and remembering: "How beautiful Ethel had looked! She was dressed in her wedding-dress—veil, wreath and all. During the service at the house, the casket had stood between the rose-covered gates, through which she should have passed, a breathing, happy bride" (*M* 340). By witnessing Ethel's and Arthur's delight in erotic expectation and their faithful Christian resolve in confronting its utter frustration, Meg sees them as exemplars of spiritual rather than romantic love. Moreover, by dying on her wedding day, Ethel is suspended eternally as a virgin bride, an absolute symbol of purity, charity, and love for both Meg and Arthur to revere.

Kelley's age was saturated with such scenes of arrested desire. Her contemporaries—black and white—had been schooled by nineteenth-century writers' and artists' depictions of young, beautiful, dead or dying women. The "dead, beautiful lady . . . [was a] 'safe' repositor[y] of unchanneled libidinal energies—and this is the important point—precisely because [she] permitted no chance for actual fulfillment" (Miller, *Dark Eden*, 34). Thus, in addition to being steeped in the cult of true womanhood, Kelley's epoch was also aesthetically, psychologically, and ideologically fascinated with the dying beauty.

Erotically charged paintings of dead or dying beauties—the Lady of Shalott, Lady Elaine of Tennyson's *Idylls of the King,* Shakespeare's Ophelia, and countless unknown "sublime consumptives"—covered the walls of museums in U.S. and European cities (Dijkstra, *Idols,* 29, 36).[20] These paintings presented "the apotheosis of an ideal of feminine passivity and helplessness" (Dijkstra, *Idols,* 36), an ideal that the dying Ethel duplicates as a "consumptive sublime." Like Ethel, these paintings of beautiful, dying or "dead women as object[s] of desire" were powerful icons of eroticism that bound the moral obligation of purity to aesthetic pleasure (Dijkstra, *Idols,* 51, 60). These icons respected the late-nineteenth-century mandate for sexual reticence and female passivity, while simultaneously expressing sexuality as arrested desire.

The bride Ethel, expiring in the loving arms of Arthur as he calls her his wife, presents a cultural icon familiar to readers of this epoch, who would have been particularly adept at detecting its sexual valences, for Kelley's contemporaries were well aware of tropes of dying as an archaic euphemism for sexual climax. The image of the deceased, pious bride both unites spiritual and sexual love and consolidates the nineteenth-century moral and aesthetic order. This scene is also magnified by material opulence—a stately parlor, a profusion of flowers, yards of "ivory white silk," a "misty bridal veil of costly lace" (*M* 334)—that further estheticizes desire.

With Ethel's removal from the triangle, the oedipal plot fades from the novel, as Meg slowly assumes Ethel's place and as Meg and Arthur display their mutual admiration and affection for one another. He "showed her plainly in a hundred little ways when with her, that he enjoyed being with her very much" (*M* 355). As for Meg, "she loved him with her whole heart, respected him above anyone she had ever known, and trusted him fully" (*M* 356). The reader realizes what as yet Meg has not, that Meg has displaced Ethel. Within a few pages the text makes that realization explicit with the chapter entitled "Mrs. Stanley," set "[t]hree years later, and once more, the twelfth of June. Just four years from the day of Ethel's wedding-day and death" (*M* 359). Meg, Dell, Laurie, and May are sitting in Laurie's parlor where they greet Meg's double, "Laurie's six-months baby girl—little Meg" (*M* 359). During this episode Ethel's ideal womanhood becomes fully integrated into Meg's character. Her "face was as fair as ever . . . but the proud, haughty look had gone, or else deepened and softened into one of sweet, grave womanliness and tender pity" (*M* 370). The text effaces Arthur's proposal to Meg, yet it exposes her thoughts: "Meg knew how much Ethel had been to Mr. Stanley, and Mr. Stanley knew that Meg knew it, and although he loved Meg deeply and tenderly now, he knew and she knew, that there was a corner of his heart where even she could never enter" (*M* 370). Thus, fully aware of his loving memory of Ethel, Meg accepts his proposal, and they look forward to sanctioning their union with the Christian sacrament of marriage.

The triangular desire among Meg, Ethel, and Arthur ultimately gives rise to the idealized love between Meg and Arthur in which spirituality and romantic ardor are fused. Because *Megda* eroticizes spirituality, the novel stimulates the reader's anticipation of the fulfillment of Meg's sexual desire by arresting the love plot while vicariously advancing it in Christian topology. The earlier episodes in which Meg pledges her love to Christ and Arthur baptizes her with extraordinary devotion serve as facsimiles of the wedding ceremony. These spiritual events gratify Meg's aspirations for piety and foreshadow her connubial bliss even as she experiences unrequited love. Yet as I explain later, the text describes such bliss not in terms of Arthur's embrace but as the plenitude of divine reward.

Megda's Unconscious Pleasure

Although *Megda* depicts Meg as Arthur's second love, she is his right love. This is the moral to the sermon that Meg fails to grasp because she is daydreaming about him. The following is a portion of that sermon:

> "Suppose that three weeks ago a lad . . . had been brought to a knowledge of the Lord Jesus Christ, and that with his heart full of love to the Lord he wanted to do something for Him. And suppose he goes to the Sunday-school superintendent and says, 'Will you have the kindness to give me a class to teach.' . . . Now this dear boy . . . begins to pray that God would convert these . . . children. . . . If these children had been converted the first week, he would take credit to himself; he would . . . attribute the conversions to his entreaties, instead of to the power of the Holy Ghost. . . . But let him patiently go on, and when his heart is prepared, God will, if

possible, give it [the conversion of the children]. Thus it is that the child of God has to wait until the heart is prepared for the blessing." (*M* 122–24)

Applying this parable to Meg, we see that had there been no obstacle in Meg's and Arthur's initial romantic attraction, the result would have failed to become Christian love. That is, if he had immediately succumbed to Meg's charm, she would have believed that her personal attributes were entirely responsible for attracting his love. She would not have regarded his love as a blessing sent to her by God. As the novel's last line insists, "Verily, He doeth all things well, and maketh all things to come right in His own good time" (*M* 394). This evangelical conviction makes Ethel's death the means to the right ending for the novel. Therefore, Ethel's death must be a source of textual pleasure. But how can such a sorrowful event be the source of pleasure? I suggest that this death contains repressed and subversive gratifying content, which can be recovered much like latent desire in a dream.

Despite the elaborate pre-oedipal plots of displacement that redirect Meg's gaze from Arthur to Ethel and blur the ego boundaries between these two female characters, the normal response of the third party in a love triangle is envy, hostility, and aggression.[21] However, the text insists that Meg is not jealous. Is the text credible? *The Interpretation of Dreams* by Sigmund Freud provides a strategy for answering this question. Here Freud explains that the prohibited and, therefore, latent content of a dream becomes conscious only when it escapes the censorship of the ego by means of disguise, "dream-work."[22]

Megda's diversionary plotting, much like the masking mechanisms of dream-work, represents Ethel's death as a consequence of a fatal illness. By applying Freud's observations on dream-work to analyze Ethel's death, which can be seen as a manifest dream, I suggest that the identity of the libidinal energy that compels Ethel's death, that indeed drives the entire novel, is not simply repressed (or latent) jealousy but murderous aggression. At the level of character development, the text has attempted to mask Meg's repressed jealousy by having her recast Ethel as the idealized pre-oedipal mother. As a result, Meg desires and identifies with Ethel. The oedipal story also motivates Meg's desire to displace Ethel and attract Arthur's attention. Although Meg's conversion and the pre-oedipalized expressions of textual pleasure partly allow her to repress her jealousy by seeking public approval, jealousy continues to exist. It resides in the novel's textuality as compulsive denials of Meg's rivalry with Ethel and erupts in the story's demand that Ethel die. The text stages this death in a way that allows Meg to retain her status as the idealized heroine by keeping her aggression and hostility toward Ethel suppressed.

Why does the text select Ethel as Arthur's beloved, a choice that seals her fate? After all, he could have fallen in love with another of Meg's pretty friends. What particular traits does she possess that makes her death produce textual pleasure for Kelley's first audience, most of whom were probably black girls and women? In answer to these questions, we must recall that Ethel is Meg's most pious friend, a quality that the text repeatedly signifies in terms of whiteness. The text has also repeatedly described Ethel as the whitest in skin color of Meg's friends and the most angelic. This pattern of signification must also possess prohibited but pleasurable content. But why would the ostensible celebration of whiteness produce pleasure in a black woman's text written during the hostile racial climate of the post-Reconstruction period? Would the death of the angelic Ethel produce pleasure for women readers who were/are not black?

I refer to Freud's "Psychopathic Characters on Stage" to explain how *Megda* preserves the innocence of Meg as well as Kelley's black and white female readers, even though all probably harbor guilty desire. In this essay Freud examines the playwright's and actor's ability to compel the spectator to identify with the hero so as to arouse the spectator's "terror and pity" and to "purge [his or her] emotions."[23] Here Freud hypothesizes that it is easy for the spectator to recognize him- or herself in the actor if the spectator is susceptible to the same conflicts that the actor experiences. But recognition can occur only when the spectator's attention has been averted, that is, when "the impulse that is struggling to consciousness, however clearly it is recognizable, is never given a definite name; so that in the spectator too the process is carried through with his attention averted" ("Psychopathic Characters," 309). Like the actor's, the spectator's emotions can also be purged because diversionary tactics, much like those of dream-work, prevent the spectator's resistance to repressing an awareness of the struggle.

These Freudian theories are also applicable to novels because the author similarly effects the reader's identification with a literary character. First, mutual "latent wishes converge on one manifest item," producing a superimposition (or overdetermination) of elements onto one (S. Mitchell, *Relational Concepts,* 21). Hence, one manifest item is saturated with the content of many wishes. Second, displacement functions to disguise items in latent dream-thoughts or narration by replacing them through a chain of associations and condensation. This stage compresses items in the latent content of the dream or narrative in associative links based on likeness and proximity to produce an overdetermined dream symbol.[24]

Overdetermination and displacement not only conceal Meg's hostility toward Ethel but provide a site for the reader's as well. Let me illustrate by referring to the novel's problematic discourse of pious whiteness.

Ethel's death is probably especially satisfying to readers who share Meg's condition—that is, for those readers who are not as white, as beautiful, or as virtuous as Ethel. Not only does Ethel's death gratify Meg's repressed jealousy of the oedipal plot; the socially sanctioned circumstances of Ethel's death also mask the murder of this exemplar of Western patriarchal femininity—the idealized white lady on the pedestal. Thus, *Megda* also gratifies readers—black and white—who share Meg's repressed hostility toward the angelic feminine ideal of patriarchal demand by allowing them degrees of pleasurable affect resulting from their aggression toward this overdetermined sexual and racial rival of white patriarchal lore.

In addition, the evangelical plot spiritualizes *Megda*'s eroticization of African Americans' political desire for racial justice and social equality. Political justice, like salvation, is initially figured in the novel as unrequited because the whitest love object secures paternal approval and affection. The darker rival is angry and jealous, but rather than harm the white other, the rival identifies with its virtues and waits for recognition, for the time when divine justice prevails. Were this a traditionally racialized novel, the wait would be very long indeed. However, the silencing of race sustains *Megda*'s happy ending by freeing it from the social hegemony of the era of its production. By reinserting *Megda* into late-nine-teenth-century African American and evangelical cultures, which form the con-textual matrix for the novel, and by engaging psychoanalytic theory to uncover its conscious and unconscious discourses of desire and aggression, we can read *Megda* as a utopian novel. Its presumptions of racelessness in connection with exaggerated whiteness deconstruct the privilege associated with fetishized white skin.

Yet there is still more pleasure inscribed in *Medga*. The novel does not termi-nate textual desire by suspending Meg in the resolved oedipal plot of fulfilled adult romance. To do so would conclude Meg's role as the novel's desiring subject. *Megda* intimates yet another plot of desire and pleasure, involving the born-again Christians, now literally symbolized as children. With Little Ethel, Little Arthur, and Little Maude as well as (big) Arthur in "a perfect little nest of beauty and com-fort," "planned by Arthur himself and built for him as a wedding present" by Ethel's father, and "furnished according to Meg's taste" by Ethel's mother, Meg "felt more satisfied with herself than she had ever felt before in her life" (*M* 377, 394). By securing Arthur, Meg gets a husband and a surrogate for the omnipotent fa-ther, God, to fill the doubly signified paternal absence in the story of fatherless Meg and in the dedication to Kelley's own widowed mother. This paternal excess concludes the oedipal conflict but not the story.

The novel's final sentence depicts Meg not only as the beloved wife but also as the idealized mother of extravagant plenitude: "Beloved by everybody, with a ten-der, loving husband to guide and protect her, Meg's heart was filled full of grati-tude to her Heavenly father" (*M* 394). By scripting Meg as "filled full," the text also satisfies its pre-oedipal fantasy of wholeness. This, I suspect, is the principal desire that propels *Megda* to closure. The text of the novel has repeatedly signified this fantasy with references to "the band of sisterhood" (*M* 249). For example, with Maude's marriage, the "first link was broken in the golden chain" (*M* 301). With Ethel's death, the "second link in the golden chain was broken" (*M* 340). The se-ries of announcements of the forthcoming nuptials of the remaining circle of girls makes "the golden chain" little more than an assortment of broken links. Whereas Jo March of *Little Women* exhorts, "'I just wish I could marry [the eldest sister] Meg myself, and keep her safe in the family'" and prevent the development of "'a hole in the family'" (250), Meg fills the center of Kelley's fantasy of wholeness.

With the psychosexual plots of the pre-oedipal and oedipal stages fulfilled, all desires in the text terminate in consummation.

Megda inscribes the patriarchal demand for the masculine designation of divine omnipotence, while describing Meg's "Heavenly Father" in the act of repeating her maternal role of nurturing her own children and the orphaned Little Maude. By describing God in the act of revealing "tender pity for all His suffering children," *Megda* assumes a maternal posture, presence, indeed character for God (*M* 394). *Four Girls at Cottage City* (1898), the sequel to *Megda,* is even more emphatic in its designation of a femininized God. This latter novel collapses woman, mother, divine intercessor, and deity into maternal omnipotence. The pervasive authority of maternal plenitude in *Megda* and maternal omnipotence in *Four Girls at Cottage City* corroborates Freud's contention that the female subject is never completely oedipalized. Freud meant this observation to identify a fundamental deficiency of female personality to support his view of female inferiority. However, *Megda* regards this so-called failure as a triumph of female subjectivity. *Megda* constitutes the daughter's desire to recuperate a primary identification with the omnipotent mother of the pre-oedipal stage, an identification that the oedipalized desire for the father cannot supplant. Detecting how the son's desire for the omnipotent mother is textually reconstituted is the problem at the center of my next two chapters, respectively about W. E. B. Du Bois's *Dark Princess* and Richard Wright's *Savage Holiday.*

CHAPTER TWO

Race and Desire

Dark Princess, A Romance,
by William Edward Burghardt Du Bois

Mother was dark shining bronze, with smooth skin and lovely eyes; there was a
tiny ripple in her black hair, and she had a heavy, kind face. She gave one the impression of infinite patience, but a curious determination was concealed in her
softness.

> —W. E. B. Du Bois, *The Autobiography of W. E. B. Du Bois* (1963)

The tale is done and night is come. Now may all the sprites who, with curled wing
and starry eyes, have clustered around my hands and helped me weave this story,
lift with deft delicacy from out the crevice where it lines my heavy flesh of fact,
that rich and colored gossamer of dreams which the Queen of Faerie lent to me
for a season. Pleat it to a shining bundle and return it, sweet elves, beneath the
moon, to her Mauve Majesty with my low and fond obeisance. Beg her, sometime, somewhere, of her abundant leisure, to tell to us hard humans: Which is really Truth—Fact or Fancy? the Dream of the Spirit or the Pain of the Bone?

> —W. E. B. Du Bois, "Envoy," *Dark Princess* (1928)

The greatest and fullest life is by definition beautiful, beautiful—beautiful as a
dark passionate woman, beautiful as a golden-hearted school girl, beautiful as a
grey haired hero.

> —William E. B. Du Bois, "Celebration of My Twenty-Fifth Birthday"
> (Journal, February 23, 1893)

Du Bois, *Crisis* Propaganda, and Desire

On December 15, 1927, Du Bois sent the final version of the manuscript of *Dark
Princess, A Romance,* his second novel, to Harcourt, Brace and Company. In the attached letter, he asked whether his prior statements about the work's social purpose were adequate for the publisher's promotional plans for the novel, which
would appear in the spring of 1928. The marketing staff at Harcourt, Brace evidently requested no additional information but drew on these statements to prepare the newspaper notices about the novel (Aptheker, Introduction, 18). This

publishing firm was well aware of Du Bois's prominence and was confident that the book would demand wide attention.

Du Bois's activist strategy in *Dark Princess* was like that in his other works. He had been agitating for racial equality by combining his rather impassioned creative compositions with social analysis since 1903, when he published *The Souls of Black Folk*. In *The Crisis,* the official publication of the National Association for the Advancement of Colored People (NAACP), which was under his editorial control from its inception in 1910, he also repeatedly referred to what he thought to be an intrinsic relationship between art and propaganda. This position, as Keith Byerman notes, "is consistent with emerging Marxist aesthetics and anticipates the black arts movement of the 1960s in its recognition of the ideological nature of art" (*Seizing,* 101). In the October 1926 issue of *The Crisis,* Du Bois published a definitive statement on this subject—"The Criteria of Negro Art." I want to address an extract from this work before turning to *Dark Princess* because it reveals a terse example of Du Bois's use of eroticism for representing racial protest that appears throughout his writings and especially in *Dark Princess*.

In "The Criteria of Negro Art," Du Bois confronts his readers' reluctance to recognize the utility of art for political activism by asking,

> How is it that an organization like this [the NAACP], a group of radicals trying to bring new things into the world, a fighting organization which has come up out of *the blood and dust of battle*, struggling for *the right of black men to be ordinary human beings*—how is it that an organization of this kind can turn aside to talk about art? (279; my emphasis)

Du Bois answers this question here by contending that "all art is propaganda and ever must be, despite the wailing of the purist" (288).

Although this excerpt has been very prominent in the scholarship on Du Bois, scholars seldom mention the three sentences, immediately following it, that bring the paragraph to closure. In them, Du Bois attests,

> I stand in *utter shamelessness* and say that whatever art I have for writing has been used always for propaganda for gaining *the right of black folk to love and enjoy*. I do not care a damn for any art that is not used for propaganda. But I do care when propaganda is confined to one side while *the other is stripped and silent*. (288; my emphasis)

Here Du Bois not only proclaims the persuasive potential of art for securing racial justice—"the right of black men to be ordinary human beings" (288). He also characterizes this objective by abandoning the public arena of social protest for the private domain of erotic pleasure. "[I]n utter shamelessness," he proclaims racial justice as "the right of black folk to love and enjoy" (288). Thus, rather than invoking the conventional and no doubt expected rhetoric of civil rights to define the objective of his social mission, he refers instead to libidinal prerogatives—indeed, to desire and gratification—to describe the goals of racial activism. Du Bois underscores this position at the end of the extract by disavowing the efficacy of any propaganda "stripped" of art and "silent" on desire and pleasure.

The complex association of propaganda with erotic delight in "The Criteria of Negro Art" illustrates a paradoxical pattern of representation that Du Bois would regularly employ in his creative writings and especially in *Dark Princess*. This pattern suggests that the public satisfaction of racial equality is connected and somewhat analogous to the private pleasure of eroticism, for eros and polity are mutually signifying. By unconsciously instilling eroticism within his understanding of propaganda, Du Bois complicates his initial equation between art and propaganda by including passion and its gratification. This conceptual framework allows him to idealize the members of the NAACP as dusty, blood-stained crusaders in a chivalric campaign of high moral significance, as the extract implies. Fighting in this crusade on the behalf of an ideal, traditionally figured as feminine, would convert the desire for freedom into liberatory action.

Du Bois's use of chivalric imagery would have been particularly meaningful for his black and white contemporaries who would have recalled D. W. Griffith's representation of the Ku Klux Klan's appropriation of chivalric zeal, codes, and images in *The Birth of a Nation* (1915).[1] Based on *The Clansman, an Historic Romance of the Ku Klux Klan* (1905) by Thomas Dixon Jr., this film championed southern, native-born, Anglo-Saxon Protestant males by depicting their violent reprisal of black(faced, white) male desire for white women and in doing so stimulated the rebirth of the "Invisible Empire" of the Ku Klux Klan.[2] Griffith appealed to white male anxiety of the years during and immediately after World War I by staging the mythic attack on the idealized symbol of white supremacy—the white woman. Defending white honor was the rallying cry of the Klan, just as it had been for the Confederacy. What had been a white male, nineteenth-century contest about capital and nation was, at the turn of the twentieth century, a more mystified struggle about white political privilege now executed as sexual authority. Hence, white male supremacists not only used white female sexuality to objectify their persecutory fantasies and to justify (or condone) the lynchings of thousands of African Americans and a few Jews and Catholics as well; many white men also exercised the presumption of their racial/sexual privilege by raping black women.

Chivalric idealization of female sexuality was the means for inciting and representing both the Klan's racist propaganda for white supremacy and Du Bois's counterpropaganda for racial equality in *The Crisis*. The Klan enhances the esteem and political power of working-class whites, who largely comprised its membership, by relying on displaced persecutory fantasies to police white female sexuality and to denigrate as well as exploit black people in general. Du Bois retaliates by using *The Crisis* to (re)appropriate chivalric imagery so as to idealize himself and others fighting for racial equality.

While Du Bois's *Crisis* readers eagerly identified with his liberational objective, they often found its eroticized expression in his writings peculiar and, as we will see, even problematic. Scholars would generally deal with this curious feature by either disregarding it or castigating Du Bois for his surplus passion. Their critical reproach was undoubtedly met with his bewilderment because Du Bois repeatedly insisted that "my writing of fiction, as well as other forms of literature, is for propaganda and reform. I make no bone on saying that art that isn't propaganda doesn't interest me" (qtd. in Aptheker, Introduction, 14). Yet as "The Criteria of Negro Art" entreats us to see, Du Bois seems unconsciously to associate propaganda for social reform with erotic desire. The eroticism is not depicted as mere sensuality; on the contrary, it is personified as a heroic ideal much like the noble and unobtainable queen of courtly romance to whom a knight would dedicate his chivalric zeal. This feminine figure is implicit in Du Bois's representation of the NAACP in "The Criteria of Negro Art," for she bids the "radicals" of this "fighting organization" to "come up out of the blood and dust of battle" and claim "the right of black men to be ordinary human beings," which is, according to Du Bois, equivalent to demanding "the right of black folk to love and enjoy" (279, 288).

The erotic relationship between art and propaganda in "The Criteria of Negro Art" is emphatic in *Dark Princess*. Here, Du Bois's chivalric tropes and passionate dedication to racial propaganda come to life to stage a romance. The "dark princess" of the title commands the protagonist's valiant fight against racism. As his reward, though, he does not triumph over racism; rather, he wins the princess and the assurance that their son will free all the dark races of the world from Western imperialism. Like "The Criteria of Negro Art," *Dark Princess* also substitutes erotic pleasure for the achievement of racial justice. This exchange suggests that the majestic female figure commanding Du Bois's activist devotion is an integral part of his imaginative process or what Roland Barthes might call Du Bois's personal "hermeneutic code" (17). This code structures his conceptual framework. I represent it with the following equations: propaganda = art = erotic desire; the goal of propaganda = freedom = erotic consummation. I will argue that *Dark Princess* relies on such figurative analogies to express racial propaganda and that they appear again and again in Du Bois's writings.

To explain, analyze, and appreciate the deep meaning of these hermeneutic equations in *Dark Princess*, I find it useful to engage the psychoanalytic model of the "fantasmatic." A fantasmatic is a "structuring action" or a recurring pattern of an individual's fantasies that "lie[s] behind such products of the unconscious as dreams, symptoms, acting out, [and] repetitive behavior" (Laplanche and Pontalis, *Language*, 317). The fantasmatic is not only an internal or masked thematic that determines a subject's unconscious associations; it is also a dynamic formation that seeks conscious expression by converting experience into action. For as the subject attaches unconscious fantasies to new experiences, she or he reproduces pleasure by copying "the patterns of previous pleasure" (Moore and Fine, *Psychoanalytic Terms*, 75). In "The Criteria of Negro Art," Du Bois discloses a brief illustration of what I suspect is his fantasmatic template for encoding racial activism—that is, his unconscious pattern of consolidating the libidinal economies of desire and freedom. This mental pattern would allow him not only to reproduce pleasure in his writings but to produce an extraordinary amount of work and to dedicate his life to laboring for racial progress as well, for he seems to have experienced the emotional effect of laboring for racial uplift like the pleasure of libidinal satisfaction. As we shall see, *Dark Princess* allows its protagonist to recover aspects of what psychoanalysis calls the lost mother (which I explain later) as an effect of black political engagement.

The symbolic function of the princess in *Dark Princess* is clearly to represent the desire to achieve racial justice. But the princess becomes detached from this objective and evolves into an autonomous and enigmatic signifier of a beloved woman. How does this signifier structure Du Bois's hermeneutic code? Recognizing the importance of this question is instructive for understanding Du Bois's unswerving devotion to racial activism. Answering this question will help us to understand the deep emotional and intellectual investments that Du Bois placed in his activist writings. Although *Dark Princess* is unquestionably a flawed novel, it provides a provocative venue for "taking a more exact measure of the range of Du Bois's interests and concerns, and of his extraordinary intellect and imagination" (Rampersad, "Du Bois's Passage," 1).

While Du Bois was apparently unaware of his tendency to eroticize racial justice in his writings, he was probably at least familiar with Sigmund Freud's basic hypotheses about unconscious desire by 1910 and certainly by the 1920s, when Freud's works were in wide circulation in the United States.[3] In spite of Du Bois's continued interest in psychology, ever since his undergraduate study with Harvard professor William James, Du Bois was reluctant to question his staunchly held conviction about the power of knowledge to eradicate social oppression.[4] He wanted to believe, to use his own words, "that race prejudice was based on widespread ignorance." Therefore, he insisted that the "long-term remedy was Truth," which he understood as "carefully gathered scientific proof that neither color nor race determined the limits of a man's capacity or desert [*sic*]" (Du Bois, "My Evolving Program," 49). For most of his life, Du Bois studied black America "with the honest hope of alleviating—through the therapy of reason and truth—the vast race hatred in America" (Allison Davis, *Love*, 130). By the early 1940s, though, he was ready to recognize "the unconscious factor," inherent not simply in all human activity but his own as well (*Autobiography*, 277). Prior to that time, as he confessed, he was not "sufficiently Freudian to understand how little human action is based on reason" ("My Evolving Program," 9). This is the observation of an elderly Du Bois.

Whether by the early 1940s Du Bois was also ready to acknowledge his chronic fixation on eros is difficult to determine, despite his admission in *The Autobiography* (written some twenty years later) that he "was a lusty man with all normal appetites" and that he "loved 'Wine, Women and Song'" (283). We do know, however, that by the mid-1910s his depictions of eroticism in *The Crisis* often confused his readers and annoyed the executive board of the NAACP. The matter first became public in 1915 when the provocative cover of the November *Crisis,* featuring the sultry portrait of a light-skinned woman, "scandalized the Boston branch of the NAACP" (Lewis, *W. E. B. Du Bois,* 498; see figure 1). Given Du Bois's fantasmatic formula, it is not difficult for us to see how he could regard this cover as an expression of his racial vision and therefore appropriate for *The Crisis.* It is easier, though, to see how his readers might fail to associate a lovely mulatta with racial uplift, for they had no means of connecting Du Bois's pattern of erotic representation to his political ambitions. I hope to make the connection clear in this chapter.

Even when Du Bois's portrayals of the erotic objective of propaganda were less tangible and confined to the rhetorical fancy of his creative writings, they undoubtedly mystified his *Crisis* readers. For were it not for the figure of a black Christ, allusions to oppression, and the personification of freedom, respectively in "The Riddle of the Sphinx," "The Princess of the Hither Isles," and "Children of the Moon," for example, his readers probably would not have been able to connect the passion in these works to racial propaganda. Despite the formidable display of eroticism in these and other creative works, Du Bois was probably unaware of the degree to which this feature controlled their development. When he wrote *Dark Princess,* the most extreme case in point, he claimed propaganda as his motivation. In explaining *Dark Princess* to his publisher, Du Bois described the novel as "a romance with a message":

> Its first aim is to tell a story: the story of a colored medical student whom race prejudice forces out of his course of study. He tries to run away from America and then learns of a union of darker peoples [led by a young, beautiful Indian Princess, the "Dark Princess"] against white imperialism. It is not a union of hatred or of offense, but of defense and self-development of the best in all races. But the problem is how such a movement can be set going. (qtd. in Aptheker, Introduction, 19)

Given the nature of this declaration, Du Bois's editors at Harcourt, Brace had to have been at least a bit surprised when they encountered more romance than message. No doubt, they hoped the passion would sell the book.

Du Bois's first readers expected *Dark Princess* to be a work by the man with whom they were familiar: Du Bois the polemicist; Du Bois the unyielding proponent for the advancement of the race. They were aware of his challenge to Booker T. Washington for the leadership of black America during the first years of the twentieth century and his central role in founding the NAACP in 1909. However, when they looked for analysis of the race problem in *Dark Princess* and for practical ways to attack Western imperialism, they were rather disappointed, for what they found was a love story that functions as a melodramatic deterrent to the novel's polemical objective. The aims of *Dark Princess* and its effects, as Arnold

The CRISIS

| Vol. 11—No. 1 | NOVEMBER, 1915 | Whole No. 61 |

ONE DOLLAR A YEAR   TEN CENTS A COPY

Figure 1. Cover of *The Crisis*, November 1915. (Courtesy of The Crisis Publishing Co., Inc., the magazine of the National Association for the Advancement of Colored People.)

Rampersad notes, "do not always succeed, and occasionally a failure is ludicrous" (*Art*, 204).[5] Still, as Rampersad adds elsewhere, Du Bois intended the novel to be "a corrective" for "the growing trend among the younger artists" who asserted "their artistic independence" by sacrificing the radical politics that defined Du Bois's own life and work ("Du Bois's Passage," 2).

Du Bois's intentions notwithstanding, the numerous reviews of *Dark Princess* characterize it as "bewildering," "an amazing mixture of fact and fancy," "a sentimental melodrama," and "the queerest sort of mixture: clear sharp observation, thoughtfully considered and carefully written, helter-skelter with Graustarkian romance" (Reitell, *Annals*, 347; see also T. S., Review, 9, and M. P. L., Review, 27).[6] Literary scholars have shared this opinion, which explains why the first printing of the novel sold poorly, rapidly went out of print, and received marginal notice in the annals of U.S. literary history.[7] For example, two scholars describe the novel as "an opera in prose," "a strange book, a strange compound of revolutionary doctrine and futilistic philosophy, refuting, it seems, Dr. Du Bois's own text of aggressive independence" (Moses, *Black Messiahs*, 154; Redding, *To Make*, 81). Another insists that "it is the only novel by an American Negro which makes an exhaustive study of the place of black folk among the darker races of the earth" (Gloster, *Negro Voices*, 153). And yet another summarizes the critical consensus by writing, "*Dark Princess*, although a poor novel, is socially, psychologically, and politically significant" (Singh, *Novels*, 126–27).

Dark Princess fictionalizes the Indian resistance to British imperialism, the rise of what would later be called the Third World, and Du Bois's actual efforts to understand "the interplay between race and politics on a global scale" (Rampersad, "Du Bois's Passage," 3). Yet the novel's focus on an emphatically sexualized messianic plot makes it deviate from the popular trends of social realism that dominated African American fiction during the New Negro Renaissance and defined the novelistic standards of Du Bois's predecessors of the post-Reconstruction period, like Sutton Griggs, Frances Harper, Charles Chesnutt, and Pauline Hopkins. While these writers emphasize the public plot of collective black polity and efface practically all references to explicit eroticism in their works, the Renaissance writers frequently address sexuality. Here, however, sexuality is presented as a repressed and frequently destructive force—for example, in Jean Toomer's *Cane* (1924) and Nella Larsen's *Quicksand* (1928) and as a pleasant complication in Jessie Fauset's *There's Confusion* (1924), all of which Du Bois admired. By contrast, the representation of black sexuality in Claude McKay's *Home to Harlem* (1928) clearly provoked Du Bois's ire. In an often cited remark, Du Bois claimed that the novel "for the most part nauseates me, and after the dirtier parts of its filth I feel distinctly like taking a bath." As far as he was concerned, *Home to Harlem* was "padded" with "utter licentiousness" to cater to the white marketplace ("Browsing Reader," 202). While *Dark Princess* is clearly a steamy novel, its propaganda, sartorial eroticism, and urbane consumption of art, music, and food as well as its focus on one extraordinary love object evidently made the novel's refined depiction of adultery appear less distasteful to Du Bois than the crass promiscuity of McKay's raunchy novel.

The reception of *Dark Princess* also reveals a historic preference for representing collective social arguments rather than personal desire in black literature. U.S. reviewers, scholars, and readers have routinely understood black novels as expressions of racial politics even when such a formulation earns reproach. Yet this audience has celebrated the highly individualistic portraits of desire in white literature (such as Edgar Allan Poe's necrophilia, Vladimir Nabokov's pedophilia, and Ernest Hemingway's infatuation with bullfighting, as well as the unique forms of eroticized passive resistance in the works of Charlotte Perkins Gilman, Kate Chopin, Edith Wharton, Virginia Woolf, and on and on the list could go) while expecting desire in black textual production to be defined by and subsumed within the political ambitions of the black masses.

Projections of Du Bois's personal desire and pleasure are certainly dominant features of *Dark Princess*—so much so that in spite of its mixed reviews, in 1940 Du Bois proclaimed it to be his "favorite book" (*Dusk of Dawn*, 270).[8] What makes this remark particularly meaningful is that at the time of its pronouncement he had been a prominent social scientist of U.S. race relations for nearly thirty years, with a spate of impressive books to his credit.[9] His prolific writings endorsed his faith in education, work, and protest as the best defenses against racial oppression. Still, he did not declare *The Souls of Black Folk* to be his favorite book, even though it endorsed such faith and "made him a leader of black Americans" (Gilroy, *Black Atlantic*, 114). Instead, this distinction he gave to his unpopular *Dark Princess*, in which the protagonist is hardly a model of success. He quits school, works at an assortment of meaningless jobs, and even fails to execute effective racial protest. Arnold Rampersad contends that *Dark Princess* "was Du Bois' favorite book because it said much of what he regarded to be essential and true [about racial politics], at a time when his effectiveness as a political and cultural leader of black America first appeared to be under serious threat" (*Art*, 204). No doubt Du Bois thought the novel would present his unfailing devotion to social activism with such passion that he could secure his role as the quintessential proponent of the race. Yet I suspect the real source of pleasure in this text for Du Bois is its emphatic manifestation of his unconscious fantasmatic processes that encode the novel's impassioned representation of racial activism.

While passion may enhance polemicism, it is a most subjective and therefore contestable form of evidence. For passion to be convincing, it needs to be attached to a rational core of information. In this regard Du Bois draws on his considerable knowledge, experience, and observations about Western imperialism to construct *Dark Princess*'s polemicism. However, he invokes a lot more passion than rational detail. Indeed, as he bolsters the justification of his argument for the inevitability of racial equality with the messianic plot, a distinct desire seizes control of the novel and especially the character of the dark princess. This type of desire has much in common with the subject's primary desire for the lost mother.

By the lost mother I mean the imaginary object that is the young child's—here the son's—earliest, principal, and most enduring attachment, one that develops over the first few years of the child's interactions with her. The feelings that bond her to him cohere into his gratifying, libidinal fantasies about her and define what Freud called the pre-oedipal stage. During the later oedipal stage,[10] Freud theorizes, the young boy becomes socialized as he represses and displaces both his strong, sexual feelings for the mother and his wishes to kill the father. In *Totem and Taboo* (1913–14) and *Civilization and Its Discontents* (1930), Freud further claims that civilization is a product of the guilty reparations of sons to their fathers.[11] The lost mother, then, is an imaginary construction of the historical mother whom the child believes is omnipotent. This, like all imagos, is generated more by the subjective dynamics of an individual's personality than actual experience. The maternal imago has two extreme forms—the idealized good mother and the persecutory bad one. Whereas fantasies of the good mother are predominant in Du Bois's writing, those of the bad mother dominate the textual unconscious of Richard Wright's fictions, as I will argue in Chapter 3.

Dark Princess depicts an oedipalized story; it is a messianic narrative about a black son's conflict with the white patriarchy. But instead of idealizing the paternal imago and making reparations to it, as discussed in Freud's *Totem and Taboo,* *Dark Princess* idealizes the maternal imago and makes the lost mother the object of the son's reparations. The emphasis that *Dark Princess* places on the protagonist's repeated acts of reparation for failed activism complicates the novel's plot and makes me wonder whether Du Bois was unconsciously associating his endeavors at working for racial uplift with reparation to one person in particular—his mother. Du Bois's mother not only helped him to define his character, genius, and social commitment; she also made it possible for him to enhance these aspects of his personality by dying at a most propitious time in his life.

As David Levering Lewis explains in his prize-winning biography on Du Bois, *W. E. B. Du Bois: Biography of a Race* (1994), his knowledge that his mother, Mary Silvina, "lived almost entirely to see him prosper in the world, that she would die for him if need be," did not lessen the fact that she became a burden to him (52; figure 2). His father Alfred's desertion of them before Du Bois was two condemned the mother and son to certain poverty. As her health rapidly failed during his senior year in high school, Willie (as Du Bois was then called) knew that his intellect would not prevent his having to work at menial jobs to support her. "But if his mother were to die," Lewis speculates, "then it surely followed that his life would make sense only if he repaid [sic] her sacrifice with extraordinary success" (52). Her death in the spring of 1885, the year after his graduation, opened the way for him to go to college: the townspeople of Great Barrington, Massachusetts, who

Figure 2. Mary Silvina Burghardt Du Bois and Baby Willie, circa 1868. (Courtesy of Special Collections and Archives, W. E. B. Du Bois Library, University of Massachusetts, Amherst. Reprinted by permission of David Graham Du Bois.)

had long marveled at his genius, took up a collection and sent him to Fisk University, thereby launching him in his career of racial uplift.

The circumstances of Du Bois's early life had to have produced his ambivalent feelings toward his mother, which would define the unique sexual constitution of his fantasmatic pattern for structuring his political attachments. Mary Silvina

Burghardt Du Bois was a member of an old Great Barrington black family that, Du Bois claimed, could trace its freedom back to the late eighteenth century. Such a background allowed Du Bois to aggrandize his maternal family as "part of a great clan" (Lewis, *W. E. B. Du Bois*, 19). Yet his mother's sexual transgression, which produced an illegitimate son five years before Du Bois's birth, embarrassed the youngster and made him silently question the legitimacy of his own birth.[12] In addition, his mother's identity as a poor dark-skinned woman, more so than his mulatto father of middle-class origins, placed Du Bois decidedly behind what he would later call the "veil" of racial difference, for his father's absence exacerbated Du Bois's insecurity, poverty, and humiliating confrontations with racial prejudice. Young Du Bois blamed his mother for his father's absence. The youngster believed that "she had deserted his father and was largely responsible for their demeaning material predicament in Great Barrington" (Lewis, *W. E. B. Du Bois*, 52). Thus, the pain caused by the absent father, "the stigma of bastardy" (already associated with his half-brother and, therefore, with himself as well), his mother's extreme poverty, and subjugation to racial prejudice had to have made his efforts to idealize his mother extremely conflicted (Lewis, *W. E. B. Du Bois*, 27; Allison Davis, *Love*, 107). Under these circumstances, we can readily imagine this very bright, ambitious, and somewhat egotistical youngster wishing for a different mother even while deeply loving the one he had.

While sociologist Allison Davis[13] does not actually use the word "hatred" to describe Du Bois's contradictory feelings for his mother, Davis suggests that Du Bois resented his mother and hid this from himself with "compensatory fantasies" (*Love*, 112). According to Davis, "Du Bois was relieved when his mother suddenly died. He felt 'free.'" She had driven him to excel. Before her death, Davis continues, Du Bois had "felt sorry" for his mother. He had "nursed her and he expressed his concern and solicitude for her. But these [responses] are not love. In fact, they might have been defensive expressions of guilt from resenting her for having disgraced him" (*Love*, 116). I extend Davis's speculation to suggest that when her death made it possible for Du Bois to accomplish what her continued existence could not, all of his prior guilty wishes to be rid of her assailed him and probably complicated his already ambivalent feelings for her. I suspect that Du Bois unconsciously transformed his guilty grief into a lifelong process of mourning and reparation in the only emotional economy that had given him sustained pleasure—the satisfaction of work. Du Bois's labor for the race would be like an act of reparation to his internalized, idealized mother and to his heroic image of himself. His writings would unconsciously inscribe his devotion to the memory of his mother and repair his assaulted ego. For these reasons his energy for accomplishment was virtually inexhaustible.

Du Bois's figurative "veil" of color is especially provocative in light of my extension of Davis's discussion of Du Bois's "compensatory fantasies" (*Love*, 112). By associating Davis's observations with what Mary Ann Doane calls "the iconography of the veil," we can understand Du Bois's veil as an overdetermined symbol for the lost mother, the racial and sexual differences she embodies, and his ambivalence toward her (*Femmes,* 52). For Du Bois, the veil locates an arbitrary and, indeed, diaphanous social barrier that represents the trivial basis of racial hierarchies. Hence, the veil of racial difference "acts as a trope that allows one [in this case Du Bois] to evade the superficial, to complicate the surface by disallowing its self-sufficiency," and to make skin color into "a secondary or surplus surface," to borrow Doane's words (*Femmes,* 55–56).[14] Du Bois's veil also acts as a trope of ambivalent feelings for the lost mother because the veil "incarnates contradictory desires" to see and not to see her racial and sexual difference (Doane, *Femmes,* 54). Thus, Du Bois's veil marks a contested site where conscious, secondary, social ambition is superimposed upon the primary desire for the mother. The veil then consolidates the libidinal economies of desire and freedom by conceptualizing the pleasure of both lifting the racial obstruction that made Du Bois see himself as a social problem and lowering the blind that shields him from his guilty feelings about the lost mother. In representing race and filial desire, the veil locates a symbolic embodiment, indeed a fetishistic form of "control over what might otherwise be terrifying ambiguities" (McClintock, *Imperial Leather,* 184).

Dark Princess lavishly inscribes the lost mother's absence as presence and eroticizes the site of racial difference. For these reasons, I suspect, this novel delighted Du Bois but estranged his critics. They identified an "unwholesome sanity" and "poisonous power" in the novel (Redding, *To Make,* 8), undoubtedly ensuing from the collapse of its exorbitant eroticism into maternal allusions. As a result, they were unable to appreciate the novel's attempt to bond "sentimental melodrama" and "poetic intensity" with Du Bois's political goals ("Day Letters" and "Throb of Dark Drums").

My objective is not to be an apologist for *Dark Princess*. Neither is it my intention to psychoanalyze Du Bois, though as a work that undeniably appears to be an extensive undertaking in sexual sublimation, *Dark Princess* invites such an endeavor.[15] Rather, my objective is to demonstrate how psychoanalysis assists me in disclosing Du Bois's conscious superimposition of propaganda onto unconscious primary desire. For the pleasure of *Dark Princess* is not simply the product of an eroticized polemic; pleasure is also inscribed in the language of the text that reproduces desire and its gratification. My psychoanalytic approach thus means that rather than depreciating, disregarding, or disparaging *Dark Princess*'s implausible plot, messianic love story, maternal allusions, and intense eroticism, to name just a few of its amazing aspects, I regard them as manifestations, indeed signifiers of Du Bois's unconscious fantasmatic template that generates the novel's imaginary discourses. These discourses play out Du Bois's deep emotional story about primary attachment, loss, and reparation.

By regarding "the structure of literature," here *Dark Princess,* as similar to "the structure of mind"—not a specific mind but what the translators of the *Standard*

Edition of the Works of Sigmund Freud call "the mental apparatus" or "the dynamic organization of the psyche," again to borrow the words of Peter Brooks—I hope to demonstrate that this novel possesses what could be called a psychic structure of subjectivity (Brooks, "Idea," 24). According to such a framework, the subjectivity of *Dark Princess* (like that of any novel) is structured by conscious, preconscious, and unconscious discourses of desire. By conscious discourses, I mean the explicit social discourses in the text. By the novel's unconscious, which I also call textual unconscious or unconscious textual desire, I mean prohibited infantile desire for primeval unity with the mother inscribed in the stylistic language and structural elements of the text (see Lacan, *Écrits*, 169). Finally, by preconscious discourses, I mean those implicit (and often figurative) discourses that, unlike the deeply obscured discourses of the unconscious, are readily accessible by means of interpretation. Even though a novel's closure is both tenuous and arbitrary, the end nevertheless claims a "final plenitude of meanings" that ensues from Du Bois's and our own determination to make even fictive experience bear meaning (Brooks, *Reading*, 314, 323). Hence, *Dark Princess*'s ending, as I shall demonstrate, gratifies and terminates its conscious desire in agitation for racial justice and its unconscious desire in a fantasy for the lost mother. Because the novel dramatizes the protagonist's political development in what resembles a series of pre-oedipal and oedipal narratives, Freudian tenets about psychosexual development complement my Lacanian rhetorical analysis of the novel's subjectivity.

To psychoanalysis I add cultural criticism to determine the social currency of the novel's discourses about decor, landscape, and fashion that are a part of the novel's preconscious textual desire. Together these stages of my discussion explain why *Dark Princess* is a work of extraordinary passion and yet unconvincing propaganda. The power of these discourses in *Dark Princess* make it a virtually unobstructed site for revealing Du Bois's fantasmatic pattern for inscribing unconscious desire that is better concealed but also operative in his more successful works, like *The Souls of Black Folk* and his first novel—*The Quest of the Silver Fleece* (1911). By analyzing *Dark Princess*'s unconscious and preconscious discourses, I hope to recuperate Du Bois's eroticized protocol of racial propaganda. I want to emphasize that the interplay between desire and race in *Dark Princess* is not simply a unique feature of this novel but a fundamental principle of black textuality that we must appreciate in conjunction with conscious expressions of politicized social desire if we want to increase our general understanding of the signifying structures of black expressive cultures.

Eroticizing Propaganda in *Dark Princess*

Du Bois clearly intended for *Dark Princess* to be a work of black heroic art and underscored that purpose by subtitling the work "a romance." The novel tells the story of "a creative spirit in [its] painful growth toward maturity and poetic power" by means of a struggle between good and evil, to borrow the words of M. H. Abrams (*Natural Supernaturalism*, 309). The plot repeats "the familiar Romantic model of a self-formative educational journey, which moves through division, exile, and solitariness toward the goal of a recovered home and restored familial relationship" (Abrams, *Natural Supernaturalism*, 225). Narrative resolution adheres to the romantic belief that love is "the only available solution to the problem of the good and evil of our mortal state" (Abrams, *Natural Supernaturalism*, 305). Du Bois, of course, racializes this basic story of moral development in *Dark Princess* so as to construct family (re)formation as the means by which to unify the dark people of the world and to recover an apocalyptic kingdom on Earth as home. As this chapter's second epigraph, from the "Envoy" of *Dark Princess*, makes clear, Du Bois fabricates the novel out of a veritable Hegelian dialectic of fancy and fact, dream and reality, spirit and bone to reveal his deep and abiding faith in the providential nature of human history, a belief that his student years at Harvard and the University of Berlin had reinforced.[16]

As a late-nineteenth-century man educated to believe in divine providence and historical progress, the genre of romance gave Du Bois the means for adapting the Hegelian model of human progress to his propaganda. Hegel furnished Du Bois with a philosophical framework for understanding black people's oppression as a part of the workings of divine providence. According to this framework, human progress evolves "through the successive histories of six world historical peoples: Chinese, Indians, Persians (culminating with the Egyptians), Greeks, Romans, and Germans" (Williamson, *Crucible*, 404). To these nationalities, Du Bois added the American Negro as "a sort of seventh son, born with a veil and gifted with second-sight in this American world" (*Souls*, in Sundquist, *Oxford*, 102). In this racialization of Hegel's model, Du Bois invested his own frustrated ambition to be "one of Hegel's world-historical-men, a dark Messiah" to redeem black America (Williamson, *Crucible*, 408).

Within *Dark Princess*, Du Bois transforms the Hegelian model of history into his passionate belief in the potential of racial propaganda to serve as the catalyst for the redemption of black people from racial oppression and the reformation of capitalism. These two objectives fulfill the novel's conscious providential design. Thus "the concept of Providence," to borrow the words of Fredric Jameson, "provide [Du Bois with] an adequate theoretical mediation between the salvational logic of the romance narrative and the nascent sense of historicity imposed by the social dynamic of capitalism" ("Magical Narratives," 132). The providential nature of the romance thus not only allows Du Bois to explain the historical relationship between racist ideology and capitalist labor exploitation but also facilitates Du Bois's conscious endeavor to preserve his faith in the inevitability of racial justice.

Despite the heroic idealism of *Dark Princess*, we should not underestimate the sheer force of conviction necessary for Du Bois to maintain his activist position, for he was not a detached observer of this battle of "two warring ideals—an American, a Negro" (*Souls,* in Sundquist, *Oxford,* 102). He was one of its most valiant warriors. Nevertheless, he possessed not only this cultural duality but complex historical, professional, and personal identities as, respectively, a Victorian and a modern, a scientist and a poet, a pragmatist and a visionary. Allison Davis provides a provocative analysis of Du Bois's complex and divided personality. Davis explains that Du Bois

> realized early that his own emotions were ambivalent and that his identity was split with regard to "race." At times he was ashamed of his color and his "race"; at other times he was proud of his "Negro blood" and aggressive in defense of the rights and abilities of his "people." In his books, he is pulled apart before our very eyes, like a man twisted on a rack.[17] (*Love,* 119–20)

Davis contends that white America's repeated refusal to recognize Du Bois's superior ability, training,[18] and herculean effort and black America's failure to grant him its steadfast support accentuated his already deeply conflicted personality. Davis further explains that Du Bois was "vain but shy, pompous but uncertain of himself, defiant but anxious to be accepted. Ambitious to lead," Davis adds, "he was essentially retiring and withdrawn. Longing to be admired and worshipped, he often was rude and scornful" (*Love,* 146). Arnold Rampersad provides a similar analysis of the powerful but conflicted sides of Du Bois's character in *The Art and the Imagination of W. E. B. Du Bois.* According to Rampersad, Du Bois was partly the empirical, practical, and tough-minded proletarian who compiled and interpreted evidence on the material conditions of black Americans. He was also the romantic, idealistic, imaginative, high-strung aristocrat who marked his writings with mythic longing and messianic prophesy. Du Bois's personality, as Davis and Rampersad explain, reveals contradictory motivations and their effects. *Dark Princess* novelizes these contradictions by relying on his penchant for combining romantic conventions with activist prose.

Such a venture in *Dark Princess* was not new for Du Bois, for he had also projected the duality of his character onto the coprotagonists—Blessed (Bles) Alwyn and Zora Cresswell—of his first novel, *The Quest of the Silver Fleece,* published in 1911. However, Matthew Townes, the protagonist of *Dark Princess,* is the most comprehensive representation of Du Bois's complex temperament, and this novel presents the most intense rendition of his fantasmatic equation for eroticized social activism. The Hegelian synthesis provided Du Bois with a model to attempt to unite not only these disparate parts of his personality but his own social alienation—his "double consciousness"—as well. This perspective also facilitated his effort to argue that black people have an essential role in human destiny and to define an important one for himself in this process.[19]

No incident in *Dark Princess* departs more extravagantly from formulating a pragmatic response to racism than the spectacular messianic masque that closes the work. This scene, reminiscent of the Magi's adoration of the Christ child, salutes the infant son of Matthew and Kautilya and consecrates the novel's conviction in its prophetic racial mission:

> There fell a silence, and then out of the gloom of the wood moved a pageant. A score of men clothed in white with shining swords walked slowly forward a space, and from their midst came three old men: one black and shaven and magnificent in raiment; one yellow and turbaned, with a white beard that swept his burning flesh; and the last naked save for a scarf about his loins. . . . They gave rice to Matthew and Kautilya. . . . Then the Brahmin took the baby from his grandmother and wound a silken turban on its little protesting head. . . . Slowly Kautilya stepped forward and turned her face eastward. She raised her son toward heaven and cried:
>
> "Brahma, Vishnu, and Siva! Lords of Sky and Light and Love! Receive from me, daughter of my fathers back to the hundredth name, his Majesty, Madhu Chandragupta Singh, by the will of God, of Bwodpur and Maharajah-dhiraja of Sindrabad."
>
> Then from the forest, with faint and silver applause of trumpets:
>
> "King of the Snows of Gaurisankar!"
>
> "Protector of Ganga the Holy!"
>
> "Incarnate Son of the Buddha!"
>
> "Grand Mughal of Utter India!"
>
> "Messenger and Messiah to all the Darker Worlds!" (*DP* 311)

This scene is a grandiose repetition of Du Bois's prophetic aspirations and wistful yearning for his infant son Burghardt, eulogized in "The Passing of the First Born" in *The Souls of Black Folk* (1903). Here, the narrator

> mused above [Burghardt's] little white bed; saw the strength of my own arm stretched onward through the ages through the newer strength of his; saw the dream of my black fathers stagger a step onward in the wild phantasm of the world; heard in his baby voice the voice of the Prophet that was to rise within the Veil. (Sundquist, *Oxford*, 209)

Whereas the narrator of *The Souls of Black Folk* is the lone listener to the "baby voice [that was to be] the voice of the Prophet," the narrator of *Dark Princess* assembles a majestic audience for the later infant that obliterates this novel's fragile construction of social realism. No wonder Du Bois's readers have failed to appreciate the novel's polemical message, for it is effaced by the spectacular masque at the novel's ending, a masque also reminiscent of the grand finale of Du Bois's pageant *Star of Ethiopia*.

Like *The Star of Ethiopia*, which was staged before 35,000 people in New York, Washington, and Philadelphia in 1915 and 1916 (Du Bois, "Drama among Black Folk," 169), the masque at the end of *Dark Princess* opts for fancy rather than fact. The spectacle of pageantry seems a curious choice for a man whose prodigious scholarship was devoted to scrupulous factual detail, yet it is remarkably consistent with the pronouncement in "The Criteria of Negro Art" that equates propaganda and eroticism. For the closing spectacles of the pageant and the novel are manifestations of Du Bois's fantasmatic template and thus reflect Du Bois's deep and steadfast devotion to the transformative power of the romantic imagination.

Dark Princess is set during the middle years of the 1920s and begins with racism frustrating Matthew Townes's dream to be an obstetrician. No longer believing that hard work and talent will enable him to achieve his ambition, Matthew leaves New York for life as an exile abroad. While in Berlin, he forestalls a white man's sexual insult of a woman of color, whom he learns is Princess Kautilya[20] of India. She is a member of an international team of dark-skinned people who are forming an organization to resist Western imperialism. Matthew immediately falls in love with the beautiful princess, who charges him, much like a knight, with the task of providing her with information in order to determine whether black Americans should be included in this organization. Kautilya departs, presumably for India, and Matthew returns to the United States and secures a job as a railway porter in order to survey the social progress of African Americans for the princess. Upon completion of this task, he is unable to contact her. When a porter is lynched, Matthew plans a porter strike to relieve his frustration, but it is unsuccessful. In another attempt to express his outrage, Matthew joins a suicidal plot to dynamite the train transporting the top officials of the Ku Klux Klan, on which he is assigned to work. When he learns that Kautilya is also on the train, he prevents the train's destruction but refuses to disclose his knowledge of the conspiracy. Kautilya tries to protect him from prosecution by telling the authorities that she informed him of the scheme, but to no avail. He is sentenced to prison for ten years, and she is deported.

Matthew's conviction attracts the attention of Sara Andrews, the secretary to a leading black politician of Chicago, the Honorable Sammy Smith (who is reminiscent of Oscar De Priest). Through a complicated exchange, they secure Matthew's speedy release from prison and make him into a local hero. Matthew deplores leading a life of unscrupulous political exchanges, but he reluctantly participates, believing that he can effect meaningful social change as an elected public servant. It is not long before Matthew marries Sara, and she manages his campaign for state legislature. After their marriage, though, he learns that her efficiency is the product of a life devoid of sexual passion. Rather than sharing the tastefully decorated house Sara has purchased for them, Matthew spends more and more time in the apartment of his bachelor days.

At the moment of his nomination to Congress, Kautilya miraculously reappears to rescue Matthew from political corruption. He abandons Sara. After Matthew and Kautilya live together for several weeks, they realize they must return to their original quest for racial justice. She departs, presumably for India. Sara sues Matthew for a divorce, and he seeks penance for his passionate excesses in the arduous labor of digging a tunnel for the new subway. However, Kautilya has not returned to India. She has gone to visit Matthew's mother on her Virginia farm. Once before, when Kautilya was deported, she returned illegally to visit Matthew's mother in order to learn about the nobility of his people. At the end of the novel Kautilya again rescues Matthew. She summons him to join her at the Virginia farm, where, after an extraordinary flight and train ride, he finds that Kautilya has given birth to his son, who is heir to her throne. In the masque, described earlier, he is proclaimed the "Messenger and Messiah to all the Darker Worlds" (*DP* 311).

Several plots of frustration motivate the plot. The first is racial, and it concerns Matthew's expulsion from medical school. He must leave the University of Manhattan because he cannot register for his third-year classes in obstetrical medicine. Despite his high class rank and honors, the school will not permit him to fulfill its clinical requirement by delivering white women's babies, a prohibition hurled at Matthew in the dean's insulting words: "Do you think white women patients are going to have a nigger doctor delivering their babies?" (*DP* 4). The novel recalls this story five times: three times in the early pages of Part 1, once in Part 2, and again in Part 4. This repetition not only underscores the severity of the racist assault on Matthew but also motivates the entire story by identifying the principal sites of Matthew's trauma and textual desire.[21] Thus, each instance of his medical school history indicates the resurgence of a conflict with prohibition consciously depicted as racism and figured, as I argue later, in the novel's textual unconscious as desire for the lost mother.

Freudian pre-oedipal and oedipal paradigms, respectively, for attachment and loss are very useful for analyzing Matthew's social aspirations and confrontations with racism and unconscious textual desire.[22] Much like the delight that Du Bois himself describes when he writes in *The Soul of Black Folk*, "I beat my mates at examination-time, or beat them at a foot-race, or even beat their stringy heads" (Sundquist, *Oxford,* 102), Matthew experiences hard-won pleasure at a northern white medical school, which supports his self-esteem. But his success comes to an abrupt end when the racist white patriarchy forbids his advancement. Racism thus presents an oedipalized assault on Matthew's ego, and he must find a way to obliterate this new threat (which Freud conceptualized as castration, the very punishment inflicted on black men who were accused of challenging racist hegemony during most of Du Bois's lifetime). What is important to see here is that the text amplifies Matthew's conscious awareness of his racial trauma with a corresponding, unconscious sexual trauma, symbolized by his aspiration to be an obstetrician.

The novel's choice of obstetrical medicine as the site for enforcing racist prohibition suggests unconscious textual desire. Given the pervasiveness of racism, Du Bois could have selected any number of situations to invoke racist proscription. But obstetrics here is particularly meaningful. By means of a displacement, the text inscribes Matthew's concealed fantasy about the mother behind his frustrated effort to enroll in a required course which dictates intimate contact with pregnant women. These women constitute an overdetermined symbol for the lost mother and a site of intense textual desire that magnify both incest and racial prohibitions. By making the women white, the text displaces the incest prohibition onto race and the specter of miscegenation. Under these circumstances Matthew's means for sublimating his primary desire—literally laying therapeutic hands on mothers—vanishes until he meets Kautilya, who is another displacement for the unobtainable mother. Prior to meeting Kautilya, though, Matthew attempts to escape the castrating effect of racism by seeking exile in Germany. The trip provides the text with another opportunity to inscribe the lost mother.

During the trans-Atlantic voyage, Matthew succumbs to the imaginary embrace of the ocean much like the infant in the arms of the omnipotent mother. Matthew is "soothed by the sea—the rhythm and song of the old, old sea. He slept and read and slept; stared at the water; lived his life again to its wild climax; put down repeatedly the cold, hard memory about the dean's insult; and drifting, slept again" (*DP* 6). This episode has much in common with the pre-oedipal bond linking the omnipotent mother and child that Freud named the *oceanic feeling*.[23] However, Matthew's pre-oedipal merger is only temporary. Just as the ship must dock, Matthew, to remain a viable character, must recover his memory of racial trauma and reenter the oedipalized plot of desire for this story to preserve its polemical objective.

At the moment he again becomes aware of his racial frustration, Kautilya enters the story. The text exchanges one form of frustration for another as Matthew now experiences surging desire for the princess whom the text describes as a "wildly beautiful phantasy," a veritable reincarnation of Scheherazade of the legendary *Tales from the Thousand and One Nights* (*DP* 8). When she enters the story, the pain of racism becomes contiguous with the agony of sexual longing as the text becomes hypnotized by desire.

The novel invigorates Kautilya's presence with erotic and political discourses. Her immediacy allows Matthew to reaffirm his racial longing for "that soft, brown world," a longing that the text constructs as a heterosexual fantasy incarnate, reminiscent of the *Crisis* cover mentioned earlier:

> First and above all came that sense of color: into this world of pale yellowish and pinkish parchment, that absence or negation of color, came, suddenly, a glow of golden brown skin. . . . It was a living, glowing crimson, *veiled* beneath brown flesh. It called for no light and suffered no shadow, but glowed softly of its own inner radiance. (*DP* 8; my emphasis)

The text goes on to describe Kautilya as a "radiantly beautiful woman" who "was colored":

> There was a hint of something foreign and exotic in her simply *draped* gown of rich, creamlike silken stuff and in the graceful coil of her hand-fashioned turban. Her gloves were hung carelessly over her arm, and he caught a glimpse of slender-heeled slippers

and sheer clinging hosiery. There was a flash of jewels on her hands and a murmur of beads in half-hidden necklaces. His young enthusiasm might overpaint and idealize her, but to the *dullest and the oldest* she was *beautiful, beautiful.* (*DP* 8; my emphasis)

Evidently, this portrait of Kautilya was especially gratifying for Du Bois, who seems to implicate himself directly in the idealization of Kautilya. Both the old and dull Du Bois and his young facsimile Matthew lavishly adore the radiantly lovely princess.

Kautilya is hardly a real woman to Matthew or to the reader. As "the high and beautiful lady whom he worshiped more and more," she is a femininized emblem for the superiority of colored people and thus an exalted symbolization of Du Bois's racial ideal (*DP* 22). However, this feminized emblem of racial loyalty fails to remain fully a political object but becomes instead an erotic object. With this transformation the novel imperils the possibility of sustaining practical propaganda. The danger becomes more pronounced when the eroticism inscribed in the settings, interior decor, and clothing amplify Kautilya's sensuality. By the last part of the novel, what was eroticized propaganda is wholly narcissistic romance. The novel's association of Kautilya with both Titania of Shakespeare's *Midsummer Night's Dream,* to whom Du Bois fondly dedicates *Dark Princess,* and with "her Mauve Majesty" of the "Envoy," to whom he appeals to endorse the novel's authority, makes Kautilya seem more a reflection of Du Bois's own erotic fixation than a political referent.

So compelling is the portrait of Kautilya that many of Du Bois's associates were prompted to speculate about the identity of the woman who may have served as the basis for her portrait. Herbert Aptheker refers to Du Bois's *Dusk of Dawn* and *Autobiography,* in which he writes about his enchantment at meeting a beautiful woman at Fisk (Introduction, 7). Mary White Ovington (a principal supporter of Du Bois and cofounder of the NAACP) suspects that Kautilya's inspiration was an Indian princess who attended the First Universal Races Congress in London in 1911 (Aptheker 7). What is important to see is that Du Bois's creative writings—published and unpublished—reveal that he had long been enchanted with the idea of such a woman. She was the muse for Du Bois's racial strivings whom he envisioned as early as 1893 in his journal.

Du Bois's Fantasmatic Pattern and Cognitive Model

On his twenty-fifth birthday, on February 23, 1893, as he reports in his journal, Du Bois consecrated his commitment to racial striving in a solitary ceremony with wine, candles, oil, and song. Alone in his room, he dedicated his library to his dead mother (Lewis, *W. E. B. Du Bois,* 134) and made a "sacrifice to the Zeitgeist" (Williamson, *Crucible,* 408). In that entry, which he entitles "Quarter-Centennial

Celebration of My Life," Du Bois defines his racial commitment: "to make a name in science, to make a name in literature and thus to raise my race." "I rejoice as a strong man to win a race," he continues, "and I am strong—is it egotism—is it assurance—or is it the silent call of the world spirit that makes me feel that I am royal and that beneath my sceptre a world of kings shall bow."[24] Such pronouncements and his wondering whether he was "a genius or a fool" (Papers, reel 88, frame 468) clearly cast him in a grandiose, indeed regal discourse.

This discourse identifies one of the great divides that Du Bois would struggle to traverse—the attempt to celebrate black folk in aristocratic terms. The fusion of the folk and the elite seems to be a defense for his own likely repressed feelings of class and caste inferiority. This journal entry also calls attention to another dilemma that would dominate Du Bois's critical vision, for in his writings and his life he would attempt to connect empiricism and romanticism. He would manage the alliance by invoking the Hegelian dialectic of synthesized opposition and by implicitly drawing on the cognitive equation between propaganda and eroticism.

Two journal entries, those of his twenty-fifth and twenty-sixth birthdays, manifest the imaginary products of Du Bois's fantasmatic pattern that cohere like a romantic narrative. In the former Du Bois writes,

> I will in this second quarter century of my life, enter the dark forest of the unknown world for which I have so many years served my apprenticeship. . . . I will seek till I find—and die. . . . What is life but life, after all? Its end is the greatest and fullest self—and this end is the Good: the Beautiful is its attribute—its soul, and Truth its being. . . . The greatest and fullest life is by definition beautiful, beautiful—beautiful as a dark passionate woman, beautiful as a golden-hearted school girl, beautiful as a grey haired hero. (Papers, reel 88, frames 469–70)

Like the extract from "The Criteria of Negro Art," this entry symbolizes racial politics as a chivalric adventure in a magic realm. His repetitive use of the word "beautiful" to describe Kautilya in *Dark Princess* reiterates the hyperbolic use of the expression "beautiful" in the description of "the dark passionate woman" in this journal entry. What Du Bois means by the "greatest and fullest life" becomes clearer in another journal entry, written on his twenty-sixth birthday, February 23, 1894. Here he writes that he spent this day "in my regular routine of work and musing." After outlining this day's itinerary, he continues, "I have finally proved to my entire satisfaction that my race forms but slight impediment between me and kindred souls. . . . Therefore I have gained for my life work new hope and zeal— the Negro people shall yet stand among the honored of the world" (Papers, reel 88, frame 490). The "greatest and the fullest life" of Du Bois's imagination is thus not constrained by race but elevated to the position of esteem by means of work, hope, and zeal among like-minded people. Such a life is not only intellectually satisfying to Du Bois but sexually gratifying as well, due to its association with the figures of the beautiful, dark, and passionate woman; the sincere, generous, and enlightened young girl; and the wise, aged hero.

What is important to observe here is that this string of images and prescriptions for the "greatest and fullest life" and "the greatest and fullest self" forms a signifying chain that intimates Du Bois's fantasmatic processes. This patterning process supplies the language for representing his racial activism. According to cognitive theorist George Lakoff, imaginative thought employs "metaphor, metonymy, and mental image to construct abstract thought—cognitive models—that exceeds the boundary of external reality" (Lakoff, *Women*, xiv). When conscious, this process is an instance of what psychoanalysts term secondary image formation, and it is conditioned by "the nature of the organism doing the thinking—including the nature of its body, its interactions in its environment, its social character, and so on" (Lakoff, *Women*, xvi). Beneath conscious imaginative thought is the unconscious fantasmatic pattern. The woman, schoolgirl, and aged hero in Du Bois's entry are metonymies of beauty, generosity, and heroism—virtues that were integral both to Du Bois's self-conception and to his vision of his racial mission. Not only do these figures define his character; they also activate by eroticizing the racial discourses in Du Bois's fiction, verse, and pageants.

These secondary images signal the latent primary fixations of Du Bois's fantasmatic. Primary and secondary process thinking and image formation not only explain the symbolization of ideas but provide gratification as well. Psychoanalyst Mardi Jon Horowitz illustrates the effects of these mental processes by referring to Freud's "The Psychical Mechanism of Forgetfulness." Here Freud describes the infant's primary association of the breast with relief from hunger. Secondary thought processes occur when the infant is hungry and the breast does not immediately appear. Freud theorizes that the infant " 'hallucinates' the absent breast" by remembering it and the associated satisfaction (Horowitz, *Image Formation*, 108). Hence, the infant's fantasy of the breast allays hunger and frustration with the illusion of satisfaction.

The pattern of image formation in the 1894 journal entry has much in common with the gratifying hallucination of the hungry infant and for this reason is very provocative. This Freudian hypothesis suggests that throughout Du Bois's life, the image of a dark, beautiful woman partly allays the conflict he encounters with racism as well as the obstacle of his passionless first wife. This image then forms an essential element of Du Bois's image schemata and the basis of an important fantasy for him. Similarly, Matthew's encounter with the beautiful princess in *Dark Princess* allows him to invigorate his activist quest with phallic authority and permits him (and Du Bois as well) to suspend the fact that the effectiveness of his role as a race leader is in question. This displacement thus enables the novel to exchange the objective of successful racial agitation for sexual gratification.

The journal entries, then, do not simply represent the musings of an ambitious man about the work of racial uplift. When placed in context with a large body of Du Bois's early unpublished writings, many of which display a preoccupation with beautiful girls, especially princesses, jewels, locked jewel cases, stolen jewels, and railroad intrigue,[25] these entries further document an erotic fantasmatic that Freud made familiar as a standard sexual iconography. This fantasmatic schema regulated Du Bois's figurative and rhetorical repertoires, represented his social ambitions, and reproduced his personal desire.

Undoubtedly, the erotic image of Kautilya serves Du Bois's ideal personification of work and pleasure. If she were an isolated case, the erotic intensity of her character would make her a curiosity. However, facsimiles of Kautilya are plentiful in Du Bois's writings. For example, a similar beautiful, dark, and passionate ideal female appears as Zora Cresswell in Du Bois's first novel, *The Quest of the Silver Fleece* (1911); the black heroine Ethiopia in his pageant *The Star of Ethiopia* (produced in 1915 and 1916; see figure 3); the woman on the cover of the November *Crisis;* the "stunning-looking" brunette with "the most wonderful misty eyes" in "The Case" (published in 1907, *The Horizon,* 2:4–10); the woman with "great eyes all full and running over with tears" in an unpublished sketch "A Woman" (dated 1893, Papers, reel 88, frame 375); and the princess in "The Princess of the Hither Isles," mentioned earlier. The recurrence of this figure in Du Bois's writing forms a personal "dialectic of style and content, sameness and difference" that coheres like an identity theme in a work of poetry or music.[26]

Such repetitions, in psychoanalysis, often indicate the site of repression for an original, idealized love object. As Freud explains in "On Narcissism," "[W]hen the original object of wishful impulses has been lost as a result of repression, it is frequently represented by an endless series of substitute objects, none of which, however, brings full satisfaction" (188–89). Whatever the explanation, some such theory of erotic displacement appears to characterize the narrative desire propelling the plot of *Dark Princess* forward in incidents that intimate Kautilya's symbolic identity as the specter of the lost mother, as I shall demonstrate in the next section. Before doing so, though, I conclude this section by exposing, first, a serious flaw in the characterization of this female ideal that symbolizes Du Bois's conception of heroic labor and, second, a discordance in his erotic symbolization of laboring for racial uplift.

Although Du Bois consciously racializes as dark the overdetermined feminine ideal in his creative writings, this intention is invaded by an effect of the white standard of female beauty.[27] For instance, Du Bois repeatedly describes *Quest*'s Zora as dark, even as he makes her a "dull-golden" mulatta with "a great mass of immovable infinitely curled hair" in "thick twisted braids" (17, 123) rather than a typical black woman with negroid features. Whether he was projecting a feminized version of his own hybridity or simply infatuated with light-skinned women is difficult to determine. The contradiction is clear. By using as uplift symbols ideal dark women who are, in actuality, golden-hued, he

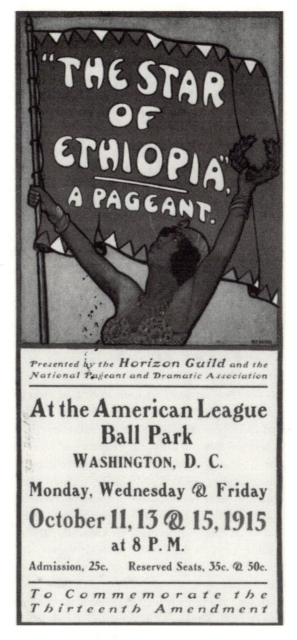

Figure 3. Handbill for *The Star of Ethiopia*. (Courtesy of Special Collections and Archives, W. E. B. Du Bois Library, University of Massachusetts, Amherst. Reprinted by permission of David Graham Du Bois.)

undermines his argument on black exceptionalism. Kautilya's portrait exacerbates this problem.

In *Black No More* (1931), George Schuyler satirized Du Bois for this inconsistency. Here Schuyler writes that Du Bois "deified the black woman but abstained from employing aught save octoroons" (90). Du Bois's preference for light-skinned women of the race is certainly not unique to him, for color prejudice in the black community has been as persistent as it has been controversial. The pervasiveness of this issue suggests that even as black Americans celebrate the physical and spiritual attributes of blackness (or what could be called a nascent black Symbolic), such celebrations are already unconsciously determined—indeed, subverted—by the white Symbolic. Despite the contradiction, this problematic love object symbolizes the imagined gratification of Du Bois's labors for racial uplift.

Indeed, Du Bois's dependency on this beloved object has much in common with Frantz Fanon's discussion of the black man's desire for the white woman in *Black Skin, White Masks*. Here the white woman becomes the signifier of racial equality for the black man because, as Fanon writes, "[b]y loving me she proves that I am worthy of white love. I am loved like a white man. I am a white man" (63). But in Du Bois's case, he abandons the white object of desire because white patriarchy uses perverse versions of this scenario to justify lynching. Yet Du Bois preserves a similar equation for racial equality by veiling the erotic object in color.

As early as 1894 Du Bois symbolically links erotic love and uplift work. In his journal entry of February 23, commemorating his twenty-sixth birthday, he associates his renewed zeal for his life's work with a romantic interlude during which, in his words, "a dear girl met and loved me" (Papers, reel 88, frame 490). To this female fantasy he attaches another about dedicated labor; thus, ideal work and ideal love become equivalent to "work and musing."[28] These identity themes and corresponding image schema (what I called a cognitive equation earlier) appear throughout Du Bois's writings and epitomize the politicized eroticism—or an eroticized politics—that energizes his quest for knowledge and social reform. As we will see, the balance between erotism and politics in the image schema becomes destabilized in *Dark Princess*. While the tension between Matthew's political commitment and sexual desire is the source of power in the novel, the schema fails to make the eroticism serve the racial politics. As a result, the alignment between the "beautiful, beautiful" dark woman as the inspiration for racial propaganda splits off from the racial plot and becomes a full-fledged love story in its own right.

I illustrate this misalignment by referring to Matthew's involvement in the train conspiracy, which he believes to be an appropriate expression of his racial outrage. However, the text does not represent this incident as radical protest but as a chivalric fantasy, again reminiscent of the tropes of valor inscribed in "The Criteria of Negro Art":

Then again came sudden boundless exaltation. He was riding the wind of a golden morning, the sense of live, rising, leaping horseflesh between his knees, the rush of tempests through his hair, and the pounding of blood—the pounding and pounding of iron and blood as the train roared through the night. He felt his great soul burst in its bonds and his body rise in the stirrups as the Hounds of God screamed to the black and silver hills. In both scarred hands he seized his sword and lifted it to the circle of its swing. (*DP* 88)

Full of the innuendo of sexual tumescence, the passage represents the attack rather than its motive or object. The reference to the "leaping horseflesh between [Matthew's] knees" and the personification of "the pounding and pounding of iron" of the train roaring "through the night" are standard Victorian icons for sexual desire moving to climax. These figurative representations call attention to an archaic euphemism—dying—for sexual climax, intimated in the extract. Hence the novel casts Matthew in the traditional chivalric pose as the valiant hero in a standardized ideational framework of sexual desire and consummation. This momentary fantasy of love and valor gratifies Matthew; however, it is at best only remotely associated with racial propaganda.

The text attempts to recover its racial plot by having Matthew attack the Klan, which is implicated in the porter's lynching. Matthew does not portray the Klan's heinous nature in either graphic detail or political terms; rather, the novel again resorts to romantic ideology. The appearance of the woman whom Matthew regards as his queen interrupts the fantasy of the charging black knight in a contest with the Klan and installs instead a tangible love story. Rather than expressing his racial commitment in terms of his devotion to this beautiful woman, at the midpoint of the novel Matthew collapses his commitment to her political ideal into his increasing erotic devotion to the woman. From there, the racial propaganda serves the novel's eroticism like metaphysical foreplay. Even when Kautilya is out of sight, she looms not only in Matthew's unconscious but in the unconscious and preconscious of the text.

Dreaming of Kautilya

Kautilya is the ubiquitous dream of the text. It projects her much like the smiling face of the mother for whom the infant longs. For example, an oriental rug that Matthew places in one of his empty rooms alludes to Kautilya like a transitional maternal object for an infant. He sits before the rug for hours and dreams unconsciously of her presence: "The rug was marvelous. It burned him with its brilliance. It sang to his eyes and hands. It was yellow and green—it was thick and soft; but all this didn't tell the subtle charm of its weaving and shadows of coloring" (*DP* 128). A second fantasy occurs while camping out on route to visit his mother. Imagining that he was "a boy again, with the world before him," Matthew "saw the sun rise, pale gold and crimson, over the eastern trees. . . . Beyond the frost, it lay magnificent—wonderful—beautiful—beautiful as one unforgettable face" (*DP* 131).

The descriptions of the rug and sunrise are not simply ancillary textual features but discourses of displaced desire for Kautilya and ultimately the lost mother that cohere into powerful fantasies. They temporarily satisfy Matthew's repressed longing for Kautilya. These allusive, figurative projections partly form the preconscious of *Dark Princess,* which is recoverable because Western culture has taught us to associate landscapes and the interior decor of residential settings with the erotic female body (Gay, *Bourgeois Experience,* 2:257). Freud was the first to call our attention to such libidinal displacements, now recognized as sublimation. Thus, to write affectionately about such a setting is "to invest [it] with the ability to receive, give, or withhold love" (Gay, *Bourgeois Experience,* 2:257). Du Bois drew on this pattern of erotic association to symbolize Matthew's unconscious desire for the princess and to inscribe latent maternal fantasies in the text of the novel.

The rug is an emphatic symbol for Kautilya; it is gorgeous, luminous, and sensual. Much like the infant in Freud's "Infantile Sexuality," mentioned earlier, Matthew searches "for some pleasure which has already been experienced and is now remembered" (181). The rug links Matthew to gratifying memories of Kautilya, who, as we shall see, is increasingly associated with the primary object she displaces—the mother. This sublimated and regressive form of eroticism inspires an extensive illusion. For as he grows increasingly more sexually frustrated and emotionally disheartened, the text expands the compensatory fantasy by adding other maternal objects. For instance, an old chair provides Matthew with comfort and security, though he remains unconscious of the maternal associations that grant it the power to console him.

In the context of Freudian dream-work,[29] Matthew's problematic response to the sunrise fantasy is particularly meaningful. As he recalls his boyhood, the memory of "one unforgettable face," projected onto the sunrise, prompts him to leap "to the ground and clench his hand. A wave of red shame smothered his heart" (*DP* 131). The text draws on the presumption that the face is Kautilya's, while simultaneously contesting that presumption with the inappropriateness of Matthew's shameful response. Matthew ought not feel guilty about his desire for this beautiful woman; nevertheless, the text is adamant. The intrusion of shame in Matthew's daydream associates Kautilya with the mother of the oedipal plot.

Embracing Prohibited Desire

The dilemma that Matthew attempts to resolve by projecting his desire onto Sara is the same struggle with desire he has repeatedly fought throughout the novel in a variety of ways but failed to master: how to embrace the prohibited object of desire by means of displacement, regardless of whether the object is racial equality or the body of a proscribed woman. In fact, *Dark Princess* constructs gratification by superimposing the racial object onto the sexual object. As a result, the censors of white hegemony and the incest taboo become mutually signifying. When the text is unable to overcome one or the other and obtain the object, it relies on passive and regressive forms of satisfaction by depicting Matthew in the act of constructing compensatory infantile fantasies of transitional maternal objects.

The text thus structures its desire in the dynamics of Matthew's pursuit of Kautilya and characterizes his devotion to her in both a pre-oedipalized plot of infantile fusion with the mother and an oedipalized racial contest for freedom, symbolized as female, between the black son and Western, white patriarchy. Hence, desire in *Dark Princess* as well as Matthew's subjectivity coheres around his aggressive drive to dedicate, indeed, attach himself to Kautilya and the text's representations of this desire by means of figurative maternal displacements.

One key incident that relies on pre-oedipal imagery follows Matthew's initial retreat from Sara. He returns to his apartment, where he sits for hours in his big, old, shabby armchair. It puts "its old worn arms so sympathetically about him" (*DP* 192). Here Matthew surrenders to an infantile fantasy of maternal holding. However, as desire develops in the text, it supplants the pre-oedipal fantasies with oedipal ones. Matthew's compulsion to purchase "a Turkish rug for the bedroom—a silken thing of dark, soft, warm coloring"—signals the onset of another oedipal allusion. When he got the rug to his apartment, he "threw it before his old bed and let it vie with the dusky gold of its Chinese mate" (*DP* 193). Much like the Freudian primal scene in which the son imagines the site of his own conception and experiences the desire to displace the father, the text here casts Matthew as the voyeur of a figurative sexual embrace that signals oedipal gratification while preserving the pre-oedipal longing for holding. The text will eventually consolidate its pre-oedipal and oedipal illusions in Kautilya, who becomes an idealized reflection but not embodiment of the lost mother. I refer to this consolidation with the term "(m)other." I will also explain the significance of this distinction at the end of this chapter. For the time being, though, what is important to see is that Matthew has transformed his apartment into a play space for his pre-oedipal and oedipal fantasies. They foreshadow Kautilya's return.

When Kautilya reappears, the text undermines its tenuous hold on the reality principle by resorting to melodrama to describe this woman, who has deliberately subjected herself to suffering as reparation for her ignorance of the history of Matthew's people. The text now sheds the golden gossamer of color that illuminated Kautilya in the first half of the novel:

A dark figure stood by the table. An old dung-colored cloak flowed down upon her, and a *veil* lay across her head. Her thin dark hands, now bare and almost clawlike, gripped each other. They were colored hands. . . . And she came like a soft mist, *un-*

veiled and *uncloaked* before him. Always she seemed to come thus suddenly into his life. . . . [S]he was different, yet every difference emphasized something eternally marvelous. Her hair was cut short. . . . [H]er hands, hard, wore no jewels, but were calloused, with broken nails. The small soft beauty of her face had become stronger and set in still lines. Only in the steadfast glory of her eyes showed unchanged the Princess. (*DP* 208–9)

Kautilya's noble endeavor to learn the effects of labor exploitation has transformed her into the emphatically dark—black—woman (Du Bois used the word "colored," which during the 1920s meant Negro). With her clawlike, calloused hands and wrinkled face, Kautilya's appearance has much in common with that of an old, poor, black woman.

The passage's references to veiling and unveiling and cloaking and uncloaking calls attention to Kautilya's bodily representation of gratified latent desire and suggests another referent for Du Bois's metaphorical veil of race. At this point in the story, Matthew no longer needs to rely on thinly veiled and overdetermined pre-oedipal and oedipal fantasies; Kautilya now clearly reflects the beloved (m)other. In grateful recognition, "[h]e lifted his hands to heaven, stretched them to touch the width of the world, and swept her into his tight embrace" (*DP* 209). The novel labels her rescue of Matthew from political corruption a "Benediction": she exhorts, "I have sought you, man of God, in the depths of hell, to bring your dead faith back to the stars." While the text insists that for Matthew "[t]he world was one woman and one cause" (*DP* 210), the reader readily discerns the woman, but the cause has become rather obscure.

The text depicts the sexual consummation of Matthew's desire as an act of artistic expression, a sacrament of shared intimacy and self-revelation. Sex for Matthew and Kautilya is transfigured as a spiritual act. Theirs is true love—"spiritual, constant and altruistic, not sensual, short-lived and egoistic" (Seidman, *Romantic Longings,* 47). The apartment, which had been a kind of womb for the vulnerable Matthew, now becomes a love nest, filled with erotic stimulants of perfumes, seductive music, and delicious foods. Moreover, this episode fuses pre-oedipal and oedipal gratification, as Matthew possesses the beloved (m)other. However, his possession of her at this point in the story is not permanent.

When Kautilya departs to resume her work for racial equality, Matthew suffers the loss of his (m)other fantasy. He tries to give meaning to his life by atoning for his activist failures and sexual indulgence. The form of reparation he chooses repeats the stages in the story when he retreats in exile and is sentenced to ten years of hard labor. He now joins a subway crew whose job is to dig subway tunnels, an activity packed with allusion to the pre-oedipal desire to return to the womb. This incident repeats not only the regression of Matthew's imprisonment but that of the ocean voyage as well. Without Kautilya, Matthew feels dead. He digs beyond the point of exhaustion and "sleep[s] like death" (*DP* 271).

And again Kautilya rescues him from an ineffective struggle to invest his life with meaning. In an urgent summons she commands that he join her at his mother's farm. In a personal letter accompanying the summons, she tells him as well that the

> Great Central Committee of Yellow, Brown, and Black is finally to meet. You are a member. The High Command is to be chosen. Ten years of preparation are set. Ten more years of final planning, and then five years of intensive struggle. In 1952, the Dark World goes free—whether in Peace and fostering Friendship with all men, or in blood and Storm—it is for Them—the Pale Masters of today to say. (*DP* 296–97)

After an extraordinary flight and train ride, full of allusions to death and rebirth, Matthew reaches his mother's farm to find that Kautilya has delivered his son, who, as the new Maharajah, has rescued her from the life of a royal consort. The child, whom Kautilya has named "Madhu" (or "Matthew" in her language), is heir to her throne (*DP* 308). After a brief wedding ceremony, the narrative explodes into the messianic masque of black supremacy discussed earlier.

Erotic Fantasy or Racial Propaganda in *Dark Princess* and Du Bois's *Quest of the Silver Fleece*

The pageantry at the end of *Dark Princess* is both a masque and a mask of optimism. However, this apocalyptic ending is not so wholly hopeful as Arnold Rampersad suggests. He regards this epic ending as an expression of Du Bois's "ecstatic optimism," "the richest dividend of his awakened political consciousness." "Applied to his writing," Rampersad continues, "this optimism was compounded by his nostalgia for a vanished innocence within both a mythic Africa and humanity as a whole, by his sense of the history of the world as the history of progress" ("W. E. B. Du Bois," 70). What Rampersad has perceived as Du Bois's "ecstatic optimism" had to have been the resolve of his extraordinary willpower and undoubtedly the pleasurable effect of the fantasies about the lost mother, for his optimism could not have existed apart from his growing despair about the intractable color line. *Dark Princess*'s pageantry implores the reader to keep the faith not by pragmatically addressing the race problem but by escaping it with divine approbation, messianic proclamation, and erotic fantasy.

The novel's tactic of masking realism with pageantry is remarkably reminiscent of the supernatural setting that closes Pauline Hopkins's serial novel *Of One Blood; Or, the Hidden Self* (1902–3). Here the black hero, conspicuously modeled on Du Bois, is anointed king of a legendary, underground African city, where he and his queen reside, waiting for God to reveal His resolution to the race conflict; for "none save Omnipotence can solve the problem." These lines conclude the story:

> To our human intelligence these truths depicted in the feeble work may seem terrible,—even horrible. But who shall judge the handiwork of God, the Great Craftsman!

Caste prejudice, race pride, boundless wealth, scintillating intellects refined by all the arts of the intellectual world, are but puppets in His hand, for His promises stand, and He will prove His words, "Of one blood have I made all races of men."[30] (Hopkins, *Of One Blood*, 621)

Dark Princess relies on similar displacements of time, place, and agency. As in *Of One Blood*, the resolution of the race problem in *Dark Princess* lies in the providential future, indeed, twenty-five years after the novel's setting, in 1952. But unlike Hopkins, Du Bois holds tenuously to human rather than divine agency. Instead of awaiting for Omnipotence to solve the race problem, Du Bois places that responsibility on a royal infant who claims divinity through Kautilya's lineage, an infant who is both a tribute to Du Bois's own dead son Burghardt and a projection of his own egotistical desire, inscribed in the journal entry of his twenty-fifth birthday.

The endings of *One Blood* and *Dark Princess* are similar because they originate in their authors' messianic racial outlook, a perspective that allowed them both to hold onto optimism even though it was tainted with continued disappointment. For during the last two decades of the nineteenth century and the first two decades of the twentieth, Hopkins and Du Bois, along with their black contemporaries, witnessed a severe re-entrenchment of racism that Rayford W. Logan called the "Dark Ages of recent American history" (*Betrayal*, 9).[31] By the onset of the 1920s the racial climate remained essentially unchanged despite the heroic efforts of legions of "race" men and women, including the monumental accomplishment of Du Bois himself, who was in his fifties. Resolving the problem of the color line no doubt seemed to defy human effort. Under these circumstances, it is not surprising that *Dark Princess*, like *Of One Blood*, maintains racial optimism by projecting it onto an apocalyptic tradition. While *Dark Princess*, unlike the earlier work, does not wholly subscribe to the existence of God, it does appeal to the ennobling potential of love, ethical conduct, and the virtues of labor, as evident in the novel's credo: "God is Love and Work is His Prophet" (*DP* 279).

Du Bois's conviction in the efficacy of education, work, and organized protest is decidedly unconvincing in *Dark Princess*. While Du Bois endorses this conviction in the novel by having Matthew make similar pronouncements, he abandons his education and fails to become involved in meaningful work or effective racial protest. This failure suggests that Du Bois himself might have been questioning the efficacy of such effort.

By contrast, his first novel, *The Quest of the Silver*, which appeared in 1911, is a more convincing work of propaganda. This novel appeared when Du Bois was also more secure in his role as race leader and thus more hopeful about the rational appeal of propaganda to mitigate the effects of racism. *Quest*, then, is a work more of reason than of passion. It focuses on the material consequences of slavery in the lives of black and white people in the context of the political economy of the cotton industry at the turn of the twentieth century. As the title suggests, the novel is a romantic, indeed, heroic quest for social justice. Despite the epic overlay, though, *Quest* is primarily a novel of social realism, grounded in the economic circumstances of black rural laborers, whose fate the central characters Zora Cresswell and Bles Alwyn share. Rather than escaping into an apocalyptic finale, they face the practical realities of achieving an educated and self-sufficient black populace in the face of severe racist oppression.

In sharp contrast, *Dark Princess* is a flight into fancy, as the novel's "Envoy" clearly indicates. *Dark Princess* turns from social realism to romance, from community enthusiasm to individual desire, from broad political objectives to narcissistic gratification. The novel's credo—"God is Love and Work is His Prophet" (*DP* 279)—is more candid than even Du Bois may have suspected, for the controlling force in this text is not reason, God, or activist labor but unquestionably erotic desire. While Du Bois explicitly states that *Dark Princess* is a romance with the "deeper aim" of explaining the "difficulties and realities of race prejudices upon many sorts of people—ambitious black American youth, educated Asiatics, selfish colored politicians, ambitious self-seekers of all races,"[32] the novel does not fulfill that aim. Rather, it fulfills an even more essential but personal need, demand, and desire that a comparison of *Quest* and *Dark Princess* makes evident.

When these novels are placed side by side, they reveal very different textual intentions determined by their conscious and unconscious discourses of desire. *Quest* looks outward to social reform. The gratification of Zora and Bles's desire involves black community development as well as personal sexual pleasure. The postscript of *Quest* emphasizes the social perspective and entreats us to "Lay not these words aside for a moment's phantasy, but lift up thine eyes upon the Horror in this land;—the maiming and mocking and murdering of my people, and the prisonment of their souls" (*DP* 434). This appeal is reminiscent of the social mission to which Du Bois dedicates his life in the journal entry written on his twenty-fifth birthday. What is important is that *Quest* depicts racial activism by relying on the same figurative elements that appear in this journal entry. By abridging it somewhat, I can emphasize Du Bois's commitment: "I will in this second quarter century of my life . . . seek . . . the greatest and fullest self—and this end is the Good: the Beautiful is its attribute—its soul, and Truth its being. . . . The greatest and fullest life is by definition beautiful, beautiful—beautiful as a dark passionate woman" (Papers, reel 88, frames 469–70). *Quest* plots a story about committed self-development by repeating the scenario of the journal entry. Such a life, to paraphrase the entry, is as good and as beautiful as a beautiful, dark passionate woman. The social and erotic discourses cohere in the extract and in *Quest*. Thus, when the novel ends by imploring us to work together for social change, it retains a social obligation by projecting its message outward to the audience. Our charge is to duplicate the commitment of Zora and Bles, one sanctified by marriage. Moreover, this novel plots realistic strategies for that undertaking, the manipulated ending notwithstanding.

By contrast, the social (conscious) and erotic (partly unconscious) discourses do not cohere in *Dark Princess*. In fact, the latter undermine the novel's social objectives. The conscious narrative claims that Matthew is a proponent of racial activism, yet he is completely ineffective in this regard. His ambitions to be a doctor, an activist, and a politician are all ultimately supplanted by his desire for Kautilya. For these reasons, eroticism in *Dark Princess* dominates the site occupied by the reformist agenda in *Quest*. Work is *Quest*'s aspiration. Love—indeed, sexual coupling—is the ambition of *Dark Princess*. To put it another way, Matthew and Kautilya (pro)create a son who is yet another displacement for racial justice. Thus, the largely realistic racial argument that controls *Quest* becomes a fantastic, regal romance in *Dark Princess*. The conscious plot of propaganda in *Quest* shatters in *Dark Princess*, leaving the fragmented discourse little recourse but to regress into messianic pageantry.

Du Bois undoubtedly believed that the genre of romance could facilitate the expression of the propaganda in both novels. But in *Dark Princess*, the ideal object of the romantic quest is eroticism instead of racial justice. The erotic, as Audre Lorde has convincingly argued in "The Uses of the Erotic," can provide the energy to pursue political change. And Du Bois no doubt believed he was tapping into that energy source with the question that concludes the novel in the "Envoy": "Which is really Truth—Fact or Fancy? the Dream of the Spirit or the Pain of the Bone?" This question invokes the novel's dedication to Du Bois's queen of fancy—Titania XXVII—and endorses what he evidently believed was the fine line between reality and providential history. However, in order for eroticism to fuel political change it must remain sublimated (or subsumed) within social activism. If the eroticism does not remain submerged within the political objective, its drive for pleasure becomes overly personalized, and its preoccupation with individual gratification subverts the collective goal. This is precisely what happens in *Dark Princess*. As a result, the novel's closing question about truth seems more the product of Du Bois's identification with Matthew's desire than with his identification with the novel's promotion of racial propaganda. *Dark Princess* more emphatically symbolizes the desire for a fulfilling, conjugal relationship and a son—two goals that in 1928 still eluded Du Bois—than for meeting the demands of political leadership. Moreover, the infant son in *Dark Princess* defines Kautilya's role as mother and thereby appeases the threat of female agency. As father and husband, Matthew holds the reigns of power until his messianic infant son is a man.

The closing question of *Dark Princess*'s "Envoy"—"Which is really Truth—Fact or Fancy? the Dream of the Spirit or the Pain of the Bone?"—seems to pertain to Du Bois's own psychological reality at the time of the novel's creation, while the truthfulness of *Quest* pertains to the historical circumstances of the real people whom the characters represent. Although we may quarrel with the bequest that sustains the optimistic ending in *Quest*, this miraculous event does not preclude a realistic program of social activism. Neither does it prophesy the eradication of racism. The fanciful ending of *Quest* seems merely to be a modest concession to optimism. By contrast, the entire story of *Dark Princess* arises from fancy—"the Dream of the Spirit." And the fantasy interrupts rather than resolves the social issues with the unrealistic demand of deferral. The novel is thus suspended between a call to action and futility, between compromised ambition and ideal aspiration, between collective politics and personal desire. The fantasy accentuates rather than conceals the fact that *Dark Princess* is weighed down in the morass of racial despair that only the hiatus of pageantry can lift.

While the novel's message lies in Du Bois's insightful observations about the effects of white supremacy on people of color, its plot seems less concerned with fashioning social reform than with painting an idealized portrait of a love object in Kautilya. This character carries the burden of the novel's mythic glorification of peoples of color, a veneration that Edward Said might have called counter-Orientalism.[33] Kautilya and the dark-skinned members of her organization seek "to discover among them the genius, gift, and ability in far larger number than among the privileged and ruling classes" (*DP* 225). That peoples of color possess such nobility (although he specifically meant the elite among them) is what Du Bois regarded as "essential and true," in Arnold Rampersad's words. According to Du Bois, such people were destined to assert their superiority. He maintained this viewpoint not only in *Dark Princess* but in all of his writings by consistently exposing the fallacious basis of white supremacy. However, rather than dismantling the ideologies of white supremacy, Du Bois inverts them to proclaim the dark "other" as the superior and foreordained leader. He clearly articulates this viewpoint in the "Credo" of *Darkwater* (1920): "the beauty of [the Negro's] genius, the sweetness of [his] soul, and [his] strength . . . shall yet inherit this turbulent earth" (3). This prophetic premise literally constructs part of the pleasure in *Dark Princess* by imagining the promise fulfilled in the birth of the messianic son. But most of the pleasure in this text is decidedly and distinctly erotic, even though Du Bois evidently believed or wanted to believe it was political.

While Du Bois took great pleasure in *Dark Princess*, his first readers, as I already indicated, did not. Like Kautilya's messenger, they perceived the novel to be a conflict "[b]etween self-indulgent phantasy and the salvation" of dark peoples (*DP* 299). I can trace their displeasure to a number of contradictory positions that the novel attempts to hold. First, it inscribes class ambivalence by appealing to the solidarity of the peoples of color with bourgeois and aristocratic leadership. Second, the novel attempts to erect black superiority while also venerating elite European art and music. Third, Du Bois's glorification of blackness is compromised by his enraptured depiction of the golden-skinned princess as the novel's ideal love object. Although the novel tries to represent all those who were not white by means of the sensuous hue of the dark princess, the polarized U.S. black/white racial discourse does not accommodate this conflation. Instead, the golden-hued princess, like Zora's mulatta background in *Quest,* endorses racial hybridity rather than blackness. This color dilemma is exacerbated by the choice of romance to structure the social message of *Dark Princess,* for implicit in romance is the ideological imperative of the status quo rather than its reformation. As Fredric Jameson has explained, the romance structure only substitutes an "enchanted space" of privilege for the "transformational scene" of the conflict ("Magical Narratives," 149). In this context the magical account and the Orientalized veiling of the dark princess are ultimately inhospitable to the novel's propagandist intent.

To be successful, to paraphrase Freud, a work must largely fuse its intellectual content and its "emotional attitude" or "mental constellation."[34] If a work achieves power, "it can only be the artist's intention, in so far as he has succeeded in expressing it in his work and in conveying it to us, that grips us so powerfully" ("Moses," 258). That intention, however, is not "merely a matter of intellectual comprehension"; intention must arise from "the meaning and content of what is represented in his work" ("Moses," 258). While Du Bois may have intended for the novel to be a powerful work of racial propaganda and indeed may have regarded it as such, the novel actually constructs a different story for those who do not share Du Bois's cognitive framework. For his rapport with *Dark Princess* is a very personal one that the reader at best can only partly share.

The ending of *Dark Princess* presents us with a dilemma. While we may generally sympathize with Matthew's frustrations and anxiety, his intense happiness at the novel's close has no corresponding significance for us. The novel's finale engenders our wonder and amazement but fails to evoke our empathy, compassion, or identification. This closed fantasy offers us no site for entry. Therefore, it certainly cannot inspire reformist zeal. In fact, the messianic ending undermines the novel's propagandist intent because it erodes the sympathy that we may have had for Matthew up to that point. The messianic ending compensates him for his suffering, as a *New York Times* reviewer points out: "it all turns out better for Matthew Townes than if he had become a doctor" (Review of *Dark Princess,* 16). The novel thus fails to keep white society's culpability for racism in the foreground and makes Matthew's reward an ironic consequence of racism. In addition, the romantic signifier and its propagandistic meaning split apart. For if Kautilya symbolizes the ascendancy of "dark peoples," the allegory falls apart when the novel grants Matthew this love object but fails to secure his racial equality. The novel tries to recover this symbolic rift by forecasting that in twenty-five years "the Dark World goes free—whether in Peace and fostering Friendship with all men, or in Blood and Storm" (*DP* 297). Rather than concluding by securing freedom as its objective, the novel sanctions the consummation of Kautilya's and Matthew's union with their marriage and celebrates the birth of their son, who will deliver freedom to the dark peoples of the world. As if the prophesy of racial liberation, which this child signifies, were not sufficiently compromised through its identification as fantasy, the novel closes with an envoy that privileges fancy over fact instead of transforming fact with fancy.

By symbolizing racial uplift as the beautiful and dark woman, Du Bois provided himself with a therapeutic mechanism for alleviating anxiety when the effects of racial trauma became severe. Because political desire assumes the cognitive form of eroticism in Du Bois's schema, overly stimulated political desire would demand intensified eroticism. This therapeutic model ultimately breaks down in *Dark Princess* because the eroticism cannot master the racial trauma. The eroticized symptoms are not contiguous with the political remedy. Thus, the trauma continues to press its demands, and despite the ultimate futility of the erotic response, the novel continues to deliver ever more extravagant images of the veiled and unveiled princess, the chivalric Matthew, and her jewels—particularly the pearl between her breasts that anticipates the suckling infant. Finally, the messianic finale abandons virtually all semblance of political association.

Because *Dark Princess* relies so heavily on Du Bois's personal erotic fantasies, it is essentially a private and, therefore, narcissistic political romance not so much about reform as the gratification of what seems to have been many of Du Bois's own personal desires: the role of race leader for himself, a fulfilling marriage with a soulmate, a son to carry forth the legacy of his leadership, his renunciation of black participation in U.S. political corruption, and his affirmation of social justice. Political scientist Harold R. Isaacs shares this viewpoint. He contends that "Du Bois poured his racial fantasies, his view of the world, his obsession with color, his public judgments and his secret hopes, and some of his own innermost dreams into [the] novel he called *Dark Princess*" (*New World,* 216). Isaacs goes on to explain that "much—if not all—of Du Bois appears in this book, his thoughts and fantasies about the world, and his dreams about himself, and about love and about fulfillment" (*New World,* 219).

The erotic display was disconcerting for the Harlem literati. Yet such symbolization is neither unusual, naive, nor absurd, for erotic energy has provided the power for social change as writers as diverse as Sigmund Freud and Audre Lorde have persistently argued. The empathic failure between Du Bois and his readers is not due to the inability of private fantasies to authorize social change but to a defect in their representation in *Dark Princess*. Du Bois fails to maintain the connection between the power of the erotic and the goal of social reform in the novel. As a result, its superfluous desire merely makes us uncomfortable.

Effective propaganda not only presents its point of view but also obliges us to share that viewpoint and become activists in its behalf. *Dark Princess* fails to accomplish such empathy because it cannot draw us into the character's obsessions; it does not "reconcile the collective nature of literary reception" with its unique logic of wish-fulfillment (Jameson, "Imaginary and Symbolic," 430). The successful writer "softens the character of his egoistic day-dreams by altering and disguising it, and he bribes us by the purely formal—that is, aesthetic—yield of pleasure which he offers us in the presentation of his phantasies" (Freud, "Creative Writers and Day-Dreaming," qtd. in Jameson, "Imaginary and Symbolic," 341).

These tactics seduce us into unconsciously recognizing our fantasies in the character's actions and emotions.[35] When this is the response, we become vicarious participants in the work's argument, and the work proves successful. This is precisely what Du Bois fails to accomplish in *Dark Princess*. Rather, the novel transforms the desire to perform racial activism into the desire to embrace the "single pearl shining at the parting of two little breasts" (*DP* 299).

Like the child in an unmediated dyad with his imaginary identifications with the mother, Matthew vacillates between two possibilities. He can be "overwhelmed by the other, crowded out, taken over (the fantasy of the devouring mother/voracious child); [or suffer] the wretched isolation and abandonment of all self-worth by the other's absence or neglect (the fantasy of the bad or selfish mother/child)" (Grosz, *Jacques Lacan*, 51). The latter describes Matthew's lot before Kautilya's restoration. To protect his fragmenting sense of self, he tries to deaden his senses with the physical exhaustion of digging subway tunnels in the bowels of the earth. This incident is full of preconscious and therefore unambiguous allusion to the regressive fantasy of being engulfed by the omnipotent mother. Kautilya rescues Matthew from mental death by offering herself as the mother surrogate. He joins her; he even marries her, but still the narrative refuses to end.

The pleasure of Matthew's embrace of Kautilya is insufficient to consummate and terminate all desire in the text because the narration continues. What else could *Dark Princess* possibly desire? Even after the wedding, the story continues by supplementing the wedding with a lavish naming ceremony for their child. Whatever final gratification the text demands is invested in this incident. What desire does this incident represent?

The naming ceremony reestablishes the formation of a nuclear family—Kautilya, Matthew, and extravagantly named child. The triangular unit disrupts Matthew's narcissistic regression into dyadic love by reestablishing individuated, parental gender roles for himself and Kautilya. Moreover, the child is the physical proof of Matthew's phallic power and his sexual difference from the mother and her surrogate. Therefore, the naming ceremony inscribes, preserves, and celebrates Matthew's masculine identity, and, I suspect, masculine textuality by symbolizing the phallus—the child, indeed a son. This incident then inscribes a defense for masculine heterosexual gender anxiety, for in desiring the fulfillment of heterosexual love, the male subject must confront the lost mother in the other woman, merge with her, *and still* preserve masculine individuation (Chodorow, *Feminism*, 73–74; Tyson and Tyson, *Psychoanalytic Theories*, 290).

When Matthew's phallic potency is evident in the infant son, the text should end. But it does not. Again, the text attempts to end after speaking the son's prophesied social role in place of his name: "'Messenger and Messiah to the Darker Worlds!'" (*DP* 311). With these words, the novel fulfills its conscious discourse of propaganda and maintains phallic difference. Therefore, the text should be ready to end. Well, almost.

The narrative now exhibits anxiety about audience response to so fanciful a story and delays the termination by appending an ancillary text in the Envoy. Here, the narrative concedes reason to desire altogether by imploring "her Mauve Majesty" to sanction the "Truth" in the novel that we mere mortal readers will undoubtedly fail fully to grasp. By offering "her Mauve Majesty," rather than us, the tale of *Dark Princess,* the narrative returns to a closed dyadic signifying system like that between the omnipotent mother and the pre-oedipal child. At this point the novel finally expresses its heavily concealed, much displaced, unconscious desire to exclude the social world and re-embrace the dyadic union with the sovereign dark matriarch, who is yet another displacement for the lost and clearly omnipotent mother.

Whereas Emma Kelley's *Megda* inscribes a fantasy of the daughter's pre-oedipal plenitude, *Dark Princess* complicates the son's oedipal resolution with residual pre-oedipal fantasies. Kelley's Meg becomes like the lost mother, while Du Bois's Matthew desires this mother and solicits her recognition. The finales of both novels symbolize the lost mother. *Megda* internalizes this figure in Meg's plenitude. The narrator of *Dark Princess* seeks the lost mother's approval in her loving gaze.

CHAPTER THREE

Rage, Race, and Desire

Savage Holiday, by Richard Wright

How could he ever explain that a daydream buried under the rigorous fiats of duty had been called forth from its thirty-six-year-old grave by a woman called Mabel Blake, and that that taunting dream had so overwhelmed him with a sense of guilt compounded of a reality which was strange and alien and which he loathed, but which, at the same time, was astonishingly familiar to him: a guilty dream which he had wanted to disown and forget, but which he had had to reenact in order to make its memory and reality clear to him!

—Richard Wright, *Savage Holiday* (1954)

At the level of concrete psychopathology, the compulsion to repeat is an ungovernable process originating in the unconscious. As a result of its action, the subject deliberately places himself in distressing situations, thereby repeating an old experience, but he does not recall this prototype; on the contrary, he has the strong impression that the situation is fully determined by the circumstances of the moment.

—J. Laplanche and J.-B. Pontalis, *The Language of Psycho-Analysis* (1973)

Gertrude: What wilt thou do? Thou wilt not murder me?
Help, help, ho!

—*Hamlet*, III, iv, 19–20

Decentering the Racial Plot in *The Outsider* and *Savage Holiday*

In 1954, one year after Harper & Brothers published Richard Wright's novel *The Outsider* (1953), Avon Books published his *Savage Holiday* as a paperback original. Harper & Brothers had first option but declined to publish *Savage Holiday* (Fabre, *Unfinished Quest,* 380). Unlike *The Outsider,* which was widely reviewed, there seem to have been no reviews of *Savage Holiday* in U.S. newspapers and magazines. Perhaps the paperback format gave book critics a reason to disregard the novel. In 1965 Award Books reissued another paperback edition of the novel. Again, there was virtually no publicity for this work. Neither has anything more than scanty scholarly attention been given to the novel over the last four decades, despite Wright's enormous popularity in African American literary scholarship.

What scholarship there is on *Savage Holiday* describes it as "a curiously incoherent little potboiler," a "schoolbook Freud," belonging "in a sleazy drugstore bookstack" (McCall, *Example*, 52; Felgar, *Richard Wright*, 121; Bell, *Afro-American Novel*, 189). In 1995 the University Press of Mississippi reissued *Savage Holiday* in hardcover and paperback. The reception of this latest reprint seems also to have stirred little attention.

Wright's critics have maintained that *Savage Holiday*'s marginality is not simply warranted but fortuitous for Wright's reputation because no response is better than negative commentary (Brignano, *Richard Wright*, 133; Margolies, *Art*, 139; McCall, *Example*, 148; Scott, *Five Approaches*, 135 n. 8; Reilly, "Richard Wright's Curious Thriller," 218). Evidently, critics found no compelling social themes in *Savage Holiday*'s bizarre story about a man who accidentally causes a young boy's death and subsequently murders the boy's mother because she reminds this man of his own promiscuous mother. Undoubtedly, they also regarded Wright's switch from black to white characters as peculiar if not problematic.

Savage Holiday seems to have entrenched the perspective that Wright's critics held about *The Outsider*. In reviews of this novel, his critics—both black and white—"seem[ed] fully agreed that as a result of leaving America he lost touch with the source of his strength as a writer, namely, his being a Negro, a man immersed in the American Negro experience, and a spokesman for black causes" (McCarthy, "Richard Wright," 68). The critics were convinced that Wright's powerful racial plots were fading from his fiction as a consequence of his permanent move to France in 1947. According to the reviews, Wright had abandoned the narrative strategies of realism and naturalism that empowered *Uncle Tom's Children* (1938), *Native Son* (1940), and *Black Boy* (1945) for the polemics of existential philosophy and Freudian psychology.

Nevertheless, Wright's white reviewers were somewhat sympathetic to Wright's casting the protagonist of *The Outsider* as "a thinking, questioning man in the perplexing twentieth century" rather than as an envoy for "the plight of the Negro," in the words of Orville Prescott of the *New York Times* (qtd. in Reilly, *Richard Wright*, 193). Granville Hicks of the *New York Times Book Review* shared this view. According to him, *The Outsider* "is only incidentally a book about Negroes" (qtd. in Reilly, *Richard Wright*, 201). This statement, though, is not as generous as it first might appear, for it assumes a totalizing "Negro" experience for a novel written by a black author and presumes such an experience to be exclusively defined by racial oppression and its effects. This viewpoint centers racial difference as the distinguishing and indeed only significant factor of black life. The views of Prescott and Hicks are not unusual. Indeed, they reflect the broadly held critical consensus about Negro literature during Wright's lifetime: race and Negro are mutually signifying; race is the central preoccupation of the black imagination; a nonracial novel is one with white characters; and presumably, only nonracial novels address so-called universal themes (Gounard and Gounard, "Richard Wright's," 344; Hakutani, *Critical Essays*, 15).

Wright's refusal to tell the conventional story of racial oppression in *The Outsider* made his black reviewers more critical of it than their white counterparts. The reviews of Arna Bontemps and Roi Ottley are typical in this regard. In the *Saturday Review*, Bontemps claims that *The Outsider* is a product of Wright's "roll in the hay with the existentialism of Sartre" (qtd. in Reilly, *Richard Wright*, 208). Like the white reviewers, Bontemps maintains that the problem of the novel's protagonist, Cross Damon, "has nothing to do with color." Bontemps goes on perceptively to identify the source of Damon's problem as "much older and even more puzzling" than race. "Its name is woman," Bontemps insists (qtd. in Reilly, *Richard Wright*, 208). Roi Ottley similarly characterizes *The Outsider* in his review in the *Chicago Sunday Tribune Magazine of Books*. Here he explains that the "main character, Cross Damon, was driven by no discernible motives—racial, political, or religious—even though the author would have us believe he is a rational person. Actually, he is not a Negro, but what Wright describes as the 'psychological man'" (qtd. in Reilly, *Richard Wright*, 205). More so than Hicks and Prescott, Ottley and Bontemps accurately identify *The Outsider*'s sites of inquiry as woman and psychology. However, they assume that these two topics are not central to Wright's artistic vision or his social and intellectual missions. As a result, neither critic pursues the implications of his observation: that irrational sexual desire and an obsession with freedom determine Damon's fate and that psychological analysis provides a strategy for interpreting the intersection of his rational and irrational motives. Rather than locating interpretative models more suited to *The Outsider*'s polemics than social realism, Wright's critics have generally lamented the absence of the familiar racial plot in this novel and the corresponding presence of tedious philosophical discourse and extravagant violence. *Savage Holiday* merely exacerbated these problems.

Despite the troublesome circumstances of the original publication of *Savage Holiday*, this work gratified Wright. Shortly after he placed the novel with Avon, Wright related his pleasure to his agent by writing, "I was proud of my effort, which began on Xmas eve day and ended on Easter Sunday, has resulted in a little 'book'" (qtd. in Fabre, *Unfinished Quest*, 380). Wright's pleasure in *Savage Holiday* probably has much in common with Du Bois's delight in *Dark Princess*. In the preceding chapter, I argue that Du Bois unconsciously and extravagantly inscribes the enigmatic presence of the lost mother at the site of racial protest and combines his protagonist's love object with this maternal enigma. In this context, Du Bois's symbolic "veil" would signify not only the stigma of racial difference, which he probably attributed more to his dark mother than to his mulatto father, but latent primary desire for the mother of his fantasies as well. In this chapter, I am arguing that while Wright's rage at social oppression determined his black protagonists' racially instigated violence throughout his writings, *Savage Holiday* more directly symbolizes another trauma of a more personal nature. This trauma incites a compulsive plot of murderous aggression that is sexual in origin. And this sexual plot forms a significant part of the subjective nucleus of Wright's stories; it is also about the lost mother.

By the lost mother, to repeat, I mean the child's earliest, principal, and most enduring erotic fantasies about the mother that are repressed—here, Du Bois's and Wright's latent fantasies about their respective mothers that characterize what Freud called the pre-oedipal stage and oedipal complex.[1] The lost mother is a representation of a maternal object, an imago, that is distinct from the real, historical mother. Du Bois's *Dark Princess* and Wright's *Savage Holiday* inscribe what seems to be their repressed, ambivalent attitudes about their respective imaginary mothers. Their compulsive repetition of strong, latent, compensatory fantasies about the lost mother and the battle to master an original psychological wound characterize much of their writings. In *Dark Princess,* this fantasy involves both the omnipotent pre-oedipal and the idealized oedipal mothers that are inscribed in the novel's textual unconscious as rhetorical features. As I explain in the previous chapter, the power of this unconscious fantasy marginalizes Du Bois's intentions to make *Dark Princess* into a novel of propaganda and transforms it instead into a passionate love story. In *Savage Holiday* textual pleasure resides not only in the inscriptions of the lost mother but also in the restaging of the fantasy of masculine phallic power. Merely fantasizing masculine power, though, is insufficient to maintain Wright's narrator's pleasure. For this task the narrator recovers the lost mother for repudiation, and this act regulates the plot of murderous violence. As I shall demonstrate, the sequence of maternal recovery, female repudiation, and murder appears in Wright's other fictions as well. Because *Savage Holiday* fantasizes the recovery of the lost maternal object for repudiation and because the repudiation is conscious in the story only insofar as it is denied, this fantasy is virtually self-evident. Wright does not rely on rhetorical devices to make allusions to the matricidal fantasy; instead, the fantasy is played out in the novel's plot.

Wright's Compulsive Plot of Violence and Its Critics

Wright wrote the first complete draft of *Savage Holiday* in one month and finished the final manuscript in less than four months (Fabre, *Unfinished Quest*, 379). When interviewed about his inspiration for the novel, he rather unconvincingly explains that he came across the idea for the story in a library, "while glancing at books naturally, casually, without any purpose. I came across a passage," he adds, "dealing with the problem of freedom. Not in a philosophical sense but in a *practical sense*" (Charbonnier, "Negro Novel," 236, qtd. in Early, Afterword, 225; my emphasis). Wright explains what he means by practical by referring to the symbolization of freedom as the central problem of his fictions. But when Wright recalls the story's origins for his compatriot Chester Himes, he abandons this vague and somewhat obligatory, intellectual account for one that is more compelling and certainly more convincing. In this instance Wright explains that the story came to him while he was sick in bed, suffering with a high fever (Himes, *Quality*, 190–91). *Savage Holiday* bears witness to this latter account, for it repeats the hallucination of "the wobbly white bags, like the full udders of cows," that threaten the ailing boy Richard of *Black Boy* (7). In *Savage Holiday* the malevolent breast fantasy reappears as the "shifting curtain of wobbly images [that] hovered before his [protagonist's] consciousness" (36). In contrast to the helpless young black boy in *Black Boy*, *Savage Holiday* presents a large and powerful white male protagonist, Erskine Fowler, whose repressed guilt for a childhood wish causes him to become the aggressor rather than a passive victim.

Savage Holiday repeats the plot of sadistic violence toward women found throughout Wright's canon.[2] What is different in this case is the absence of a racial motivation. Nevertheless, the basic outline of this plot is so constant in Wright's works that his critics routinely refer to James Baldwin's indictment of Wright's "gratuitous and compulsive" violence (Baldwin, "Alas," 188, qtd. in R. J. Butler, "Function," 9). In "Alas, Poor Richard," Baldwin claims that the root of Wright's violence is rage, but he assumes its object to be "the guilty imagination of the white people who invest him with their hates and longings" (188). While it is difficult, if not impossible, to determine the primary origin of Wright's rage by referring to his fictions, it is possible to analyze the manifestations of that rage in the series of what Malcolm Cowley has called Wright's "symbolic murders" (qtd. in R. J. Butler, "Function," 9). By doing exactly this, Diane Long Hoeveler has perceptively argued that the motivation of murderous rage in Wright's fictions appears to be "the irreconcilable oedipal dilemmas that afflict his heroes," a condition that "had preoccupied his imagination for over twenty years" ("Oedipus Agonistes," 65, 68).

The speed with which Wright completed *Savage Holiday* suggests his profound familiarity with this compulsive story, a fact that probably accounts as well for the novel's lack of subtlety and implausible narrative logic: Wright may have experienced the story as a kind of reality and therefore failed to make the subtle distinctions required to transform personal fantasy into effective communication. Again to borrow Freud's words, Wright fails to subdue his "egoistic day-dreams by altering and disguising them" so as to bribe his readers with a "purely formal—that is, aesthetic—yield of pleasure which he offers us in the presentation of his phantasies" (Freud, "Creative Writers," 152, qtd. in Jameson, "Imaginary and Symbolic in Lacan," 341). The successful rendering of this tactical bribe would entice us, according to Freud, into unconsciously recognizing our fantasies in a character's actions and emotions[3]—in Wright's case, specifically, those moments of infantile rage when we too were guilty of directing or wanting to direct our hostility at a primary parent or caretaker.

Rather than appeal to his reader's pleasure by finding the means to make them (indeed us) identify with the story, Wright seems much more preoccupied with securing his own pleasure in *Savage Holiday*. At least Du Bois believed he was addressing the race problem in *Dark Princess*, and to some extent he did. By contrast, Wright seems to have derived satisfaction in focusing on his own pleasure rather than that of his readers, for he had to have known that the novel's white characters, the matricidal plot, and the blatant Freudian symbolism would puzzle and even estrange them. When Chester Himes read the manuscript of the novel shortly after its completion, he confessed to Wright that its purpose eluded him (*Quality*, 190–91). Wright should not have been surprised by Himes's predictable response, one that his critics would share. In order to esteem Wright's other writings, they regarded *Savage Holiday* as an anomaly and suppressed it from scholarly recollection. So much so, in fact, that while we contemporary readers of U.S. literature are generally familiar with *Native Son* (1940) and *Black Boy*, Wright's best-sellers and now canonical works, many of us do not even know that Wright wrote *Savage Holiday*.

In contrast to those scholars who have labeled *Savage Holiday* an anomaly,[4] Michel Fabre and Margaret Walker, two of Wright's biographers, argue that this novel is very much a part of Wright's psycho-aesthetic landscape. They support their contention by identifying the narrative elements in *Savage Holiday* that also repeatedly appear in Wright's other works. Hence, Fabre and Walker direct their attention to analyzing the symbolism that Wright employs to relate the psychosexual experiences of his characters. Fabre associates Wright's sexual symbolism with his unique fantasy formations or what Fabre calls Wright's "phantasms" (*World*, 117), while Walker interprets this symbolization in terms of her personal knowledge of the man.

In Fabre's *World of Richard Wright*, two essays in particular focus on chronicling the imagery repeatedly associated with Wright's psychosexual fantasies. In "The Man Who Killed a Shadow: A Study in Compulsion," Fabre couches his comparison of the "crude outburst of puzzling violence" in Wright's fictions in a discussion of Wright's methodology of modeling his fictions after real-life crimes. The influence of Robert Nixon's murder trial on *Native Son* is probably the best-known case (Fabre, *Unfinished Quest*, 172–73). In addition, Fabre refers to Wright's use of aspects of the "Herbert C. Wright burglaries" in "The Man Who Lived Underground" (1944), the Julius Fisher murder case in "The Man Who Killed a Shadow" (1949), and the Clinton Brewer murder case as well as Frederic Wertham's analysis of a real case of matricide in his *Dark Legend* (1941) to write *Savage Holiday*. Fabre plots the similarities of these cases against Wright's stories but avoids interpreting the textual traces of trauma inscribed in Wright's compulsive plots of violence (*World*, 108–21).

In "Fantasies and Style in Wright's Fiction," Fabre refers to key scenes in *Savage Holiday* involving fire, voyeurism, and rhythmical beating, ticking, or chopping that also appear in *Native Son*, *Black Boy*, *The Outsider*, *The Long Dream*, "The Man Who Lived Underground," and "Tarbaby's Dawn" (*World*, 122–43). For example, in discussing *Native Son* Fabre refers to Bigger's dream in which, after his capture, he "cursed the booming bell and the white people" and "hurled the bloody head squarely in their faces *dongdongdong*" (qtd. in *World,* 126). In "The Long Black Song," which I discuss later, Fabre explains that Sarah's small daughter's striking a broken clock marks Sarah's increasing sexual tension: "a red wave of hotness drowned her in a deluge of silver and blue and boiled her blood and blistered her flesh *bangbangbang*" (qtd. in *World,* 126–27). Discussing an early draft of *Black Boy* entitled "Black Confessions," Fabre also cites Wright's depiction of himself as a small boy, "*banging* tin-cans against the pavement" just before he recounts the familiar cat-hanging episode, to which I shall return (12). In each of these incidents, rhythmical beating, bumping, banging, pounding, or striking occurs before the discharge of violence. Fabre explains that these repetitive features "create the unconscious bed-rock of the style" in Wright's fictions. "In order to dig deeply into the most personal aspects of writing," according to Fabre, "it is necessary to analyze the relations between fantasies and style" (*World,* 143). Fabre has performed the preliminary analysis. This chapter extends Fabre's argument by probing the textual desires of Wright's fictions by means of *Savage Holiday,* in search of the textual traces of the primary trauma that unifies his writings.

In *Richard Wright: Daemonic Genius,* Margaret Walker insists that *Savage Holiday* is not an aberration among Wright's writings. She contends that despite his white skin, Erskine Fowler is "the same persona as Bigger Thomas in *Native Son,* Jake Jackson in *Lawd Today,* Cross Damon in *The Outsider,* and Richard Wright in *Black Boy*" because Wright expresses his own "subliminal desires" through these personas (245, 148). Unfortunately, Walker does not identify these "desires" or the manner of their sublimation, even though she refers to the perverse preoccupations of Damon and Fowler inscribed in the anagrams comprising their names. But she does refer to numerous incidents in *Savage Holiday* that are also depicted in *Black Boy:* Fowler's hatred of his father; his conflicts with his mother, aunts, and grandmother; his fear of the " 'Biggy' Thomases of the 'big boys'; his rejection, desertion, and hunger, dread and alienation" (*Richard Wright,* 247). She concludes by asserting that

> *Savage Holiday* is the most damaging evidence of the psychosexual in Wright's fiction and perhaps the greatest exposure of Wright's own personality. As he relentlessly probes the psyche of Erskine Fowler of *Savage Holiday,* he opens wide the door to his inner self. He parades before us an embarrassment of conflicts, complexes, and complicated cycles of what we gradually recognize are Dostoevskian depths in the criminal mind. Wright is able, however, to write in a positive and healthy fashion about the anger, hostility, aggression, and anxiety that obviously plagued his psyche. (*Richard Wright,* 246)

Walker's views are resolute but also vague and undocumented. While she explains that "the wellsprings of his creativity were deep welters and dark pools of realistic and neurotic anger, which he sublimated into imaginative writing," she does not identify the suspected neuroses or explore the basis of this anger (5). Neither does she identify their manifestations in Wright's works. Instead, she repeatedly reports that four psychical devils pursued Wright for his entire life: anger, ambivalence, alienation, and aberration (*Richard Wright*, 13). While these emotional affects un-doubtedly identify aspects of Wright's personality that had specificity for Walker because she personally knew the man, they do not reveal his character to those of us who did not. In addition, she neither describes nor explains Wright's attitudes, behavior, and neuroses nor integrates them with those four psychical demons. Rather, she adds that "there are many indications of his bisexuality" (*Richard Wright*, 310) and suggests that his ambivalence toward women and his sexual ori-entation were responsible for his "sadistic" attitude toward women in general and his "hatred" of black women in particular (*Richard Wright*, 182, 179).

Both Walker and Fabre refer to Wright's fascination with the Clinton Brewer murder case, his close association with psychoanalyst Frederic Wertham, and Wertham's *Dark Legend* as important factors in the composition of *Savage Holi-day* (Fabre, *Unfinished Quest*, 378).[5] Yet neither Fabre nor Walker mentions that one of Wertham's specialties was matricide or that the psychopathic murderer of Wertham's *Dark Legend* killed his widowed mother by stabbing her thirty-two times (Wertham, *Dark Legend*, 194, 17). Fabre does mention in passing another white psychoanalyst, Benjamin Karpman, who was affiliated with Howard Uni-versity Medical School from 1921(?) to 1940 and subsequently with St. Elizabeth's Psychiatric Hospital in Washington, D.C. Wright and Karpman wrote to one an-other during the first half of the 1940s. As with his silence on Wertham's specialty, Fabre also fails to mention that the letters from Karpman to Wright suggest that Karpman's specialty was sexual perversion.[6] Walker refers to Wright's interest in the case study on the psychopathic murderer Clinton Brewer, to whom Wright dedicates *Savage Holiday*. She even goes so far as to claim that during Wright's last visit to New York, after the filming of *Native Son* in South America, "Wright had brief therapy from Wertham" (245). Because she repeatedly offers speculation as evidence, Walker undermines the significance of her conclusion about the extent of Wright's obsession with psychoanalysis (245). Fabre comes to a similar conclu-sion by stating that Wright "had outgrown" his faith in existentialism (*Unfinished Quest*, 376). He refers to Wright's letter to Paul Reynolds, his agent, about *The Out-sider*, in which Wright expresses the desire to make the novel "completely non-racial, dealing with crime *per se*" (quoted in *Unfinished Quest*, 376). What Fabre sees in *The Outsider* is Wright "settl[ing] old accounts" rather than "uncover[ing] new premises from which to start afresh" (*Unfinished Quest*, 376). As a result, Fabre does not connect the disavowal of existentialism in *The Outsider* with the authority of psychoanalysis in *Savage Holiday*. Finally, neither Fabre nor Walker sees *Savage Holiday* as the culmination of Wright's fascination with crime.

Wright invested more than intellectual curiosity in psychoanalysis. For him, psychoanalysis was a principal source of his inspiration and a genuine reflection of his faith in the power of "scientific, rational inquiry" to probe "into the nature of things"—here, specifically, the psyche, and no doubt his own (Early, Afterword, 224). Wright read widely in psychoanalysis, and he used his understanding of its tenets in his writing.[7] For example, in the typescript of his 1946 review of Jo Sinclair's *Wasteland*, entitled the "Inner Landscape of a Jewish Family," Wright argues that writers fail when they try to use psychoanalysis as a device "for novelistic structure" rather than as a methodology for "plowing up the unconscious" by means of free association "as they write" (3). Wright seems to have relied on the latter method in his own writing. Wright again refers to the unconscious in an article about the founding of the Lafargue clinic, entitled "Psychiatry Comes to Harlem." Here, in a description of repression that if personified would apply to any one of his protagonists, Wright explains that the "repressed need goes underground, gropes for an unguarded outlet in the dark and, once finding it, sneaks out, experimentally tasting the new freedom, then at last gushing forth in a wild torrent, frantic lest a new taboo deprive it of the right to exist" (49). This very process characterizes *Savage Holiday*.

Throughout Wright's unpublished manuscripts ("Memories of My Grandmother," "Personalism," and "On Literature," for instance), Wright also explicitly refers to the discursive power of the unconscious—or what he calls, in the context of *The Man Who Lived Underground*, "the recurring motif of the *strangely familiar*," a phrase that Wright repeatedly uses in his fiction and that clearly invokes Freud's "Uncanny" ("Memories," 17; my emphasis). In "On Literature," for example, Wright speculates that "all writing is a secret form of autobiography" (6). By "secret," Wright is referring not to a deliberate intention of concealing information but to an unconscious purpose, uniquely personal and inscribed in all language use by every individual. This secret marks the text with distinctive characteristics as much as an individual author's signature would.

Wright's self-conscious reliance on the creative power of his unconscious is perhaps nowhere more evident than in *Savage Holiday*. By writing this novel outside the black social milieu and protest framework, Wright accords himself greater freedom for symbolizing the "plowing up" of his own unconscious as the mode of creation. The pleasurable effect of this type of freedom on Wright probably accounts for his attachment of "so much importance to the publication of the novel" (*Unfinished Quest*, 378). Fabre suggests that Wright's attitude toward the novel was due to its depictions of "purely autobiographical touches," and Fabre suspects as well that *The Outsider* forced Wright to confront his attitude toward his mother and that this confrontation provides the emotional foundation for *Savage Holiday* (*Unfinished Quest*, 378). Fabre goes on to suggest that "Wright uses what were mere inclinations in himself to create a veritable psychosis in Fowler" (*Unfinished Quest*, 379). Fabre elaborates without additional clarification, speculating, "If it can be said the *Outsider* was a repudiation of his ideological past, it is just as true to say that the second novel [*Savage Holiday*] accomplishes on an emotional plane *what* the first had achieved on an intellectual one" (*Unfinished Quest*, 379; my emphasis). Whatever the "what" in this judgment represents is left unstated.

While we can appreciate Fabre's unwillingness to "attempt a disguised psychoanalysis of Wright," his failure to explain what he means in the preceding excerpt by Wright's "ideological past" beyond its association with existentialism, Fabre's reluctance to name or even characterize "the inclinations" in Wright that determine Fowler, or to plot their manifestations in Wright's writings seems deliberately evasive (*World*, 123).

Let me illustrate my contention by returning to Fabre's "Fantasies and Style in Wright's Fiction." Here, Fabre seems to be questioning the typical racial reading of Wright's works, which I will illustrate later by again referring to one of the most famous—"Alas Poor, Richard," by James Baldwin. Fabre extensively describes and catalogs the images, scenes, symbolic objects, and characters that repeatedly appear in Wright's fictions in order to assert that "traumatic scenes [in Wright's works] are structured by language, in particular by certain key words which serve in some way to pivot connotations according to a network specific to the writer" (*World*, 140). This statement is reminiscent both of the personal template of the fantasmatic to which I referred in analyzing *Dark Princess* and of Jacques Lacan's contention that the unconscious is structured like a language. Given Fabre's own cultural background and professional experience as a professor of African American literature in Paris, Lacan's work may have indeed influenced Fabre's understanding of a writer's linguistic network. Although Fabre seems to be inviting a psychoanalytic reading of Wright's fictions, he does not venture to offer any hypotheses himself. Rather, he states his "hope to open up this type of analysis" (*World*, 140). Prodding his reader further, Fabre demands that the "[s]tudy of Wright's writing and style must take into account the frequent eruption of groups of terms and images which can be brought to light more through a psychocritical approach than other stylistic decodings." Fabre concludes by claiming that "[i]n order to dig deeply into the most personal aspects of writing, it is necessary to analyze the relations between fantasies and style" (*World*, 143). This is precisely what this chapter attempts to do by making *Savage Holiday* the lens through which we can detect the very personal fantasies inscribed in Wright's fictions and examine the relationship of these fantasies to his racial discourses.

"Alas, Poor Richard," by James Baldwin, illustrates the racial reading typically ascribed to Wright's works and most important, I contend, its limitations. Here Baldwin argues that in "most novels written by Negroes," violence usually fills the "great space where sex ought to be." Rather than pursuing the implications of this observation—namely, that racial violence may be masking sexual content—Baldwin offers what he alleges to be "one of the severest criticisms tha[t] can be leveled against his [Wright's] work," referring to his failure to examine the root of his compulsive violence (188). Baldwin identifies the root to be racial rage, completely disregarding his own hypothesis about displaced sexuality. "Thus, when in Wright's pages a Negro male is found hacking a white woman to death," according to Baldwin, "the very gusto with which this is done, and the great attention paid to the details of physical destruction reveal a terrible attempt to break out of the cage in which the American imagination has imprisoned him for so long" (188). Unlike Baldwin, though, Margaret Walker, in particular, recognizes in Wright's works the "sexual dynamics of neurotic anger" that find "rampant articulation" in violence. Yet she too claims that "[t]he crimes are crimes of violence, not of sexual passion" (148).

Because scholars have generally understood Wright's works within the framework of racial protest, they have obscured what I am identifying as his primary narrative—plotted sequentially with maternal betrayal, filial ambivalence, and infantile rage—that lies at the heart of his protest fictions and problematic depictions of female characters. Hence, his misogynistic treatment of women is not an extraneous accessory to his racial plots; on the contrary, Wright's hostility toward women is an insistent manifestation of his primary personal narrative. It forms a ' black hole" in the constellation of Wright's fictions. I use this term because this primary narrative is the powerful but usually unseen, indeed hidden, nuclear discourse that incites the rage and murderous aggression of Wright's protagonists. This traumatic narrative determines textual desire throughout Wright's fictions. Because Wright's early works racialized this story as black and because his violent racial embellishments have historical authenticity, scholars of Wright's works have generally not looked for other factors in the works' plotting strategies. They have assumed that his works originated in racial outrage.

I am challenging the traditional racial interpretations of the compulsive plots of violence in Wright's fictions by focusing on *Savage Holiday*. I argue that this novel is a fictive recuperation of a primary sexual trauma that generates the murderous rage in Wright's writings. My argument develops in two stages. First, by using what is now a standard psychoanalytic approach of regarding the text of a novel to be similar to "the structure of mind" or "the dynamic organization of the psyche," I identify *Savage Holiday*'s conscious and unconscious plots, which restage this trauma and its narrativized symptoms (Brooks, "Idea", 24–25). Second, I refer to the classic object-relation theory of Melanie Klein in order to illuminate the novel's depictions of violent sexual conflict, for these representations are similar to the primitive model of the infantile subject who wants to attack what it perceives to be the persecutory mother. These discussions support my contention: that concealed within Wright's compulsive plots of violence is the primary story—the "urtext"—of a matricidal desire.

Unlike Baldwin, Walker, and many other critics who find racial rage at the center of Wright's writings, I am arguing that the story of racial oppression conceals Wright's heavily veiled narrative—the urtext—of the son's perception of maternal betrayal and his reactions of initial ambivalence and subsequent hostility.

To characterize the urtext further, it is necessary to ask what event it restages. I propose that it depicts the son as voyeur to the mother's real or imagined coital engagement with a man, usually the father, and the son's subsequent feelings of intense maternal betrayal. *Savage Holiday* is Wright's only work that repeatedly refers to this coital scene *and* reproduces the primary narrative of the son's betrayal, outrage, and fear. Wright's other fictions racialize this story so as to displace the sexual site of trauma onto racial violence. This racialized story recalls a more general plot of female betrayal of the male and his subsequent violent response that is masked in the other novels as racial defense. The mask arises from an overdetermined resentment toward the betraying woman and a fraudulent white society. Acting out this traumatic plot instigates the racial hostility that leads, for example, to Silas's death in "The Long Black Song" in *Uncle Tom's Children* (as I shall illustrate later), to Bobo's death in "Big Boy Leaves Home" in *Eight Men*, to Bigger's death in *Native Son*, and to the respective death and castration of Shorty in *Black Boy* and Chris in *The Long Dream*.

In *Savage Holiday*, Wright eliminates the black mask and makes his protagonist remember the primary plot of maternal betrayal by casting him as a white voyeur for its restaging in the life of another—a young, white boy. At the novel's climax the protagonist's repressed rage transforms his murderous childhood wish into the matricidal deed. By racializing the matricidal plot as white, Wright, I suspect, is not wishing that he were white, as Margaret Walker contends (*Richard Wright*, 245), but employing the censoring device of displacement. In this way the white protagonist acts out the socially prohibited feelings of murderous aggression toward the maternal object that are both silenced and repressed in *Black Boy* but nevertheless projected onto Mary and Bessie in *Native Son*, to name but two female characters in Wright's corpus who are the victims of excessive male hostility. *Savage Holiday* and *Native Son* also depict the protagonist's anger and subsequent hated at the abandoning father by depicting him as already dead. But in *Black Boy*, like the novels, the paternal hatred is resolute and not as conflicted by the guilty and ambivalent feelings of love and hate as those for the mother.

Although Margaret Walker laments that "perhaps it would have been better for Richard Wright if *Savage Holiday*, which appeared in 1954, had never been published" (244), the scholarly community has done the next best thing. It has disregarded the novel, despite Wright's persistent popularity.[8] His narrative choices all but guaranteed the novel's obscurity. In this way he could experience the secret pleasure of symbolically discharging his chronic rage toward a woman and hide the guilty evidence, thereby preventing this crime from diminishing or complicating his reputation as a racial protest writer. By identifying *Savage Holiday* as a story of symbolic matricide, I have already disclosed the novel's climax. But because this novel is not generally well-known, I will summarize its plot before continuing my discussion.

Reproducing the Primal Trauma in *Savage Holiday*

Set in New York City during the late 1940s, *Savage Holiday*, like Wright's other novels, is divided into alliterative sections—"Anxiety," "Ambush," and "Attack." Part 1, "Anxiety," begins at a testimonial dinner on a Saturday night, given in honor of Erskine Fowler's early retirement from Longevity Life Insurance Company. This celebration, though, belies the retirement's real purpose; Fowler has been forced out of the company to make his position available for the president's son. Having joined the company when he was thirteen, Fowler regards it as his family instead of his place of employment. Hence, he experiences his forced retirement as a betrayal of the "father" and sees himself as the abandoned "son." Convinced that the officers of the company do not understand the real nature of insurance or man and certain that they do not know how to spot fraudulent claimants, Fowler internalizes his rage by fantasizing their exaggerated ineptitude. His special talent for detecting the guilt in others originates in his awareness "that man was a guilty creature" (*SH* 30). Like District Attorney Houston in Wright's *Outsider*, Fowler is "an impulsive criminal," who until his forced retirement had "protected himself by hunting down other criminals" (*Outsider*, 173–74). Fowler's anger, though, is a feeble attempt to camouflage his real dilemma. He has no occupation to order his life and conceal himself from his knowledge of a guilty act he committed long ago. Facing the prospects of the extended holiday of retirement, "he was plagued by a jittery premonition that some monstrous and hoary recollection, teasing him and putting his teeth on edge because it was strange and yet somehow familiar, was about to break disastrously into his consciousness" (*SH* 32).

Fowler tries to escape to safety by returning to his apartment and preparing for bed. Just before falling asleep, he redirects his anxiety as anger at a neighbor woman, Mabel Blake, for neglecting her five-year-old son, Tony. Even though Fowler has befriended Tony, he images an appropriate punishment for her which would sacrifice Tony: "Suppose the building caught fire? Why, poor Tony would be trapped . . ." (*SH* 36; ellipsis in original). This fantasy foreshadows Tony's death and Mabel's punishment. After falling asleep, Fowler has an assortment of anxiety dreams. One assumes the form of the already mentioned malevolent breast fantasy of the "shifting curtain of wobbly images [that] hovered before his consciousness" (*SH* 36). Another is a castration dream in which a menacing man chops into a giant tree in his forest with an ax. As Fowler awakens, the imaginary hacking sounds of the ax conform to the clamor of a drum that Tony is actually beating on the balcony outside Fowler's window.[9]

Although Fowler is awake, the subsequent events have much in common with his anxiety dreams. The dreamlike scenario begins when the paperboy interrupts Fowler's preparation for his morning shower. In a state of total undress, he darts into the hall to retrieve his Sunday paper. Before he can return to his apartment, his front door slams and locks. He is trapped, naked in the hallway, like a wild animal. A "sense of hot panic flooded him; he felt as though a huge x-ray eye was glaring into his very soul; and in the same instant he felt that he had shrunk in size, had become something small, shameful" (*SH* 43). With nothing but the newspaper to conceal his nakedness, Fowler tries to reach the superintendent's apartment by concealing himself in the elevator. His anxiety intensifies as the other tenants call the elevator and make him lose control of its movement—an event that symbolizes his genital fear, for he can control neither the rising and falling elevator nor his own sexual tumescence or detumescence. As in the dream, he experiences fear in terms of a castration fantasy in which he imagines himself encircled by "hostile people armed with long, sharp knives, intent upon chopping off his arms, his legs, his genitals, his head . . ." (*SH* 50; ellipsis in original). Eventually, he stops the elevator on his floor by pushing the emergency button. As he leaps from the elevator and rushes across the hall onto the balcony outside his bathroom window, he runs into Tony, who is playing on the balcony. Tony is terrified of Fowler's nakedness and aggressive posture. Tony tries to escape but falls backward ten floors to his death. Fowler removes himself from the scene of the crime by hoisting himself through his bathroom window. While doing so, he cuts his hand on the window ledge. Throughout the text, this injury reminds Fowler of his repressed guilt. Because he conceals the wound just as he conceals his part in Tony's death, the police conclude that Tony's death was accidental. When a neighbor informs him that Mabel didn't return to her apartment until five in the morning of that fateful day and that she was accompanied by a strange man, Fowler tries to console himself by placing the blame for Tony's death on the immoral mother.

"Ambush" begins with Fowler still trying to calm his guilty feelings by going to church. After listening to scriptures about Jesus, Mary, and God's eternal family, Fowler convinces himself that his involvement in Tony's death was God's way of charging him to "help that poor Mrs. Blake . . ." (*SH* 86; ellipsis in original). He goes to her apartment to console her. While there, he becomes intensely aware of

> her cascading black hair, the creamy, satiny skin of her naked arms, the throbbing
> aliveness of her throat, the ripe fullness of her breasts, and the helpless wetness of her
> face; her right leg, tapering and slanting, almost lost in shadow, extended at an angle
> across the rug and terminated in a tiny *foot jammed tightly* into a *black pump* shoe and
> it makes *a lump rise* in his throat. . . . (*SH* 119; ellipsis in original; my emphasis)

The valences of the language—"foot jammed tightly" in the "black pump" and "a lump rise"—all signal Fowler's sexual tumescence. His lust for this seductive woman forces him to sanction his guilty feelings of sexual arousal with an impetuous marriage proposal. He pressures her into accepting it on the condition that they get to know one another better. Pursuing this end, he asks her to have dinner with him the next day. Fowler believes that by marrying Mabel, he can save this fallen women, vindicate himself from entanglement in Tony's death, erase any suspicion that Mabel may have about his guilt, and legitimate his "swelling sense of desire" (*SH* 137). Moreover, by defining himself as her husband, he can defend against seeing himself as like her son.

Before Tony's death, he had virtually no contact with Mabel; now he compulsively seeks her company. He volunteers to assist her with Tony's funeral arrangements and becomes angry when she does not act bereaved. Humiliated by guilty sexual longings, Fowler wants to both embrace and spurn her: "His desire for her was so close to his rejection of her that he couldn't separate the two" (*SH* 138). Wright accentuates Fowler's complex and contradictory feelings by engaging in (conscious or unconscious) wordplay. The name "Erskine Fowler" phonologically repeats "her skin—foul her" or "fouler" (Vassilowitch, "'Erskine Fowler,'" 206), an expression that puns the protagonist's paradoxical feelings of inseparable desire and repulsion.

Mabel's ringing telephone, which Fowler hears from his apartment, rescues him from his inability to sever his maddening emotional attachment from her. As he overhears her address a man on the phone, Fowler becomes intensely jealous. He now regards Mabel as a whore. When she is alone with him and remorseful or humiliated, Fowler regards her as an erotic object for him to redeem in marriage. The threat of another man disrupts his effort to redeem her. Consequently, he hates her and regards her as a prostitute. Hence, one moment he regards her as the loved good object, and the next he considers her the abhorred bad object. Because he cannot secure Mabel in his mind as either good or bad, he cannot stabilize his response to her. He projects his shifting estimations onto Mabel as integral to her character. She is now the frivolous, wanton woman. In his mind her behavior and not his involvement in Tony's death is the cause of his acute anxiety. As a result, he feels himself the object of an elaborate ambush, even as he plans to trap Mabel.

The opening scene of Part 3—"Attack"—begins Monday evening with Fowler "[s]till seething because of Mabel's flightiness and suffering from the stabbing pain in his left palm" (*SH* 169). In response to a note that she leaves for him, he meets her before dinner at a tavern. When he arrives, he sees that she is with some friends and has been drinking. He is disgusted and wants to escape, but he cannot. He feels himself in "a waking dream. . . . A flash of intuition went through him; yes, this woman was objectifying some fantasy of his own mind, just as he had objectified a fantasy in the mind of poor little Tony. . . . That was why Mabel held so powerful a hold over him" (*SH* 178). He wonders "how could one act without knowing why one was acting" (*SH* 178). Yet his hostile reaction to intimations of Mabel's interest in another man become so predictable that he is much like Pavlov's dog, automatically salivating on hearing the ringing bell. When she later insists that they're too different to get married, he replies that she can be any kind of person she wants to be. Still drunk, she says she cannot change. His demand that she respond to his expression of love causes her to compare him to Tony: "'This afternoon. . . . When you were angry with me. . . . You re-

minded me so much of Tony. . . . *You and Tony.* . . *.*' She leaned toward him
and touched his face. 'You need a mother'" (*SH* 183). Remembering Tony de-
presses her. As they stand outside Mabel's apartment, she feels guilty for not having been more attentive to Tony. The guilty Mabel appeals to Fowler. No sooner
than he regards her as the redeemable object, her telephone rings and a rival
threatens the redemptive role Fowler has constructed for her. As she enters the
apartment and answers the phone, he retreats to his apartment in outrage. He decides to retract his proposal. He writes a note to this effect and slides it under her
door. When Mabel retrieves the note, she becomes more convinced that his bizarre
behavior is concealing information about Tony's mysterious death. If this is not
the case, then Fowler must want sex from her. She is interested in either event.

The note, as Fowler undoubtedly expected, brings Mabel to his door late Monday night. She is dressed in only a bathrobe, and he invites her inside. The scene
is set for a seduction. Mabel locates and enters Fowler's bedroom. He follows.
When Fowler fails to approach her, he learns the other reason for her presence. She
suspects him of being involved in Tony's death. He counters her suspicion by insisting, "'It was *you* who killed your own child!'" (*SH* 196; emphasis in original).
Not understanding his accusation, she tries to reduce the rapidly rising tension between them by requesting a drink. Somewhat more relaxed, Mabel confesses, Tony
"'was an awful burden to me. . . . But I never would've killed 'im?'" (*SH* 197).
She asks Fowler to explain why he is trying to make her feel guilty. In order to
make her understand, he recalls the events of Sunday morning "in a torrent of
words." He lashes out at her, hoping "to humble her, to break her down so that he
could love her, master her, have his say-so about her" (*SH* 199). He insists that she
killed Tony by letting him repeatedly see "'her naked and making love to men,
many men . . . Tony told me so!'" (*SH* 200; emphasis in original). Fowler reveals
his own repressed fear by identifying with Tony's terror:

> "Your son was terrified of naked people, naked men in particular. . . . You made him
> feel that if he ever saw a naked man, he had to run for his life . . . for he didn't want
> that violence, that *fighting* to happen to him. . . . Tony told me that he didn't even
> want to grow up to be a man, because he felt that he'd have to *fight*—he called it [sexual
> intercourse] *fighting!*—women like his mother. . . . Mabel, you crushed that child;
> you killed him even before he fell from that balcony." (*SH* 200; emphasis in original)

Mabel does not understand his analysis of Tony's feelings; rather, she thinks that
Fowler is accusing her of being sexually involved with a man while Tony fell from
the balcony. When Mabel understands that Fowler is not referring to that fateful
Sunday morning, but "'[m]any times and *many* mornings before that!'" (*SH* 202;
emphasis in original), she becomes indignant and throws her glass at him. After
her defiance, she becomes fearful of his retaliation and crumbles to the floor. During their scuffle, her robe falls open, and subsequently she loses the robe entirely.
Again, she is a humiliated and now naked object that he can control. As he re-

turned her robe, "[s]he opened her eyes and stared at him; there was only wonder, fear, pity, humility and a kind of dread in her now. He felt that she was his, only his now" (*SH* 207). No sooner than Fowler has transformed the bad object into the redeemable one, the phone in her apartment rings. As she tries to leave to answer it, Fowler recoils in a predictable jealous rage. He attacks her, and she escapes by running into the kitchen, again losing her bathrobe. Angry and sexually aroused, Fowler grabs a butcher knife and Mabel. He bends her nude body backward over the table. "As she opened her mouth to scream, he brought the knife down hard into her nude stomach. . . . With machinelike motion, Erskine lifted the butcher knife and plunged it into her stomach again and again" (*SH* 215).

After the murder, Fowler remembers the offense that he had repressed for more than thirty years. A fantasy and the buried memory, which the fantasy had concealed, reappear in his consciousness. As clear as if it were yesterday, Fowler recalls that "*he had been playing with the little girl next door—Gladys was her name. . . . He had taken a dirty brick bat and had beaten the doll's head in, had crushed it and had told Gladys: 'There's my mama. . . . I killed her; I killed her 'cause she's a bad woman'*" (*SH* 216; emphasis in original). He then remembers that he hadn't in fact crushed the doll's head (an act reminiscent of the circumstances of Bessie's death in *Native Son*). This was merely a fantasy to conceal his real actions. He had drawn a picture of this dead, broken doll and called it his mother. Angry that she had left him alone one night when he was ill (reminiscent of an early incident in *Black Boy*), he remembers that he had violently punctured his drawing with his "colored pencils"—a doubly encoded act of his sexual and murderous violation of the mother of his memory performed with his pigmented penis substitute, the "colored pencils." He readily confesses murdering Mabel to the police. But when asked about Tony's death, "he bowed his head in his arms," unable or unwilling to explain his entanglement in that death (*SH* 222).

Early versions of the story's conclusion make Fowler's motivation clearer. A handwritten draft of this scene makes Fowler's association of Mabel and his mother even more transparent. After killing Mabel,

> he looked hard at her [dead] dark and congenial face. He knew that she was bad, but he had no feelings of fear, alarm or regret. He sighed, sank into a chair and stared at the floor.
> Suddenly he began weeping softly in mute protest. It seemed that he could see his mother standing there, just as he remembered. . . . (draft, *SH* 159)

In the first typescript of the novel, Fowler kills Mabel by stabbing her. After the deed, he looks at himself in a mirror and subsequently phones and confesses his guilt to his Aunt Tillie, admitting that he is no longer afraid. In this version Fowler erects a $20,000 monument over Tony's grave with the inscription "Don't Be Afraid," rather than a similar monument without an inscription over Mabel's grave as in the handwritten draft. The typescript closes with reports of Erskine as a model prisoner, helping out in the prison chapel and doing religious work among the inmates. In another typescript dated 1954, the novel closes with a newspaper heading: "THE MURDERER MAKES $100,000 DONATION TO THE SOCIETY FOR THE SUPPRESSION OF VICE" (all drafts of *Savage Holiday* are in Wright Papers, box 59; emphasis in original). Without a doubt, each scenario of closure as well as Wright's preliminary titles—"Monument to Memory," "The Wish and the Dream," "The Man Who Was Guilty," "Guilty Children"—focus on filial guilt and reparation (*Unfinished Quest*, 379–80; Wright Papers, box 59). The more subtle and thus less personal title "Savage Holiday" originated not with Wright but with Avon editor Oliver G. Swan (Wright Papers, box 59).

The Bad Mother

I return to my analysis of *Savage Holiday* by comparing Mabel's murder to the cat-hanging incident in *Black Boy* to suggest a conceptual identity shared by the cat, Mabel, the boy Richard, and his imaginary mother. At the conclusion of an early version of *Savage Holiday*, Fowler strangles rather than stabs Mabel (Wright Papers, box 59). These two incidents become particularly meaningful when placed in the context of an early version of *Black Boy*, a typescript entitled "Black Confessions," mentioned earlier. Here Wright describes his family's attitude toward him by explaining its determination to save him even if it meant killing him: "I felt that somehow they loved me, but in their loving me, they were determined to take me by the throat and lift me to a higher plane of living and, in lifting me, I knew that they would surely strangle me to death" (7–8). The act of strangling in the typescript is an expression of the redeeming power of an extreme form of love that Fowler also expresses toward Mabel in *Savage Holiday*, for this is precisely his attitude toward her; he prevents and, thereby, saves her from a licentious future by killing her. In both works, then, this extreme redemptive measure is a repetition and displacement that links Mabel's fate to the boy Richard's prospect at the hands of his family.

Daring to kill the cat grants the boy Richard his "first triumph over [his] father," but what is its symbolic relationship to his mother? The feline is the conventional symbol of the female. In *Black Boy*, his father may bellow, but it is actually his mother who is the rebuking, indeed persecutory parent. She reprimands him by "whack[ing him] across [his] mouth with the flat palm of her hand" (14). When she demands that he " '[g]o out there and dig a hole and bury that kitten,' " he becomes paralyzed with fear (*BB* 13). His mother's "disembodied voice" taunts him "from the menacing darkness," so much so that he is more afraid of her than the dark (*BB* 15). Only a few pages before the cat incident, the text reports, she was so relieved that the boy had not perished in the house he set afire that she "had come close to killing [him]" with her punishment (*BB* 8). These episodes are sites of a repressed guilty and hostile wish directed at the mother, a wish that would negate her demand and the boy's fear as well, a wish that he has in common with Fowler—the wish that the mother were dead. In the first incident, the boy has no recourse; he cannot escape the retaliatory mother. In the second incident, though, Wright reports, "I broke away from my mother and ran into the night, crying, shaking with dread" (*BB* 16).

In *Savage Holiday* this hostile wish reappears as Fowler's guilty childhood desire to kill his mother. This is the "daydream buried under the rigorous fiats of duty [that] had been called forth from its thirty-six-year-old grave by a woman called Mabel Blake." This is the "guilty dream which he had wanted to disown and forget, but which he had had to reenact in order to make its memory and reality clear to him!" (*SH* 220). This is the fantasy Fowler experiences by means of displacement by puncturing his drawing of his mother with his pencils. In this context, we can see Wright's central female characters—Mary, Bessie, and Mabel, for example—as his maternal surrogates, projected literally on paper and under the control of his agency. Just as Fowler kills the replicas of the mother he has created, Wright creates protagonists to kill the mother surrogates of his imagination. But unlike Fowler, whose mother dies shortly after his guilty wish, Wright must rely on his authorial power to kill and kill again the imaginary mother, whose real counterpart lives until the year before Wright's own death.

As a young boy, Wright had to have had hostile feelings toward his real mother, who fiercely chastises him, feelings that also confused him and made him feel guilty. According to *Black Boy*, she not only humiliates him with the demand that he bury the kitten; she also forces him to fight the boys who steal his grocery money and tries to make him beg his abandoning father for food. As a consequence, the boy is physically hungry, humiliated, and ultimately emotionally drained. What he hungers for is not so much food as the restoration of what psychoanalyst Melanie Klein has called "the good mother." But instead, the boy finds the mother who seems repeatedly to persecute him. When in *Black Boy* the mother suffers a paralytic stroke, the boy Richard very likely believes his guilty wish will become fact. However, she does not die, and his imagination must compensate for reality. He reports that after she suffers another stroke, she, rather than he, invites her death: "Once, in the night my mother called me to her bed and told me that she could not endure the pain, that she wanted to die" (*BB* 117). Wright's representation of her desire for death probably masks his desire to kill her in his mind: "That night I ceased to react to my mother; my feelings were frozen" (*BB* 117). Undoubtedly, even latent imaginary retaliation against the mother would cause tremendous guilt and demand reparations.

Wright met the demand. Although it is not clear exactly when Wright suspended contact with his mother, indeed fixing her in an imaginary death, sometime around 1946 he instructed his agent Paul R. Reynolds to send Ella Wright, in care of first his Aunt Maggie (Hunt) and later his brother Leon, 10 percent of his

$500 monthly salary of royalties,[10] until her death in November 1959 (Walker 308). Supporting one's mother may be an act of filial kindness, but when all relational ties are cut, the generous act becomes complicated with filial ambivalence. Reynolds became the intermediary between Wright and his mother Ella Wright. For example, when Wright's mother fell and broke her hip in May 1957, Wright's brother Leon contacted Reynolds, and Reynolds acted in Wright's behalf (Wright Papers, box 104).[11] The absence of contact between Wright and his mother, in contrast to his financial support, suggests his extremely ambivalent relationship with her. And it is not surprising that this conflict probably would form the emotional core of his fictions and become overdetermined with his authentic contempt for racism because racism creates the privation that conditions both the love and the brutality of this mother-son bond.

Object-relations paradigms help me to explain the inscription of similar filial ambivalence in *Savage Holiday*. Object-relation theory hypothesizes the subject's development as a consequence of its introjection of objects with whom it has primary and secondary infantile relationships. While Freud refers to such relationships, they have little impact on his family scenario of ego and superego formation, largely because he focuses on the oedipal stage. By contrast, object-relation theories concentrate on the earliest stages of subjective development, during which the infantile subject develops by integrating oppositional emotions. Wright's depiction of Fowler's oscillating desire to love and to repudiate Mabel corresponds to the theoretical reenactment of the primary conflict between the infant and the good/bad mother as theorized by the object-relations model. In order to appreciate this correspondence, it is necessary to summarize the model in some detail before analyzing Fowler's behavior.

Melanie Klein, one of the most influential pioneers of object-relations theory, reworks Freud's "ideas about objects, guilt, anxiety, fantasy, and the death instinct" into a theory of infantile aggression (Moore and Fine, *Psychoanalytic Terms*, 106). She identifies pre-oedipal sexuality as the "major vehicle for playing out and working through the powerful struggles between hate and love, between destructiveness and reparation, which constitute the core of early object relations" (Klein, *Love*, 95). In Klein's model, then, the superego is not a formation of the oedipal complex, as Freud theorized, but one of the pre-oedipal stage. Klein hypothesizes that during this developmental period the infant's innate aggressive impulses define two defensive positions that appear in infantile fantasies about the primary object.

The most primitive fantasies appear in what Klein names the "paranoid-schizoid position," characterized by anxieties of persecution and defenses of splitting. This position "is specific to the first four months of life" (Laplanche and Pontalis, *Language*, 298) but also occurs during the first years of childhood and under certain circumstances in later life. Klein postulates that the oral-sadistic instincts are present at birth. As a result, the infant is ambivalent about sucking, devouring, and eventually biting the sometimes good/gratifying and at other times bad/frus-trating breast. The infant eventually identifies the mother with its earlier percep-tion of her part object, the breast. As a result, the infant is now overwhelmed by anticipating both the benevolent and the malevolent mother. Apprehension causes the infant to project "the impulses to destroy the very person who is the ob-ject of all his [or her] desires and who in his [or her] mind is linked up with every-thing he [or she] experiences—good and bad alike" (Klein, *Love*, 58). The infant calms its anxiety by splitting or separating the maternal object into good and bad parts, projecting its hatred onto the bad mother and repudiating her, while mak-ing the good mother the recipient of its erotic and reparative instincts.

The next stage of Kleinian psychosexual development is the depressive position that begins to take shape around the fourth month of life, when the infant begins to perceive the mother as a whole object, and is gradually consolidated by the age one. The splitting defense is attenuated as love and aggression now focused on the same object. But during this stage the child experiences another anxiety, caused by the fear of destroying or losing the mother as the result of infantile sadistic fan-tasies. While the child tries to defend itself from the defensive mode with manic behavior, more effective protection is the product of development to the depres-sive position. This stage allows the child to defend against the anxiety of loss by learning to inhibit aggression and by fantasizing the repair of a stable identifica-tion with the loved object.

By designating these behavioral modes "positions" rather than "stages," Klein emphasizes that an individual does not pass through these stages but moves be-tween the two: at times of acute stress, the fantasies of even a mature subject as-sume paranoid-schizoid characteristics. Particularly important to remember is that the Kleinian model refers not to the child's relationship to the real parents but to "internal fantasy figures, the inner parents," the parental imagos (Moore and Fine, *Psychoanalytic Terms*, 106). As in my discussion of the difference between the lost mother and the historical mother, I maintain this latter distinction by using the possessive pronoun—*his* parents—when referring to Wright's real historical parents and by using the definite article—*the* parents—when referring to Wright's internalized or imagined parents.

Like the anxious infant, Fowler exhibits similar behavior toward Mabel. His per-ceptions of her rapidly alternate between two polar positions. At first she is his re-deemable, good object. Subsequently, she is the bad object whom he condemns as a whore. This emotional turbulence threatens Fowler's ego with fragmentation. He tries to resolve this problem just as he had the earlier problem with his mother. In the case of his mother, he kills her in his mind by puncturing his image of the bad mother, drawn on paper, and represses his guilty desire. Because his mother does soon die, he can maintain a stasis of repressed emotional turbulence by hunt-ing other guilty people—in this case, those who perpetrate insurance fraud. How-ever, when he is fired from his job and this defensive option is no longer available to him, his guilt looms large. When he encounters a scenario like the one he had repressed, he has no defenses to maintain the repression. Unable to stage a defensive response, he enacts the original wish and kills the surrogate. By committing the crime he had wanted to enact long ago, he relieves his anxiety, eliminates his guilt, and restores his good self-image, all by means of reparation. The crime also allows Fowler to satisfy his unconscious desire to have sex with Mabel, a desire that she immediately recognizes when he appears at her door with the intention of consoling her: his violent stabbing of Mabel's body with the knife symbolizes genital penetration because the knife, a displacement for the frequently recalled "colored pencils" in his pocket(!), clearly represents the revitalized and aggressive "colored" penis. Margaret Walker also identifies this correspondence by explaining that "Fowler wants to make love to Mabel in a tender fashion, but he can't; he doesn't know how. He wants to seduce her, but he can't; he doesn't know how. He wants to rape her, but again, he doesn't know how. . . . He kills because he cannot love" (247). However, Walker does not explain the symbolic logic that links Fowler's impotence to the murder.

With the assistance of object-relations theory, I can illuminate Fowler's sexual motives by referring to an important incident in which Tony asks Fowler "where babies come [from]" (*SH* 96):

> "One night I saw a big man fight mama. . . . Mama didn't have any clothes on and the man didn't have any clothes on either. After mama said that she was scared that she'd have a baby. Mr. Fowler—" Tony had paused and looked hard at Erskine, "why do they have to fight like that to make babies?" (*SH* 98)

Tony's questions make Fowler vaguely remember his own childhood experiences of observing his mother during similar sexual exploits: Like Tony, as a child Fowler evidently also believed that sexual intercourse involves fighting. This is not an unusual assumption for the young child.

In "Three Essays on the Theory of Sexuality," which greatly influenced early object-relations theory, Freud explains that the child perceives genital sexuality in terms of its own sexual development. Because the child's voyeurism occurs during the anal stage of sexuality and because the child perceives the primal scene to involve aggression, the child interprets intercourse as an anal-sadistic act. According to Klein, the "childish conception of intercourse" often appears as "[p]hantasies of the father, or of [the child] himself, ripping up the mother, beating, scratching her, cutting her into pieces" (*Love*, 176). In this context, Tony's response to Fowler's effort to explain where babies come from becomes quite clear. Tony decides, "'I don't want to grow up. . . . I don't wanna be a man. . . .'Cause I don't wanna fight. . . . I don't wanna fight ladies like my mother" (*SH* 99). Whereas Fowler resolves this conflict for Tony by accidentally causing his death, Fowler is also trapped in the anal-sadistic stage of sexuality. He has no recourse but to "fight." In the last scene, where Mabel turns away from him to answer the telephone, she becomes the object of both his sexual excitement and aggression. If his sexual development were not arrested and he were potent, he probably would have raped her. But because he can only respond within the limitations of the anal stage, he performs a perverse act of sexual penetration—the symbolized intercourse of stabbing. After its culmination, he is relieved of sexual tumult and ambivalence; he feels "a kind of sullen, stolid pride" in masculine power (*SH* 217). For these reasons Fowler can calmly confess to killing Mabel to the police, yet he cannot explain his involvement in Tony's death. To do so would demand that he acknowledge his identification with Tony.

The Kleinian model of the infant's defense of splitting corresponds to Fowler's effort to relieve his acute sexual anxiety. Klein's account of the paranoid-schizoid defense of splitting illuminates Fowler's behavior as the paradoxical affects of the son's repressed, infantile anger toward and desire for the mother. Unlike Wright's more subtle works, which also rely on the expression of these affectations, *Savage Holiday*'s textual desires of murderous aggression and incestuous union are active, explicit, indeed overstated, though projected onto a maternal surrogate, whose whiteness disavows Wright's conscious identification with the mother of his inner world. But splitting, as we shall also see, is not a feature that Wright uses only in this novel; it is a recurring strategy of characterization that he uses in his other fictions as well.

Wright's works are replete with female character pairs who illustrate maternal splitting, and the story that he compulsively rewrites has much in common with Klein's plot about the infant at the paranoid-schizoid stage of development. Much like Klein's infantile plot, Wright's obsessive narrative recalls a primary story like that of filial ambivalence toward the mother. In *Black Boy*, for example, the bad prestroke mother persecutes young Richard with a series of cruel reprimands, while the infantilized post-stroke mother is symbolically mourned by him. The imaginative schoolteacher Ella doubles for the impaired and unnamed mother, whose real name also was Ella. The favorite Aunt Maggie stands as a surrogate for the mother, who is replaced by the persecutory Aunt Addie. (We should remember that the boy Richard also threatens Addie with a knife in *Black Boy*.). In *Native Son* Bigger is a more arrogant version of the boy Richard in *Black Boy*; he can express his resentment of the conditions of his life, while Bessie and his mother are resigned to the utter futility of theirs. Bessie mirrors and thereby forces Bigger to see his own suppressed fear, while his mother reflects his utter humiliation. However, Bigger's egotism depends on disowning these parts of himself, which he splits off and projects onto these maternal objects with Mary's aid. Mary provides him with such conflicting feelings of desire and hatred that he has no margin to mediate his overpowering fear. As a result, he accidentally murders Mary. To protect himself from additional fear, he intentionally murders Bessie and disclaims his mother and her religion. "It was his life against [theirs]" (*NS* 222), and his wins.

Michel Fabre also notices that Wright splits the character of Mary as well as her more generalized facsimile in "Big Boy Leaves Home." Though the anonymous white woman of this short story is justifiably afraid given the narrative context, Fabre explains, Wright's depiction of fear in the four boys and the woman is meant to arise as a result of breaking, unintentionally or not, "the prohibition which surrounds white women, to such an extent" that Wright "seems committed, whether by conscious recourse or at a more symbolic and almost archetypal level of black/white confrontation, to reproduce this situation" as an encounter of the incest taboo. Fabre makes this point clear when he explains that the racial prohibition that surrounds the white woman is coupled with the social prohibition that surrounds the mother, who seems split into "the young woman whom the little boy dreams of possessing [the schoolteacher Ella and Mary, for example] and the older one [the corresponding Mrs. Wright and Mrs. Dalton] who incarnates the voice of conscience" (*World*, 129).

In *The Outsider*, the objects of Damon's sexual desire again repeat the splitting pattern. This novel presents not only a series of maternal objects but also paternal ones, who are not simply renounced like the women but nullified in acts of gratuitous violence even more excessive than that in *Native Son*. The split-character pairs include the wife (Gladys) and the whore (Dot), the conniving whore (Dot) and the generous one (Jenny), the idealized woman (Eva) and the vindictive one (Gladys), on the maternal side, and the liberal tyrant (Blount) and the fascist one (Herndon), the servile clown (Joe) and the vile totalitarian (Hilton), and the kindly but dangerous father surrogate (Houston) and the patronizing one (Blount), on the paternal side. This pattern of characterization distinguishes Wright's novels until the appearance in 1958 of *The Long Dream*.

The Long Dream's departure from the splitting technique of characterization suggests that stories of filial ambivalence are not static. While *Black Boy* identifies the textual origins of ambivalence and *Native Son* and *The Outsider* respectively kill the mother and father surrogates, *The Long Dream* is a novel of mourning. When the protagonist Rex "Fishbelly" Tucker awakens from what Wright terms "his long dream" of fear, shame, and hate, he needs to use neither sex nor murder for emotional release.[12] In fact, when chronologically ordered, these major works dramatize what psychoanalytic theory designates as the process of working through trauma.

Even though Wright writes a sequel to *Savage Holiday*, "A Strange Girl" (Wright Papers, box 88), that is similar to "Man, God Ain't Like That . . . ," in which the African protagonist kills a white girl rather than a white man, Wright abandons this story for *The Long Dream*. By staging the symbolic matricide in *Savage Holiday*, Wright seems to relieve his resistance to repressed anger at the mother of his memory and move toward freeing himself from compulsive repetition of homicidal violence in his fictions (a point I shall return to at the conclusion of this chapter), for Wright realized rather early in his career that writing was therapeutic.

Wright was not simply interested in psychoanalysis as an intellectual pursuit or as methods of creation and characterization. Sometime prior to 1944, Wright and analyst Fredric Wertham conducted "an experiment in the free association of ideas in the relationship between writing and psychoanalysis" (letter from Ellen Wright to Claudia Tate, November 25, 1996). Wertham presented a portion of his findings in "An Unconscious Determinant in *Native Son*."[13] During this and possibly other exchanges with Wertham, Wright undoubtedly learned much about the unconscious sources of his writings and came to understand his writing as both an encounter with his unconscious and a form of psychotherapy. Such an understanding would make his account of the origins of *Native Son* presented in "How Bigger Was Born" a rationalization designed to fit into a political argument rather than a genuine explanation of the deep emotional origins of the story.

Fiction provided Wright with a productive means of symbolizing what I suspect was his recurring and yet unacknowledged fantasy of the sexually betraying mother, a fantasy that forms the core of the subjective dynamics of all of Wright's fictions. I will illustrate this contention with a discussion of "Long Black Song," but before doing so, I want to contextualize my argument by referring to corresponding infantile sexual fantasies in Wright's autobiographical writings, in which the boy retaliates against threatening mother figures.

Wright's fantasies about the betraying mother repeatedly appear as affects of his boyhood fear of his mother and, by extension, his grandmother. Time and time again, he defends himself, particularly in *Black Boy*, by imagining one and/or the other in humiliating circumstances. He knew how they both felt about easy women, like the one who took up with his father after he had deserted the family. As a child Wright had overheard his mother and grandmother say that "that woman ought to be killed for breaking up a home" (*BB* 33). As *Black Boy* reports, the boy tells her so himself when he sees her with his father (39).

I surmise that Wright repeatedly consoled himself by consciously or unconsciously fantasizing about casting his mother or grandmother in the role they most abhorred, the prostitute, whenever he felt threatened by or was angry at one or the other, which seems to be practically all the time. In one instance, for example, the boy expresses his anger at his grandmother by telling her almost literally "to kiss his ass," while she was bathing him (*BB* 48). His grandmother accuses Ella, the schoolteacher who roomed with the family, of ruining him with "foul practices" (*BB* 48).

I want to call attention here to the facts that Ella is also his mother's name and that she had also been a rural schoolteacher. Given the repetition of the rebuke— "ruined"—and its displacement onto this other Ella, a "young woman with so remote and dreamy and silent manner that [the boy] was as much afraid of her as [he] was attracted to her" (*BB* 44), I speculate that Wright unconsciously projects his grandmother's indictment onto the overdetermined mother figure of the schoolteacher because the displacement allows him to conceal his criticism of his real mother for his blighted life. The projection would not only grant him the means of retaliation; it would also gratify Wright, who is at the time a boy in the oedipal stage, already harboring guilty fantasies about his mother.

The sexual insinuations of shame, associated with each of these illustrations, become clearer in the context of "Black Confessions." Here Wright recalls the exact

> moment when I developed a sense of shame in matters of sex; it was during the time that my mother began working. Each morning she would supervise me and my brother's going to the toilet. I had so associated my mother with the acts that I would wait for hours until she returned home before I would go again. (23)

Wright places this episode immediately before a description of how an older cousin "grabbed [him] and brought [him] close to her, holding [him] between her legs." According to Wright,

> [s]he put her finger in her vagina and pulled the lips apart, revealing red, moist depths.
> "Put your finger in," she said.
> I smelt an odor that sickened me and I broke loose with a wild wrench and ran out of the room. ("BC" 25)

A few pages later Wright recalls similar incidents which together with this one suggest that his initiation to sex was entangled with dreadful fantasies of female engulfment.

Doubleday's list of offensive words to be deleted from Wright's manuscript of *The Long Dream* also reveals his fascination with repulsive images of feces and female genitalia. This list reveals that Wright's Doubleday editor asked him to change the word "shit" almost forty times and to change or omit "cunt" nearly twenty times. Sometimes this latter word appeared as many as five times on a single double-spaced page. He was also asked to omit the phrase "mother-fucker" ten times (Wright Papers, box 96).

These obscenities conceptualize the infantile scenarios recovered in object-relations theory. "Shit" and "cunt" designate what the young child understands to be the vile contents of the bad mother's body. However, "shit" is also in the child's body; it is the gift the child delights in giving to the good mother. Hence, the child's body is also a site of ambivalence. The idiom "motherfucker" is a rather too literal reference to mother-son incest that still harbors the archaic ambivalence of the dreaded desire for the prohibited act. These obscenities, especially as they appeared in Wright's manuscripts and as they now appear in unexpurgated versions of his published works, inscribe what seem to be Wright's unconscious associations of desire, repulsion, fear, and pleasure associated with the imagined body of the good/bad mother, the mother who (according to Allison Davis and Margaret Walker) Wright felt did not love him (M. Walker, *Richard Wright*, 179).[14] The fascination with splitting the good/bad mother would defend him against guilty feelings. Moreover, by unconsciously collapsing the bad mother with white betrayal, Wright could vent his outrage at both by means of his characters' violent responses, without exposing his guilty feelings and thereby inviting public censure. Under these circumstances, his position as racial protest writer was especially efficacious.

Wright's Urtext of Matricidal Impulse

Because Wright abandoned the familiar racial plot in *Savage Holiday*, his critics, as I have already mentioned, regarded this work as an anomaly. However, I am arguing that the conspicuous Freudian plot in *Savage Holiday* embodies a primary story that Wright compulsively repeated in his works—his urtext. It not only controls the narrative of this novel; it is also the latent text of Wright's racial protest stories. For this reason *Savage Holiday* is a key for recovering the unconscious desire of his narratives. An illustration will make my contention clear.

"The Long Black Song" (published in 1938 in *Uncle Tom's Children: Four Novellas* but in near-final draft around 1936) provides an early instance of the compulsive sexual plot embedded within the text of racial protest. In this story Silas, the black protagonist, refuses to believe that Sarah, his wife, has been coerced into having sex with a traveling white salesman. Rather, Silas presumes that Sarah is a "little bitch," an inveterate whore, who has been voluntarily "layin' wid white men" (*UTC* 108, 107). To Silas, she is the "co-conspirator of [his] oppression" (Mootry, "Bitches," 118). The story insists on such an interpretation even though there is no expression of Sarah's illicit desire. Nevertheless, the narrator indicts Sarah as inherently wanton and culpable for Silas's inevitable death and underscores her guilt by claiming that "[s]he was sorry for what she had done" (*UTC* 109).

At this point in the story there is another shift in liability. The narrative shifts its focus from a sexual transgression to racial offense by displacing Silas's rage from Sarah to white men. In this way, the story superimposes Silas's racial humiliation on top of the sexual one, and the story presents itself as emphatically powerful racial protest. "The Long Black Song" celebrates Silas's heroic but doomed assault on racism by marginalizing the primary condemnation of his presumably promiscuous wife. The story's racial plot, then, masks the plot of infidelity. As the blues allusion of the title suggests, this is not an isolated incident of betrayal but a pervasive condition, encountered repeatedly by Wright's protagonists. The story's deep emotional core, I believe, is situated in Wright's repressed fantasy life about the bad mother.

Like "The Long Black Song" (1938), *Native Son* (1940) and *Black Boy* (1945) similarly recall a primary plot of female or maternal betrayal and resulting male ambivalence—the urtext—before narrating the racial plot. In these latter works, it seems that Wright's stunning expressions of outrage at racial oppression initially arise from the fury of repressed hostility toward black maternal characters. Thus, the protagonist's unrestrained, indeed primal rage seems more directly linked to

a family conflict between himself and the imaginary mother than a racist one between black and white men (see Gibson, "Richard Wright's"). This is not to say
that racism does not condition the family conflict because racism sets into motion
a sequence of events that erupts first as family violence before it permeates the society at large.

For example, in Part 1 of *Black Boy*—"Southern Night," which I examine later
in more detail—the boy Richard suppresses all expressions of anger toward his
mother, arising from a series of often cited violent conflicts between them. A similar repression of the protagonist's anger occurs in the famous opening episode of
Native Son. In this episode, in which Bigger Thomas kills the rat, he redirects toward the rat his anger at his mother's castigation of him for the wretched conditions of his family's life. Bigger not only represses his anger about the material circumstances of his life in this instance; he tries to repress all feelings about his life
in general, for "[he] knew that the moment he allowed what his life meant to enter
fully into his consciousness, he would either kill himself or someone else. So he
denied himself and acted tough" (*NS* 14). This is not to say that Bigger's rage is
not instigated by the rat's encroachment into the apartment or that the rat is not
a fitting symbol of the racist oppression to which the Thomases are subjected. For
in each instance, the response to Bigger's outrage is clearly justifiable. What I am
suggesting is that the rat and racism are overdetermined expressions for a more
deeply hidden anger. Wright's conscious and personal rage against racist persecution, which he chronicles in *Black Boy*, conceals his unconscious wrath, directed
toward the image of the persecutory mother that is inscribed in his demeaning depictions of women.

Wright's mother was locked into an oppressive situation, which Wright recalls
in *Black Boy*, that prohibited her from being an entirely nurturing mother. To the
boy Richard in *Black Boy*, she had to have seemed like both the good and bad
mother, loving and encouraging him at one moment while needlessly persecuting
him at another. Michel Fabre refers to one occasion of maternal betrayal as the
fierce beating Wright's mother gives him after he nearly burns down the house.
His discussion regards the punishment as a betrayal and his mother as the be-
trayer. However, Fabre does not give expression to what must have been Wright's
suppressed hostility toward the mother. Because Fabre's analysis of the betrayal is
very important for understanding Wright's development, I quote him at length:

> How could the source and object of all love turn into a fury, capable of punishing him
> so painfully and rejecting him so totally? This episode brutally shattered the emotional
> security he had derived from the exclusive affection of his mother. . . . The sudden
> deprivation of his mother was the first in a series of recurring experiences which, al-
> though the child was less than four years old at the time, caused a chronic frustration.
> . . . It is true, as Wilhelm Steckel maintains, that neurosis is an attempt at self-ex-
> pression, of which the man of genius is the embodiment, then it may well be that
> Wright's original estrangement and deep insecurity are rooted in this incomprehen-

sible punishment for a transgression he did not accept as such, an experience which long predated his first encounter with racism. (*Unfinished Quest*, 10)

In *Black Boy* Wright represses his ambivalent relationship to his mother and concentrates instead on making her illness, a kind of death, into the symbol of his life:

> A somberness of spirit that I was never to lose settled over me during the slow years of my mother's unrelieved suffering, a somberness that was to make me stand apart and look upon excessive joy with suspicion, that was to make me self-conscious, that was to make me keep forever on the move, as though to escape a nameless fate seeking to overtake me. (117)

Wright reformulates the symbol of maternal death into matricidal desire in *Savage Holiday*, for here Fowler experiences the symptoms of his guilty wishes in explicitly Freudian terms probably because at midcentury this was the context for their expression (see Early, Afterword, 229).

By postulating that racial rage in Wright's fictions is partly empowered by his maternal ambivalence, I am *not* suggesting that the expression of Wright's outrage at racial injustice was anything less than absolutely genuine, and it was more than justifiable. Neither am I suggesting that racism is not implicated in the primary plot of maternal betrayal. One objective of this study is to call attention to the ways in which psychoanalysis has repressed the effects of social oppression on the primary family. There are no neutral cultural contexts for plots of subjective development, even though Freud, Lacan, and Klein seem to presume them. Wright's fictions make their erroneous presumptions about cultural neutrality quite conspicuous.

The fierce beating that the mother gives the boy Richard in *Black Boy* because he set the house afire is doubly marked by her frustration. Although she is relieved that he has not died in the fire, her projection of anxiety as displaced aggression wreaks violence on his small body and probably also structures his ambivalence toward future love objects. His mother's awareness that she does not possess the means to keep him safe in a racist society also causes her to try to beat him into submission to her so that he can avoid the penalties of that society. Like the infant in the paranoid-schizoid position, the boy Richard cannot perceive the reasons for the mother's action. He only experiences the persecution of the "bad mother" and consequently tries to defend himself against such future encounters with her. This is also what Fowler attempts to do by first "disowning" the bad mother and subsequently fantasizing a series of defenses to bolster his phallic power so as to protect himself from her control.

The overdetermination of the boy Richard's (and, by implication, Wright's) primary and unconscious hatred toward the persecutory mother *and* his conscious, secondary indignation at racism superimposes boundless fury upon inexhaustible rage. When Wright's stories concern what we readily identify as racial protest, they earn him (and rightly so) the recognition of the quintessential writer of racial protest. Public recognition seems to have given him some relief for his own racial suffering. Recognition also seems to have given him some relief for the guilty affects of his unconscious, ambivalent fantasies about his mother. By writing about characters who decisively retaliate against racial assault, usually by means of initially victimizing women, Wright could defend himself against the humiliation of past, current, and future racist encounters *and* unconsciously fantasize about defending himself against maternal persecution. Moreover, the royalties from his writing gave him the means of making reparation for his guilty feelings toward his historical mother, whom he seems to have arrested in his memory. Here, she must stay for him to keep the unconscious persecutory fantasies at bay.

The need to separate the primary imago of the mother from other female love objects, I suspect, is the reason Wright selected two talented white women for wives.[15] Race here becomes one significant barrier to consciousness, and a strong personality with demonstrable talent is another. Such characteristics distinguished these women from his memory of his sick, defenseless black mother, who repeatedly humiliated him and whose dependency threatened to engulf him. With sheer force of willpower, Wright deliberately detached himself from his mother and those who reminded him of her.

Nevertheless, the displaced incest fantasy controls the plot of *Savage Holiday*. Like Shakespeare's *Hamlet* and Wertham's *Dark Legend*, *Savage Holiday* depicts the son figure encountering and subsequently being overwhelmed by the mother's desire. Her desire incites his and threatens to obliterate his identity. Wertham examines the consequences of such effects in his 1940 essay "The Matricidal Impulse: Critique of Freud's Interpretation of *Hamlet*," which he further explains in his *Dark Legend*, published one year later, in 1941. Wright read both works and probably unconsciously recognized the son's dilemma as his own.

In "The Matricidal Impulse," Wertham contests the oedipalized reading of *Hamlet* by referring to several elements of the play that challenge Freud's interpretation. Freud's reading of *Hamlet* assumes that revenge on Claudius is the impetus of the play. But Wertham insists that the play is primarily about the son's plot of "revenge for the adultery of the mother with the uncle, and is only secondarily for the murder of the father" ("Matricidal Impulse," 457). Thus, throughout the play, Hamlet's principal struggle is to suppress his impulse to punish Gertrude, the adulterous mother, for humiliating him by killing her. This intention is dramatized in the scene in which Hamlet storms so violently into her chamber that she fears he plans to kill her. (See the third epigraph at the beginning of this chapter.) In fact, only after Gertrude succumbs to the poison that Hamlet puts in the goblet, which finds its way to her mouth, can Hamlet focus his attention on Claudius and kill him. In *Dark Legend* Wertham uses his analysis of the repressed matricidal impulse in *Hamlet*, what he terms the "Orestes Complex," to contextualize his explanation of the motives for the real murder of a widow by her seventeen-year-old son, Gino. Here Wertham explains that Gino kills his mother because, according to him, she dishonored his family by having an adulterous affair with his father's brother and because she severely neglected him and his siblings. *Savage Holiday* is a similar reenactment of the matricidal scenarios in *Hamlet* and *Dark Legend*, and it probably provided Wright with the vicarious means of expressing repressed infantile hostility toward his mother through words that seemed more like action.

Prior to writing *Savage Holiday*, Wright relied on an overdetermined plot to vent his conscious rage at racial terrorism and to express his unconscious anger at the "bad mother" he had internalized. However, this anger was either so deeply concealed, as I shall demonstrate by again referring to *Black Boy*, and/or it was so displaced that it evidently gave him little satisfaction but instead became susceptible to compulsive repetition. This pattern of displaced antagonism accounts for Bigger's murders of Mary and Bessie, makes Silas believe that Sarah is a whore, incites Jake's spousal abuse in *Lawd Today*, and makes Cross regard black women as conniving bitches. However, *Savage Holiday* apparently offered Wright the best opportunity to duplicate the psychotherapeutic situation of "acting out" his repressed hostility toward the internalized persecutory mother by staging a more transparent and satisfying symbolic act: creating a facsimile of the matricidal impulse in *Savage Holiday* seems to have a therapeutic effect on the compulsive plot of violence in Wright's writing.

Textual Traces of Repressed Rage at the Mother

While the dominant and conscious plot of *Black Boy* is racial, its suppressed story is about a son's ambivalent relationship with his mother. By comparing the opening scenes of *Black Boy* to *The Autobiography of Malcolm X*, another autobiography that is unquestionably about racial outrage, I hope to demonstrate my point. The comparison is particularly pertinent because the first recollected event in each work depicts the burning down of the author's home. This first event or primal scene, as psychoanalyst Eugene Victor Wolfenstein explains in the context of *The Autobiography of Malcolm X*, "was so intense that it brought to an end the undifferentiated succession of days that had preceded it" for Malcolm.

> Measurable time, the chronological record of Malcolm's consciousness, began that night—which is also to say, Malcolm knows himself, can remember and reflect upon himself, only as the child of this moment of terror. From his own perspective, earlier events in his life are prehistoric, while all later ones will be seen in the light of this primal experience. (Wolfenstein, *Victims*, 88)

For Malcolm X the plot of racial hostility is located on this, his "earliest vivid memory":

> I remember being suddenly snatched awake into a frightening confusion of pistol shots at the two white men who had set the fire and were running away. Our home

was burning down around us. We were lunging and bumping and tumbling all over each other trying to escape. My mother, with the baby in her arms, just made it into the yard before the house crashed in, showering sparks. I remember we were outside in the night in our underwear, crying and yelling our heads off. (*Autobiography* 3)

By contrast, the opening scene in *Black Boy* depicts Wright as a four-year-old boy, standing before a fireplace with his mother's scolding words ringing in his ears: "All morning my mother had been scolding me, telling me to keep still, warning me that I must make no noise. And I was angry, fretful, and impatient" (3). Within moments, the young boy sets the curtains on fire, probably as much to entertain himself as to express his anger at his mother for mandating his silence. This episode seems remarkably similar to the apartment fire in *Savage Holiday* that Fowler imagines as punishment for Mabel's neglect of Tony. Whereas one fire teaches the young Malcolm about racism and the absolute necessity to defend oneself against racist attacks, the other teaches the boy Richard the extent of his mother's wrath. As Wright reports, his mother "stripped the leaves from a tree limb" and administered his punishment. He reports,

> I was lashed so hard and long that I lost consciousness. I was beaten out of my senses and later I found myself in bed, screaming, determined to run away, tussling with my mother and father who were trying to keep me still. I was lost in a fog of fear. A doctor was called—I was afterwards told—and he ordered that I be kept abed, that I be kept quiet, that my very life depended upon it. (*BB* 7)

This beating triggers the boy's hallucination about the wobbly bags that threaten him—what I have called a malevolent breast fantasy. At the end of this episode in *Black Boy*, Wright recalls, "I was chastened whenever I remembered that my mother had come close to killing me" (8). Anger at the persecutory mother is repressed by the "fog of fear" (*BB* 7). This is the very term Wright repeatedly uses to represent his protagonists' dreadful response to racial hostility. The unfathomable racist "fog of fear" provides the concealment that allows Wright also to vent his repressed outrage at the brutality of maternal betrayal.

While *Native Son* (1940), *The Outsider* (1953), and *Savage Holiday* (1954) are characterized by the violent acts of murder perpetrated by their respective protagonists, the protagonist of *The Long Dream* (1957) kills no one. As if awaking from a dream that has been compulsively figured as murderous desire, *The Long Dream* is a novel of mourning. In this novel Wright creates a father—whom Fishbelly, the protagonist, can love and whose death he can mourn—and a mother with maternal wisdom and sexual dignity. Indeed, mourning is the novel's most significant feature, accentuated by Fishbelly's bereavement for his father's death, his grief over his mistress's death, and the black community's collective lamentation for the scores of people who die in the fire at a nightclub. This fire is also reminiscent of Fowler's imagined punishment for Mabel and Richard's fantasy of retaliation on the chastising mother in *Black Boy*. The fiery response to fantasies of maternal persecution are replaced in *The Long Dream* with recurring depictions of mourning that suggest this novel's inscription of a more mature textual desire than longing to attack the persecutory mother of infantile fantasy, inscribed in the earlier works.

This new desire corresponds to Melanie Klein's model of the depressive-mourning position. This model characterizes Fishbelly's ability to integrate love and hate for the maternal and paternal objects as well as to display his "sorrow and concern for the loved object[s]" (Klein, *Love*, 348). This response is possible because Fishbelly's father rescues him, first, from the mother's realm by initiating the son into masculine heterosexuality and, second, from the deadly threat of racist assault. Unlike virtually all of Wright's other fictions, *The Long Dream* is a novel not about maternal betrayal and filial rage but about filial love, guilt, and reparations.

What is fascinating about the sequential plots of Wright's autobiography and the four novels that Wright published during his lifetime is that they seem to have had a therapeutic effect on their collective textual desire. Each of the first four works—*Native Son* (1940), *Black Boy* (1945), *The Outsider* (1953), and *Savage Holiday* (1954)—repeatedly symbolizes a protagonist's displaced retaliation at bad parental figures for their betrayal. *The Long Dream* (1958) depicts a protagonist who develops beyond the compulsive behavior to integrate the good and bad mother and father into the mourned father and sympathetic mother. Before this integration is possible, though, one autobiographical protagonist has to enact the full scenario of the unconscious matricidal desire by deliberately attacking the bad mother with murderous rage and incestuous aggression. Hence, one protagonist frees Wright's fiction from the compulsive matricidal plot. Erskine Fowler has this distinction. Of all of Wright's published works, the obscure and maligned *Savage Holiday* is the very work that exposes the origins of and resolves his compulsive murderous plots. Like an allegory, *Savage Holiday* presents a story so horrible that it literally awakens Wright the dreamer from a long, recurring, traumatic nightmare, inscribed in Wright's earlier works, about the paradoxical wish to express and suppress his matricidal impulses.

CHAPTER FOUR

Desire and Death

Seducing the Lost Father in *Quicksand*, by Nella Larsen

It was so easy and so pleasant to think about freedom and cities, about clothes and books, about the sweet mingled smell of Houbigant and cigarettes in softly lighted rooms filled with inconsequential chatter and laughter and sophisticated tuneless music. It was so hard to think out a feasible way of retrieving all these agreeable, desired things. Just then. Later. When she got up. By and by. She must rest. Get strong. Sleep. Then, afterwards, she could work out some arrangement. So she dozed and dreamed in snatches of sleeping and waking, letting time run on. Away.

AND HARDLY had she left her bed and become able to walk again without pain, hardly had the children returned from the homes of the neighbors, when she began to have her fifth child.

—Nella Larsen, *Quicksand* (1928)

The distinguishing mental features of melancholia are a profoundly painful dejection, abrogation of interest in the outside world, loss of the capacity to love, inhibition of all activity, and a lowering of the self-regarding feelings to a degree that finds utterance in self-reproaches and self-revilings, and culminates in a delusional expectation of punishment. . . . [T]he ego can kill itself only when . . . it can treat itself as an object. . . . The complex of melancholia behaves like an open wound, drawing to itself cathectic energy from all sides . . . and draining the ego until it is utterly depleted.

—Sigmund Freud, "Mourning and Melancholia" (1917)

Helga Crane: Desiring Subject or Desired Object?

The closing paragraphs of Nella Larsen's *Quicksand* (1928), which constitute the first epigraph of this chapter, report the fate of the mulatta protagonist, Helga Crane. Before her marriage to Reverend Pleasant Green of rural Alabama, she is charming, witty, and enterprising. At the novel's close, this once captivating woman exists only as a fading illusion in the memories, fantasies, and dreams of a despondent and debilitated wife, whom the text now designates as "'Pore Mis'

Green'" (Q 126). This extract also relates Helga's convalescence from the almost fatal consequences of childbirth and her anguished longing for a more agreeable life. This longing has regulated her predictable and yet puzzling behavior throughout the novel and has generated its plot by means of sequential stagings of Helga's search for the always more inviting home and the perfect mate. Witnessing Helga's efforts to resolve this predicament "[has] carrie[d] us forward, onward, through the text" to the novel's last sentence, which announces another pregnancy (Brooks, *Reading*, 55). When cast against the dire circumstances of Helga's prior pregnancy, the implications of this one are deadly. For this reason, readers have generally regarded its pronouncement as her death sentence.

The closing paragraphs also feature an increasingly more detached narrator, who characterizes Helga's deteriorating mental condition. Until the final three lines of the story, the narrator shares Helga's consciousness and reveals her experiences, observations, and attitudes by combining features of Helga's silent but implied direct speech and the narrator's indirect account. The narrative strategy of free, indirect speech gives the impression that Helga is recalling her own story, though she seldom speaks in the novel. Yet there is little intimacy between Helga and the narrator. With the closing three lines, the intersubjective tie between them disintegrates. The narrator deserts Helga, leaving her voiceless and pathetic. The compulsion driving the novel to this conclusion is the enigma of the text. But before pursuing it, I will summarize the story.

Quicksand's plot uses Helga's abjection to stage the conventions of protest fiction by presenting her as a product of racial oppression. She is the daughter of a Danish immigrant woman, Karen Nilssen, and an unnamed black man—"a gay suave scoundrel" and "gambler" (Q 23, 21). The text refuses to recall his name, undoubtedly because it shares Helga's conscious rage for the man who deserted her and her mother when she was a very young child. When Helga is six, her mother remarries to escape a life of "poverty, sordidness, and dissipation." Her mother's second husband is a white man who treats Helga with "jealous, malicious hatred," matched only by "the savage unkindness of her step-brothers and sisters" (Q 23). From that time Helga considered herself to be "an obscene sore" on the white skin of her family, a sore "to be hidden" from sight (Q 29). Helga identifies with the abhorrence that her white family and white society associate with her dark bodily presence. Therefore, the gaze of the racist other determines Helga's bodily ego and constitutes her subjectivity.

This process has much in common with what Jacques Lacan has called the "mirror stage," in which the subject forms its ego by constructing an imaginary identification with its reflected or specular image. However, I will argue that Helga's specular self is not simply a unified bodily image, unmarked by social meaning, as Lacan seems to suggest. Helga's imaginary identification with her bodily image also incorporates the racist attitudes of her white family. Her identity is constitutive of the misrecognition of the specular image as the self and the self-object of a racist gaze. Thus, racist self-alienation forms the most primary structures of her personality. For this reason, extreme feelings of self-loathing define Helga's character.

Helga tolerates these feelings by forming polarized defensive responses. In the context of her white family, Helga relies on masochistic self-effacement. Because she identifies with the racist gaze of her family, she cannot displace the horror of her narcissistic wound. All she can do is try to conceal it from the gaze of the racist other. However, self-effacement cannot negate her identification with the loathsome object of this gaze. For this "impossible [horror] constitutes [her] very *being*" (Kristeva, *Powers*, 5; emphasis in original). Although the damage to her ego is permanent, her mother's brother provides Helga with some relief at fifteen, when her mother dies. He sends Helga to Naxos, "a school for Negroes" in Alabama, for six years. For the first time she can "consider . . . [her]self without repulsion" (*Q* 23). "She had been happy there [at Naxos], as happy as a child unused to happiness dared be. There had been always a feeling of strangeness, of outsideness, and one of holding her breath for fear that it wouldn't last. It hadn't. It had dwindled gradually into eclipse of painful isolation" (*Q* 23–24). At Naxos, she learns anew the meaning for her skin color and curly dark hair, because what her white family repudiates is now prized in the black academic community.

Helga enhances this prized mulatta body with sartorial elegance in order to conceal her wounded self-image. However, the beautiful clothing only complicates the suffering that structures her personality, for external beauty cannot alter Helga's inner world, which has already been formed by parental neglect and racism. She can only hope to disguise her feelings of inferiority, disaffection, and vulnerability with grandiose projections of her specular body that attract masculine attention.

The text presents Helga's development in a series of her specular images, full-body mirrored projections, each within its unique scenario. Because the story uses a heterosexual economy for staging textual desire and because the novel has traditionally understood marriage as the goal of a woman's life, each scenario is overdetermined by a sexual liaison. These scenarios begin at Naxos Institute, where Helga is engaged to a colleague, James Vayle. In Chicago, she is propositioned by a white stranger as she retreats from a failed attempt to see her Uncle Peter. In Harlem, she attracts the attention of many eligible, professional black men, including Dr. Robert Anderson, the former principal of Naxos, who has relocated and who repeatedly incites "a strange ill-defined emotion, a vague yearning rising within her" (*Q* 50). Helga ignores her troubling captivation with Anderson and flees to Copenhagen in search of less conflicted attention and admiration. In accord with the wishes of her Danish aunt and uncle, she beguiles a famous artist, Axel Olsen, who paints her portrait. He attempts to arrange an informal sexual arrangement with her. When she rejects the arrangement, he proposes marriage. She rejects the proposal and returns to Harlem, where she realizes that much of her relentless yearning has been due to her denied sexual desire for Anderson. Like her mother before her, she is ready to risk "all in one blind surrender" (*Q* 23) to him, despite the fact that he is now married to her friend Ann. Helga attempts to extend a sexual overture to him but finds that his "inexorable conscience" (*Q* 94) will not permit his even considering an affair. Humiliated by the rejection, and depressed, a day later she marries a poor southern preacher, Reverend Mr. Pleasant Green, whom she meets at a storefront church in Harlem. He is "a naive creature," "a rattish yellow man" from a "tiny Alabama town where he was a pastor to a scattered and primitive flock" (*Q* 117, 118). Helga feels superior to this man whose "finger-nails were always rimmed with black" and whose "fat body" smelled like sweaty, stale clothing (*Q* 121). No doubt, she feels confident that he will not abandon her.

Returning with Green to the small Alabama town, Helga assumes the prescribed life of a minister's wife. At first, she feels virtuous, indeed magnanimous. Her "zest for the uplifting of her fellow men came back to her" (*Q* 119), a repetition reminiscent of her initial devotion to working for social uplift at Naxos. Like the earlier effort, though, this even more romanticized venture is doomed to failure. Helga's repressed racial wound returns as the overdetermined site of female vulnerability—the womb. As in Freud's description of the melancholiac in the second epigraph of this chapter, Helga's mental wound drains her ego of vitality, while her womb ravages her body.

Although represented as the space of a missing line on the page, the gap between the final paragraphs is devoid of neither desire nor gratification. The gap signals the site where Helga's desire expends her agency while effacing her responsibility in the process and thereby obscuring her role in her last impregnation. The gap is also the site of the abrupt shift in narrative tone, position, and desire. Here the narrative changes from a sympathetic rendering of Helga's longings in free-indirect discourse to a wholly detached, third-person narration that abandons her as an abject object. Moreover, the gap signals the gratification of an unnameable longing that has determined Helga's actions and propelled the narrative to closure. The change in narrative tone and the story's unnamed pleasure prompt us to question whether Helga's death fulfills her own demand, executes the narrator's desire, or symbolizes an exchange of desire between the protagonist and the narrator to effect the story's consummation. How we address the changing relationship between the protagonist and the narrator determines how we address these questions—indeed, how we read the novel's complex subjectivity and position Larsen as well within its nexus of desire.

Quicksand's subjective logic would not be so unusual were it not partly posing as a roman à clef. When a review in the *Saturday Review of Literature* stated that "most of the important incidents of the book follow [Larsen's] own life closely," it expressed the viewpoint commonly held by the novel's other reviewers and subsequent readers (896). Usually in autobiographical novels the protagonist and the narrator are veiled agents for portraying the development of the authorial persona. But because *Quicksand* intimates the termination of the protagonist's life, it subverts the narcissistic and thus reflexive relationships among the protagonist, narrator, and author typically found in such novels. The narrator's increasingly quizzical tone also unsettles the reader's sympathy for Helga and suggests that Larsen herself derived perverse pleasure from renouncing her initial emotional investment in the self-reflecting protagonist.

Larsen's dissociation from Helga centers on the pathetic consequences of her marriage to Reverend Green.[1] Thus, what is most peculiar about this autobiographical novel is the plot's enactment of the protagonist's virtual suicide. The novel seems to stage a fantasy of retaliation by implying the demand for Helga's death, a retaliation seemingly invested with sadomasochistic pleasure for Larsen. The deadly demand, though, is not fulfilled in the actual story but insinuated by a repetitive and enigmatic sequence of events that concludes with the announcement of Helga's pregnancy. Perhaps Larsen's identification with Helga prevents the narrator from foreclosing all possibility of Helga's survival by inscribing her death. Nevertheless, the last three lines of the narrative indicate the total depletion of Helga's desire.

The shifts in narrative attitude throughout the story structure complex textual desire that insinuates the affective dynamic of sadomasochistic pleasure. The sadomasochistic conflict is what has activated Helga's paradoxical character and imbued it with power, albeit self-destructive. For the text does not represent Helga's desire as female sexuality under social repression or ultimately under the control of her husband but as a wild internal repulsion like "rank weeds" that repeatedly overpowers her (Q 122). The sadomasochistic gratification has also regulated the narrator's increasing demand for the protagonist's suffering. What is important to keep in mind here and will become increasingly more evident throughout this chapter is the fact that the narrator's sadistic demand also masks Larsen's involvement with perverse pleasure in the text.

Black readers have resisted holding Helga responsible for her tragic fate, and feminist readers have cast Helga as a victim of male sexual aggression. Both groups have rightly indicted racist and sexist oppression as the causes of her tragedy. But the effects of eroticized racism in *Quicksand* are more complicated than readers have generally assumed: Helga's life is not proscribed by the typical oppression associated with black characters (like Lutie Johnson of Ann Petry's *Street* and Bigger Thomas of Richard Wright's *Native Son*, for example) whose lives are predetermined by bleak material circumstances and no liberating alternatives. Helga possesses education, mobility, and a wide array of choices. Yet an enigmatic longing makes Helga an agent in her pitiful fate.

What accounts for Helga's fate? Racism pure and simple? Sexual repression of the bourgeois, black female subject? Social alienation? Or, as I argue, a more elusive factor, a desire that inculpates race, sex, and social alienation?

Because desire, repression, and alienation are precisely the central concerns of psychoanalysis and of *Quicksand* as well, this African American novel is an exemplary work for demonstrating how the insights of psychoanalytic theory—here, Freudian and Lacanian tenets—can help to illuminate the enigmatic desire structuring this novel. By combining selected Lacanian tenets and black cultural criticism, I hope to demonstrate that *Quicksand*'s enigmatic causality is not simply the product of Helga's sexual repression and the racial protest plot.

My argument evolves in five stages. First, by addressing the novel's reception, I identify the tension between the narrative's discourse of racial protest and another of a more personal nature. Second, I identify this latter discourse by referring to two specific post-Freudian hypotheses: Lacan's understanding of "the workings of a text as psyche, based on the theory that the unconscious is structured like a language" (E. Wright, *Psychoanalytic Criticism*, 114), and his theory about the formation of subjectivity by means of self-mirroring. The first is the basis of a similar proposition which Peter Brooks propounds and to which I have referred in the first three chapters. The structural correspondence of the text as psyche allows me to analyze the implicit meaning inscribed in the stylistic language and structural elements of the text—its repetitive words, tropes, rhetorical strategies, and causal organization, for example—as a part of the textual unconscious.[2] Lacan's insight concerning the mirror stage allows me to show that Helga's personality is "excentrically layered" rather than consolidated in a unified structure and constitutive of racism (Ragland-Sullivan, *Jacques Lacan*, 20). Third, by seeking the metonymic displacements in the text of the novel or what Lacan has called the signifying chain,[3] my analysis of textual desire culminates in a theoretical recovery of the lost object of desire implicated in Helga's tragedy. Fourth, I invoke Julia Kristeva's concept of abjection to analyze Helga's ambivalence about her own biracial corporeality. And fifth, by returning to the novel's closing lines and to Helga's abjection, I explain the narrative's exchange of Helga's masochistic desire for the narrator's new sadistic fantasy of Helga's death. Together, these five stages of my analysis demonstrate that *Quicksand* is not driven primarily by racial protest or black bourgeois sexual repression. Rather, the novel is ultimately controlled by its desire to recover and forget, express and silence a lost primary love at the expense of repudiating another one and, I suspect, to reconcile Larsen with similar losses as well.

Because *Quicksand*, like the other novels in this study, has been the object of traditional racialized and/or gendered readings that have routinely disregarded the significance of those aspects of the text that exceed the lens of cultural materialism, it is an extremely provocative novel when we expose its production of meaning as a mediation of its rhetorical system, on the one hand, and as a dialectic between the protagonist's material and psychical experiences, on the other hand. By disclosing the interplay between *Quicksand*'s political and libidinal narratives, I contend that this novel and black novels in general (like the others under investigation in this study and indeed all novels) are complex discourses of desire and, therefore, quite appropriate for psychoanalytic inquiry. In the particular case of *Quicksand*, psychoanalysis allows me to demonstrate how the familiar paradigms of race and gender that it typically invites do not entirely address the novel's enigmatic causality as the history of its reception attests. While the black racialist and feminist readings, summarized later, reveal the standard interpretations of *Quicksand*'s racial and sexual thematics, a more penetrating understanding of the development of its subjectivity emerges from an intertextual reading of the novel and Lacan's rereading of Freudian tenets.

The History of *Quicksand*'s Reception

Of the five novels that I address in this study, *Quicksand* has received the most critical attention. When *Quicksand* was published in 1928, it was immediately touted as a skillful novel. William E. B. Du Bois, who at the time was the editor of *The Crisis*, contended that *Quicksand* was "the best piece of fiction that Negro America has produced since the heyday of Chesnutt" ("Browsing Reader," 202). Evidently the judges of the Harmon Foundation shared his opinion, for in 1929 it awarded Larsen the bronze medal for "Distinguished Achievement among Negroes." Black and white reviewers alike recognized *Quicksand* as one of many "sophisticated novels coming off the press" during the 1920s (Christian, *Black Women Novelists*, 48). White reviewers tended to eschew the racial factors that contributed to the protagonist's fate and focused instead on the psychological character of Helga's dilemma. The unsigned review in the *New York Times Book Review*, for example, describes *Quicksand* as "wholly free from the curse of propaganda" and continues by applauding Larsen for being "aware that a novelist's business is primarily with the individuals and not with classes" ("Mulatto Girl," 16). Although the reviewer for the *New York Herald Tribune* detected the novel's subtle arguments for racial justice, which he labeled "[b]urnt cork," he maintained that

> [t]he real charm of this book lies in Miss Larsen's delicate achievement in maintaining for a long time an indefinable, wistful feeling—that feeling of longing and at the same time a conscious realization of the impossibility of obtaining—that is contained in the idea of Helga Crane. . . . [B]ut always it is there—a wistful note of longing, of anxiety, of futile searching, of an unconscious desire. (Bradford, "Mixed Blood," 22)

The reviewer for *The Nation* understood *Quicksand* as a story about a tragic mulatta, "who is dragged one way by her Negro blood and another by her white" (Parsons, "Three Novels," 540). However, no sooner does this reviewer cite the racial origin of Helga's dilemma than she amends the judgment by explaining that "[t]he motivation of this character is not always convincingly explained; the intention of the book is not even always clear; but it is a mine of information about one human being" (Parsons, "Three Novels," 540). Writing in the *Annals of the American Academy*, Katharine Shepard Hayden similarly describes *Quicksand* as "essentially the story of [Helga Crane's] inner life; the outer events are for the most part of secondary importance, merely the result of her inner conflicts, tangles, inexplicable moods and impulses." Despite the "rich and vivid" portrait of the protagonist, this reviewer contends that the novel is "too subjective, too fragmentary, too much of a psychological study" (Review, 345).

Predictably, reviewers for African American periodicals recognized *Quicksand's* frequent protestations against racial discrimination. These reviewers also identified with Helga's efforts to define herself independently of social restrictions, because discourses universalizing blackness were a part of the conventional activist appeals for social equality. Yet *Quicksand's* psychological portrait of Helga proved somewhat problematic for black reviewers because it undercut an efficacious rendering of racial protest. Nevertheless, black reviewers fit *Quicksand* into what was by the 1920s a standardized racial interpretation. The *Crisis* review probably best illustrates this point. Here Du Bois writes that "Helga is typical of that new, honest, young fighting Negro woman—the one on whom 'race' sits negligibly and Life is always first and its wandering path is but darkened, not obliterated by the shadow of the Veil" ("Browsing Reader," 202). While Du Bois recognizes *Quicksand's* protestations against prejudice and discrimination, he also discerns that racial protest is not the novel's only focus. According to him, the novel's depiction of "Life" is larger than race. By universalizing *Quicksand's* racial focus, a conventional tactic of social criticism of the day, Du Bois attempts to incorporate race within broader human concerns so as to mitigate its power to determine the lives of African Americans.

Despite the efforts of the first reviewers to universalize race, they nevertheless cast the veil of racial protest over the novel. After all, reviewers as well as readers have understood *Quicksand* as a novel written by a black woman about a black woman; therefore, it *must* necessarily depict her efforts to escape racial oppression and its effects. Such expectations set the stage for the even more rigid racial readings that scholars would affix to *Quicksand* after its recovery in the 1970s and the somewhat prescriptive black feminist readings that would follow in the 1980s.

The 1970s racial readings of the novel regard Helga Crane as a tragic mulatta. The cover blurb of the 1971 Collier paperback perhaps best summarizes this perspective: "Taut and terrifying, this personal odyssey of an upper-class mulatto woman unveils the tortured search for identity among the racially disinherited." This "milestone novel," the caption continues, "was the first to dramatize the plight of the cultured black woman trapped between two worlds and alien to both."[4] Many literary scholars have shared this viewpoint. For instance, Nathan Huggins describes Helga as "overwhelmed by the ethnic war within her mulatto psyche" (*Harlem Renaissance*, 157). However, Arthur P. Davis offers a much needed critique of the racial reading. He advises readers "to emphasize Helga's individuality because there is a temptation to blame everything that happens to her on racial grounds" (*From the Dark Tower*, 96). After mildly chiding Robert Bone (*Negro Novel*, 1964), Saunders Redding (*To Make*, 1939), and Hugh Gloster (*Negro Voices*, 1948) for succumbing to this temptation, Davis explains that Helga "is the victim of her own inability to make the right decisions, a hang-up which the author suggests *may* come from frustrated love, or from brooding over a father who deserted his family, or from strong unsatisfied sexual urges, or from all of these causes as well as the racial situation" (*From the Dark Tower*, 96). Davis recognizes Helga's psychological dilemma, but he does not attempt to integrate it with her racial experiences. Amritjit Singh builds on Davis's observation by adding that "Helga's neurosis" (which he identifies as manic depression) is a consequence of "the emotional deprivation of her childhood." "Yet," he continues, "Helga's tragedy cannot be explained away in purely psychological terms; she is as much a victim of a self-image based on the prejudices of the people around her as a case of asphyxiation" (*Novels*, 102). This is a somewhat contradictory position. On the one hand, Singh rightly explains Helga's emotional problems as largely the consequence of her confrontation with racial prejudice. On the other hand, he erroneously assumes that Helga's self-image and her experiences of racial oppression are not intricately linked. Like Davis, he segregates Helga's psychical and material lives.

Feminist interpretations of *Quicksand* attribute Helga's tragedy not merely to race but to a uniquely gendered dialectic of desire and danger, a fateful encounter of female sexuality and biology made all the more complicated by the racial stereotype of the wanton black woman. For example, Barbara Christian explains Helga as a "pathetic mulatta" who "finds that she is seldom perceived as a person in either the black or the white world. Instead, she is an image." "Coupled with this devastating theme," Christian adds, is "Larsen's analysis of the small degree of sensuality that is allowed the lady." Christian further contends that "[Helga's] tragedy is specifically a female one. She is destroyed by her womb" (*Black Women Novelists*, 53). This viewpoint suggests that Christian regards Helga as largely a passive victim who does not share any responsibility for her fate.

In her introduction to the 1986 Rutgers University Press reprint of the novel, Deborah E. McDowell observes that "*Quicksand* likens marriage to death for women" (xxi). Like Christian, McDowell categorically indicts an oppressive marriage as the obstacle to Helga's survival, an indictment that does not question Helga's involvement in her plight. McDowell goes on to argue that "Helga's psychic struggle seems the same fought by Nella Larsen between narrative expression and repression of female sexuality as literary subject" (xvii). In this context we can see the novel's desire working against a bourgeois patriarchal economy. Such an economy is present, of course. However, gender and class codes in and of themselves do not entirely explain the novel's irrational causality. This is to say not that gender and class are unimportant but that the bourgeois patriarchal demands on the black female subject are not the novel's exclusive determining factor.

Ann E. Hostetler and Ann duCille also provide compelling yet incomplete readings of *Quicksand*. Hostetler reads the novel as cultural criticism and applauds Larsen's "stylistic experimentation and the daring self-examination of her protagonist." She also praises Larsen's "startlingly original" treatment of the black bourgeoisie "in both its narrative and its psychological insight" ("Race," 36). Ann duCille counters the basic contentions of Christian and McDowell to argue that "it is not childbirth or motherhood, or even patriarchy, that overcomes Helga as much as it is the irreconcilable social, psychosexual, and racial contradictions that become her quicksand." Helga's dilemma, duCille continues, is her inability "to *fashion* an individual identity against the competing ideological and iconographic forces that ultimately render her invisible" (*Coupling Convention*, 96; emphasis in original). While Hostetler and duCille broach Helga's problematic subjectivity, neither tries to characterize it.

Hazel V. Carby's discussion of *Quicksand* is somewhat different. By focusing her examination on the novel's social content rather than its protagonist, Carby argues that the novel presents a crisis of representing race, gender, and class in the literature of the Harlem Renaissance, a crisis that is represented on the black, female, middle-class body of the protagonist. According to Carby, the novel "did not just explore the contradictory terrain of women and romance; its sexual politics tore apart the very fabric of the romance form" (*Reconstructing Womanhood*, 168). She sees the novel as the refusal "to romanticize 'the people' as the folk," an articulation "of a woman embedded within capitalist social relations," and a representation of "the full complexity of the modern alienated individual" (*Reconstructing Womanhood*, 169–70).

These and other scholars have repeatedly mentioned *Quicksand*'s psychological content while circumscribing their discussions by the race and gender paradigm. Despite these frequent gestures toward psychology, only Barbara Johnson pursues a psychological interpretation of the novel by seeing its social content working through psychoanalytic processes.[5] By referring to Carby's discussion of Helga's alienation as "not just in her head" but produced by "existing forms of social relations" ("Quicksands," 169), Johnson argues that Larsen "does not ask the reader to *choose* between a psychic and a social model, but rather to see the articulations between them. To see Helga purely from the inside or purely from the outside is to miss the genius of the text. It is the inside/outside opposition itself that needs to be questioned" ("Quicksands," 196; emphasis in original). Johnson refers to the "self-psychology" of Heinz Kohut to read Helga as the product of a narcissistic personality disorder and charts her life as a series of unsuccessful efforts to merge her enfeebled ego with others whom she idealizes as "omnipotent selfobject[s]" ("Quicksands," 191). When Helga becomes aware of the imperfections of each of them, she abandons the merger.

Kohutian theory facilitates Johnson's analysis of Helga's originary trauma as inappropriate empathic mirroring. Johnson illustrates her argument by referring to

Helga's abandoned attempts to merge with two such objects—Robert Anderson and Axel Olsen, both of whom are urban sophisticates. Exactly how Reverend Pleasant Green fits Johnson's model of idealization is unclear. Initially described as "the man beside her," whose name she can barely remember (Q 116), Green is cast as an unlikely choice for an omnipotent other. At best, he is a displacement for divine Omnipotence, and Helga is consciously aware that her search for "perfect empathy" (Johnson, "Quicksands," 191) with him is a precarious venture.

Rather than regarding Helga as real person, suffering from traumatized empathic mirroring, as Johnson does, I refer to Lacanian theory so as to designate Helga as a signifier of the repressed conflict controlling the novel. Lacanian psychoanalysis provides a structural model for deciphering the novel's enigmatic logic as the interplay of conscious and unconscious discourses of desire that reflect the dialectical nature of Helga's personal and social conflicts. Such an analysis allows me to demonstrate that racism is not simply a secondary social trauma, as the Lacanian model suggests, but a primary misrecognition that actually structures the subject's inner world.

Desire as Unanswered Questions

Helga Crane is not the traditional, determined black character, fastened to a naturalistic plot on an oppressive social landscape, but a generally unfettered character to whom the novel grants an extraordinary range of choices and extensive freedom of movement. Yet in practically every incident Helga seems compelled to choose the wrong course of action. The narrator accentuates Helga's misfortune with recurring versions of the following rhetorical questions, which are couched not so much as verbalizations of Helga's thoughts as the perspective of a distinct narrative subjectivity, presented in an apprehensive and somewhat querulous tone:

> But just what did she want? Barring a desire for material security, gracious ways of living, a profusion of lovely clothes, and a goodly share of envious admiration, Helga Crane didn't know, couldn't tell. But there was, she knew, something else. Happiness, she supposed. Whatever that might be. What, exactly, she wondered, was happiness. Very positively she wanted it. (Q 11)

Later in the novel, the narrator reformulates these questions to expose a growing frustration with Helga:

> Frankly the question came to this: what was the matter with her? Was there, without her knowing it, some peculiar lack in her? Absurd. But she began to have a feeling of discouragement and hopelessness. Why couldn't she be happy, content, somewhere? Other people managed, somehow, to be. To put it plainly, didn't she know how? Was she incapable of it? (Q 81)

These revised questions also prompt the narrator's castigation and characterize Helga's own frustration. In addition, the questions oblige us to wonder why Helga cannot adjust pragmatically to at least some of the demands of white and black culture and be relatively happy somewhere. But she cannot accomplish this feat. The questions, then, are not attempts to prod pragmatic responses from Helga but opportunities for the narrator to reveal vague and insatiable desire as the driving force of Helga's personality. As the reception summary reveals, the white reviews generally witnessed her pain rather than offering analysis, while black reviewers and scholars have generally tended to interpret Helga's indefinite longings as largely complaints against racial segregation, discrimination, and prejudice. However, the demand for social justice establishes clear rather than obscure objectives. The typical racial reading of *Quicksand* thus makes Helga's ambiguous desire inconsistent with the very specific goals of social justice without clarifying that desire.

Insatiable desire is the dominant feature of Helga's character; it is an attribute that corresponds to the Lacanian observation that "desire is in principle insatiable" (Grosz, *Jacques Lacan*, 67). Perhaps we can understand Helga's character as an illustration of desire, for desire in *Quicksand*

> appears in the rift that separates need and demand; it cannot be reduced to need since, by definition, it is not a relation to a real object independent of the subject but a relation to phantasy; nor can it be reduced to demand, in that it seeks to impose itself without taking the language or the unconscious of the Other into account, and insists upon absolute recognition from [that Other].[6] (Laplanche and Pontalis, *Language*, 483)

Quicksand acts out the desire of the unconscious in terms of Helga's irrational and erratic actions. Because the text preserves the standard metaphor of sexuality for desire as well as for dominant cultural codes or what Lacan has termed the "Symbolic" order,[7] the text relies on sexuality to represent cultural expectations and the symptoms of unconscious desire. Under these conditions, the provocation for the unanswered questions—desire—incites Helga's romantic ventures.

These ventures form a series of perverse romances that reflect her repressed desire to express and demand love. For Helga, though, such desire is conflicted by the tension between her inner psychic world and her outer social world. While her bodily ego seeks genital sexuality, her inner self seeks to satisfy infantile longings. Alternating expressions of desire and repulsion, demonstrable in her eroticized body and reticent behavior, give expression to this conflict. Such an affective response makes Helga's involvement with men highly problematic, for she makes herself appear sexually enticing without consciously intending to attract such attention. Even when Helga is the passive aggressor, she behaves defensively in all but the last plot sequence. Until then, she projects ever more sensual, specular images of herself, seeks new occasions for idealized happiness, and usually rejects the romantic encounter before it spurns her as she anticipates it will.

This sexual pattern of representing textual desire presents Helga with a dangerous dilemma; it demands that she both seek and repel the "vile affectations" associated with the flesh (Kristeva, *Powers*, 124). In doing so Helga is bound by the
condition that Julia Kristeva has designated as the *abjection of self*: "the recognition of the *want* on which any being, meaning, language, or desire is founded" and
the repudiation of the *want* because it demeans the self with painful awareness of
imperfection (*Powers*, 5; emphasis in original). Abjection signals the subject's corporeal existence, the vulnerability that the subject wants to deny. For Helga, abjection is overdetermined and additionally perilous because her quest for the lost
father (a point I will discuss further at the conclusion of this chapter) also demands her repudiation of her partial corporeal whiteness.

Helga's desperation and sensual self-projection culminate in the storefront
church incident where she meets the Reverend Green. The text describes her as "so
broken physically, mentally, that she had given up thinking. . . . Almost," it adds,
"she wished she could die. Not quite. It wasn't that she was afraid of death, which
had, she thought, its *picturesque aspects*. It was rather that she knew she would not
die" (Q 109; my emphasis). Outfitted in a "clinging red dress" that portrays her as
a "scarlet 'oman," Helga confronts a living picture of another sort, the "rites of a
remote obscure origin," whose "horror held her" (Q 112, 113).

This scene has much in common with what Freud called the "primal scene," the
spectacle of sexual intercourse between the parents which the child observes, or
infers, and fantasizes about (Laplanche and Pontalis, *Language*, 335). In the storefront church, Helga is initially a detached and fascinated observer. Dressed as the
seductress, though, she is merely offstage, awaiting her cue to play an uncanny role
in the novel's mise-en-scène of desire. This scene repeats the dramatization of a
scenario in which the subject always has a predictable role to play; this scenario is
a part of the novel's *fantasmatic*.

A fantasmatic, as I explained in Chapter 2, is a "structuring action" or a recurring pattern of an individual's fantasies that "lie[s] behind such products of the
unconscious as dreams, symptoms, acting out, [and] repetitive behavior" (Laplanche and Pontalis, *Language*, 317). The fantasmatic is not only an internal
theme that structures a subject's unconscious associations; it is also a dynamic formation that seeks conscious expression by converting experience into language
particularly evident in literature.

Helga plays an uncanny role in the mise-en-scène of desire with Reverend
Green, who seems more present as language, conviction, and prohibition than a
corporeal entity. Given his rural simplicity, she believes that she has the advantage
in their relationship. Confident, she presses her sexual demand with the implication of having read only the literal meaning of his name—pleasant green—as
pleasing life, lasting happiness. However, the name "Pleasant Green" also signifies
symbolic meaning associated with death—pleasant green as the peaceful site of
one's final repose, a heavenly place that in February 1930 would imaginatively ma-

terialize in the Broadway opening of *The Green Pastures*, by Marc Connelly. This latter meaning of Green's name responds to the novel's unconscious desire for death, a desire that becomes increasingly more evident in the numerous references to immersion in the womblike imagery in the text. This meaning forewarns the reader that Helga's encounter with him will result in her engulfment in the symbolic and deadly "quicksand" of the novel's title.

Helga's marriage to the Reverend Green emphatically portrays her paradoxical relationship to desire, for after her demand of matrimony, desire not only remains but is exacerbated. Although the marriage is instigated by a seduction, Helga is *not* seduced, as Deborah E. McDowell contends in her introduction to *Quicksand*: "The question still remains as to why the refined Helga, who 'took to luxury as the proverbial duck to water,' participates in a religious orgy, *is seduced*, then marries a man whose 'fingernails [are] always rimmed with black,' and who smells of 'sweat and stale garments'" (xx; my emphasis). According to McDowell, the seducing agent seems to be either "the religious orgy" or the man, leaving Helga to play the role of the seduced woman. Yet the text seems to make it clear that Helga is the seducer: "Instantly across her still half-hypnotized consciousness little burning darts of fancy had shot themselves. No. She couldn't. It would be too awful" (*Q* 115). The text adds that Helga was "shocked at what she was on the verge of considering." But rather than recoiling from irrational desire, she surrenders to it and acts compulsively: "Helga Crane had deliberately stopped thinking. She had only smiled, a faint provocative smile, and *pressed her fingers deep into his arms* until a wild look had come into his slightly bloodshot eyes" (*Q* 116; my emphasis). Interpretations of Helga's sexual repression notwithstanding, the text presents her as the agent of seduction and of a symbolized sexual penetration.

Although Helga's death as desiring subject is implied in the novel's last sentence, the novel has obscured its motivation by distracting us with subtle intrusions of vague longings throughout the narrative. The object of this undefined yearning has been increasingly insinuating its presence in the story from the moment Helga expresses sympathy for her father. In this way the text aligns Helga's longing with race by seeking an identification with him. Yet after her return to Harlem, *Quicksand* loses whatever interest it may have had in staging racial protest as a vague force takes control of the novel's plot. We don't notice it at first because it hides behind the mask of race. What is it, and why must it hide?

Racial Difference as Personal Defense

One may argue, and no doubt Larsen intended to show, that the circumstances of class privilege make racial discrimination especially painful for African Americans like Helga. This negative form of social mirroring further weakens Helga's already fragile ego. What is important here is that racism does not simply affect

Helga's or any real black subject's conscious life. Racism becomes a part of the subject's unconscious because the parents consciously and unconsciously reflect the racist values of the culture onto the subject from the first moment of life. Given Helga's early life history, intense racism is constitutive of her primary processes of self-recognition and therefore a fundamental structuring principle of every aspect of subjectivity. Her successive and conscious experiences with racial trauma further exacerbate the unconscious masochism of her ego and further fragment it, producing the self-destructive behavior. She tries to protect herself from racist assault, first by seeking self-effacement and subsequently by pursuing narcissistic approval. But when this latter effort fails, the text returns to its initial defense of self-effacement, ultimately in the form of bodily self-obliteration. However, before analyzing the sadomasochistic pleasure invested in such a submission, I want to examine the racist experiences of her mature life that serve as the text's mask for prohibited content and complicate Helga's primary narcissistic injury caused by her father's abandonment, her mother's remoteness, and her stepfather's racism. These infantile injuries form the elusive factor, the invisible catalyst, that makes her identity as black and female a deadly combination for her.

Helga's defensive strategies take her as far away as Copenhagen. However, when her idealized notion of freedom and home begins to fade, she suspects that her Danish family "had been invited to look upon something in her which she had hidden away and wanted to forget" (Q 83). She saw herself once again as "an obscene sore," as abject (Q 29). Her feelings of acute unworthiness make her interpret the attention of her mother's family as the accentuation of this racial wound. No matter how she attempts to conceal it, "all along they had divined its presence, had known that in her was something, some characteristic, different from any that they themselves possessed" (Q 83). The only prior experience Helga has with her recognition by the other is racist abasement. Like the abused child, she perceives pain where pleasure should be. Helga objectifies the difference her Danish family perceives in her blackness by seeking the company of the only other black people in Copenhagen—two "gesticulating black figures" in a circus minstrel show. They epitomize the racial sore that cannot be concealed. Hence, the black figures against the ultrawhite audience reflect her own "doubts, rebellion, expediency, and urgent longings"—her racialized self-abjection (Q 83). Only able to see herself from the gaze of the racist other, Helga sees herself as despised and obscene rather than as "a precious thing, a thing to be enhanced, preserved" (Q 29). She cannot free herself from this racist self-construction despite her escape in Denmark from its gross manifestations in the United States. She is destined to perceive herself as oppressed by racism because her inner world is already constructed in these terms. With her defensive retreat, "[h]er old unhappy questioning mood came again upon her, insidiously stealing away more of the contentment from her transformed existence" (Q 83).

While Helga is suffering the anguish of racial insecurity, Olsen proposes marriage. Whereas she was able to disregard his earlier insinuation about an informal sexual arrangement, the prospect of marriage confronts Helga once again with the intimate gaze of the white other. Helga's personal history gives her good reasons to fear that such a relationship, no matter how initially self-affirming, will ultimately result in her rejection. However, her fear of rejection is displaced by her feelings of sexual aversion for Olsen, as she becomes aware of "a curious feeling of repugnance" now associated with the plainly sexualized Olsen (*Q* 85). This repudiation repeats her earlier feelings about Vayle: "a curious sensation of repugnance, for which she was at a loss to account," that gave rise to "[a]cute nausea" (*Q* 24). While she simply abandoned Vayle, she rejects Olsen to his face. He interprets her behavior as racial in nature.

Blinded by European sexual stereotypes about "the warm impulsive nature of the women of Africa," he fails to discern Helga's ambivalent sexual feelings (*Q* 87). Rather, he perceives her behavior as unduly influenced by her status-conscious aunt and the demands of the marriage market. This perspective motivates his remark "'You have been, I suspect, corrupted by the good Fru Dahl, which is perhaps as well,'" and his indictment—"'my lovely, you have, I fear, the soul of a prostitute'" (*Q* 87). Helga interprets his uncanny comment as an insult, for it reminds her and the reader of white culture's exploitative sexualization of her mulatta body, represented by the proposition of the unknown white man as well as Olsen's.

Whether consciously or unconsciously, Helga employs her racial insecurity in an offensive move to conceal her sexual discomfort. She uses race to invigorate and justify her lashing retort at Olsen. However, her show of race loyalty only partially disguises what is actually her delayed outrage caused by his earlier indecent proposition: "'I'm not for sale. Not to you. Not to any white man. . . . What I'm trying to say is this, I don't want you. I wouldn't under any circumstances marry you,' and since she was, as he put it, being brutally frank, she added: '*Now*'" (*Q* 87; emphasis in original). By responding to Olsen's honorable request as an insult, she can reject him in the manner in which she has experienced rejection throughout her life and eliminate him as an antagonistic sexual subject. Moreover, Larsen's conflation of Helga's response to Olsen's illicit proposition and his marriage proposal allows Larsen to censure the institution of marriage by casting it as a condition that renders wives as vulnerable to male caprice as prostitutes. Finally, Helga's new appreciation of racial solidarity, which has given her the means to reject Olsen's prerogatives of white male desire, allows her to bolster her self-esteem and to conceal her ambivalent feelings about sex as well as her abject corporeality.[8] Race, rather than sex, becomes the candid justification for her response: "'You see, I couldn't marry a white man. I simply couldn't. It isn't just you, not just personal, you understand. It's deeper, broader than that. It's racial'" (*Q* 88). Race, then, becomes the overdetermined basis of Helga's decision to inflict pain on Olsen, who stands as a surrogate for all those white people who have rejected her.

In addition, Helga's rejection of Olsen's proposal is the text's acknowledgment of his and Copenhagen's failure to fill what Lacan calls the gap of desire[9] propelling Helga's activity and the novel to its close. As a result, Helga seeks a newly defined, idealized object or imago that, after listening to "those wailing undertones" of "Swing Low, Sweet Chariot" in Antonin Dvorak's *New World Symphony* (1893), she identifies as an affinity with black people (*Q* 92). This bewildering and sudden awareness induces her homesickness for "Negroes" and an outpouring of sympathy for her father:

> For the first time Helga Crane felt sympathy rather than contempt and hatred for that father, who so often and so angrily she had blamed for his desertion of her mother. She understood, now, his rejection, his repudiation, of the formal calm her mother had represented. She understood his yearning, his intolerable need for the inexhaustible humor and the incessant hope of his own kind, his need for those things, not material, indigenous to all Negro environments. . . . [S]he was able to forgive him. (*Q* 92–93)

Recognizing her heretofore repressed feelings for her father is "knowledge of almost sacred importance" to Helga. By releasing her suppressed feelings for the father, she can sympathize with him, which in turn allows her to reinforce her meager self-esteem. By reclaiming and idealizing him, she begins to recover her forsaken paternal imago. However, this form of daughter-father identification, as psychoanalyst Jessica Benjamin has explained, stimulates the daughter's wish to be "recognized as like the father and to share his subjectivity, will, and desire" (*Bonds*, 115). But is his blackness what this daughter ultimately seeks?

A Lacanian Reading of *Quicksand*

The narrator manipulates Helga as an object of conscious political design, even while estranging her from the protest plot by involving her in a more primary discourse of textual desire—the daughter's unconscious desire for the father of her infantile fantasies,[10] which are lost to consciousness because guilt demands their repression. This primary discourse, I argue, regulates *Quicksand*'s unconscious discourses of desire. The demands of these unconscious fantasies expose the ego to an unconscious guilt that stimulates the sadistic demands of the censoring superego to punish the ego. At these moments in the text Helga feels a vague sense of repulsion, underscored by nausea. This is the process that Freud identified as the death drive, which is not about biological death, as the term suggests, but about the death of the ego, as Jacques Lacan has clarified.[11] The narrative transition from the sympathetic free-indirect discourse to the sadistic domination of the detached third-person narrator, who seems to sentence Helga to death, duplicates the same internal transaction within Helga's psyche as she increasingly treats her ego and body as objects.

By aligning narrative and text here I want to make clear a distinction that I have been using implicitly. By text, I mean all the language constitutive of the novel rather than the series of incidents comprising the story or narrative. "Text," then, is the term I use to refer, for example, to the novel's rhetorical, tropological, and discursive features. According to this framework, narrative desire would both culminate and terminate in the final incident, and textual desire would find satisfaction in the "occulted objects of desire" inscribed in the text's last expression (Brooks, *Reading*, 105). By definition, though, the lost objects cannot be explicitly identified; rather, they are intimated through an interplay of the desire inherent in language.

Quicksand places Helga at the center of several conflicting discourses of desire—her own as protagonist, the narrator's, the text's, and the authorial persona's. The depictions of loss inscribed in the text by means of rhetorical features ultimately dominate the racial and gender discourses. For this reason Helga cannot play out conventional female desire and select an acceptable surrogate for the lost father. Indeed, her dilemma occurs precisely because she seeks an object she cannot possess. The dialectic of desire and prohibition accounts for *Quicksand*'s elusive power and makes Helga enigmatic.

Textual meaning in *Quicksand* arises from this interplay of fear and desire, repulsion and seduction—opposing affects that both Helga and the text share. The text reinforces this interplay by projecting these affects onto the numerous portraits of Helga that appear throughout the novel. In one series of portraits, the text constructs genteel expressions of her sensuality by presenting her in gorgeous clothing largely for our appreciation. In another series, the text presents Helga as a temptress, perceivable, for example, in the observations of Olsen and the storefront churchwomen. This pattern of Helga's behavior and specular self-presentation recalls the question about whether her sexual repression is a displacement for a more deeply concealed resistance—a question whose answer, I am arguing, can be determined by deciphering the novel's unconscious desire. By unconscious desire, I mean the unstated effects created by the language in *Quicksand* and communicated in the drama of transference of affects among the protagonist, narrator, author, and reader.[12]

Quicksand uses three basic strategies to present unconscious desire. First and most obvious, the novel uses insistent repetition of single words, like "disgusting" and "tragedy." Second, the novel uses what Freud might call a slip—a curious discursive detail that seems awry. Later I will illustrate how one particular extraneous feature creates coherent meaning in this novel. And third, the novel *acts out* Helga's and the narrative's repressed desire by staging repetitive incidents and characters. These repetitions form a series of metonymic displacements—Lacanian signifying chains—to fill the lack caused by a primary loss.[13]

Quicksand gives expression to the lack in the series of unanswered questions mentioned earlier and projects the possibility of its fulfillment onto an imaginary

place where Helga would be unconditionally appreciated and understood by ad-
miring people. These instances of longings motivate Helga's self-projections and
her mobility, which in turn generate the repetitive episodes. The repetitions locate
sites of meaning that, as I argue later, make the novel *more* than a story about the
"expression and repression of female sexuality" caused by her objectification as either a "lady" or a "Jezebel" (McDowell, Introduction, xix) and *more* than a "tortured search for identity among the racially disinherited" (Collier book jacket).[14]

I return to Helga's deliberately cruel rejection of Olsen to illustrate how this pattern of repetition propels a signifying chain. Helga's rebuff of Olsen ("'I'm not for
sale. Not to you. Not to any white man'" [Q 87]) makes uncanny the site where
she castigates the unknown white man who propositions her. She replies, curiously enough, "'You're not my uncle'" (Q 29). That castigation repeats the refusal
by her Uncle Peter's new wife to acknowledge Helga as kin, recorded earlier on the
same page. (His wife spurns Helga by saying, "'He's not—,'" implying albeit il-
logically that Peter Nilssen is not really her uncle by alleging her illegitimacy.)
Helga's venture with Olsen is also a part of the repetitive romantic scenarios, during which she encounters a series of real and potential suitors. This sequence of
events calls attention to the series of repetitive specular portraits of Helga. Yet another series of repetitions concern her efforts to find a home where she would be
loved and appreciated. The novel's preoccupation with repetition is reminiscent
of Freud's theory on compulsive repetition: the compulsion to repeat signals the
resistance of repression. The repetitions therefore suggest that they are signifiers
of the repressed.

While the repressed is forever external to Helga's consciousness, it returns to
textuality with an alarming intensity in the episode in which Helga meets Reverend Green. This episode is uncanny because, to borrow Freud's words, it leads
"back to something long known to us, once very familiar" ("Uncanny," 369–70).
Reverend Green is familiar because his presence sets the stage for another repetition of the courtship scenario—now, however, a grotesque version. Green is the
magical suitor, and the church service is a bizarre courting ritual. We dread this
scenario because we recognize the face of death behind the suitor's mask of pleasure and perceive Helga's hysterical fascination with "the zealous shoutings and
groanings of the congregation," a "performance [that] took on an almost Bacchic
vehemence" of a primitive sexual climax: "Fascinated, Helga Crane watched until
there crept upon her an indistinct horror of an unknown world. . . . And as
Helga watched and listened, gradually a curious influence penetrated her; she felt
an echo of the weird orgy resound in her own heart; she felt herself possessed by
the same madness" (Q 113). The horrified fascination that Helga assumes is external to herself in this weird performance is actually within her being. She possesses the orgasmic frenzy. Overwhelmed by the repulsive, fecund bodies of the
storefront churchwomen, Helga seeks purification through the horror of abjection
of the self. Thus, when Helga "be[gins] to yell like one insane" for God's mercy,

she uses this ceremony to unburden herself of the agony inherent in desire (Q 114). Ultimately, she can transfer desire—here characterized as disgust—to socially sanctioned sexual desire only by marrying Green. Thus, by repeatedly performing desire as sexual desire, Helga condemns herself to the consequences of female biology—too-frequent pregnancies—which only worsens her abject condition.

Why does the text demand Helga's uncanny attraction to Reverend Green? As the novel moves to closure, which is the site of the culmination and the termination of textual desire, it attempts to fulfill Helga's desire with sexual relationships with James Vayle, the unknown white man, Robert Anderson, Axel Olsen, Anderson again, and Reverend Pleasant Green. These men signal the return of the repressed, figured in the text, by forming a chain of signifiers for the unnameable loss. Lacan's understanding of the signifying chain is helpful here. According to Lacan, "the displacement of the signifier [in this chain] determines the subjects in their acts, in their destiny, in their refusals, in their blindnesses, in their end and in their fate." Hence, "everything that might be considered the stuff of psychology, kit and caboodle, will follow the path of the signifier" ("Seminar," 60). By backtracking the signifiers in this chain, we can detect a textual logic that intimates an originary referent as the abandoning father.[15]

Because Helga's father abandoned her when she was an infant, he is an emphatically lost imago. The father is repressed because of the unconscious dynamics of the daughter's pre-oedipal identificatory love of the father, repressed because of the daughter's sexual repression of the father in the oedipal stage, absent because of the father's abandonment, repelled because of Helga's willful refusal to love the abandoning father, and disavowed because of her racial ambivalence. This overdetermined absence is the reason that there are so many masculine (white and black) displacements both marking and concealing the lost father: Helga's stepfather, Uncle Peter, the unknown white man, Olsen, Vayle, Anderson, and Reverend Green. Indeed, Helga's comment to the white stranger who propositions her—"'You're not my uncle'"—is the awry response that calls attention to the signifying chain of repressed, incestuous, and thus prohibited desire leading back to the father. This may very well be the shameful incestuous impulse that the text both conceals and reveals.

When these repressions return to textual consciousness, they rebound with multiple forcefulness as Helga's sexual, paternal, and racial longings. Thus, Green, as the final suitor, becomes the last displacement for Helga's father, and as a minister he is also a displacement for cultural paternity—God—and the signifier of divine prohibition. Her reckless response to Green also repeats her mother's reaction to Helga's father, an uncanny repetition that underscores Green's identification with the lost paternal imago. For despite Helga's uncle's warning not to repeat her mother's mistakes, Helga's life seems curiously determined by the scenario of her mother's desire, a tragic predetermination that feminist scholars identify with the consequences of expressing female desire in patriarchal cultures. The novel's textual logic establishes the chain of male signifiers that attempts to fill narrative desire. This chain calls attention to a personal conflict in Larsen's life.

Thadious M. Davis, Larsen's biographer, explains that Larsen's historical father takes on a number of identities in relationship to her. At her birth, her father is the "Colored" Peter Walker (*Nella Larsen*, 21). When Larsen enters grade school a few years later, the school records indicate a change in her surname, suggesting that her father has changed his name to Peter Larson. His new name appears on the records, while the mother's name is not simply effaced but marked with an *X* (*Nella Larsen*, 24). However, the signifier *X* in Nella Larsen's school records is not Larsen's own expression but that of her father. Davis then goes on to argue that this record suggests that he, not the mother, is Larsen's real "primary, public parent": "From Nellie [Larsen's] earliest years in public school, then, there is an unaccounted for distance between the child and the mother, and an obvious connection between the child and father whose own self-invention emerges from his public records" (*Nella Larsen*, 24). Davis does not explain the difference between the "primary, public parent[al]" role of the father and the "central [maternal] figure in textual relation to Helga," which (according to Davis) is the one held accountable for Helga's adult condition, for Davis claims that *Quicksand*'s "power emanates from the core of Helga's existence and from the interpolation of her mother's story into Helga's own" (*Nella Larsen*, 255).[16]

But Davis also states that Larsen's social identity and name were determined by the father, which had to have included the changes in his racial self-fashioning. For this reason, Larsen's identity had to have been regulated successively by paternal affection, mutual racial recognition, and growing racial alienation. When Peter Lar*son* becomes the fully white Peter Lar*sen*, as Davis explains, he "not only left behind his old name"; "he also made what now appears to be a conscious effort to disassociate himself from his old [racial] identity" by passing as white (*Nella Larsen*, 43). His new life demands the termination of his paternal relationship to the visibly dark daughter. Consequently, the primary social parent cruelly expels the dark Nellie from the reformulated white family. Davis presents further evidence to this effect, adding that on learning of Nella Larsen's death, her sister Anna (who was only two years younger than Larsen herself) was unaware that she had a sister. Davis correctly assumes that "[i]t would appear that there was a conspiracy of silence and deception surrounding Nella Larsen's relationship not only to Anna" but to her parents as well (*Nella Larsen*, 47). I would argue that this deception seems to resonate in Helga's curious retort—"'You're not my uncle'"—to the unknown white man, after her encounter with Uncle Peter's wife (*Q* 29). Could this be a veiled rebuke directed at the historical father, also named Peter, who may have passed off his daughter Nellie Larsen as his illegitimate and partly black niece? Could the novel, signed in the surname that she and her father shared, be a veiled demand for recognition from him?

Davis aptly speculates that if Larsen's father were passing for white, "then Larsen's presentation of a dead father would be a metaphorical rendering of his death as a black person" (*Nella Larsen*, 48) and, I suggest, a decisive breach between them. Larsen lavishly repeats such ruptures in *Quicksand*, first by having Helga's father abandon her; second, by having Helga assume that her father is deceased; third, by having the white stepfather treat her cruelly; and fourth, by having Uncle Peter send her to a black school. In each instance the text separates Helga from the man who is to her an important relational object. Davis goes on to speculate that the racial alienation of Larsen's historical father further complicated his abandonment of her and undoubtedly caused her additional suffering:

> Nella Larsen's background may well have been even more traumatic than she would claim and more complicated than others could comprehend. In her version of her parentage, Nella Larsen could well have been symbolically addressing an even more grievous alienation from a father who, while passing himself, sent her off to become a completely black person. (*Nella Larsen*, 49)

But before Davis considers the implications of her speculation, she deserts the father for the more conventional designation of the mother as the child's primary relational object. Consequently, Davis abruptly shifts her focus from the passing father to the obscure white mother and designates the mother as the "central figure" in *Quicksand* without offering any justification beyond the presumption that the mother must reflect this relation to the fictive daughter (*Nella Larsen*, 255).

By contrast, I am arguing that it is the unnamed father who is *Quicksand*'s object of desire generating its plot. While I agree that the mother forms the basis of another problematic relationship for Helga, she does not ground Helga's *repressed* identification, for the text names her. This naming is evidence of less narrative repression and therefore less narrative ambivalence organizing the representation of the mother. In addition, the text does not long for the fictive mother, as Helga's numerous and conscious repudiations of the mother suggest. Whether Nella Larsen's father was her primary caretaker or merely the surrogate of her public persona is difficult to determine from the information Davis supplies. Yet it is clear that as Larsen's father, Peter Larsen would define Nella Larsen's social identity.

Helga's representation of her mother has much in common with the boy Richard's clear repudiations of his father in Wright's *Black Boy*. Both Helga and Richard harbor less ambivalence toward these respective parental imagos. For this reason Helga can name her mother and Richard can say that he hates his father. But Helga cannot name the father or recognize her desire for him. Similarly, Wright cannot consciously depict hostility toward the mother, as I discussed in Chapter 3. Just as ambivalence toward the lost mother controls Wright's fictions, desire for the lost father haunts *Quicksand*. Signifiers pertaining to him are pervasive and uncanny in the novel.

Helga's repressed desire and disavowed affection for the father determines her puzzling behavior, for when she embraces the symbolic father, figured as Reverend Green, she accomplishes exactly what Larsen's historical father attempted to effect by sending her to Fisk University—the construction of a black daughter. Hence the daughter-father plot, to invoke and revise Marianne Hirsh's term, locates a deeper basis for explaining Helga's inconstant symptoms of sexual repression, staged as the effects of the daughter's suppression of paternal identificatory love and desire for the father.

Since Helga proves incapable of constructing a coherent life story for herself as a member of the bourgeois intelligentsia, she chooses a life predetermined by religious fundamentalism. By marrying Green, she exchanges the ambiguity of her background, reflected in the "sophisticated, tuneless music" of the northern urbane, for a predictable life defined by the gospel beat of a southern, rural, folk community. Thus, she exchanges her unanchored and fragmented life of erratic movement, possibility, and uncertainty for constancy, restriction, and certitude.

Before I refer to Lacan's mirror stage to characterize further Helga's subjective development, I take a moment to comment on Larsen's depiction of the corresponding mother-daughter plot in *Passing*, her second and last published novel.[17] *Passing*, *Quicksand*'s immediate sequel (published a year later, in 1929), reveals the other half of this daughter's dilemma: her identification with, idealization of, and rivalry with the maternal imago. I suspect that Larsen's highly masked expression of repressed paternal love in *Quicksand* allowed her to write and thereby give similar expression to repressed desire for the mother in *Passing*. For the unconscious desire in this second novel is a conflict between the daughter's repressed desire to possess, idealize, and identify with the lost mother, on the one hand, and the daughter's jealousy of and hatred for her, on the other. *Quicksand* dramatizes the daughter-father pre-oedipal and oedipal plots, and *Passing* dramatizes the corresponding daughter-mother plots.

Passing begins with protagonist Irene Redfield reestablishing contact with her childhood friend Clare Kendry, whose smiling gaze at Irene is reminiscent of that of the lost mother. While Irene has a loving, responsible, and living father, Clare's father was a drunkard who was "killed in a silly saloon-fight" when Clare was fifteen, the same age Helga is when her mother dies (*P* 144; *Q* 23). Irene's mother seems to have recently died, while Clare's mother is not mentioned. The familial backgrounds of these two women set the stage for the novel's interplay of pre-oedipal and oedipal discourses. One prominent scholar identifies the relationship between Irene and Clare as homoerotic,[18] while most resist this interpretation by referring to Irene's heterosexual jealousy, staged as her unfounded suspicion that Clare is having an affair with her husband, Brian.

Irene's spoken words to Clare and internalized language about Clare is certainly sexually suggestive, but it encodes what I suspect is infantile sexuality. That is, Irene's speech delineates the daughter's desire for the lost mother by displacing it onto the (pre-oedipal) idealization and (oedipal) jealousy of Clare. As a result, Irene unconsciously alternates between the longing to possess the mother and the urge to express murderous aggression toward her. These two desires structure the text. At the novel's climax, Irene must choose whether to relinquish her ego by fusing with the always smiling mother surrogate or to preserve her individual self by repudiating Clare. Even when she chooses the latter, the text still refuses to resolve Irene's ambivalence. Not only does she still love and hate the surrogate; the ambiguous circumstances surrounding Clare's death underscore her conflict. Moreover, rather than secure Irene's mature identity, *Passing* problematizes her subjectivity by ending the story at the moment of her psychical engulfment, which the text characterizes as submersion, drowning, and darkness, much like the end of *Quicksand.*

By contrast, *Quicksand* minimizes female rivalry and displaces Helga's expression of desire for the lost father onto a chain of male signifiers rather than one father surrogate. Although the final displacement, Reverend Pleasant Green, is not "a gay suave scoundrel" (*Q* 23) and "gambler" (*Q* 21) like her father but a crude, "naive creature" (*Q* 117), their similarity becomes clear when we regard them as linguistic signifiers. Despite their physical dissimilarity, their surnames—Green and Crane—are slant rhymes, which suggests an equation between them.[19] The play of signification in the characters' names in *Quicksand* exceeds this one slant rhyme. Helga's name—Helga Crane—also splits her identity between the mother's northern European identity and the abandoning black father's name, Crane. As a signifier, the Reverend Green encodes both the deferred desire of locating the ever greater gratification of green(er) pastures as well as the final resting place. His very name, then, inscribes desire and death. Corresponding wordplay appears in *Passing.* For example, Clare Kendry is *clear kindred.* By referring to the playful naming, I want to emphasize the fact that these characters not only function as dramatic actors in the novels' respective plots; more important, they are also linguistic signifiers—in a quasi-allegorical way—of unconscious textual desire.

Whereas *Quicksand* constructs Helga Crane in terms of alienated self-specularity, *Passing* casts Irene Redfield against the mirroring ambivalence of the (m)other. Helga is virtually all specular body, as I will explain later, and Irene is virtually all voice. However, Helga's fate is even more tragic than Irene's. While both novels conclude with the protagonists' psychic deaths, Irene is "dimly conscious of strong arms lifting her up" (*P* 242). Therefore, *Passing* suggests the possibility of the reintegration of her psychic life beyond the novel's close. In addition, because *Passing* continues to report Irene's perceptions from her point of view, she remains the novel's desiring subject even though she is temporarily submerged in darkness. Thus, the narrator and Irene preserve their empathic tie at the novel's close. By contrast, the ending of *Quicksand* splits the shared perspective of the protagonist and the narrator. The wretched Helga is the object that satisfies the sadistic desire of the narrator and of Larsen as well.

With Larsen's daughter-mother and daughter-father plots characterized and separated, I return to Helga's problematic subjectivity. I understand her conflicted agency as the failure to integrate body and voice and thus as the failure of the subject to sustain an imaginary unity, by referring to Lacan's essay "The Mirror Stage as Formative of the Function of the I as Revealed in Psychoanalytic Experience." Here Lacan postulates that the infant celebrates the recognition of its own specular image. This image of the infant in the mirror not only offers a unified vision of the self, a picture of wholeness in contrast to the fragmented body discernible through self-examination, but also identifies one's unique individuality, soon to be designated by the first-person pronouns "I" and "me"—the two components of the Lacanian human subject ("Mirror Stage," 2). "I" refers to the speaking subject, which gives expression to its conscious and unconscious longings. "Me" refers to a corporeal sense of being, reflected in the specular self, and forms the narcissistic self or bodily ego.

In the context of Lacan's mirror stage, Helga's enigmatic character seems a product of a personality that fails to discern itself as distinct from its surroundings. This condition is reflected in the novel's contradictory plot. Both the story and Helga develop as the narrator manipulates her as an object of conscious political design, even while estranging her from the protest plot by unconsciously investing her in another story about her own self-division, evidenced in her reticent voice and seductive appearance. As both the object of the racial plot and the subject of this other unconscious discourse of desire, Helga's very character complicates the novel. The narrative explicitly repudiates the racial oppression that traumatized her childhood and frustrates her professional ambitions. These actions serve the novel's protest mission. Yet Helga's unconscious speaking self paradoxically implicates her sympathies with those who harbor prejudice against her. Although Helga largely adopts bourgeois sexual and racial proprieties, her highly demonstrative narcissistic bodily ego is governed not by those social codes but by a particular drive for pleasure whose origins lie in her painful childhood of racial oppression and parental neglect. As a result, these latter elements of her subjectivity create a compelling urge for sensual gratification that undermines her concern with decorum and subverts the novel's expressions of racial protest.

The opening scene of the novel, for instance, provides a stunning portrait of Helga's narcissistic bodily ego. Here Helga sits like a "small oasis in a desert of darkness . . . in a big high-backed chair, against whose tapestry her sharply cut face, with skin like yellow satin, was distinctly outlined" (Q 1–2). Helga appears as a pleasing specular image for an observer's and the narrator's gaze. This portrait calls attention to the story's reliance on visual rather than oral subjectivity for characterizing Helga. This feature undermines the novel's racial protest by entrusting its argument to her ineffectual voice and overly eroticized body.

Olsen's painting of Helga provides another instance of Helga's specularity from multiple points of view—his, hers, the text's, and ours. Although Helga rejects the portrait as not her "but some disgusting sensual creature with her features," she is compelled to stand "for a long time before it" (*Q* 90). The compulsion to stare at her portrait is reminiscent of an earlier episode on the train ride to Chicago. Here "her eyes were constantly, involuntarily straying" to the "disgusting door panel" soiled with the white man's spittle (*Q* 25). As in Lacan's description of the child who jubilantly assumes its specular image and uses it to form the "agency of the ego," Helga continues to internalize the repulsion associated with her blackness ("Mirror Stage," 2). Whereas Lacan's infant constructs its bodily ego by introjecting its unified image reflected in the mirror, Helga internalizes the disgust, loathing, and revulsion that the racist other projects onto her. The jubilation of Lacan's infant is masochistic pleasure for Helga. As a result Helga cannot resist the insistent mirrorlike surface of the "disgusting" portrait any more than she can resist the similar surface of the "disgusting" door panel. Each repeats the emphatically racialized and sexualized gaze of the racist other with whom Helga identifies.

Even though Helga rejects Olsen's portrait of herself, it compels her expression of desire. After viewing it, Helga abandons the excessive preoccupation with propriety in dress and bourgeois decorum that had dominated her character and constructs a new self-image, one that is "more charming [and] more aware of her power" (*Q* 95). This change in Helga's character challenges the traditional black feminist view that defines her as sexually repressed and reads Helga as the simple product of historical, racialized sexual oppression. Rather, Helga's new alluring self-image arises from her tremendous appetite for pleasure and an extremely meager capacity for consuming the pleasure so long sought after.[20] Much like an infant who establishes self-esteem by demanding parental recognition of exuberant behavior, Helga exhibits her elegantly attired and enticing body in search of long-overdue admiration. Yet with no prior experience of gratification, she is unable to experience the satisfaction of the recognition she craves. As a result, she becomes obsessed with desire and fashions her body with more and more seductive appeal.

If textual desire is indicative of Helga's desire, then how does Reverend Green signify gratification? The text can only perform pleasure and its prohibition; it cannot state such affects explicitly. Therefore, Helga embraces Green as both the censor and the signifier of desire.[21] Green is the last displacement for the lost object of her desire, which is unrecoverable, and for the figure of God, whom she believes to define the conditions of her life. Helga's realization that the lost object is forever unsalvageable is the novel's final tragedy, thematized in the incident in which the nurse reads Anatole France's "Procurator of Judea." The incident underscores Helga's discovery that she could not "even blame God" for her tragedy "now that she knew that He didn't exist" (*Q* 130). Like God, the lost father is for her only a fantasy.

Helga's inability to locate an external object of reproach not only conditions her dilemma but also gives expression to an indictment of Western culture. Helga's repudiation of the existence of God indicts patriarchal law, racist attitudes, and sexist convention, what Lacan calls "the Law of the Father," as an arbitrary system of social fantasies and master plots of hegemonic desire that categorically compound the adversity of women of color. This indictment recalls the suppositions of recent social theorists (like Louis Althusser and Slovoj Žižek), who repeatedly refer to "the imaginary foundations of ideology" (Elliot, *Social Theory*, 163).[22] What a culture esteems, indeed recognizes as reality, then, is always structured by and within dominant social practices and political relations, for the bodily "me" and the speaking "I" are never culturally neutral. The reflecting surface of Lacan's "mirror stage" is located in culture. Although Lacan refers to cultural rather than biological determinants in personality development, he is somewhat reticent in his articulation of cultural variables. The status quo fills that gap and undermines the revolutionary ambition of Lacanian theory.

The Last Look at Helga

I return to Olsen's portrait of Helga to emphasize how the sequence of Helga's specular images form cultural signifiers that construct meaning by displacing the fundamental lack of desire. This portrait not only represents Helga's sensual nature without the mask of sexual repression, thus anticipating her dress and manner in the storefront church; it also calls attention to another image in a scenario or what might be termed *Quicksand*'s originary scene and its repetition in the mise-en-scène. The text emphatically stages the mise-en-scène in the storefront church. It is the scene of seduction that attempts paradoxically to present and conceal the novel's unacceptable libidinal impulses.

The numerous specular images of Helga also suggest this mise-en-scène of seduction that generates her desire, and textual desire as well. Successive stagings of her body attempt to nullify her social alienation and bring the text to closure by gratifying her unconscious desire to seduce the other whose gaze rests on her body. This scene is surmisable in the sequence of these images. The first reported image depicts Helga at Naxos, where she "sat alone in her room," framed in "light and shade" (Q 1–2). This scene suggests her unspecified longing by referring to its gratification in "forgetfulness, complete mental relaxation, rest from thought of any kind. . . . [S]he wanted an even more soothing darkness" (Q 2–3). The scene initiates the succession of images of Helga, and it is reminiscent of her "own childish self-effacement" during the numerous ugly family arguments about Helga's racial heritage (Q 23). This self-effacement is also repeated in the episode at the Negro Episcopal church in Chicago, where Helga projects "the self-sufficient uninterested manner adopted instinctively as a protective measure for her acute sensitiveness" (Q 34).

After her fateful pregnancy, representations of Helga's effacement—"[s]ilent and listless"—abound in the novel's final pages. One memorable instance recalls that

[n]othing penetrated the kind darkness into which her bruised spirit had retreated. . . . While she had gone down into that appalling blackness of pain, the ballast of her brain had got loose and she hovered for a long time somewhere in that delightful borderland on the edge of unconsciousness, an enchanted and blissful place where peace and incredible quiet encompassed her. (Q 127–28)

Helga wants "to linger forever in that serene haven," but consciousness returns (Q 128). Reprieve is only temporary, as "she sought refuge in sleep" (Q 131). At the novel's close, though, Helga again seeks an emotional retreat, this time instigated by Green's gaze:

Reluctantly he [Green] went from the room with a *last* look at Helga, who was lying on her back with one frail, pale hand under her small head, her curly black hair scattered loose on the pillow. She regarded him from behind dropped lids. The day was hot, her breasts were covered only by a nightgown of filmy *crepe*, a relic of prematrimonial days, which had slipped from one carved shoulder. He flinched. Helga's petulant lip curled, for she well knew that this fresh reminder of her desirability was like the flick of a whip. (Q 129; emphasis added)

From Green's perspective, this scene suggests Helga's sexual desirability, thereby implying that she is the object of Green's desire. But Helga herself longs to retire to the serene haven where her inner self could again become detached from her material body. This "enchanted and blissful place" would satisfy her longing of the opening scene: "She wanted forgetfulness, complete mental relaxation, rest from thought from any kind. . . . [S]he wanted an even more soothing darkness" (Q 2, 3). Trying to fulfill this desire has caused her frantic movement throughout the novel, all the while displaying her specular body.

Although we do not see Helga after the bedroom scene, the text implies that she did not remain inactive. While Green's gaze in the quoted passage has suggested to many readers that Helga is a passive victim of male sexual oppression, the novel does not corroborate this reading, for Helga has been the sexual aggressor. We should remember that she seduced him before the marriage, and it is her desire that the text portrays as irrational and all-consuming: "Emotional, palpitating, amorous, all that was living in her sprang like rank weeds at the tingling thought of night, with a vitality so strong that it devoured all shoots of reason" (Q 122). Indeed, the novel has often commented on Helga's looking and feeling like the "veritable savage" (Q 69). She is, as the text insists, "[c]harming, yes. But insufficiently, civilized. Impulsive. Imprudent. Selfish" (Q 91). By repeatedly foregrounding her desire as irrational, unpredictable, and reckless, the text anticipates Helga's irrational and final pursuit of a man whom she later says she hates, a pursuit staged as a performance of desire and repudiation.

At *Quicksand*'s close, her frantic mobility terminates. The last time we see Helga's now very still specular body, we cannot fail to notice that she is even more provocatively dressed in the filmy nightgown than in the "clinging red dress" of the storefront church episode (Q 112). The "filmy crepe" nightgown is curious sickbed apparel. Yet the text's accentuation of the word "crepe" signifies the death and mourning associated with the text's unconscious desire. Peculiar language again inscribes the unconscious. Helga's red attire in the storefront church has foreshadowed her initial seduction of Reverend Green; the filmy nightgown of her final appearance anticipates a repeat performance. In the first instance the seduction is elided in the space between the last sentence of one paragraph—as Helga "pressed her fingers deep into his arms until a wild look had come into his slightly bloodshot eyes"—and the beginning of the next, which announces "[t]he next morning" (Q 116). The elision between these paragraphs is repeated in the last two of the novel.

The gratification of desire occurs in the gap, and the text implies its consequence to be fatal. While readers have understood Helga's death as a racial and sexual tragedy, the text portrays her death as the event for which the text longs, the event that produces "an enchanted and blissful place" (Q 128), a place of "forgetfulness, complete mental relaxation, rest from thought of any kind," "an even more soothing darkness," a womb- or tomblike place where desire no longer exists (Q 2, 3).

What feminist critics have recognized as the symptoms of Helga's sexual repression have a more primary origin in an incestuous impulse that the text paradoxically conceals and reveals. When she finally embraces this last signifier of the lost father, she fulfills the desire of the text, if not her own. Experiencing the irrational pleasure of embracing the symbolized black father by means of Reverend Green ultimately means that Helga must desire and repudiate Green's physical abhorrence as well as reject her mother's whiteness, while still sharing her "corporeal contiguity with her own mother" (Grosz, "Body of Signification," 96). The text stages these conflicting acts of self-repudiation and self-affirmation by having Helga induce her own death in childbirth.

In the final three lines of the novel, the narrator withdraws Helga's body from view and grants her desire for absolute fulfillment, "an impossible plenitude" (Grosz, *Jacques Lacan*, 62). Helga's desire is filled by that of the narrator, and such fullness "paradoxically entails [Helga's] own annihilation, for it demands a fullness of the other to stop up the lack that conditions [her] existence as a subject" (Grosz, *Jacques Lacan*, 62). This lack is filled by the change in narrative perspective and by the displacement of Helga's prolonged wound with her plentiful but deadly womb. Helga fills the womb and the demand of the other inscribed in the narrator's new perspective. Helga is the narrator's gratifying masochistic object and probably Larsen's therapeutic sacrifice. Now that the unconscious demand of textual desire has been consummated through Helga's last impregnation, all narrative desire is gratified. But we resist an identification with the text's repeated associations of pleasure with sleep, indeed death, even from the very first scene. The text dramatizes the paradox of subjectivity by defining endless pleasure as death.

CHAPTER FIVE

Mourning, Humor, and Reparation

Detecting the Joke in *Seraph on the Suwanee,* by Zora Neale Hurston

JIM MERCHANT is always in good humor—even with his wife. He says he fell in love with her at first sight. That was some years ago. She has had all her teeth pulled out, but they still get along splendidly.

He says the first time he called on her he found out that she was subject to fits. This didn't cool his love, however. She had several in his presence.

One Sunday, while he was there, she had one, and her mother tried to give her a dose of turpentine to stop it. Accidentally, she spilled it in her eye and it cured her. She never had another fit, so they got married and have kept each other in good humor ever since.

—Zora Neale Hurston, "Turpentine Love,"
from "The Eatonville Anthology" (1926)

I HAVE BEEN AMAZED by the Anglo-Saxon's lack of curiosity about the internal lives and emotions of the Negroes.

—Zora Neale Hurston, "What White Publishers Won't Print" (1950)

I wrote "Their Eyes Were Watching God" in Haiti. It was dammed up in me, and I wrote it under internal pressure in seven weeks. I wish that I could write it again. In fact, I regret all my books.

—Zora Neale Hurston, *Dust Tracks on a Road* (1942)

Reading the Playful Judgment of *Seraph*

In "Books and Things" in *Dust Tracks on a Road* (1942), Zora Neale Hurston expressed her desire to rewrite *Their Eyes Were Watching God* (1937), the novel that critics castigated during her lifetime and began to applaud two decades after her death. Published in 1948, eleven years after *Their Eyes, Seraph on the Suwanee* was probably the product of that revisionary ambition.[1] But unlike *Their Eyes, Seraph* has never enchanted its readers. In this novel Hurston returned to the topic that claimed her lifelong interest—probing "what makes a man or a woman do such-and-so, regardless of his [or her] color" (*DT* 151). Hurston's reference to skin color is especially pertinent to *Seraph* because here the man and woman are character-ized as white.

Like *Their Eyes* and Hurston's first novel, *Jonah's Gourd Vine* (1934), *Seraph* in-vestigates the nature of erotic love. This objective seems to have originated in Hurston's wish to know how her father felt about her mother when she died, a wish Hurston records in *Dust Tracks* (64–65). Her need for erotic knowledge was undoubtedly intensified by her own disappointments with love and matched only by her need to absolve her guilt for failing to fulfill her promise to her dying mother and be her voice. Although Hurston never discovered her father's feelings at that fateful moment and evidently never experienced an enduring love affair, she repeatedly used fiction to probe the complexity of heterosexual attachment and loss. In *Seraph*, she returns to this topic by imagining the conditions of ulti-mate romantic fulfillment. In what seems to be an act of self-consolation, Hurston also depicts the fictive daughter of this novel gratifying her mother's dying wish.

In *Dust Tracks*, Hurston confesses that *Their Eyes* is the product of one special experience with love as well as a work that she specifically regretted. "It is one of the tragedies of life," she explains in *Dust Tracks*, "that one cannot have all the wis-dom one is ever to possess in the beginning" (155). This general complaint does not identify a specific defect in wisdom in this novel. Yet when we examine the ef-fort of the novel's central character, Janie Crawford, to define love, we find that she offers little substantial information. In fact, when *Their Eyes* does not altogether efface Janie's observations on love, it presents erotic knowledge by means of provocative though mystifying imagery rather than lucid language. For example, at the novel's close Janie tells her friend Phoebe, "'Love is lak de sea. It's uh movin' thing, but still and all, it takes its shape from de shore it meets, and it's different with every shore.'" "'Two things,'" she adds, "'everybody's got tuh do fuh theyselves. They got tuh go tuh God, and they got tuh find out about livin' fuh theyselves'" (*TE* 182, 183). The flowery but imprecise prose suggests that like Janie, Hurston is more successful at describing desire than its gratification. No doubt Hurston later realized that many of the charming expressions characterizing love in *Their Eyes* are somewhat obscure. With the wisdom of an additional decade, Hurston set out to "write it again" (*DT* 155). When she finished *Seraph*, she had written a story that explicitly analyzes the bondage of romantic passion, a form of sexual love that her epoch particularly idealized in stories of female submission.

While *Seraph* examines female desire, much like *Jonah's Gourd Vine* and *Their Eyes*, it often does so by inverting many of the discourses of these earlier novels. *Seraph* is a story about female desire gratified. Unlike Isis and Lucy Pearson of *Jonah's Gourd Vine* and Janie Crawford of *Their Eyes*, who are rural, black south-erners, Arvay Henson of *Seraph* is the daughter of a poor white "Cracker from way back" (*S* 8). She is also what Lucy Pearson, the fictive mother in *Jonah's Gourd Vine*, refuses to be and what Hurston does not permit Janie to become—a fool for love. Yet Arvay does not suffer the "resounding smack" that further taints Lucy's love for her husband, John, or the "two or three face slaps" that Tea Cake gives Janie "to show he was boss" (*Jonah,* 129; *TE* 140). In fact, Arvay "slapped Jim's [her future husband's] face with all her might and main" without the physical retaliation that Hurston received on a similar occasion from A. W. P., the love of her life (*S* 17; *DT* 188). Arvay also does not have to tolerate a philandering husband like Lucy Pearson does. In addition, the social privilege of Jim's whiteness—combined with his congeniality, discipline, and hard work—allow him to provide for some two decades the material comfort for Arvay that Lucy never experiences and Janie does not especially value. Lucy's death ends twenty years of turbulent marriage in *Jonah's Gourd Vine.* In *Their Eyes* Joe Starks's death terminates twenty years of oppressive wedlock for Janie and frees her to achieve mutual, conjugal pleasure with Tea Cake. But Tea Cake's early death cuts their pleasure short. *Their Eyes* is like a pretty love song about romantic desire; *Seraph* is a veritable treatise on heterosexual love, but a treatise with a twist.

More so than Hurston's other novels, *Seraph* depends on rhetorical and dramatic jest to construct textual meaning. The novel suggests that a jesting rapport is a therapeutic means for working through conjugal conflict because it engenders mutual recognition. This is the erotic dynamic found in *Their Eyes*—indeed, the very model of intersubjective gratification that feminist psychoanalysts like Jessica Benjamin endorse. *Their Eyes* depicts this tactic by relying on the narrative structure of the romantic quest and by internalizing verbal jesting as a minor discursive element. When read against Hurston's other novels, *Seraph* appears as a text of contradictory stories that produces coherent meaning only when we detect its jesting nature. *Seraph,* then, is structured as an extended joke. Indeed, there are two basic jokes in this novel, literally composed of verbal jest: one about whiteness and another about female submission to romantic passion. Both jokes deliver "a *playful* judgement," to invoke Freud, that is trivial or tendentious, depending on the disposition of the listener (*Jokes,* 10).

Hurston's expansive use of humor has invited others to make similar observations. In a recent biographical essay on Hurston, Craig Werner argues that *Seraph* "requires a special reading" and "an ability to understand the shifting, masked nature of black humorous traditions" to reveal "the novel's narrative strategy" ("Zora Neale Hurston," 259). Werner refers to Hurston's "use of stereotypical masks to deflect attention away from subversive subtexts" and to create "a dense and shifting rhetorical texture that challenges readers to abandon preconceptions concerning the desirability of a unified or theoretically consistent narrative voice" ("Zora Neale Hurston," 230–31). He also argues that applications of Freudian psychology to Arvay's personality has "contribute[d] directly to a crucial misreading of the significance of African American tradition in the novel" ("Zora Neale Hurston," 230). In *Jump at the Sun: Zora Neale Hurston's Cosmic Comedy,* John Lowe cites Werner's observations as he examines the novel's discursive processes and multiple levels of humor by referring to Mikhail Bakhtin's theory about the spurious cultural inversions of the carnivalesque masquerade. Lowe, though, shifts his focus from Bakhtin's theory to a Freudian analysis of Arvay's personality. Such a reading distracts Lowe from the goal both he and Werner seek—a reading strategy that frames *Seraph*'s black folk humor and sees beyond its "conventional white surface of reality" ("Zora Neale Hurston," Werner, 231), a surface that seems to be a part of Hurston's concession to the patriarchal demands for female submission.[2]

Hurston's use of jest in *Seraph* troubles its conservative, white, bourgeois love story with cunning critiques of racial segregation and female idealization of romantic submission. Thus, if readers focus on the novel's explicit plot, *Seraph* seems to support the dominant culture's presumptions about whiteness and patriarchal virtue. The literal meaning of the hero's surname "Meserve"—"me serve" or "serve me"—underscores the demand for Arvay's obsequiousness, for attending to Jim Meserve's needs is Arvay's most consistent objective. But if we probe *Seraph*'s transgression of the expected black social setting and its repudiation of the masochistic female desire that sustains patriarchal constructions of romantic love, we will find that a more subversive story emerges from the novel's conservative surface. This new story censures binary constructions of race and reveals the death of female desire in the fulfillment of romantic love. Thus, the text undermines the conservative plot by subverting or carnivalizing the racial and gender politics that the plot explicitly supports.[3] As a result, *Seraph* is both conservative and revolutionary.

Readers have tended to miss *Seraph*'s guile by failing to detect its complex jest. Rather than probe this anomalous novel's conspicuous contradictions, prior readers have tended to assume that Hurston exchanged the celebration of freedom, desire, and self-definition in *Their Eyes* and *Jonah's Gourd Vine* for erotic bondage in *Seraph*. Just as *Their Eyes* had a special purpose, "to embalm all the tenderness" of Hurston's passion for A. W. P., so too did *Seraph*. This last published novel allowed Hurston to circumvent both the inability of white publishers to fathom middle-class black characters and their lack of curiosity about the internal lives of black people in general. *Seraph* was also Hurston's calculated effort to make some money, for with *Seraph* she tried to please a white popular audience and herself as well by conspicuously constructing *and* subtly deconstructing the novel's white, patriarchal, erotic narrative with a couple of canny jokes about the dominant culture's ideal of female desire and its conflation of race and class.

Seraph's anomalous whiteness and female investment in masochistic desire are textual enigmas that complicate this novel. By using psychoanalysis, a strategy specifically devoted to interpreting concealed meaning, I attempt to unveil these enigmas so as to construct the meaning of this text. Psychoanalysis allows me to establish a dialectic between *Seraph*'s explicit surface meaning and its implicit deep meaning, in much the same way that the human psyche constructs intelligible performance by mediating between its conscious and unconscious desire. By seeing a correspondence between the structure of *Seraph* and the organization of the mind (Brooks, "Idea," 24–25), we can regard the discourses of *Seraph* as functioning like the conscious, preconscious, and unconscious domains of the psyche.

By extending this argument, I will consider the novel's explicit and implicit features as analogous to those of Freudian "joke-work," which explains how the joke moves from bewilderment (the unconscious) to illumination (consciousness) through the act of telling it. Like Freud's understanding of the tendentious joke, *Seraph* has similar functions: to evoke pleasure in ourselves and our listeners by exploiting "something ridiculous in our enemy which we could not, on account of obstacles in the way, bring forward openly or consciously." Thus, "the jokes *will evade restrictions and open sources of pleasure that have become inaccessible*" (Freud, *Jokes*, 103; original emphasis). By using joke-work, Hurston repeatedly critiqued the dominant understanding of race and female desire in her writings. *Seraph* is the culmination of this endeavor.

According the Freud, "jokes are formed in the first person" as "*a preconscious thought is given over for a moment to unconscious revision and the outcome of this is at once grasped by conscious perception*" (*Jokes*, 166; original emphasis). *Seraph's* joke about whiteness is the bewildering discourse; it is a part of the text's preconscious, undergoing revision in the novel's unconscious. Its unconscious is constitutive of stylistic language and structural elements. Although jesting, or what Freud called joke-work, and unconscious discourses make use of the same structural devices of condensation, indirect representation, and displacement, in jokes "the techniques are explicit and overt and their opposition to accepted modes of conscious thought [is] clearly recognizable" (Oring, *Jokes of Sigmund Freud*, 7). The pleasure of the fully formed joke results from its circumventing the censor of consciousness to express a prohibited thought. In contrast to striving for intelligibility, like the joke, the unconscious discourses paradoxically seek and elude expression. For this reason they are more heavily veiled.

Freudian psychoanalytic tenets about compulsive repetition can also help us to identify *Seraph's* recurring sentence—"I can read your writing"—as the inscription of the text's unstated desire that directs my reading of *Seraph's* textual enigmas.[4] This sentence discloses Jim's ability to detect Arvay's desire despite her sexually repressed behavior. This sentence also identifies the demand that Arvay fulfills at the novel's close when she accurately interprets Jim's concealed desire beneath his jesting, defensive behavior. Most important, though, this sentence insinuates the demand that we carefully examine *Seraph's* textuality, which, like Jim's joking behavior, is not transparent. By realizing that *Seraph* is a carnivalesque text of tendentious, subversive jest, we can mediate the incongruity of the novel's plot, surface elements, and rhetorical features to clarify the novel's social critique. In psychoanalytic literary terms, we can interpret the novel's meaning not only by reading its conscious or explicit plot and dialogue but also by deciphering its unconscious discourses of desire. Like Arvay, however, we readers will have to sweat because *Seraph* refuses to deliver its meaning in any simple way.

Despite Hurston's tremendous popularity over the last two decades, *Seraph* has remained a problematic novel, indeed an anomaly in Hurston's canon and in African American literary scholarship. I hope to dispute this view by demonstrating that *Seraph* offers a critique of fixed racial identities and patriarchy by making these themes the butt of its jokes. Psychoanalysis gives us a model for uncovering this critique; it helps us to clarify the meanings of the novel's enigmatic whiteness and its depiction of female masochism. Before I continue my discussion about how this jesting text deconstructs female masochism and racial purity, I need to outline the plot of this marginal novel and contextualize the incidents that form the novel's denouement.

Seraph begins in 1905 in Sawley, a poor white Florida town whose life "streamed out from the sawmill and the 'teppentime' still" and concludes around 1927 at sea, off the western coast of the state (*S* 1). The opening incident portrays the whole town's amusement in watching Jim Meserve "scorch" the peculiar Arvay Henson. The vernacular expression—"scorch"—is particularly appropriate in this case for describing the local courting ritual because it suggests the intensity of Jim's ardor and Arvay's resistance. Jim is a young, bold, and handsome stranger with "Black Irish in his ancestry somewhere" (*S* 7). Although he arrives in Sawley with only a small bundle, his ancestors had been plantation owners before the Civil War. According to the narrator, who reveals Arvay's thoughts, "[t]his was the prettiest man that she had ever laid eyes on . . . no common Cracker boy whatsoever" (*S* 24). On first seeing Arvay, Jim is sure that "[s]he just suited him . . . and was worth the trouble of breaking in" (*S* 8). However, Arvay believes that "this pretty, laughing fellow was far out of her reach," since she "was born to take other people's leavings" (*S* 24). To make matters worse, Arvay also suffers guilt from secretly "living in mental adultery with her sister's husband," Reverend Carl Middleton (*S* 34). Five years earlier she had developed a crush on him. When he married her sister Larraine, however, whose robust manner and appearance everyone, including her parents, preferred to Arvay's slight form and timid manner, Arvay concealed her hurt feelings by "turning from the world" with "religious fervor" and thus unconsciously repressing her sexual desire by developing hysterical convulsions (*S* 3).

In record time Jim proposes to Arvay, and she accepts even though she expects him to jilt her. Her insecurity makes her behavior contradictory and causes Jim to think she has insufficient love for him. To remedy this dilemma, two weeks before their wedding day, Jim rapes Arvay and marries her immediately afterward without coercion. Arvay does not realize that this scenario is Jim's attempt to show his satisfaction with her and to bind her to him. She merely concludes that his extravagant charity causes him to marry her. Their failure to recognize their mutual insecurities binds them in a sadomasochistic cycle of sexual aggression and submission, which the rape foreshadows. This defensive pattern of sexual attachment defines their marriage for more than twenty years.

Their first child, Earl, probably conceived during the rape, is retarded and slightly deformed. His abnormality suggests Hurston's censure of the rape. Weak and fearful of almost everything, he projects Arvay's insecurity. Even though she and Jim have two more children, Angeline and James Kenneth—called Angie and Kenny—who are not just normal but smart, very good-looking, and self-confident, Arvay devotes most of her energy to Earl, as her penance for "the way [she] used to be" (*S* 69). Because she cannot recognize her own virtues or appreciate her pretty appearance, she regards Earl as her child, while perceiving Angie and Kenny as Jim's children. When Earl is about eighteen, he sexually assaults a neighbor girl and is killed in an attempt to escape. Earl's death frees Arvay of one guilty burden.

During the marriage, Jim pushes his family up the social ladder. He moves Arvay away from Sawley to "Citrabelle, a bright-looking flowery town," and takes on a number of jobs, some legal, some not (*S* 72). Eventually, he becomes an entrepreneur in the citrus fruit business. Although Arvay enjoys the financial security of Jim's ambition, she recognizes neither his motive nor his struggle to succeed. Entrenched in the passive-masochistic role of sexual submission, she cannot be confident of Jim's love. After Angie marries and Kenny goes to college, Arvay is relieved of most of her domestic duties. With more time to reflect, she has more opportunity to justify her lack of esteem and to fantasize about Jim's abandoning her. According to her reasoning, she would then be free to return to her kind of folk in Sawley and live in confidence. Frustrated by Arvay's defensive behavior, Jim devotes more and more time to developing a shrimping business that takes him out of town. He also tries to invigorate the marriage by performing a stunt with a rattlesnake, but like his effort to bind Arvay to him with rape, all he ends up doing is terrifying her. This final failure convinces him that he must do something desperate if Arvay is to renounce her "stand-still, hap-hazard kind of love" (*S* 262). He decides to leave her. Though he will support her indefinitely, he gives her one year to surrender passivity for "a knowing and a doing love" to save their marriage (*S* 262).

Before Arvay can plan a course of action, she receives a telegram from her sister, stating that their mother is ill. Her mother's illness, which Arvay initially believes is not fatal, overshadows her "happy anticipation" of returning to Sawley. In her mind "[t]he corroding poverty of her childhood became a glowing virtue, and a state to be desired" (*S* 272). This idealization allows her to deny the pain of Jim's abandonment. Instead, she imagines that she will leave him by returning to Sawley. When Arvay arrives at her former home, her idealization confronts reality. Her sister Larraine is a "ton of coarse-looking flesh," Carl is a "drab creature," and their daughters are "mule-faced and ugly enough" (*S* 274, 275, 276). If the Middletons' appearances and the dilapidated childhood home, with its odor of rat urine, are insufficient to make Arvay consider her life with Jim a tremendous improvement, the invectives of Arvay's dying mother, Maria Henson, sharpens the comparison. She tells Arvay, "'You and Jim sure is raised your chaps to be nice and kind.' 'Tain't that a'way with Larraine nor none of her whelps.'" She and Carl, Maria insists, are just "'like turkey buzzards'" (*S* 280, 278).

In Arvay's presence, her mother confesses a lifetime of unfulfilled desire. Moments before she dies, Maria makes a deathbed request. She asks to be "'put away nice'" on Sunday "'with a heap of flowers on my coffin and a church full of folks marching around to say me farewell.'" Arvay assures her that she can put her "dying dependence" in her (*S* 280). When Carl learns that his mother-in-law is dead, he rudely refuses to take any responsibility for Maria's funeral. But knowing that she has the means to fulfill her mother's request, Arvay does not cower but retorts, "'I come prepared to do whatever was necessary to be done. I got a *husband*! He covers the ground he stands on. He ain't never let me know what a hard day means'" (*S* 284; emphasis in original). Her reference to Jim identifies the source of her presumed independence and makes Carl angry. Shortly thereafter, she learns that Carl has been jealous of Jim and resentful of her marriage for years. Back when Arvay had a crush on him, he had actually preferred Arvay to Larraine, but Larraine conspired to redirect his attention to herself. "But for 'Raine's intervention," Arvay now realizes, she might have been married to Carl. "Been the mother of those awful-looking young men and women that he had fathered. Had to get in the bed with something like that! Do, Jesus!" (*S* 289). Her latter remark repeats Janie's judgment on Logan Killicks, when she says that "'some folks never was meant to be loved and he's one of 'em'" (*TE* 22).

By keeping her "sacred promise" to her mother, Arvay nourishes her self-confidence, and "[s]he came away from her mother's funeral changed inside" (*S* 297, 298). This climatic event makes Arvay realize she has "sense enough to appreciate what [Jim has] done, and [is] still trying to do for [her]" (*S* 309). Consequently, she resolves to try to get Jim back. Arvay soon joins Jim on board his shrimp boat, named the *Arvay Henson*. She displays her courage and tells him how proud she is of him. To say that he is glad to welcome Arvay is an understatement. While the final incident depicts the gratification of their sexual desire, the narrative does not end with depictions of erotic pleasure. Through indirect discourse, the text reveals that Arvay at last perceives the insecurity behind Jim's aggressive mask. She sees that on the "[i]nside he was nothing but a little boy to take care of, and he hungered for her hovering" (*S* 351). She realizes that she was just as unaware of his inner self as she had been of her own ability.

The final words of the novel describe Arvay meeting "the look of the sun with confidence. Yes, she was doing what the big light had told her to do. She was serving and meant to serve. She made the sun welcome to come on in, then snuggled down again beside her husband" (*S* 352). This ending suggests that Hurston is offering her readers the conventional notion of conjugal happiness by regarding a woman as a mother figure for her husband. This entreaty may be just another instance of Hurston's often-cited and puzzling political conservatism (Hemenway, *Zora Neale Hurston*, 333–37). For unlike Janie, who is neither wife nor mother at the close of *Their Eyes*, *Seraph* seems to endorse the ever popular, essentialized viewpoint of woman as perpetual mother. Yet by redefining the object of maternal desire as the husband instead of the child, Hurston subverts this reductive position and its patriarchal authority by infantilizing the man. This displacement, as Nancy Chodorow argues, does not simply reproduce mothering but also reproduces and complicates heterosexual eroticism.

By using a combination of Freudian and Lacanian psychoanalytic theory, I detect the social critique beneath *Seraph*'s surface whiteness and Arvay's romantic servility. These surface features form the novel's conscious discourses of desire. Its corresponding unconscious and preconscious discourses construct the novel's critique. While I will fully explain my methodology as I proceed, at this point in my discussion I need briefly to define these forms of textual desire. By *unconscious desire*, I mean the novel's insinuation of unstated demands and longings inscribed in rhetorical features of the text. *Preconscious desire* refers to similar longings that become explicit in the narrative, like the punch line of a joke. Because the pleasure of the text terminates in gratification at its closure, the last incident intimates the objects of conscious and unconscious desire.

At *Seraph*'s close Arvay confidently assumes the role of the omnipotent mother. This feature presents a clue about the novel's unconscious pleasure, though we do not yet know the specific desire that this pleasurable event gratifies. But before addressing this dilemma, I return to two pronouncements that recur in Hurston's writings: first, her confession that her writings inscribe her observations about the experience of love, and second, her repeated references to the daughter's desire to fulfill the mother's dying wish, the desire that *Seraph* gratifies.

Seraph not only draws on Hurston's personal observations about the slavery of love; it also presents a critique of the orthodox Freudian viewpoint about masochism "as an expression of feminine nature" ("Economic Problem," 257), a perspective with which Hurston was undoubtedly familiar. As John Lowe explains, "Freud was a favorite topic during the Harlem Renaissance and in New York intellectual society in general during the twenties and thirties" (*Jump*, 271). "Hurston's mentor Boas," Lowe adds, "no doubt introduced her to Freud as early as the twenties, but other friends like Van Vechten were aficionados as well" (*Jump*, 273).

Ironically, just when Freud began to question his established views on female subjectivity in "Female Sexuality" (1931) by proposing "that the pre-Oedipus phase in women is more important than we have hitherto supposed" (253), Helene Deutsch and Marie Bonaparte, his major female proponents, endorsed his earlier presumption of the inherent basis of female masochism.[5] This endorsement further standardized female masochism as the expression of female sexuality. *Seraph* reflects what seems to be Hurston's interrogation of this presumption.

Deutsch's "Significance of Masochism in the Mental Life of Women" and "Female Sexuality" appeared respectively, in 1930 and 1933, and Bonaparte published "Passivity, Masochism and Femininity" in 1935. There was persistent resistance in psychoanalytic circles to the passive-masochistic construction of female personality during this period, but when Deutsch published her two-volume study *The Psychology of Women* in 1944 and 1947, respectively, she made this construct the normative behavioral model for (white) women. In "Feminine Masochism," Deutsch partly documented this contention by referring to her clinical work, in which she found that girls at puberty repeatedly reveal masochistic rape fantasies involving their mental constructions of their fathers. According to Deutsch, the fantasies usually have two parts. The masochistic rape fantasy produces the sexual tension, and the ensuing sexual encounter provides the unconscious "delights of being loved and desired" by the internalized father (255).

Other psychoanalysts, principally Karen Horney and Melanie Klein, question Deutsch's failure to examine the cultural implications of her construction of female personality. But during the decade of the 1940s, Deutsch's contention that passive-masochistic rape fantasies were constitutive of female desire held sway ("Feminine Masochism," 239–78). As Karen Horney explains, Deutsch's model of female personality promotes the belief that "[w]hat the woman secretly desires in intercourse is rape and violence" ("Problem," 215). This construct also endorses "the naive, dependent, childlike, self-abnegating model of femininity" and bolstered the patriarchal privilege of U.S. (white) servicemen returning to civilian life after World War II (Honey, *Creating Rosie*, 1–2). No wonder Deutsch achieved popularity in U.S. culture during the late 1940s and 1950s.

Although we do not need to know that the Freudian construction of female passive masochism was the orthodox model of female subjectivity at the time Hurston wrote *Seraph* to recognize Arvay's masochistic disposition, such knowledge helps us contextualize the novel's argument. For most of her marriage, Arvay deludes herself with the impression that all she need do to fulfill her marital responsibility is to be a submissive wife. For her, this is a deadly serious obligation that renders her unable to detect Jim's jokes because she habitually sees herself as their butt. To use Arvay's own words, she feels "like a fool at a funeral" (*S* 18; I will return to this curious expression). Jim supplies the other half of this model; he is the active sadist of this dyad. Their unconscious devotion to sadomasochistic love undermines their marriage by scripting their oppressive sexual roles. Although they are aware that something is missing from their marriage—a mutual understanding—they do not know how to achieve it.

Seraph rejects the passive-masochistic construction of normative female personality by demanding that Arvay act in her own best interest with confidence, courage, and most of all with humor. At the end of the novel, she tells Jim, "'I ain't near so dumb as I used to be. I can read your writing. Actions speak louder than words'" (*S* 347). She emphasizes the wisdom of her hard-won lessons by further insisting, "'Just lemme tell you one thing more, Jim. You—I want you to overlook how dumb I used to be. But, Jim, I just wasn't wise of things. Like Mama used to say, being dumb never kilt nobody. All it did was to make you sweat, and Jim, since I've been with you, I done sweated mightily'" (*S* 348). Arvay saves her marriage by learning how to read Jim's writing—that is, how to interpret the incongruity between his actions and words in order to construct coherent meaning about the nature of his character. This she does by coming to appreciate Jim's jesting nature and by learning to jest in return so as to negotiate a space for both her desire and pleasure. In a like manner, to construct *Seraph*'s meaning, we readers must also come to appreciate the jesting textuality of this novel—its subtle, silenced, and often subversive meaning masked by its teasing signs.

Arvay acquires the confidence jesting requires by gratifying her dying mother's wish. *Seraph* thus depicts the daughter's success in keeping her promise to the dying mother, while failure marks the daughter's similar efforts in *Jonah's Gourd Vine* and *Dust Tracks*. In these latter works Hurston claims her failure to execute her mother's last wishes by repeating the death scene as if to convince herself of the impossibility of carrying out the promised task. In *Jonah's Gourd Vine*, Hurston fictionalizes this event:

> They had turned Lucy's bed so that her face was to the East. . . . Great drops of sweat stood out on her forehead and trickled upon the quilt and Isis saw a pool of sweat standing in a hollow at the elbow. She was breathing hard, and Isis saw her set eyes fasten on her as she came into the room. She thought that she tried to say something to her as she stood over her mother's head, weeping with her heart.
>
> "Get her head offa dat pillow!" Mattie Mosely ordered. "Let her head down so she kin die easy."
>
> Hoyt Thomas moved to do it, but Isis objected. "No, no, don't touch her pillow! Mama don't want de pillow from under her head!"
>
> "Hush Isie!" Emmeline chided, "and let mama die easy. You makin' her suffer."
>
> "Naw, naw! she said *not* tuh!" As her father pulled her away from her place above Lucy's head, Isis thought her mother's eyes followed her and she strained her ears to catch her words. But none came. (132–33)

Isis's resistance to her community's death ritual literally makes her "look like a fool at a funeral," to invoke *Seraph*'s curious description for being the butt of a joke (18). Perhaps this phrase verbalizes Hurston's own feelings when she attempted to execute her mother's wishes, feelings that she had to acknowledge before she could imagine their gratification in fiction.

Dust Tracks recalls rather than dramatizes this mortifying event by explaining that Hurston's father "restrained [her] physically from outraging the ceremonies established for the dying" (64). While the text does not use the word "fool" to describe the thwarted effort of the nine-year-old Hurston, it does characterize her acute feelings of dejection, resulting from her failure:

> I was old before my time with grief of loss, of failure, and of remorse. No matter what the others did, my mother had put her trust in me. She had felt that I could and would carry out her wishes, and I had not. . . . I failed her. *It seemed as she died that the sun went down on purpose to flee away from me.* (*DT* 64–65; my emphasis)

Equally important in describing Hurston's acute despair is her connecting the failed promise to the need to read her father's feelings, which the text cites:

> But she [Hurston's mother] looked at me, or so I felt, to speak for her. She depended on me for a voice. . . . If there is any consciousness after death, I hope that Mama knows that I did my best. She must know how I have suffered for my failure. . . . Mama died at sundown and changed a world. That is, the world which had been built out of her body and her heart. Even the physical aspects fell apart with the suddenness that was startling. . . . I have often wished I had been old enough at the time to look into Papa's heart that night. If I could know what that moment meant to him, I could have set my compass toward him and been sure. (*DT* 64–65)

The repetition of this incident in Hurston's works indicates its centrality in her life. In fact, this may be one trauma that she attempts to defeat with the jesting humor that characterized her life. For humor, as Freud recognized, defends the ego by deflecting painful assault. This traumatic incident may also have engendered Hurston's devotion to investigating the dynamics of heterosexual relationships and recording rural black folklore, itself steeped in defensive humor, for these two interests dominated her life and work.

The representations of the mother's death in *Jonah's Gourd Vine* and *Dust Tracks* reveal Hurston's recollection that the failed promise not only disappointed her mother but also profoundly disillusioned her own childhood fantasy of grandiosity. Prior to her mother's death, as Hurston recalls in both works, she reveled in imposing fantasies about her childhood feats. For example, she recalls in *Dust Tracks* that the moon had been her own private playmate, following her "like a pretty puppy dog" (26). She also refers to her amazing talent to delight white travelers. They almost always invited her to "ride up the road for perhaps a half mile" (*DT* 43). Most important, though, Hurston exults in being "Mama's baby." But on the day of her mother's death, this favorite child could not fulfill her mother's wish. Hurston "set [her] will against [her] father, the village dames and village custom," but she lost this battle of wills (*DT* 22, 63). Not only does she lose her mother to death; she also imagines a corresponding loss of the sun to express her devastation, for as Hurston reports in *Dust Tracks*, "the sun went down on purpose to flee away from [this unworthy daughter] me" (65).

Common sense should have told the dying woman that a nine-year-old child could not possibly intercede on her behalf and forestall the execution of the local death rituals. Perhaps this demand was not the mother's expectation but an expression of the daughter's resistance to her mother's death. After all, *Jonah's Gourd Vine* and *Dust Tracks* are the daughter's narratives. In these works Hurston imputes her desire for magnificent ability onto the mother. According to Hurston, Lucy Potts Hurston desperately wanted to believe in the power of her daughter's "brazen" self-assurance, and she encouraged her ambition by challenging her "to jump at de sun" (*DT* 34, 13). By depicting the mother placing her dying confidence in the daughter, Hurston not only illustrates the extent of the mother's love for her but also uses that love to sanction her own ambition. Despite these achievements, Hurston's failure to abort the death rituals makes her feel guilty. Together guilt and grief transform her ambition into reparations—works in honor of the mother. They preserve the mother's voice.

The passage from *Dust Tracks* connects Hurston's sun imagery to her mother. In this context, completing the impossible trip to the horizon so as to greet the sun at its origination and destination would represent the desire to recover the mother lost to her in death. As the Freudian tenet of compulsive repetition suggests, the recurring projections of such a journey throughout her works signal sites of desire in Hurston's writings. In addition, Freud's "Theme of the Three Caskets" (1913) identifies the place where textual pleasure is most intense—its closure: here the narrative anticipates both gratifying and terminating desire. The final sentences in Hurston's two erotic novels—*Their Eyes* and *Seraph*—do not, as we might expect, address the heterosexual love objects of the stories. Rather, Janie and Arvay encounter the sun and the horizon, respectively. In *Their Eyes* Janie drapes the horizon over her shoulders: "She pulled in her horizon like a great fish-net. Pulled it from around the world and draped it over her shoulder. So much of life in its meshes! She called in her soul to come and see" (184). In *Seraph* Arvay greets the sun: "Yes, she was doing what the big light had told her to do. She was serving and meant to serve. She made the sun welcome to come on in, then snuggled down again beside her husband" (352). In *Dust Tracks,* the association of the sun with the deceased mother invites us to see the closing lines of these novels as inscriptions of latent primary desire for the mother, lost to the daughter due to the normal repression of infantile desire and lost to death. The final lines of these novels inscribe desire gratified with the mother's imaginary return, symbolized as the sun.

Scholars have frequently referred to the death of Hurston's mother as the genesis of her professional ambition to be a folklorist. As an anthropologist, she belatedly speaks for her mother by collecting and preserving the folklore of her mother's speech community. In this way Hurston seems to work through the trauma of her mother's death and her failed promise by professionalizing its execution in another venue. In this context her professional devotion would be more than a vocation; it would be a means of mourning and reparation.

The emphasis Hurston places on the failed promise partly obscures two additional promises that Hurston evidently made to her dying mother that are also directly related to her career. Hurston suggests their content in *Jonah's Gourd Vine* by depicting her fictive mother, Lucy Potts Pearson, on her deathbed, imploring her daughter Isis to "'get all de education you kin'" and to "love nobody better'd you do yo'self" (130). Hurston kept these promises with vigilance, and they defined her life. With great effort and virtually no money, she managed to graduate from Morgan Academy in Baltimore, receive an associate degree from Howard

University in the District of Columbia, and study anthropology at Barnard College with Franz Boas. Hurston also seemed determined to love herself more than a man. Again and again, she made her career her priority. According to *Dust Tracks*, three years after her divorce from Herbert Sheen, she met A. W. P. and experienced the "real love affair" of her life (185). However, she was steadfast to her ambition and used the Guggenheim Fellowship she had recently received to free herself from love's bondage. While on a research trip for the Guggenheim project, she reports, she "*tried* to *embalm* all the tenderness of [her] passion for him in 'Their Eyes Were Watching God'" (*DT* 189; my emphasis). As her language suggests, Hurston is aware that she was not entirely successful in accomplishing her goal in this novel of overdetermined mourning. While we do not know if she was pleased with the repeated effort in *Seraph*, her readers have been ambivalent at best.

The Reception History of *Seraph on the Suwanee*

When *Seraph on the Suwanee* appeared in 1948, Hurston's white reviewers were much more amenable to her writing about white folks, whom she called "Crackers," and her dabbling in Freudian psychology than black scholars would be over the next four decades. Frank G. Slaughter of the *New York Times Book Review* regarded the heroine as "a textbook picture of a hysterical neurotic. . . . One gets the impression that [Hurston] took a textbook on Freudian psychology and adapted it to her needs" ("Freud," 24). The reviewer for *Library Journal* reported that "[t]he colorful Florida 'Cracker' language holds the mood throughout, and the total effect is one of charm and readability" (Whitmore, Review, 1193). Worth Tuttle Hedden of the *New York Herald Tribune* contended that the novel was "[e]motional, expository; meandering, unified; naive, sophisticated; sympathetic, caustic; comic, tragic; lewd, chaste." Hedden added,

> one could go on indefinitely reiterating this novel's contradictions and still end helplessly with the adjective unique. Incomparable strains in the novel mirror the complexity of the author. Miss Hurston shuttles between the sexes, the professions, and the races as if she were man and woman, scientist and creative writer, white and Negro. ("Turpentine," 2)

Hedden's remarks anticipate the now familiar decentered narrative that repudiates fixed meaning. But during the 1940s, the subject was presumed to be unified, and meaning was not supposed to be problematic. Harnett T. Kane of the *Chicago Sun-Times* contended that even when "[Hurston] is guilty of bad writing, overstraining, overtelling, she gives page after page of powerful, impassioned observation" (Review, 58). Herschel Brickell of the *Saturday Evening Review* perhaps best summarized the general attitude of her white reviewers with his insistence that "[a]ll

of Miss Hurston's fiction has had warmth of feeling, a happy combination of lusti-
ness and tenderness, that gives it an appeal too often missing from much of the
day's bloodless writing, which is sexless in spite of its frequently overpowering
sexiness" (Review, 31). These reviewers were sympathetic to *Seraph* probably because, first, Hurston did not feature the explicit racial polemics that persistently
appeared in African American writing of the 1930s and 1940s (especially that by
Richard Wright) and, second, *Seraph* depicts the familiar seduction-rape fantasy
that Freudian analysts made popular by ascribing it to the feminine woman. Both
characteristics make *Seraph* appear to endorse traditional racial and gender roles.

If African American scholars mention *Seraph* at all, and many have not, they
categorically regard it as the least of Hurston's works. For example, three black
scholars writing in the wake of the Black Power and Black Aesthetic movements
tie the novel's defects to its racial posture. Arthur P. Davis contends that

> an author writes best about his own group, and this is true of Zora Neale Hurston. *Ser-
> aph on the Suwanee* does not move as freely as her two "Negro" works of fiction; it lacks
> the racy Negro folk speech and seems more highly contrived. No matter how much
> Miss Hurston knew about Florida poor whites, she instinctively and naturally knew
> more about Florida Negroes, and the difference shows in this novel. (*From the Dark
> Tower*, 118)

Even though Davis argues that Hurston did what "[Frank] Yerby and [Willard]
Motley did exclusively and what Richard Wright, William Gardner Smith, Ann
Petry, and others did from time to time, which was to leave the Negro problem
and write simply as Americans," he, like other black scholars, was much more
critical of Hurston than of these other writers (*From the Dark Tower*, 118).

More recently, feminist literary scholars Cheryl A. Wall and Mary Helen Washington have endorsed Davis's viewpoint. Wall contends that *Seraph* "represents an
artistic decline" and that "Hurston was at her best when she drew her material directly from black folklore; it was the source of her creative power" ("Zora Neale
Hurston," 391). Washington speculates that Hurston wrote

> this strange book to prove that she was capable of writing about white people. The in-
> tent may have been admirable, but all the white characters in *Seraph* sound exactly like
> the Eatonville folks sitting on Joe Clarke's front porch. The result is an awkward and
> contrived novel, as vacuous as a soap opera. It was as though, in abandoning the source
> of her unique esthetic—the black cultural tradition—she also submerged her power
> and creativity. (*Invented Lives*, 21)

While these scholars agree that the novel is flawed, they disagree on whether the
white characters speak in "Eatonvillese." Yet this is precisely what they do. In fact,
many of the most distinctive expressions in *Seraph* appear not only in Hurston's
first two novels—*Jonah's Gourd Vine* (1934) and *Their Eyes Were Watching God*
(1937)—but throughout her other works as well. Wall concurs: "Though black
characters play minor roles in the novel, black cultural traditions permeate the

narrative. They influence everyone's speech, so much so that at times the whites sound suspiciously like the storytellers in Eatonville" ("Zora Neale Hurston," 391). While Washington also recognizes the emphatic presence of the black vernacular in a white cultural setting, she contends that this strategy is a contrivance. By contrast, Arthur Davis dismisses the possibility that black cultural idioms pervade the novel because the words come out of white instead of black mouths. Whether rural black and white Floridians actually speak the same dialect is not really the point, for even if they speak the same dialect with differences in intonation, timing, and gesture, the real issue is Hurston's failure to fulfill her black readers' expectations by writing about a white instead of a black woman.

Is *Seraph* "awkward and contrived, as vacuous as a soap opera," as Washington has contended? Many literary scholars seem to think so. Karla Holloway describes the novel as "encumbered by clashes of class and gender," weighed down by "psychological portraiture" of "a woman's repression and submission and a family's dissolution" in "deathlike images of dead values, lost ambition and thwarted goals" (*Character*, 42, 44). Alice Walker goes so far as to insist that *Seraph* is "reactionary, static, shockingly misguided and timid" (Foreword, xvi). Janet St. Clair takes a different position. She argues that the narrative "inconsistencies are the result of a subversive feminist substory that has so far gone unrecognized, a narrative of resistance and self-discovery that exists not between the lines but solidly on every page" ("Courageous Undertow," 38). While St. Clair analyzes Arvay's achievement of self-respect and self-worth in the context of sadomasochism, she does not probe the psychological or cultural dynamics of this perversion; neither does she question Hurston's decision to cast the novel in whiteface.

Ann duCille and John Lowe specifically address the issue of race. DuCille argues that Hurston's use of white characters allows her to address "misogynistic attitudes and the issue of sexual violence in courtship and marriage without *directly* assigning to black men the politically and racially charged label of racist" (*Coupling Convention*, 127). Lowe argues that *Seraph*'s racial difference gives Hurston an opportunity to expose class difference, memorialize her beloved state of Florida, and provide "more background on the black folk culture" and thereby explain "some other factors that had entered into making Zora, Zora" (*Jump*, 263).

Racial whiteness, I would add, allows Hurston the opportunity to explore the effects of love's bondage without having to defend the freedom and dignity of her fictive, black heroines, with whom she probably identified. Like the whiteness of Richard Wright's Erskine Fowler in *Savage Holiday*, Arvay's whiteness is probably a defense. It allows Hurston to examine issues, behavior, and desire she too possessed without recognizing or acknowledging it as her own. The shift in racial focus is also a part of Hurston's pragmatic attempt to secure a Hollywood contract for writing screenplays[6] and, therefore, her bid to hit a straight lick at white publishers (as well as her white and black readers) with a crooked stick, to invoke one of her favorite sayings.

Regardless of Hurston's motives, though, *Seraph* is the most comprehensive, published account of the subject that continued to fascinate her—erotic love. As Ann duCille remarks, the novel's "brilliant narrative strategy" engages Hurston's female readers with the same internal conflict between erotic pleasure and humiliation that Arvay experiences (*Coupling Convention*, 131), for women readers find themselves in the awkward position of feeling like traitors to their sex if they like this novel. More so than *Jonah's Gourd Vine* and *Their Eyes*, *Seraph* analyzes the demands of heterosexual love as well as the degrading effects of both childhood poverty and parental preference for a sibling on one's self-esteem. In addition, this novel provided Hurston with a therapeutic opportunity to work through the trauma of the failed promise to her mother, for *Seraph* inscribes the fulfillment of the traumatic promise. The satisfaction of this promise repairs Arvay's ego and allows her to surrender her defensive effort to idealize a poor "Cracker" background. Because Arvay's experience indirectly corresponds to Hurston's, this text insinuates what many have long suspected—that Hurston's idealization of her southern roots was a defense that she was unable to relinquish. These inner-world narratives are not associated with Lucy Pearson, Isis, and Janie, probably because they would interfere with Hurston's idealization of these characters.

"A Straight Lick with a Crooked Stick"

Seraph's white social milieu was probably the result not just of Hurston's effort to attract a movie contract but also of a deliberate concession to publishers, who could not imagine a novel about a middle-class black family.[7] Shortly before she began working on this novel, Hurston tried to interest her publisher, Lippincott, in "a serious book [about a middle-class black woman] to be called *Mrs. Doctor*" (Hemenway, *Zora Neale Hurston*, 303).[8] No doubt, Ann Petry and Dorothy West encountered similar reluctance on the part of white publishers because they too were exploring the possibility of writing serious novels about the black middle class. West's *Living Is Easy* and Petry's *Narrows* appeared in 1948 and 1953, respectively. However, both works went out of print soon after their first printings.[9] These circumstances suggest that the black and white reading public not only expected black characters in novels by black authors; they also expected them to represent a homogeneous black folk. While black stereotypes were undoubtedly a part of Hurston's problem with Lippincott, her biographer, Robert Hemenway, refers to her editor's disappointment with "the sloppiness of the writing" and the "strained quality in the prose." Hemenway then explains that Hurston blamed the rejection on Lippincott's decision "that the American public was not ready" for a book on "the upper strata of Negro life" (*Zora Neale Hurston*, 393). Hurston gave up on the book, and on Lippincott, to write *Seraph* for Scribner's. While Hurston's hope to make money off an enlarged audience for the book no doubt was another reason for contextualizing the novel as white, the effect of the white racialized focus on the text is not a simple contrivance, as many scholars have argued, but the complex product of Hurston's conscious reflection and unconscious longings.

When Hurston identifies Jim as Black Irish, she partly clarifies how to read the novel's racial identity. In Emma Kelley's *Megda* (see Chapter 1 of this study), the label "Black Irish" refers to a mixed black/white heritage, resulting from what David Roediger contends was the preponderance of Irish "intermixing with ship-wrecked slaves" (*Wages*, 4). The label also invokes the mid-nineteenth-century racial stereotypes associated with the Irish. Insofar as popular racial wisdom was concerned, "an Irishman was a 'nigger', inside out" (qtd. in Roediger, *Wages*, 133). Hurston's use of the term "Black Irish" suggests her familiarity with such stereotypes. *Seraph* draws on the derisive banter associated with the racialization of this ethnic stereotype to portray Jim and Arvay with white bodies and what her readers identify as black voices, because these characters speak recognizable Eatonville idioms. Thus, Jim and Arvay seem to possess white exteriors and black interiors. In this respect, *Seraph* has two layers of meaning, which I attempt to read as a subversive and parodic joke by mediating the gap between these racial codes. The novel's unstated joke deconstructs absolute racial distinctions and facilitates the exposure of the harmful psychological effects of defining normative female desire as passive and masochistic.

According to John Lowe, however, Jim and Arvay are decidedly white. Lowe insists that *Seraph* "is not simply a whitewashing of black characters," because "Crackers don't have a folk culture that memorializes actual events in history. Their stories and idioms bespeak a repository of folk wisdom, but one unconnected with history" (*Jump*, 266). As evidence of this questionable insight, Lowe cites the following passage that appears early in *Seraph*:

> Few were concerned with the past. They had heard that the stubbornly resisting Indians had been there where they now lived, but they were dead and gone. Osceola, Miccanope, Billy Bow-Legs were nothing more than names that had even lost their bitter favor. The conquering Spaniards had done their murdering, robbing, and raping and had long ago withdrawn from the Floridas. Few knew and nobody cared that Hidalgos under De Sota had moved westward along this very route. (*Jump*, 2)

Lowe argues that *Seraph*'s lack of concern with the area's local history is indicative of its white social context: "Obviously, African Americans would have more cultural strength in this connection, as so much of their oral tradition is tied to history." He concludes that Arvay's "family in Sawley seems adrift in time, much like the Lesters of Caldwell's *Tobacco Road*" (*Jump*, 266).

I find Lowe's conclusion curious and inaccurate. Hurston's other novels do not seem intricately tied to history. Each focuses on character development; thus, historical events are not foregrounded. In *Their Eyes*, Nanny's "highway through de wilderness" speech situates the novel at the turn of the century, the identical time frame as *Seraph*. After this temporal reference, this novel is also "adrift in time"—indeed, so much so that if it were not for surmising Janie's age in relation to Nanny, the courthouse scene could be set in either 1910 or 1930. The only way that we can approximate dates is by referring to the novel's internal generational history in relationship to the Emancipation. The same is true of *Jonah's Gourd Vine*: slavery is the only historical marker. In fact, the novel withholds the date of Lucy's death, telling us instead that Isis is nine when her mother dies. In *Seraph*, like the other two novels, the narrator identifies a post-Reconstruction setting by referring to Jim's background: "fortunes of the War had wiped Jim's grand-father clean" (*S* 7). The narrator also informs us that Jim is twenty-five when he arrives in Sawley and near fifty when he leaves Arvay. Moreover, the inscription of Arvay and Jim's children's birth dates in a family Bible provides clear historical markers. For example, this ritual informs us that Earl is born in 1906, nine months after the story begins.

Rather than being cast adrift in time, then, this novel is more attentive to dates than are the others. In addition, Lowe does not present any examples of this historically informed black folklore from Hurston's other works to support his argument. He simply assumes that the "black oral tradition is tied to history" (266). Hurston's works reveal black and white folk life as tied to the historical facts of slavery and the Emancipation, on the one hand, and the consequences of Civil War, on the other. On the basis of narrative evidence in Hurston's three novels, there seems to be no reason to conclude that white culture is any more or less ahistorical than black culture.

We do know, however, that Hurston was emphatic in her denunciation of stereotyped presumption. She contended that poor rural residents in and around Eatonville, Florida—black and white—share the same dialect. In *Dust Tracks*, she further explains that all southerners have "the map of Dixie on [their] tongue[s]." The "average Southern child, white or black, is raised on simile and invective. . . . Since that stratum of the Southern population is not given to book-reading, they take their comparisons right out of the barnyard and the woods" (*DT* 98–99). Given her reluctance to racialize southern dialect, it must have been Hurston's intention to have *Seraph's* white characters sound like the Eatonville blacks. This was William Faulkner's intention in *The Sound and the Fury* (1929), too, when he has two unnamed white northern characters tell Quentin Compson that "[h]e talks like they do in minstrel shows," by which they mean that Quentin "talks like a colored man" (137). Similarly, as urban blacks readily attest, when one of them speaks the dialect associated with professional whites, they are accused of speaking "white." Thus, when Jim and Arvay speak the phrases that the Eatonville blacks have already spoken in Hurston's earlier works, they are speaking "black." Whether Sawley whites sounded like Eatonville blacks seems a moot issue because the racial valence of the Eatonville dialect, which was designated as black in Hurston's prior publications, remains black regardless of the (presumed) racial identity of the speaker.

According to Hurston, poor blacks and whites living in the rural South speak the same dialect. She also maintained that race is cultural rather than biological. In the unexpurgated version of "My People, My People," she insists that "you can't tell who my people are by skin color" (*DT* 216). If appearance is an unreliable indication of race, what can be said of speech, especially that of characters in a novel? For Hurston, race would seem to be an altogether questionable category. Hurston's manipulation of the slippage of presumably fixed racial designations of the body and the voice probably gave her a great deal of pleasure. Whereas "My People" (as well as "How It Feels to Be Colored Me," discussed later) draws on racial banter for its humor, *Seraph* constructs the jest into a full-fledged joke. Here she transgresses multiple racial expectations. Still, since the characters in *Seraph* sound black, Hurston did not really abandon "the source of her unique esthetic—black cultural tradition," inasmuch as language is the medium of culture.

Despite Hurston's adoption of what we ultimately recognize as black vernacular for her white characters, she nonetheless relied on the assumptions associated with the privilege of whiteness to stage her critique of masochistic female desire. This setting facilitates her representation of the patriarchal demands of romantic love because it avoids black people's problematic relationship to masculine authority. In this way Hurston can connect Jim's love of Arvay and his financial success in Florida without taxing the credibility of her white and black readers. Hurston uses money similarly in "The Gilded Six Bits." But the few coins that Joe can bestow on Missie May make the act symbolic, whereas in *Seraph* Jim's economic gain is the physical proof that allows Arvay to set herself apart from her Cracker background, a developmental process that John Lowe has explained with the assistance of Freudian theory on melancholia and joking.

While Lowe's analysis is, in my estimation, generally accurate[10] if one wants to analyze a character like a person, I am arguing that Hurston's application of Freudian psychology to Arvay is part of her deliberate and subversive commentary on female masochism. By realizing that *Seraph* also has textual subjectivity that is analyzable, we can both construct the meaning of the text and appreciate Arvay's flawed personality. She is, after all, merely a textual signifier whose newfound wisdom at the novel's close informs the reader how to decipher *Seraph*'s meaning. Just as she learns to read Jim's jesting words, we must detect and read the novel's joking humor, for *Seraph* is a long satirical joke about notions of cultural and biological purity that serve Arvay's (and possibly Hurston's) aggressive ego defenses with pleasurable effect (Oring, *Jokes and Their Relations*, 97).

Psychoanalysis facilitates the construction of the textual meaning of this metahumorous novel by allowing us to appreciate the double valences inscribed in its carnivalesque discourses. In addition to producing humor, these conciliatory and subversive discourses engender parody. In this way *Seraph* unsettles the unquestioned social relationships between blacks and whites, women and men. The novel foregrounds Jim and Arvay's unacknowledged dependency on black idiom, labor, companionship, and folk wisdom as well as their reliance on sadomasochism and sexual bondage. By also acknowledging Jim's successful business endeavors in language that seems like flattery, indeed cajolery, Arvay learns to manage Jim to her advantage. When compared to the spirited, aggressive, and censoring humor of Arvay's invectives, however, her new language of sweet regard seems rather shallow.[11] In addition, the novel's happily-ever-after conclusion seems more like an afterlife in heaven than a continuing marital relationship on Earth.

While the external whiteness of the novel's central protagonists controls the discourse of social mobility, the desire of Jim and Arvay to exploit black folk wisdom controls the novel's plot. For example, after listening to Joe, Jim's black friend, Jim finds what he believes to be a way to make Arvay love him, which I discuss later. This event prefigures their marriage. For instance, when Arvay returns from her mother's funeral, determined to win her husband back, she seeks the assistance of Joe's son Jeff and his wife Janie by taking up "an attitude that she would have died before adopting before she went away" (*S* 313). They respond to the changed Arvay by commenting:

> "I declare, Miss Arvay, but you sure is folks."
> "Sure is," Jeff added sincerely. "Just like Mister Jim, ain't she, Janie? And everybody knows that Mister Jim is quality first-class. Knows how to carry hisself, and then how to treat everybody. Miss Arvay's done come to be just like him."
> The reflection upon her past condition escaped Arvay in the shine and the gleaming of the present. (*S* 314)

While the text preserves the class entitlements for racial demarcation, it signifies the mutual respect between the Meserves and the Kelseys, a perspective that is further emphasized on Jim's shrimp boats. When Arvay boards the boats, for example, she notices that "white and Negro captains were friendly together and compared notes. Some boats had mixed crews" (*S* 323). These factors, combined with the protagonists speaking black but appearing white, suggest a masquerade. We see a connection here between the protagonists' affective and social identities that becomes problematic when we try to place them in the novel's racially defined and polarized codes of the real South of Hurston's epoch.

Not only does racism segregate black people from white in the real South during this era; it also prescribes servility for all black subjects. For them to appear equal to white subjects in Western culture, they would have to assume white masks, as psychoanalyst Frantz Fanon has argued in *Black Skin, White Masks* (1952). Undoubtedly, Hurston would appreciate Fanon's contention because she seems to have masked Arvay and Jim in a related way.

Arvay's observations about her own changed racial perspective and the racial equality on the microcosmic boats are a part of *Seraph*'s racial fantasy. Hurston constructs this fantasy by violating the presumption of a black social context, complicating the white social context with parodic inversion in ways that resemble Bakhtin's carnival. Here the masquerade works out "a *new mode of interrelationship between individuals*, counterpoised to the all-powerful socio-hierarchical relationship of noncarnival life" (Bakhtin, *Problems*, 123; emphasis in original). Like the participants of the Bakhtinian carnival, the appearances, gestures, and discourse of Arvay and Jim "are freed from the authority of all hierarchial positions" (Bakhtin, *Problems*, 123).

Seraph's refusal to center a black social milieu and its corresponding delight in repeatedly calling the white characters "Crackers" while self-consciously placing black folk idioms in their mouths carnivalizes the presumption that discernible racial difference is the natural basis of segregation and discrimination. These racist conventions oppressed Hurston all her life. For this reason, flaunting her transgression of the racist social censor must have given Hurston a great deal of pleasure.

Hurston seems to be virtually the only one to have appreciated *Seraph*'s racial transgressions. Her black readers have been much too troubled by her switch to white characters to share this pleasure. And her white readers, who already enjoyed her apparent endorsement of dominant cultural myths about patriarchal virtue and female romantic submission in *Seraph*, probably would have liked it even better if she had published the work under another name and thereby made the novel's connection to black culture less tangible.

Whether Hurston calculated correctly on the novel's appeal to dominant culture, we will never know. Hurston was falsely arrested for sexual misconduct shortly after the novel's publication. When the *Baltimore Afro-American* published a sensational account of the indictment by referring to an excerpt from *Seraph* (Jim's statement "I'm just as hungry as a dog for a knowing and a doing love") as an allegation of Hurston's perverse sexual aggression, and subsequently defended its position by presuming Hurston's guilt, *Seraph* became entangled in the controversy. By the time the charge was dismissed, the damage was irreparable: Hurston and her readers neglected the novel.[12]

By reexamining this anomalous novel in the context of the subversive jest of the carnivalesque, we can see *Seraph* as a mediation (indeed, a deconstruction) of modern racial binary classifications. What initially appears as a regressive racial fantasy is actually a revolutionary text that condemns racial categories and restrictions. Like the "carnivalized" body described by Bakhtin, the external bodies of *Seraph*'s protagonists and their black speaking voices are not closed, complete, defined, or totalized social entities. Since Arvay and Jim repeatedly transgress the boundaries of their presumed racial categories, they are neither entirely white nor black. Yet this radical commentary is lost on those who do not recall that all of Hurston's works refuse to consider race as a serious category.

In "How It Feels to Be Colored Me," for example, Hurston insisted that "[a]t certain times I have no race, I am *me*," and "in the main, I feel like a brown bag of miscellany propped against a wall" (*DT* 155). She further trivialized race by regarding it as a contest and by describing her colored body as painted: "My face is painted red and yellow and my body is painted blue" (*DT* 153, 154). *Seraph's* whiteface masquerade is typical of such racial bantering. Even as this masquerade reifies the presumption of racial difference, it also symbolizes a revised social self and a reformed society in which race is not the quintessential distinguishing characteristic.[13] The indeterminacy of race and the refusal, indeed the inability, of this novel to validate absolute racial distinctions among black and white dialect, culture, and people is the basis of *Seraph's* subversion—its subtle joke on both black and white readers.

To be a joke, *Seraph* must have a punch line that defeats the censor—here, the racist ideology. For "[a] joke without a punchline is no joke" (Oring, *Jokes and Their Relations*, 82). We can detect the punch line by looking for the place where "what is seemingly incongruous" becomes "appropriate" (Oring, *Jokes and Their Relations*, 83). This novel appears to sanction two contradictory racial conventions: the segregation of black and white bodies and the "one drop" law, endorsed in the United States of Hurston's epoch, on the one hand, and white bodies talking black, on the other hand. White readers have tended to read Jim's and Arvay's bodies as racially white and to disregard their black voices even though both are effects of language. Black readers have read these incongruities as contrivances to justify marginalizing the novel altogether. Both groups of readers know how to interpret these apparent contradictions, however. For these characteristics identify racial hybridity that has been projected onto, and therefore inscribed in, textuality. According to real, time-honored racial conventions, white-black racial hybrids *must be* black. The punch line is, then, that these white folks are black! Much like Mark Twain's *Puddn'head Wilson* (1894), in which the presumptions about the absolute meaning of racial difference turn out to be a cultural fiction, *Seraph* unsettles the validity of time-honored racial ideologies. This is *Seraph's* seditious jest on racialism, matched by its subtle but nonetheless radical critique of romantic love, analyzed later. In both instances, Hurston appears to uphold the racial and sexual conventions of her day. Yet she presents them in such a way that they insinuate their own internal contradictions.

Love's Bondage

To defend themselves against their insecurities, Jim and Arvay bind themselves together in the sadomasochistic cycle of oppression and submission. Jim repeatedly supplies the aggression for Arvay's humiliating submission, making her feel like his slave. Although in each instance she initially resists his aggression, she cannot ultimately withstand its intensity because she regards him as virtually omnipotent.

Submission also allows Arvay to display her devotion to him, partially absolves her guilt, and compensates for her feelings of unworthiness. Jim experiences her surrender as an expression of intense ardor, which he recognizes by the appearance of a "mysterious green light [that] appeared in Arvay's blue eyes. . . . Each time that she succumbed to his love making, Arvay's eyes gradually changed from the placid blue to a misty greenish-blue like the waters of the sea at times and at places. It warmed him, it burned him and bound him" (*S* 106). The novel's climax arises from Jim's steadfast belief that his demand for her submission will lead Arvay to what he calls a "sufficient understanding" of their marriage (*S* 104). However, his means and his goal operate at cross-purposes. He attempts to teach Arvay how to become a part of an erotic union—that is, how to share the erotic experience of "mutual recognition in which both partners lose themselves in each other without loss of self," to borrow the words of psychoanalyst Jessica Benjamin (*Bonds*, 29). However, his demand for submission erodes Arvay's ego and ability to achieve the mutual recognition he seeks. Herein lies the paradox of the sadomasochist dynamic. The "sadist, who seems so desirous of control, secretly crave[s] *resistance* to, and challenges of, his . . . authority. If the masochist resists, the sadist can then go on taking pleasure in asserting power anew, over and over, thus prolonging and sustaining the dynamic" (Chancer, *Sadomasochism*, 50; emphasis in original). This is precisely what happens in the novel. Over the course of twenty years of marriage, Arvay fails to detect Jim's jokes, and he exerts more and more sadistic aggression, verbal and physical, in an ill-fated attempt to secure Arvay's resistance until he literally immobilizes her with the snake stunt. As a result of this incident, he leaves Arvay.

On one prior occasion, Jim considers leaving her just for a moment. However, the thought of life without her makes him realize the origin of his love for Arvay, a realization that

> had been dodging around in his mind for years. There was something about Arvay that put him in mind of his mother. They didn't favor each other in the face, but there was something there just the same. Maybe that was what had caught his attention the first time he had laid eyes on Arvay. Maybe that was why he had never missed his family since he had married her. All the agony of his lost mother was gone when he could rest his head on Arvay's bosom and go to sleep of nights. . . . There was something about Arvay besides her good looks. Something like a vapor, which reached to him and delivered him to her hands *tied and bound*. (*S* 105, my emphasis)

Rather than acknowledge his dependency on Arvay, Jim diverts his attention to jealousy by imagining that "some other man should find out what he knew about Arvay, and be soothing his trashy head on Arvay's soft and comforting bosom" (*S* 106). "[I]t was his privilege to do for her" (*S* 105). By doing so, he defines himself, reclaims the wealth and stature of his "ancestors [who] had held plantations upon Alabama River before the War" (*S* 7), and transforms Arvay into his version of "a king's daughter out of a story-book" (*S* 263). Like Arvay, he imagines the possibility of a sexual opponent to bolster his aggressive competition. Because Arvay cannot strengthen her self-confidence, her imagined competitor seems more real to her and, therefore, more threatening.

Jim's comment about postcoital repose, which the novel repeats two more times (*S* 219, 349; cited later) suggests the origin of Jim's sadism. It originates in his intense feelings of maternal loss, associated with the sexual repression of the son's desire for the mother during the oedipal stage and his bereavement over his mother's death.

Effective mourning, as Freud explains in "Mourning and Melancholia," "requires forthwith that all the [mourner's] libido shall be withdrawn from its attachments to [the loved] object" and reinvested into the ego (154). When Jim first sees Arvay, he becomes "stuck on" her (*S* 8), as he somehow recognizes her as the lost mother he has never been able to release. The more he controls her, the more she confirms his belief that she is the fantasy object that he has lost. Consequently, he is "tied and bound" to her. Unwilling to entertain the possibility of suffering another erotic loss, though, Jim unconsciously binds her to him with the sadomasochistic dynamic of love, which he rationalizes as his effort to teach her "sufficient understanding" in their marriage (*S* 105). Arvay then not only fulfills his unconscious needs by replacing the lost mother (that is, his memory of his historical mother); she also stimulates his latent desire for maternal reparation. For this reason, he works and schemes to give her the rewards of his labor. Unfortunately, Jim's repressed fear of losing Arvay causes him to increase the tension in their sadomasochistic marriage and threaten the very object that he desperately struggles to possess.

Two other incidents illustrate their sadomasochistic bondage. The first is the rape incident that occurs right before their marriage, and the second is a bedroom scene in which Jim humiliates her by ripping off all her clothing and demanding that she stand before him "naked as she had been born" (*S* 217). In the first incident, while Arvay held two limbs of the mulberry tree and swang, she was suddenly

> snatched from the sky to the ground. Her skirts were being roughly jerked upwards, and Jim was fumbling wildly at her thighs. . . . Arvay opened her mouth to scream, but no sound emerged. Her mouth was closed by Jim's passionate kisses, and in a moment more, despite her struggles, Arvay knew a pain remorseless sweet. (*S* 51)

Arvay reacts much like an abused child who suspends its ego during an assault, and "[n]ot until Jim lay limp and motionless upon her body, did Arvay return to herself and begin to think, and with thinking all of her old feelings of defeat and inadequacy came back on her." "She was terribly afraid. She had been taken for a fool, and now her condition was worse than before" (*S* 51). Not realizing that Jim intends to marry her, she unconsciously struggles to find some way to bind him to her:

Some unknown power took hold of Arvay. . . . A terrible fear came over her that he might somehow vanish away from her arms, and she sought to hold him by the tightness of her embrace and her flood of kisses. It seemed a great act of mercy when she found herself stretched on the ground again with Jim's body weighing down upon her. Even then she was not satisfied. . . . She must eat him up, and absorb him within herself. Then he could never leave her again. (*S* 53–54)

Arvay's romantic passion culminates in intense humiliation and submission, which Jim experiences as love. When Jim marries Arvay, rather than welcoming his love with confidence, she feels unworthy and in need of compensating him for his act of extravagant charity. She repeatedly pays with eroticized self-abasement that defines her as a female masochist. In contrast to Freudian psychology that normalizes female masochism, *Seraph* questions and ultimately rejects it as the normal expression of feminine passion.[14] The novel reveals that Arvay feels neither normal nor satisfied. Rather, she "hungered and retreated inside of herself with her fears" (*S* 65).

The second incident occurs after more than twenty years of marriage. One night Arvay's jealousy incites an argument with Jim that compels her to make a stand. Jim responds by explaining, "Where I made my big mistake was in not starting you off with a good beating just as soon as I married you. . . . [Y]ou done got beside yourself. What you mean by sitting there [on the bed?] . . . [G]et out of those clothes" (*S* 215–16). Arvay tries to bolster her courage, only to have Jim rip off her dress. "'Don't you move!' Jim bellowed harshly. 'You're my damn property, and I want you right where you are, and I want you naked. Stand right there in your tracks until I tell you that you can move.'" (*S* 216). In a few moments he lets her get in bed, and he gets into bed beside her. Although the text has baited our expectations for another rape, Jim merely demands that she hug his neck. As a result, Arvay "flung her arms around Jim's neck with gladness" (*S* 217). She "hugged and hugged and kissed and kissed for what she decided was abundant and sufficient time," inciting no response from Jim. "She kissed him violently and hungrily for a minute, then braced her hands against his shoulders and did all she could to shove him away from her." She then started to scream and cry.

> "I can't stand this *bondage* you got me in. I can't endure no more! I can't never feel satisfied that I got *you tied to me*, and I can't leave you, and I can't kill you nor hurt you in no way at all. *I'm tied and bound down* in a burning Hell and no way out that I can see. I can't see never no peace of mind." (*S* 218; my emphasis)

The repetition of the language of bondage underscores the sadomasochistic dynamic of this incident. Arvay's increased masochistic humiliation reveals their immense discharge of emotional energy, after which their relationship takes on the character of the pre-oedipal relationship between mother and infant.

During this stage of infantile development, the child perceives the mother to be all-powerful, and attachment to her dominates the child's subjectivity. When Jim takes "[Arvay's] face between his hands and looked down in her eyes" and sees once again "that greenish infusion creep in and mingle with the sky blue of her eyes," he becomes reattached to this mother surrogate, as evident by his snuggling "his head down on her breast in that way he had that Arvay thought was so much like a helpless child, and went off into peaceful sleep" (S 219). Not only does Jim achieve unspoken gratification; the narrator also suggests that the change in the color of Arvay's eyes is a physical manifestation of her corresponding unconscious desire for a similar union.

The climax to their sadomasochistic bondage occurs when Jim substitutes a sexually symbolic and potentially deadly test for the explicitly sexual assaults on Arvay's ego. Jim attempts to wrestle an eight-foot rattlesnake as proof of his love for her, an incident that Hurston variously depicts in *Jonah's Gourd Vine* and *Dust Tracks*. When the snake overpowers him, Jim reverses the roles of the sado-masochistic dynamic and assumes masochistic jeopardy in a desperate attempt to force Arvay to display heroic courage. Hence, Jim revises the sadomasochistic dynamic in the hope of producing mutual recognition even as he resorts to the same pattern of behavior, albeit with the roles reversed. However, Arvay has no ego strength left, and fear predictably immobilizes her. Jeff comes to Jim's rescue. Arvay's failure to respond leaves Jim convinced that her love for him is deficient, and he leaves her.

By breaking the link with his masochistic other, Jim does what a sadist seldom does. He redirects his interest to another object, the sea. Here he unconsciously attempts to replace his dependency on the mysterious "greenish infusion [that] cre[pt] in and mingled with the sky blue of her eyes" with his appreciation of the magnitude of the ocean: "The [blue-green] colors [of the sea] charmed and pleased him. . . . [A]nd where the sun rested on it, it seemed to be over-laid by a silvery veil" (S 219, 224). Whether he can maintain the sublimation of his desire is a question that the text ultimately does not answer, for by the end of the novel Arvay joins him.

The last incident in *Seraph* ends with Arvay's sexual gratification and permits her to realize that the self-assured Jim Meserve is "nothing but a little boy" on the inside (S 351). If we see Arvay as a person rather than the text's principal signifier, we will see her at the center of a marital relationship bound by patriarchal law. But I have defined her as an element in a sexual fantasy. Arvay adrift on the sea is not a person to be read mimetically; she is an overdetermined image. Recall that Arvay's eyes reflect the sea, which the text repeatedly associates with Jim's fantasy of the lost mother; that he names his ship after Arvay; and that at the novel's close she is in the ship that bears her name, aimlessly drifting toward the horizon. Insofar as the text is concerned, Arvay signifies desire, and desire is terminated in this oceanic incident, to invoke Freud's famous term (*Civilization*, 64–65). This final incident presents her suspended in the pleasure of her realization of Jim's desire to be bound to her, a role that casts her as an all-knowing mother.

With Arvay's desire terminated in romantic bondage, the novel turns to satisfying its unconscious desire, reflected in the last words of the narrative. They report that she met "the look of the sun with confidence. Yes, she was doing what the big light had told her to do. She was serving and meant to serve. She made the sun welcome to come on in, then snuggled down again beside her husband" (*S* 352). Whereas in *Dust Tracks* the child Zora believes "the sun went down on purpose to flee away from [her]" on the day her mother dies (64–65), Arvay "made the sun welcome to come on in" (*S* 352). Hence, *Seraph* symbolizes the return of the daughter's primary love object as the overdetermined maternal image of the sun. Heterosexual pleasure gratifies the novel's conscious narrative, and the pleasure of the gaze of the lost mother, symbolized as the sun, satisfies and terminates unconscious textual desire (and probably Hurston's as well).

Their Eyes relies on a similar figure at its close—the draped horizon—to express the termination of textual desire, but this mystified ending is problematic. Moments before the closing scene, Janie emphatically professes abiding satisfaction and tranquility to Phoeby in the absence of explicit textual representation of erotic gratification. While Phoeby is convinced by Janie's story, readers long before us have been troubled by the novel's ending. Experience has taught us that suspended erotic longing intensifies rather than diminishes desire. Thus, we certainly do not expect frustrated desire to engender serenity or fulfillment, despite Janie's words. For Janie to achieve satisfaction, we would have to imagine Janie forever remembering Tea Cake and equating recalled pleasure with immediate sensual delight. In addition, Janie's mourning would have to be interminable to perpetuate the attachment of her libidinal energy to Tea Cake's memory and not to reinvest that energy in her own pleasure.

By concluding with Janie in mourning, *Their Eyes* preserves and commemorates, rather than terminating Janie's position as the novel's desiring subject. She signifies freedom and possibility beyond the novel's close. Such an ending creates a fantasy of everlasting desire—indeed, immortality—by privileging fancy over fact. The conflict between desire and reality makes the novel's ending problematic and yet pleasurable because it violates the Real by appealing to the Imaginary. This appeal to the Imaginary has engendered critical accolades for *Their Eyes* because it reflects our desire. While *Seraph* also appeals to the Imaginary, our cultural understanding of romantic ecstasy as the ultimate pleasure paradoxically links such pleasure to the death of desire, indeed to the death of the desiring subject. Because *Seraph* has no social desire, like that in Du Bois's *Dark Princess*, to displace the now realized erotic pleasure, all desire in *Seraph* is consummated. Arvay and Jim are symbolically dead, as their oceanic slumber at the novel's end suggests.

The Silent Protest

While *Their Eyes* sustains romantic passion, *Seraph* celebrates its gratification. Whereas *Their Eyes* depicts the experience of romantic love as psychically enhancing, *Seraph* dramatizes it as sadomasochistic and regressive. Whereas Janie is always self-assured, Arvay struggles to develop this trait. Because Arvay is ultimately willing to make Jim her entire life, they develop a relationship without the intersubjective conflicts that marred Hurston's relationship with A. W. P. Unlike the mocked dreamer on the opening page of *Their Eyes*, Arvay's wish does not "sail forever on the horizon, never out of sight, never landing until the Watcher turns his eyes away in resignation, his dreams mocked to death by Time" (1). At the end of *Seraph* Arvay recovers Jim's embrace and perceives her newly discovered self-confidence, not so much as an independent woman but as an omnipotent mother. More important, she is literally sailing out to meet one wish on the horizon, with the other embraced literally within her grasp. While Janie gives birth to a new desiring self by internalizing the memory of Tea Cake, Arvay gives birth to herself as the knowing mother. She feels herself "stretching and expanding" with the vastness of the sea and "the unobstructed glory of the rising sun" (*S* 331, 330).

Seraph's closing rhetorical question, "What more could any woman want or need?" (351)—reminiscent of Freud's famous question "What does woman want?"—is not an affirmation of Arvay's subjectivity but an ironic question that invites a querulous response. For certainly, Arvay should want more than a cajoling romantic relationship, no matter how sexually pleasurable, to sustain her identity as a speaking subject. The implication of a negative response to this question confirms the surrender of Arvay's personal ambitions and longings—her desire. No longer a subject of desire, Arvay forsakes the exhilarating humor of her verbal bouts with Jim. Just when she learns to use joking to sustain her ego and becomes a spirited character who can make us laugh (see, for example, the episode with Carl in the hotel lobby, just after her mother's death), the narrative makes her relinquish her ego by literally killing it with pleasure. The irony of this situation suggests that the patriarchal notion of romantic love plays a joke on women. To invoke Roberta Flack's lyrics, such love kills women *softly*. At the novel's close Arvay is the beloved maternal object who retires with Jim in an oceanic realm suggestive of heaven. While Janie is exuberant with anticipation at the end of *Their Eyes*, Arvay is languid with inner harmony at the end of *Seraph*.

Their Eyes possesses a story beyond its ending because the novel preserves Janie's status as a desiring subject. By contrast, Jim and Arvay each surrender their desiring selves by merging with the other. For this reason it is appropriate that Jim is already asleep and Arvay will join him. By merging with the figure of the preoedipal mother, a plot underscored in oceanic imagery, Jim no longer needs to comfort himself with sadistic aggression toward Arvay, and she no longer needs to make masochistic reparation to him. Erotic bondage is not necessary when desire has terminated. The symbolically dead need no chains. The text encourages Arvay to develop her self-awareness, only to render it irrelevant with the demands of romantic love.

Seraph dramatizes the theme that appears throughout Hurston's works, whether intentional or not. This theme expresses Hurston's ambivalence toward a woman's pursuit of romantic love. Indeed, the theme suggests that romantic love is a deterrent for female self-discovery. *Seraph* is more emphatic in this determination than Hurston's other novels. It reveals that romantic submission ultimately demands the death of female subjectivity, much like the death of O's ego in Pauline Reage's *Story of O*.[15] As Janie's life in *Their Eyes* reveals, if female subjectivity survives, it must mourn romance.

Seraph's joke, then, is on Hurston's female readers who are lured into thinking that it is possible to set a story of female development within the context of romantic love. *Seraph* dramatizes the opposition of these two plots, for even when Arvay achieves a fully developed self, indeed the self whom Jim claims he wants, by relinquishing what he condemns as a "stand-still, hap-hazard kind of love" (*S* 262), she must abandon that self to win him back. What he really wants in Arvay is a wife who not only tolerates but invites his domination, a viewpoint he clearly expresses at the novel's close:

> "You brought this on yourself. You could have stayed away from me, but you didn't. So you're planted here now forever. You're going to do just what I say do, and you better not let me hear you part your lips in a grumble. Do you hear me, Arvay?"
> "Yes, Jim, I hear you." (*S* 349)

This knowledge is *Seraph's* critique on romantic love. Jim has not changed. His last demand is reminiscent of an earlier one, where he told Arvay she was his "damned property." He wanted her still and naked (*S* 216). Whereas she resisted the demand in the earlier incident, she now submits. According to the text, "[t]he sweetness of the moments swept over Arvay so that she almost lost consciousness" (349).

This passionate but disturbing final incident emphasizes the text's patriarchal vision of romantic love, which it critiques by asking, "What more could any woman want or need?" (*S* 351). The text responds for Arvay: "She was serving and meant to serve" (*S* 352). While female servility is Arvay's response to the ironic question, it certainly was not Hurston's. The silent resistance to the dramatic answer to this question is a part of the text's revolutionary unconscious. Hurston represents her critique by projecting it onto a frail, white, blue-eyed, pretty, blond woman—white society's ideal of femininity. Arvay is a fictive displacement that allows Hurston to dramatize the stories she denied to her other black female protagonists. In plotting the fateful course of romantic love in *Seraph*, Hurston can reassure herself that even if the happily-ever-after romance had been possible, it would not have fulfilled her passionate desire for self-definition.

Conclusion

Plenitude in Black Textuality

> She did not try to make me perfect. To her I was already perfect.
> —William E. B. Du Bois, *Darkwater* (1920)

> I remember well when the shadow swept across me. I was a little thing away up in the hills of New England, where the dark Housatonic winds between Hoosac and Taghkanic to the sea. In a wee wooden schoolhouse, something put it into the boys' and girls' heads to buy gorgeous visiting-cards—ten cents a package—and exchange. The exchange was merry, till one girl, a tall newcomer, refused my card,—refused it peremptorily, with a glance.
> —William E. B. Du Bois, *The Souls of Black Folk* (1903)

> Even in the matter of girls my peculiar phantasy asserted itself. Naturally, it was in our town voted bad form for boys of twelve and fourteen to show any evident weakness for girls. We tolerated them loftily, and now and then they played in our games, when I joined in quite as naturally as the rest. It was when strangers came, or when the oldest girls grew up that my sharp senses noted little hesitancies in public and searching for possible public opinion. Then I flamed! I lifted my chin and strode off to the mountains, where I viewed the world at my feet and strained my eyes across the shadow of the hills.
> —William E. B. Du Bois, *Darkwater* (1920)

> Later, in the high school, there came some rather puzzling distinctions which I can see now were social and racial; but the racial angle was more clearly defined against the Irish than against me. It was a matter of income and ancestry more than color. I have written elsewhere of the case of our exchanging visiting cards when one girl, a new-comer, did not seem to want mine, to my vast surprise.
> —William E. B. Du Bois, *The Autobiography of W. E. B. Du Bois* (1968)

This study proposes a critical strategy for analyzing a unique form of desire—the implicit wishes, unstated longings, and vague hungers inscribed in the rhetorical elements of novels written by African Americans. These textual features insinuate puzzling emotional meaning that seems superfluous to the novel's explicit social content. Such surplus meaning is not unique to black novels or black textuality, as I have explained, but is an intrinsic condition of language that Jacques Lacan has identified as the implicit expression of the unconscious desire of the speaking/writing subject. Yet scholars of African American literature have routinely disregarded this aspect of black textuality, undoubtedly because it complicates the production of coherent social protest against racial injustice. This response is understandable. It has produced a black literary canon in which the politics of race forms the manifest text; at the same time, it has repressed problematic personal discourses of desire. However, to ignore the workings of the unconscious in language and its effects on black texts negates neither its presence nor its power to influence textual meaning.

Because the unconscious in language cannot explicitly communicate its meaning, it stages desire in a metaphoric/metonymic dumb show in which awry and excessive signification encodes the implied meaning. The more opaque this signifying performance, the more repressed the desire. The greater the density of the enigmatic signifiers, the more compelling the desire to reveal some censored content.

By desire, as I have explained throughout this study, I do not simply mean the sensual craving of adult sexuality or the social demands for racial equality typically associated with African American novels. Instead, I mean the unique, personal fantasies of the narrator—what I have termed the *discourses of unconscious desire*. These discourses allow the author to express unacknowledged and socially censored wishes by inscribing them in the novel's rhetorical features. In addition to repetition and the meaningful selection and arrangement of narrative elements, the discourses of the unconscious also rely on tropes to signify the censored content. Hence, figures of speech in the novel express the prohibited wish much like a Freudian slip. We can, then, understand unconscious discourses as compromise formations "between the wish to communicate and the wish to conceal, whereas the wish to conceal, not to know, is the more conscious" (Hook, "Psychoanalysis," 121). The language of a text performs this paradoxical mediation of speaking and muting, disclosing and masking, in much the same way that hysterical symptoms conspicuously stage the hidden obsession of the neurotic subject.

As I have demonstrated, textual meaning is a dialectic of a work's implicit and explicit expressions. We have typically associated the explicit discourses of a work with its stated social themes, while attributing the implied meaning inscribed in its rhetorical strategies to its aesthetic design rather than to its conceptual propositions. Such a separation of form and content has been particularly troublesome in African American literature because it has produced a reception history marked by the color line. Black reviewers have generally applauded those works by African Americans that emphatically focus on the political aspirations of racial equality. And white reviewers have tended to applaud those corresponding works that concentrate on their aesthetic development. Each group has made black texts fit its own expectations rather than perceiving how form and content mediate the production of textual meaning.

My objective has been to demonstrate how the five black novels at the center of this study negotiate the paradoxical symptoms of speaking and muting desire so as to produce meaning that is social, emotional, and personal. I selected these five novels precisely because they exaggerate the process of performing unconscious desire. Their representation of repressed discourses of desire is so heavily veiled that they seem opaque. Consequently, the latent discourses interfere with the presentation of each novel's social message to the extent that they undermine the work's credibility. Because it has had no strategy for synthesizing the social and latent content, African American literary scholarship has relegated Du Bois's *Dark Princess*, Wright's *Savage Holiday*, and Hurston's *Seraph on the Suwanee* to its margins, even though their respective authors are otherwise famous. In the case of Larsen's *Quicksand*, black feminist readings promote the prominence of this work while simultaneously disregarding its troublesome content. As for Kelley's *Megda*, the fifth novel, anachronistic cultural meaning complicates this recently recovered work by making the typical feminist and racial paradigms of social inequity inappropriate.

The production of textual meaning is a complex process. Just as texts have distinctive signifying properties, readers have specific emotional and experiential histories. For this reason, novels and readers form very personal rapports. In the event that there is an affinity between a text and a reader, it is largely a factor of that reader's conscious or unconscious recognition and subsequent identification with the various inscriptions of desire and pleasure in the text. But this relationship is a very complicated process. For example, we readers may be well aware that we like a work and just as well unaware of the reasons why. Even if we probe our affinity, we are likely not to discover its intricate origins but, rather, to find justifications that are culturally determined displacements for our pleasures in the text.

Having said this, I am aware that I am inviting my readers to see some connection between myself and the five anomalous novels that structure this study. Certainly, this is true. I do not believe that I could have devoted years of my life to a project for which I felt no compelling passion—conscious and unconscious. And it is likely that the latter is what has driven me to produce this study. Such is the origin of all creative production. But rather than probe the basis of my desire, I'd rather invite my readers to explore the covert expressions of desire in the textuality of African American literature and to investigate the relationship between desire and race in all types of cultural texts, especially that between the canonical and the noncanonical.

While all novels inscribe desire, the five black novels that form the sites of my investigation accentuate this paradoxical process by creating enigmas we can detect but seldom interpret. Because these enigmas disrupt our efforts to construct the racially sanctioned social meaning for the novels, we have marginalized them as anomalies. By referring to psychoanalysis, I have attempted to name the veiled desire that enacts the textual enigma of each novel and to integrate its personal and social longings into a coherent critical narrative. Psychoanalysis has helped me recognize an originary experience of desire in each of these novels by facilitating my identification of textual signifiers that repeat a narrative of primary loss—what psychoanalysis has termed the oedipal story. This story presupposes another about primary attachment and the plenitude of gratification—the pre-oedipal story. Because such signification is culturally determined, I have accentuated the effects of cultural difference in my rendering of psychoanalysis so as to attach the signifiers of racial traumas and resulting anxieties depicted in the novels to their compulsive stories of primary loss and desire and to their fantasies of recovered plenitude. Thus, by recognizing the muted but performative expressions of desire and gratification in the rhetorical elements and stylistic features of the five novels, I have attempted to produce comprehensive readings of them that evolve as a dialectic of social demands and personal desire.

As I have demonstrated throughout this study, my critical model is particularly useful for analyzing black texts that do not depict conventional racial discourses and therefore do not privilege the expectation that black novels directly portray black people's lived experiences with racial oppression. My model is also applicable to all types of black texts because it recovers a peculiar excess of meaning embodied in them that is usually disregarded. I will suggest the implications of my model at the close of this study by referring to an often cited episode in Du Bois's life. But before doing so, I want to refer to several of the previous chapters to summarize how my model differs from other critical paradigms.

More comprehensive than linguistic analyses of vernacular or signifying speech acts, on the one hand, and material analyses of social concerns, on the other hand, my model offers an understanding of the complex linkage between personal expressions of unacknowledged wishes and collective social appeals. I am not saying that vernacular strategies do not provide informative readings of black texts but that they do not address the textual conflicts that frequently compete with and often overpower a work's social logic. Scholars of African American literature have usually disregarded such conflicts or attributed them to aesthetic defects because they disrupt the sanctioned social meanings of black texts.

For example, as I explain in Chapter 3, we scholars have generally not probed the misogynistic basis of Richard Wright's racial protest stories. Rather, we have usually subsumed this persistent feature of Wright's fictions in discussions about his outrage at racism. As a result, we have not explored the relationship between Wright's plots of racial outrage and his repeated use of narrative fragments about female entrapment or betrayal. When these elements become so overwhelming that they disrupt our expectations of black textuality, as in the case of Wright's matricidal, whitefaced novel *Savage Holiday* or his depiction of marital discord in "The Long Black Song," we either marginalize the entire work, as in the case of this novel, or dismiss the presumably minor elements, like those in this story, so as to preserve an uncontested racial interpretation.

In the case of black canonical novels, like Wright's *Native Son*, the scholarship seems preoccupied with identifying expressions of racial strife, so much so that it effaces other personal conflicts. For example, scholars have routinely pointed to Bigger Thomas's murder of Mary Dalton as problematic. They recognize the social logic that defines the accidental nature of her death, but they also repeatedly refer to Bigger's decapitation of Mary and the incineration of her body as gratuitous violence. Rather than focusing on the sexual meaning associated with these excessively brutal acts, scholarly analysis has routinely turned to explicating Bigger's racial rage. As I explain in Chapter 3, James Baldwin's remark in "Alas, Poor Richard" is typical. Here he counsels critics/scholars to examine Wright's "gratuitous and compulsive" violence as the mask of sexual trauma (188). But no sooner does he make this entreaty than he abandons it for the typical social argument of racial outrage. To examine the gratuitous violent excess in Wright's works seems as threatening as gazing into the face of the Medusa. Baldwin dares to identify the feared object as sexual but refuses to investigate it.

Shouldn't we question our reluctance to explore these sexual conflicts and our reflexive maskings of them with race? Granted, there is a long and traumatic history associated with the hypersexualized black body. But does this history mean that we must continue to cover black sexuality with explications of racial oppression because we fear that others will pathologize, victimize, and in some way punish black subjects with racist activity?

In writing about desire and black textuality and by using the language of psychoanalysis, I have situated my study in this tabooed site of black sexuality. Each of the novels in this book suffers from eruptions of desire that are external to racial and/or social narratives and generate serious logical problems for the novels. We could even say that the dis-ease is fatal in almost every instance. The eruptions inhabit the novels' sexual tropes and obscure the works' social argument. But rather than exploring these problematic features as important sites of analysis, we have either dismissed the conflict so as to make the work fit racial protocols, as in the case of Nella Larsen's *Quicksand*, or obscured the work altogether, as in the instances of the other four novels of my study—Zora Neale Hurston's *Seraph on the Suwanee*, W. E. B. Du Bois's *Dark Princess*, Emma Kelley's *Megda*, and Richard Wright's *Savage Holiday*.

The last four works exhibit so many disruptions that the works fail to fit the familiar racial and gendered models of social protest. But as I have argued, such eruptions are important elements in the production of meaning for these and other novels. Their implicit personal desire and explicit social demands coexist in the novels' narratives. Not to examine this relationship is to dismiss a key factor of textual meaning and a probable motivation for the production of the work as well.

By investigating how collective demand and personal desire—or, more generally, the social and psychological effects of race and sex—are embedded in the texts' signifying operations, I have attempted to explain how figurative patterns, rhetorical strategies, and causality in these texts imply meaning that is distinct from that located in their dialogues, plotlines, and thematic content. The latter elements constitute a work's explicit and manifest argument about social recognition and justice, while the stylistic features express a surplus and masked desire about a lost and irrational longing that is symbolically fulfilled at the close of each novel.

For example, in Chapter 5, on *Seraph on the Suwanee*, I explain the imaginary plenitude structured in the final scene of the novel as the recovery of the gaze of the (m)other. Thus, instead of regarding the description of the sunrise as a neutral setting for the novel's finale, I question the profusion of images for describing the sun and their referents in the hope of locating aspects of the text's unstated but intimated desire invested in this language. In Chapter 1, on *Medga*, I view the excessive signification of pleasure at the close of this novel as a site for investigation rather than as a justification for dismissing the work as a puerile domestic fantasy. Instead of regarding this trait as flawed writing, I regard it as a clue for identifying the desire that is signified in each novel. Such desire regulates the production of textual meanings.

Let me illustrate this process by referring to the discussion in Chapter 2. Here I explain that Du Bois considered *Dark Princess* a work of racial propaganda. For him the novel's eroticism advanced its social argument. But for his readers, the eroticism unsettles and even overpowers the propaganda. Rather than regarding the eroticism as simply an ineffective metaphor for social meaning, I examine the profuse inscriptions of erotic passion as sites of conflicted expression, indeed exhibitions of conflicted desire, that erupt in and subsequently disrupt the racial narrative. I make these sites the focus of my analysis. To disregard them as simply instances of writing defects or inadequate artistic vision makes us prescribe rather than analyze black textuality. This is precisely what has happened. Ironically, this endeavor also results in our reifying what we want to protest by locking black writers into perpetuating the very racial arguments that we and they want to relinquish as anachronisms.

What makes the novels that form the core of my study problematic, then, is their failure to make their unique personal logic inscribed in their rhetorical designs—what I have been calling "textual desire"—serve their social message. Rather than disregard these troublesome features, I have made them the objects of my analysis so as to expose their masked insinuations.

Such content is not simply a consistent product of the writer's mental conflicts; more significantly, it is an expression of cultural tensions that are reproduced not only in individuals and their works but also in social relationships. Hence, the canonical imperatives of different historical moments reflect the changing needs, demands, and desires of dominant power relationships by sanctioning or censuring the problematic content. As I have argued throughout this study, modernist canonical imperatives on African American literary scholarship have denounced by marginalizing the surplus expression that unsettles its master narratives of race, while postmodernist canonical exigencies acknowledge the glut of excess meaning and complicate what we mean by race. Moreover, by studying the marginal works of an epoch, we can get a clearer understanding of its conscious cultural preoccupations and suppressions as well as its unconscious obsessions.

I want to conclude my study by illustrating how the interrogation of desire can reveal concealed meaning in familiar places rather than anomalous ones. I do so by referring to three pieces of information about W. E. B. Du Bois's life in broad circulation. I selected him to illustrate the implications of my model because he left behind an extensive personal archive that makes efficacious my attempt to investigate desire as an object of analysis. Even more important, though, the three biographical texts suggests significant information about Du Bois, but it is only accessible if we ask new questions of the texts. The first piece of information concerns the story about "when the shadow [of the 'vast veil' of race] swept across [him]" (*Souls*, in Sundquist, *Oxford*, 101), a traumatic event that he repeatedly inscribes in his autobiographical writings, to which I refer in the second, third, and fourth epigraphs at the beginning of the Conclusion. The other two pieces of information are well-known photographs. One is labeled "Willie Du Bois 4 years old" (see figure 4). The other is a photograph of his mother Mary Silvina Burghardt Du Bois holding her infant son (see figure 2). It was probably taken in 1868, the year of Du Bois's birth. These two photographs are frequently reproduced as sites of factual information about Du Bois's early life. Their meaning is assumed to be transparent. It is precisely this presumption that I want to interrogate in the concluding discussion of this study.

In the second epigraph Du Bois recalls an incident in high school that he associated with his painful discovery of the social meaning attached to his dark skin color: "one girl, a tall newcomer, refused my card,—refused it peremptorily, with a glance" (*Souls*, in Sundquist, *Oxford*, 101). I want to use my model to question the manner in which Du Bois chooses to represent his encounter with racial proscriptions rather than read the event as simply a neutral conveyor of historical fact.

Given the innumerable types of racial assault that a young, poor, fatherless black boy was likely to suffer in a northern town during the onset of the post-Reconstruction era, I want to ponder the meaning of Du Bois's selection of female rejection to represent his first memorable encounter with racism. According to Du Bois's biographer David Levering Lewis, before entering high school Du Bois "came to have an informed idea of what being a black male meant even in the relatively tolerant New England" (*W. E. B. Du Bois*, 34). According to Lewis, one of Du Bois's white neighbors was nearly successful in sending him to reform school for stealing grapes from someone else's yard. Had it not been for Frank Hosmer, the high school principal, the bright young Du Bois would have found himself "learning a trade under lock and key" (Lewis, *W. E. B. Du Bois*, 34). On this occasion, Du Bois became painfully aware, in his own words, that many whites "actually

Figure 4. Willie Du Bois, four years old. (Courtesy of Special Collections and Archives, W. E. B. Du Bois Library, University of Massachusetts, Amherst. Reprinted by permission of David Graham Du Bois.)

considered . . . brown skin a misfortune"; others "even thought it a crime" (qtd. in Lewis, *W. E. B. Du Bois*, 34). This event would seem to have constituted a much more serious "wake-up call" for Du Bois about the consequences of race than being slighted by a white girl. But as I will argue, Du Bois's temperament seems to have been much more vulnerable to female rejection than to the threat of reform school. For this reason, the girl's refusal to accept his visiting card comes as a "vast surprise," a traumatic event that disrupts his admirable self-image (Du Bois, *Autobiography*, 94)

The girl's refusal to accept his visiting card was probably particularly meaningful to Du Bois because it contests the perfect image of himself his mother seems to have reflected for him. As he informs his readers in *Darkwater,* "She did not try to make me perfect. To her I was already perfect" (11). The idealizing gaze of Mary Silvina seems to have structured her son's ego as "a fantasy of narcissistic completion" (Spitz, "Reflections," 236–37), a fantasy that he repeats in his novels, especially *Dark Princess.* The alarming contrast between these two feminine gazes is probably what made the spurning one so disturbing that Du Bois repeatedly recalled it. This latter one undermines his image of himself as the perfect object of female desire, deserving unquestioned affection, admiration, and sympathy—in short, the object of uncontested love he imagines his mother sees when she looks at him.

But what is particularly fascinating about the mother's idealizing gaze is the fact that she finds the means in photography to objectify, preserve, and endow her gaze with power and immortality. The evidence of her effort is clearly visible, though we have not perceived it. Before focusing on the two photographs of her fabrication, I want to refer once again to another one that we have no trouble comprehending.

The desire invested in the photograph that constitutes the cover of *The Crisis* of November 1915 (see figure 1) is obvious to us. We have been well trained in recognizing sexual desire on the sultry face and partially revealed body of a pretty young woman. And like Du Bois's 1915 *Crisis* audience, as discussed in Chapter 2, we probably also question the apparent incongruence of the magazine's intended focus on racial propaganda and its signifier posed as female sexual longing on the magazine's cover. Indeed, the provocative photograph and the title *The Crisis* create a site of ruptured meaning, and we clearly discern the gap between the signifier and its referent.

By contrast, the desire of the gaze invested and preserved in the two familiar photographs of Du Bois as a child is much more subtle and therefore not so noticeable. These photographs allow us to see that his mother was dark-skinned, with typical Negroid features, and that Du Bois consistently looked more like his mulatto father as a baby and at four. Any other meaning they might bear has been beyond our perception because we have presumed that nothing else is there.

Undoubtedly, Mary Silvina arranged to have the photograph taken of the four-year-old Du Bois, wearing long twist curls and decked out in a velvet suit, a formal jacket, lace collar and cuffs, sheer light-colored stockings, shiny elegant ankle-pumps, a ring, a broach, and a necklace. Whether she purchased these items or rented them like a costume, she projected her ambitions on the child's body by posing him like a little lord of an imaginary estate. But unlike the conventional photographs of the bourgeois subject that displayed the material evidence of class status as backdrop, a dark cloth draped over an indiscernible object forms the background for this photograph and effaces all references to class. Given the extreme poverty of this abandoned mother and child, posing Du Bois in aristocratic finery was no small feat. Reflected in the extravagance of the child's appearance is the wealth of the mother's imagination, inversely matched by their material impoverishment. The photograph reveals the child as the perfect object of his mother's desire. Her gaze and its object, immortalized by photography, invite us to envision a poor black woman's fantasy of accomplishment for her son.

While the photograph stages the child returning his mother's gaze, his sultry countenance reflects no demonstrable pleasure. Rather, the young Du Bois exhibits what he would later describe as the "Dutch taciturnity" of his mother and the black Burghardts (*Autobiography*, 93). He would also attribute this mien to his "hard, domineering, unyielding" paternal grandfather Alexander Du Bois, whom Du Bois idealized and who facilitates his construction of a noble ancestry. The reason Du Bois is successful at embracing his grandfather's heroic character is probably due to his mother. She had already prepared fertile sites for the development of his heroic vision by defining it in her gaze of him and preserving it by means of photography.

The photograph of him at four aggressively presents her aspiration for her son, an aspiration she was determined to make real. For "[w]hat gave Mary Silvina the greatest of all pleasures" was Willie Du Bois's academic performance, and it pleased Du Bois to please her (Lewis, *W. E. B. Du Bois*, 30). When he graduated from elementary school, Du Bois recalled, she "rather insisted on his" not simply attending but completing high school (qtd. in Lewis, *W. E. B. Du Bois*, 31). She defined for him a resolute belief in education as the means of self-perfection. Du Bois soon became aware, to invoke his own words, that rather than going to work like most of his white cohorts and all of the few other black teenagers who lived in Great Barrington, "I sort of had to justify myself" (qtd. in Lewis, *W. E. B. Du Bois*, 31). When he later writes to his mother about entering his "illustrious name" on the registry at the capitol building in Hartford, on his way to visit her grandfather Alexander Du Bois, it is not simply his ego speaking but his mother's as well (qtd. in Lewis, *W. E. B. Du Bois*, 41).

Photography was an agent for consolidating Mary Silvina's idealized aspirations for her son and endowing him with a sense of self-importance, for "[t]o photograph is to confer importance" (Sontag, *On Photography*, 28). In 1872, when Du Bois was four, photography was not commonplace, especially among African Americans. They might be the objects of someone else's photographic gaze, constructing another's conception of reality, but seldom were poor black people the subjects of their own self-fashioning. In this regard Mary Silvina seems to have been quite unique. She must have seen the standard photographs of members of the white bourgeois households in which she worked. These photographs functioned "to confirm an ideal of the sitter" by "embellishing personal appearance" to proclaim social standing (Sontag, *On Photography*, 165). But what seems unusual about Mary Silvina is her ability to imagine herself as the photograph's desiring subject.

Mary Silvina not only conferred importance on her son by posing him as a bourgeois subject; she also fashioned herself in the pose of a madonna with child—Du Bois as a baby of about six months. Like the standard photographs of bourgeois individuals, by the last third of the nineteenth century "Renaissanced" representations of the Madonna become cultural icons in the West. The Madonna photographs of Julia Margaret Cameron, in particular, entered circulation in 1864 (Mavor, *Pleasures*, 44, 42). Such portraiture probably allowed Mary Silvina to reconstruct both her compromised womanhood and motherhood.

By the time she posed for her madonna photograph, she had already given birth to one son, Adlebert, outside of wedlock, five years before Du Bois's birth. When Du Bois's father, Alfred, deserted her shortly after their marriage, she probably began to suspect this second son's legitimacy. Exactly when she learned that Alfred was already married is uncertain. Lewis deduces the acrimony between the black Burghardts and Alfred as evidence of this knowledge (*W. E. B. Du Bois*, 23).

By the moral conventions of her age, Mary Silvina must have seen herself at best a compromised woman, and her second son, through no fault of the mother, was similarly dishonored. What better way to refashion herself than to sit for a photograph in which she and her baby posed as madonna and child? But while Cameron's madonnas staged sentimentality, the photographic portrait of Mary Silvina and her baby reflected this mother's stern determination to invest "what was left of herself" in her son (Lewis, *W. E. B. Du Bois*, 30). Her vision would define Du Bois's character, whether he liked it or not. For this reason, I suspect that Du Bois repeatedly and unconsciously associated female approval with his achievement, which he would later define as working for racial uplift. Inversely, he would associate female rejection with the suffering of racial assault.

If we identify the gaze of female approval as a central feature of Du Bois's unique fantasmatic code for structuring his fantasies and other products of his conscious and unconscious, then it is not surprising that he would use such a gaze to represent the achievement of social equality. As I argue in Chapter 2, Du Bois repeatedly associates social equality with the presence of this erotic feminine gaze. The structural similarity of political and erotic satisfaction in Du Bois's fantasmatic schema is probably the reason why they become mutually signifying especially in *Dark Princess*, and why he proclaimed that novel his favorite work.

Throughout this study, I have argued that the inscriptions of personal desire and its gratification in black textuality must be objects of critical investigation, even though neither is entirely governed by the social codes of race, gender, or class. As the previous chapters illustrate, the plenitude of a writer's fantasmatic pleasure also exceeds reason, prohibition, and indeed possibility. This radical fantasy of surplus delight uses enigmatic discourses to embrace traces of the first beloved other. Because this first object has been female, the pleasure is gendered. In *Megda* and *Seraph on the Suwanee*, the fantasy of gratification reproduces the daughter's extravagant delight in identifying with and/or recognizing a symbolization of the mother. In *Quicksand*, the daughter symbolically embraces both of her abandoning parents by playing out a fateful and erotic scenario in which she performs the maternal role to seduce the lost father. In *Dark Princess* and *Savage Holiday*, the imaginary gratification reproduces the sons' satisfaction in reclaiming another like the lost mother. The mother is an object of repudiation in *Savage Holiday*. In *Dark Princess*, the mother is an object of ideal devotion.

What has become absolutely clear to me and I hope to my readers as well is the necessity of including the analysis of the enigmatic expressions of emotional meaning in African American literary and cultural criticism. These expressions signal silent performances of desire and fantasies of fulfillment. Their inscriptions in a work's rhetorical design help us produce textual meaning that is a dialectic of the work's material and psychical elements. Such meaning is not only pertinent to an individual work but particularly meaningful in the context of a writer's entire corpus of works, for a writer's figurative schematic—her or his fantasmatic template—tends to be remarkably consistent, much like an identity theme.

My strategy for constructing meaning from synthesizing the psychical and the cultural factors of a text also eliminates a tendency to make the social meaning of a black text a reductive understanding of black people's historical ambitions for racial justice. This goal remains as important as ever. However, it has become increasingly more complicated in its articulation, let alone its realization.

This study demonstrates how the fantasy of personal plenitude complicates expressions of the elusive goal of freedom in black texts. This study also asks that we question the consequences of conceptualizing race as always the driving force of black textuality. If we expect black textual desire always to reenact the commonplace scripts of social oppression, any construction of textual meaning we may offer will already be a reinscription of the status quo rather than a sign of possibility.

Notes

Introduction

1. This question rests on the premise of the pervasiveness of racialisms in U.S. culture. For this reason, I summarize the premise in this endnote: American literature, like every aspect of society in the United States, is racialized. This is to say not that racializations are essentially identical, easily quantifiable, or readily apparent but, rather, that they are always present and ever variable. Consequently, the ubiquity of the ideologies of white supremacy in the United States over the last five hundred years has produced a national literature that is inextricably tied to racial difference.

2. For example, at the turn of the century, Paul Laurence Dunbar's "The Poet" immortalizes his critique of the white literary establishment's inability to regard black poetry as other than dialect poetry. Langston Hughes's "Negro Artist and the Racial Mountain" (1926) and Ralph Ellison's "Twentieth-Century Fiction and the Black Mask of Humanity" (1953) both critique white literary culture's presumption that artistic representations of blackness do not depict universal concerns. More recently, Joyce A. Joyce, Henry Louis Gates Jr., and Houston A. Baker Jr. question what constitutes appropriate black critical models. Respectively, see Dunbar, "The Poet"; Hughes, "Negro Artist"; Ellison, "Twentieth-Century Fiction"; Joyce, "Black Canon" and "'Who the Cap Fit'"; Gates, "What's Love,"; and Baker, "In Dubious Battle."

3. I present an extended discussion of Wright's *Outsider* in Chapter 3, which focuses on *Savage Holiday.*

4. Paul Gilroy has made a similar observation about Wright's major protagonists. According to Gilroy, they are characterized by racial selves "performatively constituted in the special dramaturgy of colonial and postcolonial settings" that include "the experience of the Southern United States." "Behind this self, barely in control of its scripts and gestures, is a

fragmented humanity that exceeds the limits of merely racial subjectivity and can only be narrated with the benefit of hindsight" ("Racial and Ethnic Identity," 24).

5. See Hogue, *Discourse,* for a discussion that surveys the demands made on black texts by the white literary mainstream.

6. I am well aware that there are many who would contend that the imposition of psychoanalytic theory on African American literature advances Western hegemony over the cultural production of black Americans, indeed over black subjectivity. This is a curious defense in light of the fact that black literary criticism often regards black characters as signifiers of racial ideologies rather than as subjects, even as it focuses on the psychological trauma of racism. Arnold Rampersad, for one, responds to such complaints by contending that "any analysis is better than none" and that "anti-Freudian blacks have offered no countersystem or antisystem worthy of the name." Rampersad adds that "the Freud–Erik Erikson model does not so much declare itself as final truth as it raises questions of enormous value" ("Psychology," 11).

When I recently mentioned to the members of an Internet list about African American culture that I was reading black novels by referring to psychoanalysis, a presumably black respondent questioned my use of psychoanalysis, posting, "You mean wanting to sleep with 'Mommy and Daddy'? That's a white thing." Whether the other members of this list agreed or disagreed with this reply, I don't know. No one else offered a comment. I started to ask this respondent about the incestuous desire in two black novels—Ralph Ellison's *Invisible Man* (1952) and Carolivia Herron's *Thereafter Johnny* (1991). But I decided that while the Internet was a good medium for determining attitudes, it was not so good for probing complicated issues.

7. Frances Cress Welsing and James Comer, two prominent black psychiatrists, argue that racism constitutes a reaction-formation defense mechanism (Greene, "Considerations," 391). James Comer explains racism as "a low level defense and adjustment mechanism utilized by groups to deal with psychological and social insecurities similar to the manner in which individuals utilize psychic defenses and adjustment mechanisms to deal with anxiety. A given society may promote and reward racism to enable members of the group in control to obtain a sense of personal adequacy and security at the expense of the group with less control" (qtd. in Greene, "Considerations," 391).

8. The citation is in the name of Goldberg, the organizer of the discussion. The quotation is from the presentation by Percy Hintzen.

9. Freud's *Psychopathology of Everyday Life* is helpful for explaining what is meant by unconscious expressions, whether they are single words or extended narratives. Here Freud argues that slips of the tongue, errors, memory lapses, and other behavioral and linguistic symptoms are manifestations of unconscious motives: "they are compromise formations between forbidden impulses or ideas and the censorship imposed upon them" (Moore and Fine, *Psychoanalytic Terms,* 139). By referring to the structural linguistics of Ferdinand de Saussure and the structural anthropology of Claude Lévi-Strauss, Jacques Lacan reinterprets Freudian theory on language to postulate what he calls the "Symbolic Order." The Symbolic Order "refers quite simply to language itself and the entire realm of culture, conceived as a symbol system structured on the model of language" (Childers and Hentzi, *New Columbia Dictionary,* 299). When the subject enters the Symbolic, she or he functions in culture by means of language. Although language articulates the subject's needs and de-

mands, "it cannot deliver desire in its transparency." Desire is displaced "in (and by) language" (J. Butler, "Desire," 370).

10. The most famous of Freud's essays about the unconscious and creativity is "Creative Writers and Day-Dreaming." I plot many of the expressions of conscious and unconscious desire in detail in Chapter 2 on Du Bois's *Dark Princess*.

11. Freud's developmental scheme identifies the oedipal complex as the key stage in which the child heeds the demands of the father to separate from the mother, so as to become individuated and socialized. Because Freud presumes the child to be male, these goals are frequently obscured in Freud's writings by the more sensational and reductive plot of the young son's incestuous desire for the mother and his fear of the father's retaliation in the form of the threat of castration. Freud's selection of the symbolic term "castration" also obscures the actual object that creates anxiety—partriarchal power. The terminology indicates that Freud's own subjectivity dominates his effort to plot a universal story of personality development, for Freud's bourgeois individuation (which is under paternal regulation) and his Jewish alienation in anti-Semitic Austria greatly influence the structure of the oedipal scenario.

By recognizing that the oedipal scenario arises from the social repressions of the bourgeois-family structure rather than a universal psychical structure, as Freud's colleague Wilhelm Reich contended and Deleuze and Guattari further clarify, we can see that "psychic repression depend[s] on social repression" (*Anti-Oedipus*, 118). There is a distinction between psychic and social repression. Because they are linked together, much like the proverbial chicken and the egg, we frequently misunderstand which repression is actually primary. According to Deleuze and Guattari, "social repression needs psychic repression precisely in order to form docile subjects and to ensure the reproduction of the social formation, including its repressive structures. But social repression should not be understood by using as a starting point a familial repression coextensive with civilization—far from it; it is civilization that must be understood in terms of a social repression inherent to a given form of social production. Social repression bears on desire—and not solely on needs or interests—only by means of sexual repression. The family is indeed the delegated agent of this psychic repression, insofar as it ensures 'a mass psychological reproduction of the economic system of a society'" (*Anti-Oedipus*, 118). Psychic repression, then, is the primary emotional energy that mobilizes the social repression that is constitutive of civilization. "[T]he social repression of desire or sexual repression—that is the *stasis* of libidinal energy"—energizes the oedipal plot (Deleuze and Guattari, *Anti-Oedipus*, 118). This plot is a secondary formation, indeed a cultural myth that structures the effects of the already present bourgeois social repression on the subject.

The family is the appointed site of psychic repression, and the father is the delegated agent for carrying out this function by means of prohibitions, or what Lacan would call "the Law of the Father." The "incestuous drives are the disfigured image of the repressed." The "process of oedipalization is therefore the result of this double operation. *It is in one and the same movement that the repressive social production is replaced by the repressing family, and that the latter offers a displaced image of desiring-production that represents the repressed as incestuous familial drives. In this way the family/drives relationship is substituted for the relationship between the two orders of production*"—the family and civilization (Deleuze and Guattari, *Anti-Oedipus*, 119–20; emphasis in original). Freudian psychoanalysis misreads this relationship as an originary phenomenon, when in actuality it is the effect of transference.

Rather than understanding the resolution of the oedipal conflict as the child's repression of desire for the mother in the Freudian context, we can see it as the child's recognition of the demands of civilization to repress all prohibited desire. This process constructs a subject "that radically transcends the Cartesian understanding of the ego as a fixed, indivisible, and permanent whole" (Elliott, *Social Theory*, 29). Despite Freud's personal obsessions and presumptions, he advances our understanding of subject formation by seeing it as a relationship among "the self, the body, others, and culture itself" (Elliott, *Social Theory*, 29).

Object-relations theory, a post-Freudian division (or school) of psychoanalysis (called Kleinian theory in its early formulation) began in the late 1920s with the works of British analyst Melanie Klein, who studied with Freud in Vienna. Klein's hypotheses center on the infantile stage of psychosexual development, which Freud had already labeled as the pre-oedipal stage. Rather than focus on the guilt and repression of the later oedipal stage, Klein observed the play of young children and discovered their inner worlds of primary identifications with "objects"—"entities perceived as separate from the self, either whole persons or parts of the body, either existing in the external world or internalized as mental representations"—that structure their personalities (Elizabeth Wright, *Feminism and Psychoanalysis*, 284). In their play, Klein found unconscious and primitive fantasies, anxieties, and defenses that arise as a result of internalized relationships between the infantile self and external objects. These responses form identifications that define personality development. According to Klein, the goal of the young subject is to move from the *paranoid-schizoid position*, during which fantasies of persecution and aggressive splitting are dominant, to the *depressive position*, in which love, guilt, and reparations are predominant. Whereas Freudian theory regards both male and female children as little males until the oedipal complex, Klein postulates a primary femininity for both sexes because both identify with the mother. However, Klein theorizes sexually specific paths of socialization during the oedipal stage, where "womb envy" for boys corresponds to "penis envy" for girls. Unlike Freudian theory, which conceives of the oedipal stage as a developmental process that achieves termination, Kleinian (and later object-relations) theory contends that the subject never fully achieves the depressive position. During intense conflict, Klein argues, the subject reverts to the symptomatic behavior of the paranoid-schizoid position. Throughout the life span, then, individuals move between the two positions.

Lacanian psychoanalysis began in the 1930s with the works of French psychoanalyst Jacques Lacan, who revitalized psychoanalysis by rereading the works of Freud in the context of the structural linguistics theory of Swiss linguist Ferdinand de Saussure. Basically, Lacanian theory claims "that the self is a misrecognized object of the imaginary; that primary narcissism is fundamental to the structuration of subjectivity; that the other (person) is unknowable to the self; and that the unconscious is an effect of the internal differences of a universal structure of language" (Elliot, *Social Theory*, 123). Lacanian precepts place the self in three realms of perceivable experience—the Real, Imaginary, and Symbolic. The Real is not a reformulation of Freud's reality principle, which is a regulatory demand to conform to social constraints in order to achieve satisfaction. Lacan's Real is "brute reality" or material entities that are left behind after the subject has internalized the object or the experience. The Real then "resists the imposition" or the mediating processes of the Imaginary

(Elizabeth Wright, *Feminism and Psychoanalysis,* 375). By Imaginary, Lacan does not mean the imagination but rather the subject's internalization of an image.

The most important instance of the Imaginary occurs during what Lacan terms the "mirror stage," at which time the subject is between the ages of six and eighteen months. The subject realizes an imaginary or illusory unification of the body by means of identifying with its own reflection in a mirror. The child identifies the self with its specular image in the mirror, and this image "situates the agency of the ego" (Lacan, *Écrits,* 2). By means of this identification, which is based on a misrecognition of the self, the "specular I" anticipates the "social I" (Lacan, *Écrits,* 5). Thus, central to the Imaginary realm is the subject in the act of filling the lack that is constitutive of its already perceived fragmented body. Lacanian and Freudian constructions of the subject designate identification as the basis of ego formation. According to Freud, the social identification of consciousness (the ego) arises from the unconscious, which is the primary structure, as a consequence of the repression of the oedipus complex. For Lacan, the emergence of consciousness of the social self occurs during the mirror phase. This identification is the product of imaginary reflections and not the unconscious because for Lacan there is no unconscious prior to language or entry into what he calls the Symbolic.

With language the subject achieves individuation, identity, and the logic of socialization, or what Lacan calls the "Law of the Father." The Symbolic, then, mediates the expression of need, demand, and desire originating in childhood. While need and demand have specific objects of fulfillment, desire cannot be satisfied because it is a part of the primary lack of the unconscious that the Imaginary covers over and that language speaks in slips and rhetorical devices. Subjects can be said, then, to speak their subjectivity in conscious and unconscious discourses. The correspondence between language and subjectivity allows Lacan to hypothesize that "in the unconscious is the whole structure of language" (Lacan, *Écrits,* 147). The importance of Lacanian theory in its relationship to literary scholarship "lies in its transformation of the psychoanalytic problematic into a theory of subjectivity as it is constituted by and through language" (Brenkman, *Culture,* 142).

Because Lacanian theory designates subjectivity as structured in and by language, it is especially pertinent to literary criticism. Lacanian theory identifies the rhetorical structure of the text itself as the appropriate object of the psychoanalytic critical enterprise. Therefore, the subjectivity of a text is constitutive of the attributes of language in that text.

12. For example, in "The Quicksands of the Self: Nella Larsen and Heinz Kohut," Barbara Johnson performs an intertextual reading of *Quicksand* and Heinz Kohut's theories on narcissistic personality disorder. Here Johnson analyzes the disintegration of the protagonist's ego and exposes Kohut's failure to appreciate the effects of the institutional, narcissistic structures of racism and race pride on subject formation. Johnson argues that Kohut "generally neglects or subsumes the *social* mirroring environment in favor of the dynamics of the nuclear family" ("Quicksands," 194; emphasis in original). Like Johnson and others, I am imploring scholars and critics of African American culture to interrogate the racial assumptions of self-identified white theoretical paradigms.

13. For example, Nancy Chodorow combines Freudian and object-relations models in her works (*The Reproduction of Mothering* [1978], *Feminism and Psychoanalytic Theory* [1989], and *Femininities, Masculinities, Sexualities* [1994]) and regards Elizabeth Abel's "psychoanalytic interpretative approaches" (derived from both Lacanian psychoanalysis

and from object-relations theory) in "Race, Class, and Psychoanalysis?: Opening Questions" (1990) as "a stunning example" of how theoretical models can be modified to fit culturally diverse circumstances of analysis ("Gender," 523). Jessica Benjamin also extends her use of combined schools of psychoanalytic theory even "further than some explicit advocates of the relationship perspective might" (*Like Subjects,* 4).

14. Erich Fromm repeatedly identified this fallacy of classic psychoanalysis. See, for example, "Psychoanalysis and Sociology," "Politics and Psychoanalysis," and "The Crisis of Psychoanalysis" in Bronner and Kellner, *Critical Theory.*

15. In 1989 Modern Language Association presented a panel on psychoanalysis and race. The program was arranged by the Division on Psychological Approaches to Literature. Jane Gallop presided over the panel of three presenters: Henry Louis Gates Jr., Barbara E. Johnson, and Hortense J. Spillers. The 1996 Modern Language Association presented another panel on psychoanalysis and race. Claire Kahane presided over a panel of four presenters: Mark Bracher, Barbara E. Johnson, Hortense J. Spillers, and me.

16. See Abel, "Black Writing" and "Race," and J. Walton, "Re-Placing Race."

Chapter 1

1. Johnson's *Martina Merida; or, What Is My Motive* (1901) is no longer extant.

2. See Molly Hite's introduction to the 1988 Oxford University Press edition of *Megda.* Here she rightly explains that as "a novel by a black woman," *Megda* "perhaps inevitably . . . encodes tensions about being black and female" (xxvii). However, rather than following this line of inquiry and situate her reading within a textual system that negotiates that complex identity, Hite relies on (white bourgeois) feminist paradigms to read *Megda.* She associates the novel with the white American subgenre of girls' fiction, "the female Christian *Bildungsroman*" (xxxii), and reads accordingly. As a consequence, Hite privileges a white cultural feminist analysis of gender inequity to the degree that she suppresses the novel's representations of female authority and fails to query the consequences of black and white people's different cultural relationships to domesticity and patriarchy. According to this model, *Megda*'s thematics seem to conform to the goal of this subgenre, namely to form "a Christian marriage in which the wife is entirely subordinated to her husband" (xxxiv). Such a reading, Hite explains, "may well strike twentieth-century readers as a regression, inasmuch as it takes her [Meg] away from leadership, self-reliance, and personal responsibility for her actions—away, that is, from precisely those qualities that made her an attractive heroine" (xxxiii). Hite acknowledges that *Megda* engenders "some resistance to the patriarchal thrust of the female Christian *Bildungsroman*" through the presence of maternal figures. Yet, she continues, the conventions of this plot make Meg's "growing up seem oddly like growing *down*, a diminution" (xxxiii). Hite's reading fits Alcott's *Little Women.* Clearly, it is my purpose in this chapter to demonstrate that *Megda* presents enough resistance to the traditional female Christian *Bildungsroman* to preserve and further develop Meg's subjectivity.

3. To illustrate this point, I refer to the Irish because they constituted the largest group of nineteenth-century European immigrants. Among European immigrants, the Irish were the most frequent targets of ethnic humor during the late eighteenth and nineteenth cen-

turies (Secor, "Ethnic Humor," 177). The largest wave of Irish immigration occurred shortly after the 1845 potato blight. As David Roediger has explained, these new immigrants learned to capitalize on the chronic fear of black-white miscegenation to protect them from job competition (*Wages*, 133–66). Their demands for segregated workplaces produced "white" laboring jobs, and employment segregation in turn constructed them as white. By means of manipulating the racial and labor discourses, then, the mid-nineteenth-century Irish immigrants initiated their variation of the so-called melting process that had already transformed eighteenth-century Irish immigrants into white U.S. citizens.

4. For a discussion of desire, see E. Wright, *Feminism and Psychoanalysis*, 63–68, and Lacan, "Subversion."

5. The name Megda seems to be a conflation of two names: Magda, which is a condensed form of the biblical Magdalene, and Meg (March), Jo March's sister in *Little Women*.

6. Kelley's black contemporaries resisted the nineteenth-century positivist viewpoint that racial identity was an objective classification. Rather, her contemporaries regarded race as a designator of cultural and not biological difference. Thus, the white-mulatto characters were counterarguments to the positivist racial science.

7. bell hooks cites white supremacy as the force suppressing the linguistic marker— "white"—in dominant discourse. "In a racially imperialist nation such as ours," she explains, "it is the dominant race that reserves for itself the luxury of dismissing racial identity while the oppressed race is made daily aware of their racial identity. It is the dominant race that can make it seem that their experience is representative" (*Ain't I a Woman*, 138).

8. Kelley selected excerpts from Act II, scenes 2 and 3 of *Macbeth*. As Alcott's Jo March explains, these scenes comprise "the killing part," the scenes she has always wanted to perform (*Little Women*, 14).

9. Female narratology designates the conventional narrative strategies found in works in which the authority is female and not necessarily those works of a female writer.

10. The "classic" conversion narrative of the nineteenth century follows a predictable outline (Brereton, *From Sin*, 6). Usually, such narratives treat five stages of the conversion experience: (1) life before the conversion process begins, when narrators more or less ignore the question of salvation; (2) a period when narrators become acutely aware of their sinfulness and of the possibility that they will be damned forever; (3) the surrender to God's will in conversion proper, during which converts feel relief from the oppressive sense of sinfulness and gain confidence or at least hope that they are saved; (4) a description of the narrator's changed behavior and attitudes, resulting from conversion; and (5) an account of periods of discouragement and low spiritual energy followed by renewals of dedication until salvation is attained.

11. Gay explains that the additions of erotic love and spiritual conversion to the Victorian novel of development assured its popularity.

12. Kelley has a central character in her *Four Girls at Cottage City* refer to this popular evangelical novel. Phelps's other best-selling novels included *The Gates Ajar* (1868), *The Gates Between* (1887), and *Within the Gates* (1901). See McDowell's introduction to *Four Girls at Cottage City*, xxxiii.

13. Good taste and the accoutrements of bourgeois respectability were particularly meaningful for African Americans of the post-Reconstruction era. The acquisition of the means to display refinement, domesticity, and piety became symbols for reflecting their

readiness for racial equality. Black people's alterity to white culture's ideology of true womanhood produced idealized constructions of femininity and domesticity in post-Reconstruction African American culture that represented emancipatory optimism. Its expression was bound by two cultural extremes—one conceptually symbolic and the other socially performative. Idealized expressions of black domestic ideology symbolically endorsed the political aspirations of African Americans to become assimilated in the dominant society as full-fledged citizens and to participate in class mobility. Their adoption of genteel domesticity was the sign of their civic worthiness, as they asserted social parity in terms of gender and class rather than race. Not only was bourgeois domesticity a part of a theoretical emancipatory discourse; in practice, domesticity was less confining in African American culture because it was subject to greater female mediation than its white counterpart. Even when black gender and class ideologies adopted many of the regulations of the dominant culture at the turn of the twentieth century, such as restricting black women's access to higher education (which prompted the criticism of Anna Cooper, Gertrude Mossell, and Pauline Hopkins, for example), these restrictions were seldom as rigid as those in white society. Second-class citizenship undermined patriarchal power among African Americans and subsequently made black gender and class conventions more pliable than their white counterparts. Therefore, gender and class discourses became available for symbolizing black civil desire, as the novels of black writers of the post-Reconstruction era demonstrate. See Tate, *Domestic Allegories,* 97–123.

14. "Pre-oedipal" here refers to "the period of psychosexual development" in which one's "attachment to the mother predominates both sexes." See Laplanche and Pontalis, *Language,* 328.

15. Miller's citation in this passage references the iconography of landscape; however, his explanation is equally pertinent for other beautiful objects of erotic displacement. See Miller, *Dark Eden,* 152.

16. On Easter, for example, the narrator exhorts, "I must tell about Meg's dress; it was the prettiest one of all. . . . It was one of those beautiful, delicate shades of 'apple green.' . . . She wore a small hat covered entirely with apple blossoms—delicate pink and white beauties" (*M* 226). On another occasion she "wore a pale-blue cheese-cloth dress, and a large black hat with slightly rolling brim, and a wreath of yellow daises around the crown. She had a great sheaf of yellow daises [*sic*] over her left shoulder. A wide band of black velvet was around her white throat" (*M* 266).

17. The symmetry between textual and human subjectivity suggests that similar psychosexual experience structures desire in both the text and the human subject. Psychoanalysis has identified that experience for humans as the pre-oedipal mother-child dyad and the oedipal conflict among the child, the mother, and the father. My use of the article "the" is meant to indicate the unconscious, internalized construction of the parent or parental imago and not the historical parent, which I shall indicate by using the possessive pronouns "her" or "his." Because these primary relationships play out integral roles in the formation of the personality and in the orientation of desire, I hypothesize that they also characterize primary textual desire. Unfortunately, when the oedipal complex moved into U.S. currency in the 1920s, popular culture trivialized this hypothesis about "the organised body of loving and hostile wishes which the child experiences toward its parents" into

the child's desire to "sleep with Mommy or Daddy" (Laplanche and Pontalis, *Language*, 282–83). While reductive versions of the oedipal complex circulate in U.S. popular culture, the pre-oedipal stage is virtually unknown in popular currency. As the suffix "pre" indicates, this period of psychosexual development precedes the oedipal stage and is characterized by the attachment to and fantasies about the mother that predominates the internal life of children of both sexes. The incest prohibition causes the love objects of both the pre-oedipal and oedipal stages to become a part of the child's unconscious desire, which is later displaced onto appropriate surrogates.

Because women mother, women figure as the primary love objects for both sexes. Consequently, heterosexual males have a more direct route for satisfying unconscious primary desire for the mother, by means of female surrogates, than do heterosexual females, who partly displace primary desire onto the father and eventually onto other male surrogates (Chodorow, *Feminism*, 76–78). However, "the primary, profound, primeval oneness with mother" that is "buried but active in the core of one's identity," as analyst Robert Stoller explains, poses a fundamental but latent threat to masculinity, as we shall see in the following chapters on Du Bois and Wright (qtd. in Sprengnether, *Spectral Mother*, 198). In order to preserve their individuation, males must defend themselves against the powerful but latent primary desire to identify with the mother and her surrogate in the female other. By contrast, such desire is tempered for heterosexual females, who displace desire onto a discontinuous masculine other. Despite the displacement, though, heterosexual females continue unconsciously to desire the primary object, as Chodorow suggests (see the third epigraph at the beginning of this chapter). I suspect that this difference in structuring desire for heterosexual males and females also structures textual desire in *Megda* and other novels that inscribe heterosexual desire, as I will demonstrate in this and the succeeding chapters.

18. The substitution of the homonym "bare" for "bear" also suggests sexual intimacy. I thank Vicki Arana for this observation.

19. I thank Ann Kelly and Vicki Arana for these observations.

20. We should recall that Ethel was to play the role of Ophelia in the youth theatrical until she gives up such vanities as a sign of her spiritual conversion.

21. See Freud, "Family Romances"; Klein, "Early Stages of the Oedipus Conflict," in *Love*.

22. See Freud's "Dream-Work" in *Interpretation of Dreams*, 277–310.

23. In "Psychopathic Characters on Stage," Freud contextualizes his analysis within Greek classical drama. He analyzes an extreme form of neurosis (even psychosis) as a model for explaining how the normal psyche responds in similar cases of unconscious identification. My application of psychopathic empathy to *Megda* is not meant to imply that this novel dramatizes psychopathology. Rather, I refer to the reader's likely recognition of the representation of unconscious aggression in the text as responsible for Ethel's death.

24. Jean Laplanche and J.-B. Pontalis explain "over-determination" as "a consequence of the [dream-]work of condensation. It is not only expressed on the level of isolated elements of the dream—the dream as a whole may be over-determined." They emphasize that this process does not mean that the dream image may be interpreted variably but that the context, the intonation, and the superfluous signifiers of the dream identify its specific meaning. See Laplanche and Pontalis, *Language*, 292.

Chapter 2

1. Griffith and Dixon appropriated the chivalric imagery and discourses of Sir Walter Scott's *Ivanhoe* (1819) to structure their portraits of the "Old South."

2. For a history of the Ku Klux Klan, see, for example, Chalmers, *Hooded Americanism.*

3. In 1909, Freud was invited to lecture at Clark University in Worcester, Massachusetts. During this first trans-Atlantic trip, Freud met with William James, one of Du Bois's favorite Harvard professors. James knew German (as did Du Bois) and had already been reading Freud's lectures with "great interest." James accorded the "future of psychology" to Freud's work (Jones, *Life,* 2:57). Inasmuch as Du Bois maintained contact with James long after he left Harvard and James was clearly impressed with Freud's work, I suspect that the two were likely to have discussed Freud's hypotheses (Lewis, *W. E. B. Du Bois,* 225, 294, 366, 371, 565).

4. Conversation of January 20, 1994, with David Levering Lewis, Du Bois's principal biographer.

5. Aptheker provides an excellent summary of the reviews of *Dark Princess* in his introduction to the novel. See Aptheker, Introduction, 21–29.

6. "Graustarkian" refers to the well-known romantic novel *Graustark* (1901), by George Barr McCutcheon, about the military and courtly adventures of a group of valiant characters in the fictional kingdom of Graustark. Another reviewer labels *Dark Princess* a "skyscraper problem novel of the Negro intellectual and the world radical," filled with "overelaboration" and "an epic theme . . . befogged by false romanticism" (Locke, "Negro Intellectual," 12). Another states that this "is by no means a dull novel, for the author's passion alone is enough to give it vigor and interest. . . . [T]he book judged as a novel has only the slightest merit. As a document, as a program, as an exhortation, it has interest and value, but one can readily imagine the mirth it will provoke among the Harlem literati" (Review of *Dark Princess, Springfield Republican,* 216). And another reviewer asserts that the novel is "well written, but there is enough material in it for several novels and the plot is flamboyant and unconvincing" (Review of *Dark Princess, New York Times,* 19). Still another refers to the novel's "fantastic plot" and "Du Bois's old white-hot indignation against racial oppression and also his fierce pride in the beauty and deep tragic joy and rich loveliness of the dark peoples" ("Throb of Dark Drums," 12). The reviewer for *The Crisis* applauds *Dark Princess* for raising "the dead weight of our solid depression by propaganda at once eloquent and sane" (Allison Davis, "Browsing Reader," 339). The reviewers generally agree, though, in the words of one, that *Dark Princess* "is not wholly successful" (Locke, "Negro Intellectual," 12).

7. After decades of neglect, Herbert Aptheker had the novel reprinted in 1971 as a part of a mammoth project to republish all of Du Bois's writings for library holdings. Even then, only a few scholars of African American culture became acquainted with this obscure work. Consequently, *Dark Princess* has been a marginal novel despite the fame of its author. In 1995 the University Press of Mississippi reissued the novel and thereby provides contemporary readers with an opportunity to observe the passion of Du Bois's commitment to racial progress, manifested in the eroticism of *Dark Princess.*

8. Here Du Bois exclaims that "'Dark Princess' [is] my favorite book." Herbert Aptheker, a friend and colleague of Du Bois, has corroborated Du Bois's affection for this work, re-

calling that he quite often "spoke [of the novel] with a special fondness" (Aptheker, Introduction, 29).

I am indebted to my colleague Marshall Alcorn for pointing out that the novel's failure arises not from Du Bois's choice of fusing erotic fantasy with political activism but from his inability to involve his reader in this fantasy.

9. By 1940 Du Bois had written the following books: *The Suppression of the African Slave Trade to the United States of America, 1638–1870* (1896); *The Philadelphia Negro: A Social Study* (1900); *The Souls of Black Folk* (1903); *John Brown* (1909); *The Quest of the Silver Fleece* (1911); *The Negro* (1915); *Darkwater: Voices from within the Veil* (1920); *The Gift of Black Folk* (1924); *Black Reconstruction in America* (1935); and *Black Folk, Then and Now: An Essay in the History and Sociology of the Negro Race* (1939).

In addition to these nine books, between 1897 and 1915 Du Bois edited fifteen volumes on the study of Negro life that evolved from the proceedings of Annual Conferences on the Negro Problem at Atlanta University, which were published by Atlanta University Press: *Social and Physical Condition of Negroes in Cities* (1897); *Some Efforts of American Negroes for Their Own Social Betterment* (1898); *The Negro in Business* (1899); *The College-Bred Negro* (1900); *The Negro Common School* (1901); *The Negro Artisan* (1902); *The Negro Church* (1903); *Some Notes on Negro Crime, Particularly in Georgia* (1904); *The Health and Physique of the Negro American* (1906); *Economic Cooperation among Negro Americans* (1907); *The Negro American Family* (1908); *Efforts for Social Betterment among Negro Americans* (1910); *The Common School and the Negro American* (1912); *The Negro American Artisan* (1913); and *Morals and Manners among Negro Americans* (1915).

After *Dusk of Dawn* appeared, Du Bois wrote eight more books, three of which were novels that were written in the eighth decade of his life. These works include *Encyclopedia of the Negro: Preparatory Volume with Reference Lists and Reports* (1945); *Color and Democracy: Colonies and Peace* (1945); *The World and Africa: An Inquiry into the Part which Africa Has Played in World History* (1947); *Battle for Peace: The Story of My 83rd Birthday* (1952); The Black Flame Trilogy (*The Ordeal of Mansart* [1957], *Mansart Builds a School* [1959], and *Worlds of Color* [1961]); and *An ABC of Color: Selections from over a Half Century of the Writings of W. E. B. Du Bois* (1963, the year of his death).

The term "Negro" is a European historical designation for African peoples. Throughout this book, I will use several terms in addition to Negro—colored, black, Afro-American, and African American—to designate New World people of African descent of different historical periods and political persuasions.

10. The term "oedipus complex" first appears in Freud's "Special Type of Object Choice Made by Men," published in 1910. The oedipus complex became linked with the nuclear family and what Freud called "family romances" (1909) when Jung began to question Freud's theories on the sexual etiology of neuroses. By 1920 the term had become the identifying feature that distinguished Freud's adherents from his opponents.

11. Freud's gender presumptions are a product of the patriarchal demands of his age and his own awareness of oedipalized conflicts with his father, whose death evidently exacerbated Freud's guilt.

12. In 1940 Du Bois attempts to alleviate the anxiety about the circumstances of his birth by inserting into his autobiographical record reference to the 1867 marriage registry for his parents at the Great Barrington Town Hall (*Dusk,* 109; Lewis, *W. E. B. Du Bois,* 588).

13. Allison Davis (1902–83) a psychologist and educator, received a B.A. from Williams College in 1924, an M.A. from Howard University in 1925, and a Ph.D. from the University of Chicago in 1942. Davis knew Du Bois personally and reviewed *Dark Princess* for *The Crisis*. Davis was professor of sociology and educational psychology at the University of Chicago, where he taught from 1942 to 1965. His most famous book (coauthored with John Dollard) is *Children of Bondage* (1940).

14. Priscilla Wald associates Du Bois's symbolic use of the veil, especially his reference to the story "Of the Coming of John" in *The Souls of Black Folk* as a "tale twice told," with Nathaniel Hawthorne's *Twice-Told Tales,* published in 1837. Wald also notes an earlier prototype of the veil in Query 14 of Thomas Jefferson's *Notes on the State of Virginia* (Wald, *Constituting Americans,* 182–83). References to veiled female faces also appear in Du Bois's unpublished sketches, written while he was studying in Berlin, and later in the *Dark Princess.*

15. At the time Du Bois wrote this novel, he had already devoted thirty years of his life to his marriage to Nina Gomer Du Bois. He characterizes this marriage as "not . . . absolutely ideal" (*Autobiography,* 280). According to him, he had been "literally frightened into marriage" to a woman whose "life-long training as a virgin, made it almost impossible for her ever to regard sexual intercourse as not fundamentally indecent." Du Bois goes on to explain that "[i]t took careful restraint on my part not to make her unhappy at this most beautiful of human experiences. It was no easy task for a normal and lusty young man" (*Autobiography* 281). "To the world," Du Bois adds in another context, "I was nearly always the isolated outsider looking in and seldom part of that inner life [of human beings]. Partly that role was thrust upon me because of the color of my skin. But I was not a prig. I was a lusty man with all normal appetites. I loved 'Wine, Women and Song'" (*Autobiography,* 283).

16. During his years at Harvard in the late 1880s, Du Bois was a committed student of philosophy. He planned to study under George Herbert Palmer, who was a "profound and devoted Hegelian" (Williamson, *Crucible,* 406); however, Palmer went on sabbatical. Consequently, Du Bois enrolled in the class of William James, who at that time was developing a Hegelian counterdiscourse in "pragmatic philosophy" (Williamson, *Crucible,* 406). No doubt, James's pragmatism fueled the dialectical dynamic of Hegelian metaphysics for Du Bois. Under the instruction of George Santayana, Du Bois also studied Immanuel Kant's *Critique of Pure Reason* (*Autobiography,* 143). Two other professors, Nathaniel Southgate Shaler and Albert Bushnell Hart, reaffirmed Du Bois's belief (which appears throughout *The Souls of Black Folk*) that each race has distinctive traits for fostering human progress. Du Bois's study at the University of Berlin would further develop this concept. Although Du Bois did not study philosophy at the University of Berlin, he arrived at a time when "Berlin was in the midst of a Hegelian revival" (Williamson, *Crucible,* 407). Hegel provided Du Bois with a philosophical model that influenced his thinking. This model explains the truth of human history as the positive or negative progressive reconciliation of contradictory propositions.

17. Davis's portrait of the man on the rack in this citation is particularly meaningful, given the frequency that Du Bois uses the word "writhe" in his unpublished fiction. Davis knew Du Bois personally and therefore had the opportunity to observe him. His portrait of Du Bois has much in common with the biographical sketch of him that appears in *The*

New Worlds of Negro Americans by Harold R. Isaacs. Isaacs includes transcriptions from an interview that he conducted with Du Bois when he was ninety-two. What is remarkable about the excerpts from this interview is that just as Du Bois had earlier predicted that the problem of the twentieth-century was the color line, he predicts here that in the twenty-first century the next stage in the battle would be for human dignity.

18. At sixteen, in 1885, Du Bois went to Fisk University, where he earned his A.B. He then fulfilled his childhood ambition to enter Harvard College. In 1888 he enrolled at Harvard as a junior. In 1890 he graduated cum laude and was one of six commencement speakers. In 1892 he secured the Slater Fund Fellowship for two years of study at the University of Berlin. In 1896 he received a Ph.D. from Harvard. His dissertation, *The Suppression of the African Slave-Trade to the United States of America, 1638–1870,* was published as the first volume in the Harvard Historical Series. He referred to this early period of extraordinary success and achievement as "the age of miracles." Unfortunately, despite his brilliance and labor, he was never to recover the eminence of these early years.

19. For example, see Du Bois's famous *Souls of Black Folk* and *Darkwater* as well as the more obscure 1915 sociological treatise *The Negro* and reviews of his extravagant pageant *The Star of Ethiopia,* also staged that year.

20. Kautilya is the name of a well-known adviser of a Hindu kingdom before the Arabian invasion. Kautilya is also, as Arnold Rampersad points out, the name of the male author of the *Artha-sastra,* a political treatise written between 326 and 291 B.C. ("Du Bois's Passage," 11). Rampersad further identifies Du Bois's familiarity with Indian culture by referring to the respective Sanskrit and Hindi words for "black" and "the black one"— "Krishna" and "Kali"—as terms of endearment that he uses in *Dark Princess* ("Du Bois's Passage," 20).

21. Psychoanalyst Gilbert J. Rose explains in *Trauma and Mastery in Life and Art* that "creative and clinical processes follow the fundamental psychic principle of attempting to master passively experienced trauma by active repetition" (44).

22. For a provocative essay that uses psychoanalytic theory to analyze *The Scarlet Letter,* see Diehl, "Re-Reading," 235–51. This essay focuses on Hawthorne's "repressed authorial desires" to expose "a subtext that links [Hawthorne's] motives for writing to a search for the lost mother" (237, 236). Diehl hypothesizes Hawthorne's "deep authorial conflict toward Hester as lover/mother" ("Re-Reading," 236). This is a deep-rooted conflict of male psychical development that Freud chronicled as the oedipal stage and that Du Bois symbolizes in *Dark Princess* with Matthew's attachment to Kautilya.

23. For discussion of the oceanic feeling, see Freud, *Civilization and Its Discontents,* 64–65, 72.

24. The Papers of William E. B. Du Bois, reel 88, frames 468, 472, 473. Du Bois included the text of this entry in his autobiography. See *Autobiography,* 170–71.

25. Du Bois often wrote about girls in his weekly expository writing assignments for English 12 at Harvard. See, for example, those dated October 31, 1890 (Papers, reel 88, frame 329), January 21, 1891 (reel 88, frame 357), February 24, 1891 (reel 88, frame 362), and undated (reel 88, frames 350–51). He also made beautiful women, often in conjunction with stolen jewels and railroad intrigue, the subject of many of his early stories, published and unpublished. For unpublished examples, see "Fables from within the Veil" (reel 88, frames 970–71), "Princess Wata" (reel 88, frames 927–28), "The Necklace of Emeralds"

(reel 88, frames 1117–21), "The Diamond Earring" (reel 88, frames 1058–62), and "The Jewel" (reel 88, frames 1235–42). For published examples, see "The Shaven Lady" and "The Case." The woman in "The Case" seems to be a replica of one in the unpublished sketch "A Woman."

Du Bois was also fond of the cloak-and-dagger story and plots of railroad intrigue. "The Case" and "The Shaven Lady" also employ these narrative devices. For representative published stories about princesses and noble women who rescue or are rescued by noble men, see "The Woman" and "The Princess of the Hither Isles."

Representative messianic scenarios include Du Bois's staged pageant *The Star of Ethiopia,* which he says attracted audiences of 14,000. For details about this work see Du Bois, *"Star of Ethiopia,";* a detailed review in the *Washington Bee* (October 23, 1915) included in the Papers at the Library of Congress (reel 87, frames 1535, 1536), and the program (reel 88, frames, 1528, 1529). Also see Du Bois's "Three Wise Men"; "Second Coming"; "Flight into Egypt"; "Gospel According to Mary Brown"; and "Black Man Brings His Gifts" in *The Creative Writings of W. E. B. Du Bois.*

Several of the above unpublished sketches also feature princesses; see, for example, "Princess Watta" (frames 928–29) and "Fables from within the Veil" (frames 970–71) in reel 88 of his Papers. Others feature mystery stories about jewels and jewel cachets; see "The Necklace of Emeralds" (frames 1059–63), and "The Jewels" (frames 1236–43), all in reel 88. In addition, see these representative fragments of unpublished pageants: "The Jewel of Ethiopia" (undated, reel 87, frame 1421) and "A Pageant of Negro History" (1913, reel 88, frames 1443–59). For similar plays, see "The Christ of the Andes/Christ on the Andes" (undated, reel 87, frames 428–645) and "The Darker Wisdom: Prophecies in the Tale and Play, Seeking to Pierce the Gloom of 1940 . . ." (reel 87, frames 646–916).

26. For a discussion of the personal dialectic, see Heinz Lichtenstein, *Dilemma of Human Identity,* 258–60. For a discussion of the identity theme, see Norman N. Holland, *Brain of Robert Frost,* 38.

27. I appreciate Nell Painter's prompting me to focus on this issue and thereby to address the degree to which African Americans unconsciously struggle with the cultural duality Du Bois describes in *Souls.* This "two-ness" or hybridity of the Lacanian white Symbolic and the desire for a black counterpart manifests itself in Du Bois's (and in some other black people's) appreciation of selected white cultural artifacts (like classical music, European art, and Western fashion, for example), to say nothing of white values, especially Eurocentric beauty standards.

28. On his twenty-sixth birthday, Du Bois wrote in his journal, "This is my twenty-sixth birthday—a fresh cold sunshiny day spent most in my regular routine of work and musing" (Papers, reel 88, frame 489). For Du Bois, working seems very similar to musing, day dreaming.

29. In *The Interpretation of Dreams* Freud explains dreams as expressions of unconscious desire that cannot be fulfilled in the state of consciousness. Because such desire cannot seek satisfaction through action, dreams project satisfaction by encoding gratification in cryptic strings of images. Freud identified the stages of dream-work that produce the imagery as (1) condensation, (2) displacement, (3) considerations of representability, and (4) secondary revision. The first stage produces the overdetermined image by converging several latent wishes onto one manifest item. The second stage disguises elements in latent dream-thoughts by replacing them through a chain of associations. Condensation also occurs dur-

ing this stage; it compresses elements in the latent content of the dream in associative links based on likeness and proximity. In speech, metaphor and metonymy embody these processes. The third stage translates dream-thoughts into manifest images. The fourth stage, known as secondary revision, imposes order, logic, and language on the manifest content of the dream in order to make it into a cohesive narrative. Because the manifest dream is a mediated formation, it bears a direct relationship to the demands of desire and the intensity of repression. Thus, the more obscure the encodings of dream-work, "the more intense the force of repression" (Elizabeth Wright, *Psychoanalytic Criticism*, 19). But without repression, there would be shame.

30. Du Bois seems to be the model for the heroes of Hopkins's *Of One Blood*, as well as her first novel, *Contending Forces* (1900). Hopkins lived in Cambridge during the period in which Du Bois attended Harvard, and I suspect that she came into contact with him then. She covered the 1900 Pan-African Conference for the *Colored American Magazine* (September 1900): 223–31. For a discussion of *One Blood*, see Chapter 7 in my *Domestic Allegories*.

31. See Chapter 7 of my *Domestic Allegories* for a discussion of the terms of representing the growing racial despair in the writings of Pauline Hopkins.

32. This statement is an extract from the second of two descriptions that Du Bois prepared describing the novel. In a letter of December 15, 1927, to Harcourt, Brace and Company, Du Bois inscribes a "general statement about the novel for your [the publisher's] use," which he sent "some time ago." Wondering whether that statement was adequate, he included another with the final manuscript. See Aptheker, Introduction, 18–20.

33. In *Orientalism*, Said defines Orientalism as "a style of thought based upon an ontological and epistemological distinction made between 'the Orient' and (most of the time) 'the Occident' in which the latter is implicitly and explicitly understood as superior" (2). We late-twentieth-century readers no doubt recognize Orientalism as a discourse about the sovereignty of Western consciousness, a discourse about its "desires, repressions, investments, and projections" (*Orientalism* 8). This cultural discourse was/is intrinsic to the ideology of white supremacy that undergirded U.S. slavery and post-Reconstruction black disenfranchisement and racial segregation, as well as Western imperialism.

34. This is a paraphrase of Freud's thesis expressed in "The Moses of Michelangelo," *Collected Papers*, 4:258.

35. For a description of this process see Freud, "Psychopathic Characters on Stage," 305, 310.

Chapter 3

1. See note 10 in Chapter 2.

2. Wright's own discussions of the novel are not particularly convincing or informative. In one interview, Wright struggles to account rationally for the story that controls *Savage Holiday* rather than explore its dreamlike qualities. I suspect this is so because he has no access to the repressed plot that empowers the novel. By contrast, he can talk about racism. For this reason he can both understand and explain his black fictions as works of racial protest. See Charbonnier, "Negro Novel."

3. For a description of this process see Freud, "Psychopathic Characters on Stage," 305, 310.

4. See, for example, McCall, *Example*; Brignano, *Richard Wright*; Margolies, *Art*; and Felgar, *Richard Wright*.

5. Wertham wrote a very provocative essay, "An Unconscious Determinant in *Native Son*," published in the *Journal of Clinical and Experimental Psychopathology* in 1944. Here he links the scene in which "Bigger Thomas unintentionally kills Mary Dalton in the presence of her blind mother" to Wright's repressed dream fragments" produced during Wertham's experiment of free association with Wright (112, 113). In one fragment, Wright recalls working for a white couple while a teenager. One day, when carrying an armful of wood, he "came suddenly upon the lady of the house before she had dressed" (113). Also see Hoeveler, "Oedipus Agonistes." Hoeveler also refers to the Clinton Brewer murder case, Wright's friendship with Frederic Wertham, and Wertham's *Dark Legend* as greatly influential on Wright's *Savage Holiday*.

6. The letters from Karpman in Wright's private papers at Yale University also suggest a rather curious relationship between the two men. Whereas Wright's relationship with Wertham seems to have been one of mutual trust and respect, a friendship that slowly waned after the founding of the Lafargue Psychiatric Clinic in Harlem in 1946 and Wright's departure from the United States, the Wright-Karpman association seems characterized by mutual self-interest. Karpman's letters address the vicissitudes of the oedipal complex, psychopathology, criminality, black homosexuality, and female alcoholism and promiscuity.

7. The following books on psychoanalysis were a part of Wright's library: Karl Abraham's *Selected Papers on Psycho-analysis*, Clifford Allen's *Sexual Perversions and Abnormalities: A Study in the Psychology of Paraphilia*, Josef Freuer and Sigmund Freud's *Studies in Hysteria*, and Anna Freud's *Ego and the Mechanisms of Defense*. Wright possessed several works by Sigmund Freud: *Basic Writings, Civilization, War and Death: Selections from the Three Works of Sigmund Freud, Collected Papers* (all five volumes), *The Future of an Illusion, Interpretation of Dreams, Leonardo da Vinci, A Psycho-Sexual Study of an Infantile Reminiscence, Moses and Monotheism, The Question of Lay Analysis: An Introduction to Psychoanalysis*, and *Totem and Taboo*. His library also included the works of his friend Frederic Wertham (*Dark Legend: A Study of Murder, Seduction of the Innocent*, and *The Show of Violence*) and Ben Karpman (*Case Studies in the Psychopathology of Crime* [three volumes] and *The Individual Criminal: Studies in the Psychogenetics of Crime*). See Fabre, *Books and Writers*.

8. The 1995 PBS special entitled *Black Boy* mentions all of Wright's writings with the exception of *Savage Holiday*.

9. Michel Fabre explains that the drum-beating scene corresponds to an unpublished episode in *Black Boy* in which his father bans young Richard from playing a drum. This scene precedes the one where Richard kills the black kitten (*World*, 127).

10. Financial statements appear in Wright's papers. In addition, there are numerous letters to Reynolds from immediate members of Wright's maternal family that indicate Reynolds's role as the mediator between Wright and his mother. All of her petitions went to Reynolds. Wright would give him instructions, and Reynolds would carry them out.

11. In a letter of May 5, 1957, written by Reynolds to Wright, Reynolds advises Wright that Maggie Hunt, his aunt, sent him a telegram informing him that Wright's mother was in a clinic due to a hip fracture and that she needed $130 immediately. Reynolds writes that

he has wired her to expect the money. Reynolds's letter reveals his respect for Wright's decisions regarding his mother and Reynold's willingness to assist him in that matter.

12. Quite interestingly, *The Long Dream* repeatedly uses the word "cut" as a verb and a noun in lieu for the more widely used term "screw" to designate the act of sexual intercourse. This term seems to be an overdetermined signifier—a regional euphemism as well as Wright's personal metaphor for the textual desire of *Savage Holiday*. See Folb, *Running Down Some Lines*, and Major, *From Juba to Jive*.

13. See note 5.

14. In *Love, Leadership, and Aggression*, Allison Davis writes that one need only read *Black Boy* to "understand that Wright considered his family the primary source of his anger and his hatred" (156n). Davis analyzes Wright's personality and concludes that "Wright's hostile 'death wishes' toward his mother and grandmother were very powerful and lasted throughout his life" (*Love*, 176). Davis explains that usually these wishes were unconscious. By contrast, Wright's feelings toward his father were less ambivalent and, therefore, conscious. Davis also states that he "deals entirely with the influence of Wright's personality upon his fiction." The problem with Davis's analysis is that he presents little tangible evidence about the man Richard Wright. For example, Davis describes one instance in which he observes Wright at a social gathering. Davis refers to the experiences of poor, black southerners to explain Wright's behavior. By and large, though, Davis relies on a rather transparent reading of *Black Boy* for the basis of his analysis of Wright's personality. Davis subsequently uses his analysis to explain the relationship between Wright's personality and a few of his other works, which Davis mentions more than analyzes. By referring to "the fantasy of the bad tit," Davis relies on a popular rendering of the primary relationship between the subject and a maternal object of Kleinian theory. Although Davis's analysis is generally credible, it is decidedly circular and reductive.

15. Wright married two Jewish women. In 1939 he married Dhimah Rose Meadman, and in 1941 he married Ellen Poplar. Before his marriages to these women, Wright was engaged in 1938 to Marion Sawyer, a frail, self-effacing mulatta, who he learned had congenital syphilis. Wright broke off the engagement. See Fabre, *Unfinished Quest*, 196–220. Also, around this time he and Margaret Walker were friends. See Walker, *Richard Wright*, 89–150.

Chapter 4

1. Critics first assumed that the Copenhagen scenario is factual, then regarded it as an embellishment, and now once again consider it probable. Prior to Charles Larson's introduction, every biography on Larsen assumes that she not only visited Copenhagen but also attended the university there (Larson, *Intimation*, xx). These studies include Arthur P. Davis, *From the Dark Tower*, 95; Lewis, *When Harlem*, 231; Christian, *Black Woman Novelists*, 47; McDowell, Introduction; Thadious Davis, "Nella Larsen," 183; and Washington, *Invented Lives*, 161. In her 1994 biography on Larsen, Thadious Davis speculates that it is possible that Larsen may have traveled to Denmark between 1908 and 1912, "even though no passport records exist" (*Nella Larsen*, 67). Most recently, George Hutchinson contends that Larsen did indeed travel to Denmark, perhaps twice, as she reported. According to Hutchinson and his examination of a 1912 Baedeker guide to Scandinavia, American citizens did

not need a passport to go to Denmark during the years Larsen would have visited. See Hutchinson, "Nella Larsen and the Veil of Race." I thank George for making this information available to me.

2. According to Lacan's "Agency of the Letter in the Unconscious," such rhetorical features would include "periphrasis, hyperbaton ellipsis, suspension, anticipation, retraction, negation, digression, [and] irony" (*Écrits*, 169).

3. Lacan discusses the chain of signification in his readings of *Hamlet* in Felman, "Turning the Screws," and Poe's "Purloined Letter" in *French Freud*.

4. This edition was published by Collier Books, a division of Collier-Macmillan Limited, London, in 1971.

5. An early version of this chapter, "Desire and Death in *Quicksand*, by Nella Larsen," appears in *American Literary History* 7, no. 2 (Summer 1995): 234–60. The *ALH* version does not refer to Barbara Johnson's "Quicksands of the Self: Nella Larsen and Heinz Kohut" because I was not aware of it at the time of my article's composition.

6. I substitute "that other" for "him" in the original quotation in order to eliminate the presumption of masculine specular agency.

7. Here the Lacanian Symbolic draws on the structural linguistics of Ferdinand de Saussure and the cultural anthropology of Claude Lévi-Strauss. In *Course in General Linguistics*, Saussure argues that the linguistic signifier has no intrinsic tie to the signified. The signifier has meaning only insofar as it is a part of a system of signification defined by differential opposition. Lévi-Strauss uses this structural relationship to analyze culture. In *Structural Anthropology*, he explains that the system that determines linguistic signification is like the system that determines cultural meaning: "Any culture may be looked upon as an ensemble of symbolic systems, in the front rank of which are to be found language, marriage laws, economic relations, art, science and religion" (qtd. in Laplanche and Pontalis, *Language*, 440).

8. Hortense E. Thornton also makes this observation. She writes, "It is significant that in her rejection of Olsen [Helga] stresses their racial differences, causing one to question the extent to which her acknowledgment of race is used as a mask for her sexual repression" ("Sexism," 299).

9. Lacan remarks in his second seminar, "Desire is a relation of being to lack. This lack is the lack of being properly speaking. It isn't that lack of this or that, but lack of being whereby the being exists" (qtd. in Silverman, *Male Subjectivity*, 20).

10. My presumption of the daughter's heterosexuality is not meant to define lesbian desire as aberrant. Rather, the narrative details of *Quicksand* designate Helga's heterosexuality.

11. See Lacan, "Function and Field of Speech and Language," in *Écrits*, 101–2. Also see Boothby, *Death*, 10–20, 84–97.

12. Here I rely on the arguments about the textual unconscious, presented in Mellard, *Using Lacan*, 36, 55.

13. My argument draws on Shoshana Felman's Lacanian methodology in "Turning the Screws," 119.

14. See Freud's "Remembering, Repeating, and Working-Through," *SE* 12:147–56.

15. This interpretation rests on two central hypotheses of psychoanalytic theory. The first identifies the pre-oedipal daughter's identificatory love for the father as "the basis for later

heterosexual love" (Benjamin, *Bonds*, 110). The second designates the oedipal stage as the reinforcement of heterosexual desire. See also Freud's "Transformations of Puberty."

16. George Hutchinson maintains a similar conviction about the centrality of the mother to Helga's life. During a discussion with me on November 15, 1995, he maintained that when she hears her children's "cry of 'Mummy, Mummy, Mummy,' through sleepless nights" (Q 135), she is recalling her own longing for her real mother. The difference between Hutchinson's reading and mine is that I am not so much regarding Helga as like a real person, who would certainly duplicate Larsen's despair over her mother's abandonment of her. Rather, I am reading Helga as a signifier in a fantasy. As a result, she signifies textual desire rather than projecting her own. The chain of signifiers is more elaborate around the paternal imago than the maternal one. For this reason, I focus on the desire for the lost father as the force driving this novel.

17. Larsen's biographer reaches a similar conclusion; however, she sees Clare Kendry of *Passing* as a re-embodiment of Larsen's virtually white father rather than her white mother, as I suggest. Regardless of whether Clare is symbolized as father or mother or even both, Helga and Irene are daughters who seek lost parent figures. See T. Davis, *Nella Larsen*, 327.

18. See McDowell, Introduction, xxx.

19. I thank Ann Kelly for pointing out all the wordplay in the names of the central characters of *Quicksand* and *Passing*.

20. Psychoanalyst D. F. Klein's theory of appetitive and consummatory pleasures is helpful here for appreciating Helga's dysfunction. Klein, by way of psychiatrist Norman Doidge, "asserts that there are at least two broad, independent pleasure systems. One regulates appetitive pleasure and in normal situations acts to boost energy for the pleasurable pursuit of a goal. A second system of consummatory pleasure underlies the pleasurable enjoyment of food, sex, and other interests already obtained" (Doidge, "Appetitive Pleasure States," 146).

21. I thank Marshall Alcorn for this observation.

22. The Imaginary here is a Lacanian concept that identifies all perception, understanding, and observation associated with an awareness of the self as a mental (or imaginary) mediation of a priori conditions—what Lacan calls the Real—that lies beyond and thereby resists conceptualization. Human experience cannot engage the Real except by means of imaginary intervention of the self (which Freud called the ego), even though paradoxically such intervention always seems *un*mediated and therefore objective to the subject. What is commonly known as reality, then, cannot be assumed as given; it is constituted "in the ideological formations" in which we recognize it (Althusser, "Freud and Lacan," 219).

Chapter 5

1. John Lowe also comes to this conclusion. Referring to the section on love in *Dust Tracks* in which Hurston describes her slavery to A. W. P., Lowe writes, "[T]he love affair that supposedly prompted the scenario for *Their Eyes* perhaps played a larger role in shaping *Seraph*, for Zora and A. W. P. epitomize Strindberg's version of Hell—a man and woman desperately unhappy together who are yet unable to part" (*Jump*, 299).

2. As social historians Mintz and Kellogg have argued, at the end of World War II "Rosie

the Riveter" had to return to her role as wife and mother. "National magazines were saturated with Freudian notions of 'penis envy' and the sexual origins of neurosis and argued that women could only achieve happiness by accepting roles of wife and mother and rejecting 'masculine strivings'" (*Domestic Revolutions*, 182). For example, they refer to one best-seller of that era, *Modern Woman: The Lost Sex*, which circulated a warning about the dangerous consequences of higher education and careers on women. Such a path would promote the "masculination of women with enormously dangerous consequences to the home, the children dependent on it, and the ability of the woman, as well as her husband, to obtain sexual gratification" (*Domestic Revolutions*, 182). Insofar as black people were concerned, their servile places awaited them as well. The war was over, FDR was dead, and "blacks need not apply." This viewpoint was repeatedly endorsed in popular culture.

3. Here I borrow Linda Hutcheon's analysis of subversive effects of the carnivalesque. See "Modern Parody and Bakhtin" in Morson and Emerson, *Rethinking Bakhtin*, 99.

4. For elaboration on the compulsion to repeat, see Freud's *Beyond the Pleasure Principle* and "Remembering, Repeating and Working-Through," *SE* 12:147–56.

5. Freud retains the primacy of the oedipal stage and marginalizes the implications of his new hypothesis by (mis)naming this period for the girl the "pre-oedipal phase." Nina Lykke breaks with the oedipalized containment of the girl's development by naming this stage the "Antigone phase" (qtd. in *Daughtering and Mothering*, 16).

6. In *Zora Neale Hurston: A Literary Biography*, Robert E. Hemenway explains that "[a]s early as 1942 [Hurston] had told Carl Van Vechten that her 'tiny wedge' in Hollywood gave her 'hopes of breaking that old silly rule about Negroes not writing about white people. . . . I am working on a story now'" (303). This story seems to have evolved into *Seraph*.

7. Wallace Thurman wrote several Hollywood screenplays in which he featured white characters to address class issues. As Phyllis Klotman explains, Thurman, Langston Hughes, and Hurston learned "that the 'Negro' may have been in vogue in Hollywood in the thirties, but it was still the cardboard Negro, the Imitation-Judge Priest-Green Pastures GWTW Negro" ("Black Writer," 80–92; quotation appears on 91).

8. According to Hemenway, no extant copy of the manuscript exists.

9. *The Living Is Easy* (1948) and *The Narrows* (1953) were reissued in 1975 and 1971, respectively, with the resurgence of black nationalism and the women's movement. Both novels are currently in print.

10. Arvay displays an assortment of symptoms. *New York Times* reviewer Frank Slaughter identifies her as a hysterical neurotic. Since her feelings of dejection arise from narcissistic deficiencies, I would instead perhaps identify her core problem as a narcissistic personality disorder. A manifestation of this problem would include melancholy and other neuroses.

11. Ann duCille also comments on Arvay's altered speech pattern. According to duCille, Arvay has abandoned the speech pattern of a Cracker and assumed the discourse of a coquette or a "southern belle." Moreover, she uses her newfound language to flatter Jim's ego (*Coupling Convention*, 140).

12. For an account of the trial that also includes the coverage in the *Baltimore Afro-American*, see Hemenway, *Zora Neale Hurston*, 319–25.

13. Here I adapt Castle's argument: "Even as the masquerade assumed its place in English society, it reified a sometimes devolutionary, sometimes revolutionary, anti-society founded

on collective gratification. Its profuse, exquisite, difficult imagery symbolized a revision, not just of the psyche, but of culture itself " (*Masquerade*, 74).

14. Freud argues in "Female Sexuality," "Femininity," and "The Economic Problem of Masochism" that female masochism is a normal response to feminine passivity. However, Freudian revisionists like Karen Horney and Jessica Benjamin explain female masochism as ultimately a consequence of patriarchal culture. See Horney's "Problem of Female Masochism" and Benjamin's *Bonds of Love*.

15. For a psychoanalytic reading of this work, see Benjamin, *Bonds of Love*, 50–84.

Bibliography

Abel, Elizabeth. "Black Writing, White Reading: Race and the Politics of Feminist Interpretation." *Critical Inquiry* 19, no. 3 (Spring 1993): 470–98.

———. "Race, Class, and Psychoanalysis?: Opening Questions." In *Conflicts in Feminism*, edited by Marianne Hirsch and Evelyn Fox Keller, 184–204. New York: Routledge, 1990.

Abrams, M. H. *Natural Supernaturalism: Tradition and Revolution in Romantic Literature.* New York: W. W. Norton, 1971.

Alcott, Louisa May. *Little Women, I and II.* 1868, 1869. Reprinted in 1 vol. New York: Modern Library, 1983.

Althusser, Louis. "Freud and Lacan." In *Lenin and Philosophy and Other Essays*, 189–219. New York: Monthly Review Press, 1971.

Anderson, Victor. *Beyond Ontological Blackness: An Essay on African American Religious and Cultural Criticism.* New York: Continuum, 1995.

Andrews, William L. Introduction. In *Sisters of the Spirit: Three Black Women's Autobiographies of the Nineteenth Century*, 1–22. Bloomington: Indiana University Press, 1986.

Aptheker, Herbert. Introduction to *Dark Princess: A Romance*, 1–33. 1928. Reprint. Millwood, N.Y.: Kraus-Thomson Organization, 1974.

Awkward, Michael. *Inspiriting Influence: Tradition, Revision, and Afro-American Women's Novels.* New York: Columbia University Press, 1989.

———. Introduction to *New Essays on* Their Eyes Were Watching God. New York: Cambridge University Press, 1990.

Baker, Houston A., Jr. *Blues, Ideology, and Afro-American Literature: A Vernacular Theory.* Chicago: University of Chicago Press, 1984.

———. "In Dubious Battle." *New Literary History: A Journal of Theory and Interpretation* 18, no. 2 (Winter 1987): 363–69.

Bakhtin, Mikhail. *Problems of Dostoevsky's Poetics.* Edited and translated by Caryl Emerson. Minneapolis: University of Minnesota Press, 1984.

———. *Rabelais and His World.* Translated by Helene Iswolsky. Cambridge, Mass.: M.I.T. Press, 1968.

Baldick, Chris. *The Concise Oxford Dictionary of Literary Terms.* New York: Oxford University Press, 1991.

Baldwin, James. "Alas, Poor Richard." In *Nobody Knows My Name: More Notes of a Native Son,* 181–215. New York: Dell, 1961.

Barthes, Roland. *S/Z: An Essay.* Translated by Richard Miller. 1974. Reprint. New York: Hill and Wang, 1974.

Baym, Nina. *Woman's Fiction: A Guide to Novels by and about Women in America, 1820–1870.* Ithaca, N.Y.: Cornell University Press, 1978.

Bedell, Madelon. Introduction to *Little Women,* by Louisa May Alcott, ix–1. New York: Modern Library, 1983.

Bell, Bernard W. *The Afro-American Novel and Its Tradition.* Amherst: University of Massachusetts Press, 1989.

Benjamin, Jessica. *The Bonds of Love: Psychoanalysis, Feminism, and the Problem of Domination.* New York: Pantheon Books, 1988.

———. *Like Subjects, Love Objects: Essays on Recognition and Sexual Difference.* New Haven, Conn.: Yale University Press, 1995.

Bergner, Gwen. "Who Is That Masked Woman? or, The Role of Gender in Fanon's *Black Sin, White Masks.*" *PMLA* 110, no. 1 (January 1995): 75–87.

Bettelheim, Bruno. *The Uses of Enchantment.* New York: Alfred A. Knopf, 1976.

"The Black Man Brings His Gifts." *The Survey* 53 (March 1, 1925): 655–57, 710.

Bonaparte, Marie. *Life and Works of Edgar Allan Poe: A Psycho-Analytic Interpretation.* London: Imago, 1949.

Bone, Robert A. *The Negro Novel in America.* 1958. Rev. ed. New Haven, Conn.: Yale University Press, 1964.

Book Review Digest, 1928. New York: H. W. Wilson Company, 1929.

Boone, Joseph Allen. *Tradition Counter Tradition: Love and the Form of Fiction.* Chicago: University of Chicago Press, 1987.

Boothby, Richard. *Death and Desire: Psychoanalytic Theory in Lacan's Return to Freud.* New York: Routledge, 1991.

Bradford, Roark. "Mixed Blood." *New York Herald Tribune,* May 13, 1928, 22.

Brenkman, John. *Culture and Domination.* Ithaca, N.Y.: Cornell University Press, 1987.

———. *Straight, Male Modern: A Cultural Critique of Psychoanalysis.* New York: Routledge, 1993.

Brereton, Virginia Lieson. *From Sin to Salvation: Stories of Women's Conversions, 1800 to the Present.* Bloomington: Indiana University Press, 1991.

Brickell, Herschel. Review of *Seraph on the Suwanee. Saturday Review of Literature,* November 6, 1948, 31.

Brignano, Russell Carl. *Richard Wright: An Introduction to the Man and His Works.* Pittsburgh, Pa.: University of Pittsburgh Press, 1970.

Bronner, Stephen Eric, and Douglas MacKay Kellner, eds. *Critical Theory and Society: A Reader.* New York: Routledge, 1989.

Brooks, Peter. "The Idea of a Psychoanalytic Literary Criticism." In *Psychoanalysis and Storytelling,* 20–45. Cambridge, Mass.: Blackwell, 1994.

———. *Reading for the Plot: Design and Intention in Narrative.* New York: Random House, 1984.

Butler, Judith. *Bodies That Matter: On the Discursive Limits of Sex.* New York: Routledge, 1993.

———. "Desire." In *Critical Terms for Literary Study*, edited by Frank Lentricchia and Thomas McLaughlin, 369–86. Chicago: University of Chicago Press, 1995.

Butler, Robert James. "The Function of Violence in Richard Wright's *Native Son.*" *Black American Literature Forum* 20 (Spring–Summer 1986): 9–26.

Byerman, Keith E. *Seizing the Word: History, Art, and Self in the Work of W. E. B. Du Bois.* Athens: University of Georgia Press, 1994.

Carby, Hazel V. *Reconstructing Womanhood: The Emergence of the Afro-American Woman Novelist.* New York: Oxford University Press, 1987.

Castle, Terry. *Masquerade and Civilization: The Carnivalesque in Eighteenth-Century English Culture and Fiction.* Stanford, Calif.: Stanford University Press, 1986.

Chalmers, David M. *Hooded Americanism: The History of the Ku Klux Klan.* Durham, N.C.: Duke University Press, 1987.

Chancer, Lynn S. *Sadomasochism in Everyday Life: The Dynamics of Power and Powerlessness.* New Brunswick, N.J.: Rutgers University Press, 1992.

Charbonnier, George. "A Negro Novel about White People." In *Conversations with Richard Wright*, edited by Kenneth Kinnamon and Michel Fabre, 220–23. Jackson: University Press of Mississippi.

Childers, Joseph, and Gary Hentzi, eds. *The New Columbia Dictionary of Modern Literary and Cultural Criticism.* New York: Columbia University Press, 1995.

Chodorow, Nancy J. *Femininities, Masculinities, Sexualities: Freud and Beyond.* Lexington: University Press of Kentucky, 1994.

———. *Feminism and Psychoanalytic Theory.* New Haven, Conn.: Yale University Press, 1989.

———. "Gender as Personal and Cultural Construction." *Signs* 20, no. 3 (Spring 1995): 516–44.

———. *The Reproduction of Mothering: Psychoanalysis and the Sociology of Gender.* Berkeley: University of California Press, 1978.

Christian, Barbara. *Black Women Novelists: The Development of a Tradition, 1892–1976.* Westport, Conn: Greenwood Press, 1980.

Davis, Allison. "The Browsing Reader." *The Crisis* 35 (November 1928): 339.

———. *Love, Leadership, and Aggression.* San Diego, Calif: Harcourt, Brace, Jovanovich, 1983.

Davis, Arthur P. *From the Dark Tower: Afro-American Writers 1900 to 1960.* Washington, D.C.: Howard University Press, 1974.

Davis, Charles T., and Michel Fabre. *Richard Wright: A Primary Bibliography.* Boston: G. K. Hall, 1982.

Davis, Thadious. "Nella Larsen." In *Dictionary of Literary Biography*, edited by Trudier Harris. Detroit: Gale, 1987.

———. *Nella Larsen: Novelist of the Harlem Renaissance.* Baton Rouge: Louisiana State University Press, 1994.

"Day Letters." Review of *Dark Princess*, by W. E. B. Du Bois. *New York Evening Post*, May 12, 1928, 9.

Deleuze, Gilles, and Felix Guattari. *Anti-Oedipus: Capitalism and Schizophrenia.* Minneapolis: University of Minnesota Press, 1983.

Deutsch, Helene. "Feminine Masochism." In *The Psychology of Women: A Psychoanalytic Interpretation*, 1:239–78. New York: Grune & Stratton, 1944.

———. *The Psychology of Women: A Psychoanalytic Interpretation.* Vol. 1. New York: Grune & Stratton, 1944.

Diehl, Joanne Feit. "Re-Reading *The Letter*: Hawthorne, the Fetish, and the (Family) Romance." In *The Scarlet Letter by Nathaniel Hawthorne*, edited by Ross C. Martin, 235–51. Boston: St. Martin's, 1991.

Dijkstra, Bram. *Idols of Perversity: Fantasies of Feminine Evil in Fin-de-Siècle Culture*. New York: Oxford University Press, 1986.

Doane, Mary Ann. "Dark Continents: Epistemologies of Racial and Sexual Difference in Psychoanalysis and the Cinema." In *Femme Fatales*, 209–48. New York: Routledge, 1991.

———. *Femmes Fatales: Feminism, Film Theory, Psychoanalysis*. New York: Routledge, 1991.

Doidge, Norman. "Appetitive Pleasure States: A Biopsychoanalytic Model of the Pleasure Threshold, Mental Representation, and Defense." In *Pleasure beyond the Pleasure Principle: The Role of Affect in Motivation*, edited by Robert A. Glick and Stanley Bone, 138–76. New Haven, Conn.: Yale University Press, 1990.

Du Bois, W[illiam]. E. B. *The Autobiography of W. E. B. Du Bois: A Soliloquy on Viewing My Life from the Last Decade of Its First Century*. New York: International Publishers, 1968.

———. "The Black Man Brings His Gifts." In *The Creative Writings of W. E. B. Du Bois: A Pageant, Poems, Short Stories, and Playlets*, compiled and edited by Herbert Aptheker, 139. White Plains, N.Y.: Kraus-Thomson Organization Ltd., 1974.

———. "The Browsing Reader." *The Crisis* 35 (June 1928): 202.

———. "The Case." *The Horizon* 2 (July 1907): 4–10.

———. "Criteria of Negro Art." In *W. E. B. Du Bois: The Crisis Writings*, edited by Daniel Walden, 279–89. Greenwich, Conn.: Fawcett Publications, 1972.

———. *Dark Princess, A Romance*. 1928. Reprint. Jackson: University Press of Mississippi, 1995.

———. "The Drama among Black Folk." *The Crisis* 12 (August 1916): 169, 171–72.

———. *Dusk of Dawn: An Essay toward an Autobiography of a Race Concept*. New York: Harcourt, Brace and World, 1940.

———. "The Flight into Egypt." In *The Creative Writings of W. E. B. Du Bois*, 101.

———. "The Gospel According to Mary Brown." in *The Creative Writings of W. E. B. Du Bois*, 106.

———. "Jesus Christ in Georgia." In *The Creative Writings of W. E. B. Du Bois*, 79.

———. "My Evolving Program for Negro Freedom." In *What the Negro Wants*, edited by Rayford W. Logan, 37–70. Chapel Hill: University of North Carolina Press, 1944.

———. The Papers of William E. B. Du Bois. Microfilm. Manuscript Division, Library of Congress, Washington D.C.

———. "The Princess of the Hither Isles." *The Crisis* 6 (October 1913): 285, 288–89.

———. *The Quest of the Silver Fleece*. 1911. Reprint. Boston: Northeastern University Press, 1989.

———. "The Second Coming." In *The Creative Writings of W. E. B. Du Bois*, 103.

———. "The Shaven Lady." *The Horizon* 2 (August 1907): 5–10.

———. *The Souls of Black Folk*. 1903. Reprinted in *The Oxford W. E. B. Du Bois Reader*, edited by Eric Sundquist, 97–241.

———. "*The Star of Ethiopia*." *The Crisis* 9 (December 1915): 90–94.

———. "Two Novels." *The Crisis* 35 (June 1928): 202.

———. "The Woman." *The Crisis* 2 (May 1911): 12.

DuCille, Ann. *The Coupling Convention: Sex, Text, and Tradition in Black Women's Fiction*. New York: Oxford University Press, 1993.

Dunbar, Paul Laurence. "The Poet." In *The Black Poets*, edited by Dudley Randall, 52. New York: Bantam Books, 1971.

Early, Gerald. Afterword to *Savage Holiday* by Richard Wright, 223–35. Jackson: University Press of Mississippi, 1994.

Elliot, Anthony. *Social Theory and Psychoanalysis in Transition: Self and Society from Freud to Kristeva*. Oxford, U.K.: Basil Blackwell, 1992.

Ellison, Ralph. "Twentieth-Century Fiction and the Black Mask of Humanity." 1953. Reprinted in *Within the Circle: An Anthology of African American Literary Criticism from the Harlem Renaissance to the Present*, edited by Angelyn Mitchell, 134–48. Durham, N.C.: Duke University Press, 1994.

Fabre, Michel. *Books and Writers*. Jackson: University Press of Mississippi, 1990.

———. *The Unfinished Quest of Richard Wright*. Translated by Isabel Barzun. New York: William Morrow, 1973.

———. *The World of Richard Wright*. Jackson: University Press of Mississippi, 1985.

Fanon, Frantz. *Black Skin, White Masks*. 1952. Reprint, translated by Charles Lam Markmann. New York: Grove Press, 1967.

———. *The Wretched of the Earth*. 1961. Reprint, translated by Constance Farrington. New York: Grove Press, 1963.

Faulkner, William. *The Sound and the Fury*. 1929. Reprint. New York: Vintage Books, 1987.

Felgar, Robert. *Richard Wright*. Boston: G. K. Hall, 1980.

Felman, Shoshana. "Turning the Screws of Interpretation." *Literature and Psychoanalysis: The Question of Reading Otherwise*, 94–207. Baltimore: Johns Hopkins University Press, 1982.

Felski, Rita. *Beyond Feminist Aesthetics: Feminist Literature and Social Change*. Cambridge, Mass.: Harvard University Press, 1989.

Fiedler, Leslie. *Love and Death in the American Novel*. New York: Criterion Books, 1960.

Fisher, Dexter, and Robert B. Stepto, eds. *Afro-American Literature: The Reconstruction of Instruction*. New York: Modern Language Association, 1978.

Flieger, Jerry Aline. "Trial and Error: The Case of the Textual Unconscious." *Diacritics: A Review of Contemporary Literature* 11, no. 1 (Spring 1981): 56–67.

"The Flight into Egypt." *The Crisis* 17 (December 1918): 59.

Folb, Edith. *Running Down Some Lines: Language and Culture of Black Teenagers*. Cambridge, Mass.: Harvard University Press, 1980.

Freud, Sigmund. *Beyond the Pleasure Principle*. 1922. In *The Standard Edition of the Complete Works of Sigmund Freud*, translated by James Strachey et al. (*SE*), 18:7–64. London: Hogarth Press and the Institute of Psycho-Analysis, 1953–73.

———. *Civilization and Its Discontents*. 1930. *SE*, 21:57–146.

———. *The Complete Letters of Sigmund Freud to Wilhelm Fleiss, 1897–1904*. Cambridge, Mass.: Harvard University Press, 1985.

———. "Creative Writers and Day-Dreaming." *SE*, 9:143–53.

———. "The Economic Problem of Masochism." 1924. *SE*, 9:157–70.

———. *The Ego and the Id*. 1923. *SE*, 16:1–66.

———. "Family Romances." 1909. *SE*, 9:237–41.

———. "Female Sexuality." 1931. *SE*, 21:225–43.

———. "Femininity." 1933. *SE*, 22:112–35.

———. "Fetishism." 1927. *SE*, 21:149–58.

———. "Fragment of an Analysis of a Case of Hysteria." 1905. *SE*, 7:1–122.

———. "Infantile Sexuality." *Three Essays on Sexuality*. 1905. *SE*, 7:173–206.

———. *The Interpretation of Dreams*. 1900. *SE*, 4–5.

———. *Jokes and Their Relation to the Unconscious.* 1916. *SE*, 23:7–140.

———. "The Moses of Michelangelo." 1914. *SE*, 23. Reprinted in *The Collected Papers of Sigmund Freud,* translated by Joan Riviere et al. (*CP*), 4:257–88. New York: Basic Books, 1959.

———. "The Most Prevalent Form of Degradation in Erotic Life." Contributions to the Psychology of Love. 1912. *SE*, 11. Reprinted as "On the Universal Tendency to Debasement in the Sphere of Love," in *CP*, 4:203–16.

———. "Mourning and Melancholia." 1917. *SE*, 14:237–59.

———. "On Narcissism: An Introduction." 1914. *SE*, 14:111–40.

———. "Psychopathic Characters on Stage." 1942 (1905–6). *SE*, 7:305–10.

———. "The Question of Lay Analysis: Conversations with an Impartial Person." 1926. *SE*, 20:212.

———. "The Relation of the Poet to Day-Dreaming." 1908. *CP* 4:173–83.

———. "The Splitting of the Ego in the Process of Defense." 1938. *CP*, 5:372–75.

———. "The Theme of the Three Caskets." 1913. *CP*, 4:244–56.

———. "Transformations of Puberty." In *Three Essays on Sexuality.* 1905. *SE*, 7:207–30.

———. "The Uncanny." 1919. *SE*, 17:217–56.

Fromm, Erich. "Psychoanalysis and Sociology," "Politics and Psychoanalysis," and "The Crisis of Psychoanalysis." In *Critical Theory and Society: A Reader,* edited by Stephen Eric Bronner and Douglas MacKay Kellner, 37–40; 213–18; 247–54. New York: Routledge, 1989.

Frye, Northrop. *The Anatomy of Criticism.* Princeton, N.J.: Princeton University Press, 1957.

Fuss, Diana. "Interior Colonies: Frantz Fanon and the Politics of Identification." *Diacritics* 24, nos. 2–3 (Summer–Fall 1994): 20–42.

Gallop, Jane. *The Daughter's Seduction: Feminism and Psychoanalysis.* Ithaca, N.Y.: Cornell University Press, 1982.

Gates, Henry Louis, Jr. "African American Criticism." In *Redrawing the Boundaries: The Transformations of English and American Literary Studies,* edited by Stephen Greenblatt and Giles Gunn, 303–19. New York: Modern Language Association, 1992.

———. "Critical Fanonism." *Critical Inquiry* 17, no. 3 (Spring 1991): 457–70.

———. *The Signifying Monkey: A Theory of Afro-American Literary Criticism.* New York: Oxford University Press, 1987.

———. "Talking Black: Critical Signs of the Times." In *Loose Canons: Notes on the Culture Wars.* New York: Oxford University Press, 1992.

———. " 'What's Love Got to Do with It?': Critical Theory, Integrity, and the Black Idiom." *New Literary History: A Journal of Theory and Interpretation* 18, no. 2 (Winter 1987): 345–62.

———, ed. *Black Literature and Literary Theory.* New York: Methuen, 1984.

Gay, Peter. *The Bourgeois Experience: Victoria to Freud.* Vol. 1, *Education of the Senses.* New York: Oxford University Press, 1984.

———. *The Bourgeois Experience: Victoria to Freud.* Vol. 2, *The Tender Passion.* New York: Oxford University Press, 1986.

Gayle, Addison, Jr. *The Black Aesthetic.* New York: Doubleday, 1971.

Gibson, Donald B. "Richard Wright's *Black Boy* and the Trauma of Autobiographical Rebirth." *Callaloo* 9, no. 3 (Summer 1986): 492–98.

Gilman, Sander L. *The Case of Sigmund Freud: Medicine and Identity at the Fin de Siècle.* Baltimore: Johns Hopkins University Press, 1993.

———. *Freud, Race and Gender.* Princeton, N.J.: Princeton University Press, 1993.

————. *The Jew's Body.* New York: Routledge, 1991.

Gilroy, Paul. *The Black Atlantic: Modernity and Double Consciousness.* Cambridge, Mass.: Harvard University Press, 1993.

————. "Roots and Routes: Black Identity as an Outernational Project." In *Racial and Ethnic Identity: Psychological Development and Creative Expression*, edited by Herbert W. Harris, Howard C. Blue, and Ezra E. H. Griffith, 15–30. New York: Routledge, 1995.

Glick, Robert A., and Stanley Bone, eds. *Pleasure beyond the Pleasure Principle: The Role of Affect in Motivation.* New Haven, Conn.: Yale University Press, 1990.

Gloster, Hugh. *Negro Voices in American Fiction.* 1948. Reprint. New York: Russell and Russell, 1965.

Goldberg, D. T. "Conversation: Facial Formation in Contemporary American National Identity." *Social Identities: Journal for the Study of Race, Nation and Culture* 2, no. 1 (February 1996): 169–91.

"The Gospel According to Mary Brown." *The Crisis* 19 (December 1919): 41–43.

Gounard, J. F., and Beverley Roberts Gounard. "Richard Wright's *Savage Holiday*: Use or Abuse of Psychoanalysis." *C.L.A. Journal* 22 (June 1979): 344–49.

Greene, Beverly A. "Black Feminist Psychotherapy." In *Feminism and Psychoanalysis: A Critical Dictionary*, edited by Elizabeth Wright, 34–35. Cambridge, Mass.: Blackwell, 1992.

————. "Considerations in the Treatment of Black Patients by White Therapists." *Psychotherapy*, 2d ser., 22 (Summer 1985): 389–93.

Grosz, Elizabeth. "The Body of Signification." In *Abjection, Melancholia and Love: The Work of Julia Kristeva*, edited by John Fletcher and Andrew Benjamin, 80–103. New York: Routledge, 1990.

————. *Jacques Lacan: A Feminist Introduction.* New York: Routledge, 1990.

————. *Space, Time, and Perversion.* New York: Routledge, 1995.

Hakutani, Yoshinobu. *Critical Essays on Richard Wright.* Boston: G. K. Hall, 1982.

Harper, Frances Ellen Watkins. *Iola Leroy, or the Shadows Uplifted.* 1892. Reprint. New York: Oxford University Press, 1988.

Hayden, Katharine Shepard. Review of *Quicksand. Annals of the American Academy* 140 (November 1928): 345.

Heald, Suzette, and Ariane Deluz, eds. *Anthropology and Psychoanalysis: An Encounter through Culture.* New York: Routledge, 1994.

Hedden, Worth Tuttle. "Turpentine and Moonshine." *New York Herald Tribune Weekly Book Review*, October 10, 1948, 2.

Hemenway, Robert E. *Zora Neale Hurston: A Literary Biography.* Urbana: University of Illinois Press, 1977.

Himes, Chester. *The Quality of Hurt.* New York: Doubleday, 1972.

Hirsh, Marianne. *The Mother/Daughter Plot: Narrative, Psychoanalysis, Feminism.* Bloomington: University of Indiana Press, 1989.

Hite, Molly. Introduction to *Megda.* New York: Oxford University Press, 1988.

Hoeveler, Diane Long. "Oedipus Agonistes: Mothers and Sons in Richard Wright's Fiction." *Black American Literature Forum* 13, no. 2 (Summer 1979): 65–68.

Hogue, W. Lawrence. *Discourse and the Other: The Production of the Afro-American Text.* Durham, N.C.: Duke University Press, 1986.

Holland, Norman N. *The Brain of Robert Frost: A Cognitive Approach to Literature.* New York: Routledge, 1988.

————. *The Shakespearean Imagination.* Bloomington: University of Indiana Press, 1968.

Holloway, Karla F. C. *The Character of the Word: The Texts of Zora Neale Hurston.* Westport, N.Y.: Greenwood Press, 1987.

Holmes, Dorothy Evans. "Race and Transference in Psychoanalysis and Psychotherapy." *International Journal of Psycho-Analysis* 73, no. 1 (1992): 1–11.

Honey, Maureen. *Creating Rosie the Riveter: Class, Gender, and Propaganda during World War II.* Amherst: University of Massachusetts Press, 1984.

Hook, R. H. "Psychoanalysis, unconscious phantasy and interpretation." In *Anthropology and Psychoanalysis: An Encounter through Culture,* edited by Suzette Heald and Ariane Deluz, 114–30. New York: Routledge, 1994.

hooks, bell. *Ain't I a Woman.* Boston: South End Press, 1981.

———. *Yearnings: Race, Gender and Cultural Politics.* Boston: South End Press, 1990.

Hopkins, Pauline E. *Contending Forces.* 1900. Reprint. New York: Oxford University Press, 1989.

———. *Of One Blood: Or, the Hidden Self.* In *The Magazine Novels of Pauline Hopkins.* 1903. Reprint. New York: Oxford University Press, 1988.

Horney, Karen. "The Problem of Female Masochism." In *Feminine Psychology.* New York: W. W. Norton, 1967.

Horowitz, Mardi Jon. *Image Formation and Psychotherapy.* New York: Janson Aronson, 1983.

Hostetler, Ann E. "Race and Gender in Nella Larsen's *Quicksand.*" *PMLA* 105 (1990): 35–46.

Huggins, Nathan Irwin. *Harlem Renaissance.* New York: Oxford University Press, 1971.

Hughes, Langston. "The Negro Artist and the Racial Mountain." 1926. Reprinted in *Within the Circle: An Anthology of African American Literary Criticism from the Harlem Renaissance to the Present,* edited by Angelyn Mitchell, 55–59. Durham, N.C.: Duke University Press, 1994.

Hurston, Nora Neale. *Dust Tracks on a Road.* 1942. Reprint. New York: Harper Perennial, 1991.

———. "How It Feels to Be Colored Me." 1928. Reprinted in *I Love Myself When I Am Laughing . . . : A Zora Neale Hurston Reader,* edited by Alice Walker, 152–56. Old Westbury, N.Y.: Feminist Press, 1979.

———. *Jonah's Gourd Vine.* 1934. Reprint. New York: Harper Perennial, 1991.

———. *Seraph on the Suwanee.* 1948. Reprint. New York: Harper Perennial, 1991.

———. *Their Eyes Were Watching God.* 1937. Reprint. New York: Harper Perennial, 1990.

———. "Turpentine Love" from "The Eatonville Anthology." In *I Love Myself When I Am Laughing . . . ,* edited by Alice Walker, 169–73. Old Westbury, N.Y.: Feminist Press, 1979.

———. "What White Publishers Won't Print." In *I Love Myself When I Am Laughing . . . ,* 169–73.

Hutcheon, Linda. "Modern Parody and Bakhtin." *Rethinking Bakhtin: Extensions and Challenges,* edited by Gary Saul Morson and Caryl Emerson, 87–104. Evanston, Ill.: Northwestern University Press, 1989.

Hutchinson, George. *The Harlem Renaissance in Black and White.* Cambridge, Mass.: Harvard University Press, 1996.

———. "Nella Larsen and the Veil of Race." *American Literary History* 9, no. 2 (Summer 1997): 329–49.

Isaacs, Harold. *The New World of Negro Americans.* New York: John Day, 1963.

Jameson, Fredric. "Imaginary and Symbolic in Lacan: Marxism, Psychoanalytic Criticism, and the Problem of the Subject." In *Literature and Psychoanalysis: The Question of Reading, Otherwise,* edited by Shoshana Felman, 338–95. Baltimore: Johns Hopkins University Press, 1978.

———. "Magical Narratives." In *The Political Unconscious: Narrative as Socially Symbolic Act*, 103–50. Ithaca, N.Y.: Cornell University Press, 1981.

Johnson, Barbara. "The Frame of Reference: Poe, Lacan, Derrida." In *Literature and Psychoanalysis: The Question of Reading, Otherwise*, edited by Shoshana Felman, 457–505. Baltimore: Johns Hopkins University Press, 1978.

———. "Metaphor, Metonymy, and Voice." In *A World of Difference*, 155–71. Baltimore: Johns Hopkins University Press, 1987.

———. "The Quicksands of the Self: Nella Larsen and Heinz Kohut." In *Telling Facts: History and Narratives in Psychoanalysis*, edited by Joseph H. Smith, 184–99. Baltimore: Johns Hopkins University Press, 1992.

Jones, Ernest. *The Life and Works of Sigmund Freud*. Vol. 2. New York: Basic, 1957.

Jordan, Jennifer. "Feminist Fantasies." *Tulsa Studies in Women's Literature* 7, no. 1 (Spring 1988): 105–17.

Joyce, Joyce A. "The Black Canon: Reconstructing Black American Literary Criticism." *New Literary History: A Journal of Theory and Interpretation* 18, no. 2 (Winter, 1987): 335–44.

———. "'Who the Cap Fit': Unconsciousness and Unconscionableness in the Criticism of Houston A. Baker, Jr., and Henry Louis Gates, Jr." *New Literary History: A Journal of Theory and Interpretation* 18, no. 2 (Winter 1987): 370–83.

Jung, Carl G. *The Archetypes and the Collective Unconscious*. 2d ed. Translated by R. F. C. Hull. Princeton, N.J.: Princeton University Press, 1980.

Kane, Harnett T. Review of *Seraph on the Suwanee*. *Chicago Sun-Times*, November 17, 1948, 58.

Kelley, Emma Dunham. *Megda*. 1891. Reprint. New York: Oxford University Press, 1988.

Kent, George E. "On the Future Study of Richard Wright." *C.L.A. Journal* 12 (June 1969): 366–70.

Kinnamon, Kenneth, and Michel Fabre, eds. *Conversations with Richard Wright*. Jackson: University Press of Mississippi, 1993.

Klein, Melanie. *Love, Guilt and Reparation: And Other Works, 1921–1945*. New York: Free Press, 1975.

Klotman, Phyllis. "The Black Writer in Hollywood, Circa 1930: The Case of Wallace Thurman." In *Black American Cinema*, edited by Manthia Diawara, 80–92. New York: Routledge, 1993.

Kohut, Heinz. *The Analysis of the Self: A Systematic Approach to the Psychoanalytic Treatment of Narcissistic Personality Disorders*. New York: International Universities Press, 1971.

Kostelanetz, Richard. *Politics in the African-American Novel: James Weldon Johnson, W. E. B. Du Bois, Richard Wright, and Ralph Ellison*. Westport, Conn.: Greenwood Press, 1991.

Kristeva, Julia. *Powers of Horror: An Essay on Abjection*. Translated by Leon S. Roudiez. New York: Columbia University Press, 1982.

Lacan, Jacques. "Agency of the Letter in the Unconscious." In *Écrits*, 146–78.

———. "Desire and Interpretation of Desire in *Hamlet*." In *Literature and Psychoanalysis: The Question of Reading, Otherwise*, edited by Shoshana Felman, 11–52. Baltimore: Johns Hopkins University Press, 1982.

———. *Écrits: A Selection*. Translated by Alan Sheridan. New York: W. W. Norton, 1977.

———. The Function and Field of Speech and the Language of Psychoanalysis. In *Écrits*, 30–113.

———. "The Mirror Stage as Formative of the Function of the I." In *Écrits*, 1–7.

———. "The Seminar on the *Purloined Letter.*" In *The French Freud*, Yale French Studies 48, 38–72. 1973.

———. "The Subversion of the Subject and the Dialectic of Desire in the Freudian Unconscious." In *Écrits*, 292–326.

Lakoff, George. *Women, Fire, and Dangerous Things: What Categories Reveal about the Mind.* Chicago: University of Chicago Press, 1987.

Laplanche, L., and J.-B. Pontalis. *The Language of Psycho-Analysis.* Translated by Donald Nicholson-Smith. New York: W. W. Norton, 1973.

Larsen, Nella. *Quicksand.* 1928. Reprint. New York: Collier Books, 1971.

———. *Quicksand and Passing.* 1928 and 1929. Reprinted in 1 vol. Edited by Deborah E. McDowell. New Brunswick, N.J.: Rutgers University Press, 1986.

Larson, Charles, ed. *An Intimation of Things Distant: The Collected Fiction of Nella Larsen.* New York: Anchor, 1992.

Layton, Lynne, and Barbara Ann Schapiro, eds. *Narcissism and the Text: Studies in Literature and the Psychology of Self.* New York: New York University Press, 1986.

Leach, William. *The Land of Desire: Merchants, Power, and the Rise of a New American Culture.* New York: Pantheon Books, 1993.

———. *True Love and Perfect Union: The Feminist Reform of Sex and Society.* New York: Basic Books, 1980.

Lewis, David Levering. *W. E. B. Du Bois: Biography of a Race, 1868–1919.* New York: Henry Holt, 1993.

———. *When Harlem Was in Vogue.* New York: Oxford University Press, 1979.

Lichtenstein, Heinz. *The Dilemma of Human Identity.* New York: Hason Aronson, 1977.

Locke, Alain. "The Negro Intellectual." *New York Herald Tribune*, May 20, 1928, 12.

Logan, Rayford W. *The Betrayal of the Negro.* New York: Collier, 1965.

Lorde, Audre. "The Use of the Erotic: The Erotic as Power." In *Sister Outsider*, 53–59. Trumansburg, N.Y.: Crossing Press, 1984.

Lott, Eric. *Love and Theft: Blackface Minstrelsy and the American Working Class.* New York: Oxford University Press, 1993.

Lowe, John. *Jump at the Sun: Zora Neale Hurston's Cosmic Comedy.* Urbana: University of Illinois Press, 1994.

Lukacher, Ned. *Primal Scenes: Literature, Philosophy, Psychoanalysis.* Ithaca, N.Y.: Cornell University Press, 1986.

Lurie, Alison. *The Language of Clothes.* New York: Random House, 1981.

M. P. L. Review of *Dark Princess: A Romance*, by W. E. B. Du Bois. *New Republic*, August 22, 1928, 27.

Major, Clarence. *From Juba to Jive: A Dictionary of African-American Slang.* New York: Penguin, 1994.

Margolies, Edward. *The Art of Richard Wright.* Carbondale: Southern Illinois University Press, 1969.

Matthews, Victoria Earle. *The Value of Race Literature: An Address.* Boston: First Congress of Colored Women of the United States, July 30, 1895. Reprinted in *Massachusetts Review* 27 (Summer 1986): 169–92.

Mavor, Carol. *Pleasures Taken: Performances of Sexuality and Loss in Victorian Photography.* Durham, N.C.: Duke University Press, 1995.

McCall, Dan. *The Example of Richard Wright.* New York: Harcourt, Brace and World, Inc., 1969.

McCarthy, Harold T. "Richard Wright: The Expatriate as Native Son." In *Richard Wright: A Collection of Critical Essays*, edited by Richard Macksey and Frank E. Moorer, 97–117. Englewood Cliffs, N.J.: Prentice-Hall, 1984.

McClintock, Anne. *Imperial Leather: Race, Gender and Sexuality in the Colonial Contest.* New York: Routledge, 1995.

McDowell, Deborah E. Introduction to *Quicksand,* ix–xxxvii. New Brunswick, N.J.: Rutgers University Press, 1986.

Mellard, James M. "Fanon's Confession: *Black Skin, White Masks* as Talking Cure." Paper delivered at the first annual conference of the Association for the Psychoanalysis of Culture and Society, Washington, D.C., 1995.

———. *Using Lacan, Reading Fiction.* Urbana: University of Illinois Press, 1991.

Miller, David C. *Dark Eden: The Swamp in Nineteenth-Century American Culture.* New York: Cambridge University Press, 1989.

Mintz, Steven, and Susan Kellogg. *Domestic Revolutions: A Social History of American Family Life.* New York: Free Press, 1988.

Mitchell, Angelyn, ed. *Within the Circle: An Anthology of African American Literary Criticism from the Harlem Renaissance to the Present.* Durham, N.C.: Duke University Press, 1994.

Mitchell, Stephen A. *Relational Concepts in Psychoanalysis: An Integration.* Cambridge, Mass.: Harvard University Press, 1988.

Mitchell, W. J. T. *Iconology: Image, Text, Ideology.* Chicago: University of Chicago Press, 1986.

Moore, Burness E., and Bernard D. Fine. *Psychoanalytic Terms and Concepts.* New Haven, Conn.: American Psychoanalytic Association and Yale University Press, 1990.

Mootry, Maria K. "Bitches, Whores, and Woman Haters: Archetypes and Typologies in the Art of Richard Wright." In *Richard Wright: A Collection of Critical Essays,* edited by Richard Macksey and Frank E. Moorer, 117–27. Englewood Cliffs, N.J.: Prentice-Hall, 1984.

Morrison, Toni. *Playing in the Dark.* Cambridge, Mass.: Harvard University Press, 1992.

Morson, Gary Saul, and Caryl Emerson, eds. *Rethinking Bakhtin: Extensions and Challenges.* Evanston, Ill.: Northwestern University Press, 1989.

Moses, Wilson, J. *Black Messiahs and Uncle Toms: Social and Literary Manipulations of a Religious Myth.* University Park: Pennsylvania State University Press, 1982.

Moynihan, Daniel Patrick. "Moynihan Report." In *The Negro Family: The Case for National Action.* Washington, D.C.: Department of Labor, Office of Policy, Planning and Research, 1965.

"A Mulatto Girl." *New York Times Book Review,* April 8, 1928, 16.

Oring, Elliott. *Jokes and Their Relations.* Lexington: University Press of Kentucky, 1992.

———. *The Jokes of Sigmund Freud: A Study in Humor and Jewish Identity.* Philadelphia: University of Pennsylvania Press, 1984.

Parsons, Alice Beal. "Three Novels." *Nation,* May 9, 1928, 540.

Polhemus, Robert M. *Erotic Faith: Being in Love from Jane Austen to D. H. Lawrence.* Chicago: University of Chicago Press, 1990.

Prager, Jeffrey. "Self Reflection(s): Subjectivity and Racial Subordination in the Contemporary African-American Writer." *Social Identities* 1, no. 2 (1995): 355–71.

Ragland-Sullivan, Ellie. *Jacques Lacan and the Philosophy of Psychoanalysis.* Urbana: University of Illinois Press, 1986.

Rampersad, Arnold. *The Art and the Imagination of W. E. B. Du Bois.* Cambridge, Mass.: Harvard University Press, 1976.

———. "Biography and Afro-American Culture." In *Afro-American Literary Study in the 1990s,* edited by Houston A. Baker Jr. and Patricia Redmond, 194–207. Chicago: University of Chicago Press, 1989.

———. "Du Bois's Passage to India: *Dark Princess.*" Unpublished manuscript.

————. "Psychology and Afro-American Biography." *Yale Review* 78 (Autumn 1989): 1–18.

————. "W. E. B. Du Bois as a Man of Literature." In *Critical Essays on W. E. B. Du Bois*, edited by William L. Andrews, 50–68. Boston: G. K. Hall, 1985.

Rank, Otto. *Beyond Psychology.* New York: Dover Publications, 1941.

Reage, Pauline. *Story of O.* New York: Grove Press, 1965.

Redding, Saunders. *To Make a Poet Black.* Chapel Hill: University of North Carolina Press, 1948.

Reilly, John. "Richard Wright's Curious Thriller." *C.L.A. Journal* 21 (December 1977): 218–23.

————, ed. *Richard Wright: The Critical Reception.* New York: B. Franklin, 1978.

Reitell, Jane. Review of *Dark Princess. The Annals of the American Academy of Political and Social Science* 140 (November 1928): 347.

Review of *Dark Princess: A Romance,* by W. E. B. Du Bois. *New York Times,* May 13, 1928, 19.

Review of *Dark Princess: A Romance,* by W. E. B. Du Bois. Extract from *Springfield Republican,* May 28, 1928. Quoted in *Book Review Digest, 1928,* 216. New York: H. W. Wilson Company, 1929.

Review of *Quicksand,* by Nella Larsen. *Saturday Review of Literature,* May 19, 1928, 896.

Review of *The Star of Ethiopia,* by W. E. B. Du Bois. *The Washington Bee,* October 23, 1915. Reprinted in *The Papers of W. E. B. Du Bois,* reel 87, frames 1535–36.

Roediger, David R. *The Wages of Whiteness: Race and the Making of the American Working Class.* London: Verso, 1992.

Rogin, Michael. "Blackface, White Noise: The Jewish Jazz Singer Finds His Voice." *Critical Inquiry* 18, no. 3 (Spring 1992): 417–53.

Rose, Gilbert J. *Trauma and Mastery in Life and Art.* New Haven, Conn.: Yale University Press, 1987.

Rubin, Joan Shelley. *The Making of Middlebrow Culture.* Chapel Hill: University of North Carolina Press, 1992.

Said, Edward. *Orientalism.* New York: Pantheon, 1978.

St. Clair, Janet. "The Courageous Undertow of Zora Neal Hurston's *Seraph on the Suwanee.*" *Modern Language Quarterly* 50 (March 1989): 38–57.

Schuyler, George. *Black No More.* 1931. Reprint. Evanston: Northeastern University Press, 1989.

Scott, Wilbur. *Five Approaches of Literary Criticism: An Arrangement of Contemporary Critical Essays.* New York: Collier Books, 1962.

"The Second Coming." *The Crisis* 15 (December 1917): 59–60.

Secor, Robert. "Ethnic Humor in Early American Jest Books." In *A Mixed Race: Ethnicity in Early America,* edited by Frank Shuffelton, 163–93. New York: Oxford University Press, 1993.

Seidman, Steven. *Romantic Longings: Love in America, 1830–1980.* New York: Routledge, 1991.

Showalter, Elaine. "Feminist Criticism in the Wilderness." *The New Feminist Criticism: Essays on Women, Literature and Theory,* edited by Elaine Showalter. New York: Pantheon Books, 1985.

Silverman, Kaja. *The Acoustic Mirror: The Female Voice in Psychoanalysis and Cinema.* Bloomington: University of Indiana Press, 1988.

————. *Male Subjectivity at the Margins.* New York: Routledge, 1992.

————. *The Threshold of the Visible World.* New York: Routledge, 1996.

Sinclair, Alison. *The Deceived Husband: A Kleinian Approach to the Literature of Infidelity.* Oxford, U.K.: Clarendon Press, 1993.

Singh, Amrijit. *The Novels of the Harlem Renaissance: Twelve Black Writers, 1923–1933.* University Parks: Pennsylvania State University Press, 1976.

Skura, Meredith Anne. *The Literary Use of the Psychoanalytic Process.* New Haven, Conn.: Yale University Press, 1981.

———. "Psychoanalytic Criticism." In *Redrawing the Boundaries: The Transformation of English and American Literary Studies,* edited by Stephen Greenblatt and Giles Gunn, 349–73. New York: Modern Language Association of America, 1992.

Slaughter, Frank G. "Freud in Turpentine." *New York Times Book Review,* October 31, 1948, 24.

Sontag, Susan. *On Photography.* New York: Anchor Books, 1977.

Spritz, Ellen Handler. "Reflections on Psychoanalysis and Aesthetic Pleasure: Looking and Longing." In *Pleasure beyond the Pleasure Principal: The Role of Affect in Motivation,* edited by Robert A. Glick and Stanley Bone, 221–38. New Haven, Conn.: Yale University Press, 1990.

Sprengnether, Madelon. *The Spectral Mother: Freud, Feminism, and Psychoanalysis.* Ithaca, N.Y.: Cornell University Press, 1990.

Steele, Valerie. *Fashion and Eroticism: Ideals of Feminine Beauty from the Victorian Era to the Jazz Age.* New York: Oxford University Press, 1985.

Stepto, Robert B. *From Behind the Veil: A Study of Afro-American Narrative.* Urbana: University of Illinois Press, 1979.

Sundquist, Eric J., ed. *The Oxford W. E. B. Du Bois Reader.* New York: Oxford University Press, 1996.

T. S. Review of *Dark Princess,* by W. E. B. Du Bois. *New York Evening Post,* May 12, 1928, 9.

Tate, Claudia. *Domestic Allegories of Political Desire: The Black Heroine's Text at the Turn of the Century.* New York: Oxford University Press, 1992.

———. "Freud and His 'Negro': Psychoanalysis as Ally and Enemy of African Americans." *Journal for the Psychoanalysis of Culture and Society* 1, no. 1 (Spring 1996): 53–62.

Thornton, Hortense E. "Sexism and Quagmire." *C.L.A. Journal* 16 (March 1973): 299.

"The Three Wise Men." *The Crisis* 7 (December 1913): 80–82.

"The Throb of Dark Drums in Du Bois's Novel." *Honolulu Star Bulletin,* June 16, 1928, 12.

Toll, Robert C. *Blackening Up: The Minstrel Show in Nineteenth-Century America.* New York: Oxford University Press, 1974.

Tyson, Phyllis, and Robert L. Tyson. *Psychoanalytic Theories of Development: An Integration.* New Haven, Conn.: Yale University Press, 1990.

Van Mens-Verhulst, Janneke, Sarlein Schreurs, and Liesbeth Woertman. *Daughtering and Mothering: Female Subjectivity Reanalysed.* New York: Routledge, 1993.

Vassilowitch, John, Jr. "'Erskine Fowler'": A Key Freudian Pun in *Savage Holiday. English Language Notes* 18 (March 1981): 206–8.

Wald, Priscilla. *Constituting Americans: Cultural Anxiety and Narrative Form.* Durham, N.C.: Duke University Press, 1995.

Walker, Alice. Foreword to *Zora Neale Hurston: A Literary Biography,* by Robert E. Hemenway. Urbana: University of Illinois Press, 1977.

Walker, Margaret. *Richard Wright: The Daemonic Genius, a Portrait of the Man; A Critical Look at His Work.* New York: Amistad, 1988.

Wall, Cheryl A. "Zora Neal Hurston: Changing Her Own Words." In *American Novelists Revisited: Essays in Feminist Criticism,* edited by Fritz Fleischmann, 370–93. Boston: G. K. Hall, 1982.

Walton, Eda Lou. Review of *Quicksand. Opportunity* 7 (July 1928): 212.

Walton, Jean. "Re-Placing Race in (White) Psychoanalytic Discourse: Founding Narratives of Feminism." *Critical Inquiry* 21, no. 4 (Summer 1995): 775–804.

Washington, Mary Helen. *Invented Lives: Narratives of Black Women, 1860–1960.* New York: Anchor/Doubleday, 1987.

———. "A Woman Half in Shadow." In *I Love Myself When I Am Laughing . . . A Zora Neale Hurston Reader,* edited by Alice Walker. Old Westbury, N.Y.: Feminist Press, 1979.

Wellek, Rene, and Austin Warren. *Theory of Literature.* 3d ed. New York: Harcourt, Brace & World, 1956.

Welsing, Frances Cress. "The Cress Theory of Color Confrontation." In *The Isis Papers: The Keys to the Colors,* 1–16. Chicago: Third World Press, 1991.

Welter, Barbara. "The Cult of True Womanhood, 1820–1860." In *Dimity Convictions.* Athens: Ohio State University Press, 1976.

Werner, Craig. "Zora Neale Hurston." In *Modern American Women Writers,* edited by Elaine Showalter, Lea Baechler, and A. Walton Litz, 221–33. New York: Charles Scribner's Sons, 1991.

Wertham, Frederic. *Dark Legend: A Study in Murder.* New York: Doubleday, 1941.

———. "The Matricidal Impulse." *Journal of Criminal Psychopathology* 2, no. 3 (July 1940): 455–64.

———. "An Unconscious Determinant in *Native Son.*" *Journal of Clinical Psychopathology* 6, no. 1 (July 1944): 111–15.

Whitmore, Ann. Review of *Seraph on the Suwanee. Library Journal* 73 (September 1, 1948): 1193.

Williamson, Joel. *The Crucible of Race: Black-White Relations in the American South since Emancipation.* New York: Oxford University Press, 1984.

Winnicott, D[onald]. W. *Playing and Reality.* 1971. Reprint. New York: Routledge, 1989.

Wolfenstein, Eugene Victor. *The Victims of Democracy: Malcolm X and the Black Revolution.* 1981. Reprint. New York: Guilford Press, 1993.

Woll, Allan. *Black Musical Theatre: From Coontown to Dreamgirls.* Baton Rouge: Louisiana State University Press, 1989.

Wright, Elizabeth. *Psychoanalytic Criticism: Theory in Practice.* London: Methuen, 1984.

———. *Feminism and Psychoanalysis: A Critical Dictionary.* Cambridge, Mass.: Blackwell, 1992.

Wright, Ellen. Letter to Claudia Tate, November 25, 1996.

Wright, Richard. *Black Boy.* 1945. Reprint. New York: Harper Perennial, 1993.

———. "Black Confessions." Unpublished manuscript. Wright Archive, James Weldon Johnson Collection, Beinecke Library, Yale University (Wright Papers), box 9, folders 202–8.

———. *Black Power: A Record of Reactions in a Land of Pathos.* New York: Harper & Brothers, 1954.

———. *Eight Men.* New York: Pyramid Books, 1961.

———. "Inner Landscape of a Jewish Family." Review of *Wasteland,* by Jo Sinclair. Wright Archive, box 86, folder 9.

———. *Lawd Today.* New York: Avon Books, 1963.

———. *The Long Dream.* 1958. Reprint. New York: Doubleday, 1958.

———. "Man, God Ain't Like That . . ." In *Eight Men.*

———. *Native Son.* New York: Harper & Row, 1940.

———. *The Outsider.* 1953. Reprint. New York: Harper Perennial, 1993.

———. "Psychiatry Comes to Harlem." *Free World* 12 (September 1946): 49–51.

———. *Savage Holiday.* 1954. Reprint. Jackson: University Press of Mississippi, 1994.

———. *Uncle Tom's Children.* 1938. Reprint. New York: New American Library, 1963.

———. *White Man, Listen!* 1957. Reprint. New York: Anchor Books, 1964.

Wyatt, Jean. *Reconstructing Desire: The Role of the Unconscious in Women's Reading and Writing.* Chapel Hill: University of North Carolina Press, 1990.

Young, Robert M. *Mental Space.* London: Process Press, 1994.

Index